Intercultural Communication

Language in Society

GENERAL EDITOR
Peter Trudgill, Chair of English Linguistics,
University of Fribourg

ADVISORY EDITORS
J. K. Chambers, Professor of Linguistics,
University of Toronto

Ralph Fasold, Professor of Linguistics,
Georgetown University

William Labov, Professor of Linguistics,
University of Pennsylvania

Lesley Milroy, Professor of Linguistics,
University of Michigan, Ann Arbor

Intercultural Communication

A DISCOURSE APPROACH

THIRD EDITION

Ron Scollon, Suzanne Wong Scollon, and
Rodney H. Jones

A John Wiley & Sons, Ltd., Publication

This third edition first published 2012
© 2012 John Wiley & Sons, Inc

Edition History: Basil Blackwell Ltd (1e 1995); Blackwell Publishing Ltd (2e 2001)

Wiley-Blackwell is an imprint of John Wiley & Sons, formed by the merger of Wiley's global Scientific, Technical and Medical business with Blackwell Publishing.

Registered Office
John Wiley & Sons Ltd, The Atrium, Southern Gate, Chichester, West Sussex, PO19 8SQ, UK

Editorial Offices
350 Main Street, Malden, MA 02148-5020, USA
9600 Garsington Road, Oxford, OX4 2DQ, UK
The Atrium, Southern Gate, Chichester, West Sussex, PO19 8SQ, UK

For details of our global editorial offices, for customer services, and for information about how to apply for permission to reuse the copyright material in this book please see our website at www.wiley.com/wiley-blackwell.

The right of Ron Scollon, Suzanne Wong Scollon, and Rodney H. Jones to be identified as the authors of this work has been asserted in accordance with the UK Copyright, Designs and Patents Act 1988.

Library of Congress Cataloging-in-Publication Data
9780470656402 (paperback ISBN)
Scollon, Ronald, 1939–
Intercultural communication : a discourse approach / Ron Scollon, Suzanne Wong Scollon, and Rodney H. Jones. – 3rd ed.
p. cm.
Includes bibliographical references and index.
ISBN 978-0-470-65640-2 (pbk. : alk. paper)   1. Intercultural communication.
I. Scollon, Suzanne B. K.   II. Jones, Rodney H.   III. Title.
P94.6.S36 2012
–dc23
2011023904

A catalogue record for this book is available from the British Library.

This book is published in the following electronic formats: ePDFs 978-1-118-14968-3; ePub 978-1-118-14969-0; Mobi 978-1-118-14970-6

Set in 10/12 pt Ehrhardt by Toppan Best-set Premedia Limited

1   2012

Contents

Figures

Series Editor's Preface

A number of books in the Language in Society series have dealt with topics in the field of the ethnography of speaking, broadly defined. The present volume, now in its third updated and expanded edition, draws on theoretical advances that have been made in this field over the past three decades, but also makes a very valuable contribution based on important descriptive work, including the authors' own, in the field of cross-cultural communication. This new edition is, too, notable for its extended and very helpful discussion of the terms *cross-cultural communication*, *intercultural communication*, and *interdiscourse communication*. The book is perhaps most noticeable, however, for the extent to which it represents an essay in applied sociolinguistics. Although theoretically founded and descriptively rich, *Intercultural Communication* also examines what conclusions can be drawn from sociolinguistic research for the practice of professional communication, something which is now in this third edition greatly enhanced by the addition of the new chapter, "Doing 'Intercultural Communication'" – see for example the section on "Avoiding Miscommunication." The emphasis on practice makes the book a pioneering work which will continue to have an impact well beyond the fields of sociolinguistics and foreign-language teaching, as the amount of interest in, and enthusiasm for, the first two editions makes very clear. As in the earlier editions, the authors' final conclusions are sober and paradoxical, namely that expert professional communicators are those who have come to appreciate their lack of expertise. Readers of *Intercultural Communication* will nevertheless come to appreciate not only the amount of variation to be found between human discourse systems – as well as their similarities, as the authors point out - but also the amount of progress that has been made by sociolinguistic researchers such as the Scollons and Rodney Jones in describing and understanding such systems.

Peter Trudgill

Preface to the First Edition

This book is about professional communication between people who are members of different groups. When as westerners or Asians we do business together, when as men or women we work together in an office, or when as members of senior or junior generations we develop a product together we engage in what we call "interdiscourse communication." That is to say, the discourse of westerners or of Asians, the discourse of men or women, the corporate discourse or the discourse of our professional organizations enfolds us within an envelope of language which gives us an identity and which makes it easier to communicate with those who are like us. By the same token, however, the discourses of our cultural groups, our corporate cultures, our professional specializations, or our gender or generation groups make it more difficult for us to interpret those who are members of different groups. We call these enveloping discourses "discourse systems."

Interdiscourse communication is a term we use to include the entire range of communications across boundaries of groups or discourse systems from the most inclusive of those groups, cultural groups, to the communications which take place between men and women or between colleagues who have been born into different generations. In interdiscourse analysis we consider the ways in which discourses are created and interpreted when those discourses cross the boundaries of group membership. We also consider the ways in which we use communication to claim and to display our own complex and multiple identities as communicating professionals.

This is a book on intercultural professional communication in English between westerners and East Asians, especially Chinese; but it is more than that. This book is on organizational communication, especially where conflicts arise between identity in the corporate culture and in one's professional specialization; but it is more than that. This book is about communication across the so-called generations gap; but it is more than that. This book is about miscommunications which occur between men and women; but it is more than that. This book is an interactive sociolinguistic framework for analyzing discourse which crosses the boundaries between these discourse systems. Because each professional communicator is simultaneously a member of a corporate, a professional, a generational, a gender, a cultural, and even other discourse systems, the focus of this book is on how those multiple memberships provide a framework within which all professional communication takes place.

Discourse analysis in professional communication is a new and rapidly developing field which integrates aspects of intercultural communication studies, applied interactional sociolinguistics, and discourse analysis. We have written this book to meet the needs of students and teachers in courses in English for professional communication, English for special purposes, or other such courses where the central focus is on communication in professional or business contexts. The book is designed for either classroom use or self-study, since many of those who are involved in intercultural professional communication have already completed their courses of study and are actively engaged in their professional work.

We have two main audiences in mind: (1) professional communicators who are East Asian speakers of English, and their teachers in courses on professional communication, whether in Asia or elsewhere, and (2) professional communicators who are concerned with any communications which cross the lines of discourse systems. The book has been field-tested in Hong Kong and therefore tends to emphasize examples of most direct relevance to Chinese (Cantonese) speakers of English. Nevertheless, the research on which this book is based covers a much broader range of East Asian English communication including Taiwan, Korea, Japan, Singapore, Mainland China, North America, Great Britain, and Australia.

In over twenty years of research on intercultural intra-organizational communication in North America as well as in Taiwan and in Korea, we have seen that most miscommunication does not arise through mispronunciations or through poor uses of grammar, important as those aspects of language learning are. The major sources of miscommunication in intercultural contexts lie in differences in patterns of discourse. In our consulting work with major business, governmental, and educational organizations in North America and in Asia we have found that frequently intergroup miscommunication and even hostility arise when each group has failed to interpret the intentions of the other group as a result of misinterpreting its discourse conventions. In teaching a range of courses, from "cultural differences in institutional settings" to courses on discourse, sociolinguistics, and first and second language acquisition, we have found that careful attention to communication at this higher level of discourse analysis leads to an ability to return to original statements and to do the repair work that is needed to improve cross-group communication. In this book we have for the first time organized course topics from a range of diverse fields into a unified presentation specifically designed for the professional communicator.

Our research in Taiwan was supported by Providence University (Ching Yi Ta Hsueh), Shalu, Taiwan, and in Korea by the Sogang Institute for English as an International Language, Sogang University, Seoul, Korea. It received continued funding from the Alaska Humanities Forum, Anchorage, Alaska (a program of the National Endowment for the Humanities), and Lynn Canal Conservation, Haines, Alaska. We wish to thank these two universities as well as the two funding agencies for their support of our work. Of course, the ideas expressed in this book are not the responsibility of any of these agencies.

The principal foundation upon which we write is the ongoing discourse about discourse among our colleagues. We owe much of our general approach to discussions of intergroup discourse with John Gumperz. We wish to thank Deborah Tannen for critical reading and lively discussion of not only this manuscript but the many other papers upon which this book is based. We also thank Tim Boswood, Coordinator of the English for Professional Communication program at City Polytechnic of Hong Kong, for the pleasure of many thoughtful conversations about this material.

This book has been used in manuscript form as the textbook for several courses which we have taught at City Polytechnic of Hong Kong and Hong Kong Baptist College. Our students in those courses have provided many useful comments, raised important questions, and suggested further examples which have materially improved the clarity of this text. We wish to thank them for their interest and for their astute observations. We are indebted to David Li Chor Shing for many suggestions which have clarified our statements regarding Chinese cultural matters as well as for improvements in style. We have benefited greatly too from discussions with him of the book's contents. Judy Ho Woon Yee and Vicki Yung Kit Yee have also given critical and helpful readings. As well, we thank Tom Scollon for his assistance in preparing the figures and Rachel Scollon for her editorial assistance. While we are deeply indebted to all of these people as well as to many others for their help in making our ideas clearer, we ourselves remain responsible for infelicities, eccentricities, and failures to get it right.

Preface to the Second Edition

Intercultural Communication: A Discourse Approach first appeared in 1995. We were pleased to see it come into print as we had used the substance of the book in manuscript form for two years before that with classes at the City University of Hong Kong (then Polytechnic) and at Hong Kong Baptist University (then College). We were confident that the book would find an audience in Asia and in North America, the UK, and Europe where readers had a concern with intercultural communication dealing with Chinese and other Asians. Where we have been pleasantly surprised in the five years since the book's first appearance is with the widespread appeal the book has had for readers quite outside this primary audience for which we had imagined it. We have now heard from readers and from teachers of intercultural communication in many parts of the world who have used the book to good effect and who have also sent us questions and comments which have been most helpful in shaping this revised edition. We wish, then, to begin by acknowledging these many correspondents for their help in focusing our attention on points which needed clarification and, in particular, in helping us to see how to shape the entirely new chapter 12 with which the book now ends.

This revised edition retains substantially the full text of the original edition. To this text we have added clarifications of points for which readers have asked for further elaboration. The first chapter now includes a section in which we set out our distinction between *cross-cultural communication* and *intercultural communication* or, as we prefer to call it in most cases, *interdiscourse communication*. There is another section which outlines the methodology of ethnography which is the practical basis of our research. In the full new final chapter, chapter 12, we return to this methodology and show how we and others have been able to use it and this book to do new research in intercultural communication and how this work has been used in conducting training and consultation programs.

Preface to the Third Edition

A lot has changed in the world since the first edition of *Intercultural Communication* was published in 1995. Dramatic advances in information technology, especially the growth of the World Wide Web, and the rapid globalization of the world's economy have in many ways brought people closer together, while at the same time, wars, terrorism, environmental devastation, and massive changes in the world economic order have resulted in greater political and social fragmentation. There have also been considerable advances in the fields of anthropology and linguistics, which lie at the heart of the work described in this book, particularly in fields dealing with things like gender, sexuality, and computer mediated communication. Finally, our own thinking and research has also evolved since the notion of *discourse systems* was proposed in this book more than fifteen years ago. Perhaps the most significant aspect of this evolution has been our development over the past decade of the theoretical framework of *mediated discourse analysis*, an approach to discourse which focuses less on broad constructs like "culture" and more on the everyday concrete actions though which culture is produced.

It would be impossible to account thoroughly for all of these changes without writing an entirely new book. What we have tried to do in this new edition is to strengthen the theoretical framework and make it more user friendly and relevant to the present day. The source of these revisions comes not just from our own continued research in the fields of intercultural communication and discourse analysis, but also from many years of experience using this book with our students, as well as the valuable feedback from many others who have made use of it in their teaching and research.

Although we have tried to preserve as much as possible of the original line of argument and most of the material from the original text, this edition does represent a substantial revision. The changes are of three types. First, we have tried to improve on the organization of the material, specifically by introducing the framework of *discourse systems* earlier and devoting a full chapter to each of the four components of this framework: face systems, ideology, forms of discourse, and socialization. Second, we have tried to make the book more useful for students by adding at the end of each chapter a section giving step-by-step advice on how to apply the concepts developed in that chapter to a research project on interdiscourse communication. We have also added at the end of each chapter a list of questions to guide classroom discussions and a list of references for further study. Finally, we have tried to develop the material from the first two editions by updating it to take into consideration the social and technological changes that have more recently affected intercultural communication as well as new research by us and others. This includes especially the addition of new material in the chapter on Generational Discourse describing the generations currently entering the workforce and analyzing generational shifts in China, and the addition of new material in the chapter on Gender Discourse, giving a more balanced account of the debates around discourse and gender and adding a section on discourse and sexuality. Especially in the last two chapters we have attempted to problematize and refine the framework of *discourse systems* in line with our current thinking around mediated discourse analysis.

It is fitting that we finished this manuscript on the second anniversary of Ron Scollon's death. From the start we approached this project first and foremost as a tribute to Ron's life and work, and as much as possible we have tried to be true to the spirit if not the letter of Ron's thinking as it developed in the last years of his life. One of the advantages of collaborating with a dead man is that he cannot object to your editorial decisions. While we must give Ron full credit for the strength and flexibility of the argument that is at the core of this book, we take full responsibility for any omissions, distortions, or factual errors in this revision.

We must also take this opportunity to thank those who share with us Ron's intellectual legacy and have given us invaluable advice and support along the way, especially his students Najma Al Zidjaly, Cecilia Castillo-Ayometzi, Ingrid de Saint-Georges, Andy Jocuns, Jackie Jia Lou, Sigrid Norris, and many others. As always, while we are deeply indebted to these people, the responsibility for any inaccuracies or infidelities in this work is ours alone.

Rodney H. Jones, Hong Kong
Suzanne Wong Scollon, Seattle
July, 2011

1

What Is a Discourse Approach?

Ho Man is a university student in Hong Kong majoring in English for Professional Communication. Late in the evenings after she has finished her schoolwork she likes to catch up with her friends on Facebook. Her grandmother, who has no idea what Facebook is, sometimes scolds Ho Man for staying up so late and spending so much time "playing" on her computer. One of Ho Man's best friends is Steven, a university student in Southern California who is majoring in environmental science. They met on an online fan forum devoted to a Japanese anime called Vampire Hunter D, and when they write on each other's Facebook walls much of what they post has to do with this anime. This is not, however, their only topic of conversation. Sometimes they use the chat function on Facebook to talk about more private things like their families, their boyfriends (Steven is gay), and even religion. Ho Man is still mystified by the fact that her friend in America is a Buddhist. Ho Man is a Christian and has been since she entered university two years ago. She goes to church every Sunday and belongs to a Bible study group on campus. As far as she is concerned, people should be able to believe in any religion they want. On the other hand, she still has trouble understanding why her friend, who is the same age that she is, believes in the same religion that her grandmother does.

The short anecdote above is an illustration of "intercultural communication," that is, it is an example of communication between an American from California and a Chinese living in Hong Kong. The fact that Ho Man is Chinese and Steven is American, however, seems to be, if not the least significant, perhaps the least interesting aspect of this situation. In any case, it does not seem to interfere at all with their ability to communicate.

There are also other ways Ho Man and her friend Steven are different. Ho Man is female and Steven is male. Ho Man is heterosexual and Steven is homosexual. Ho Man is an English major and Steven is a science major. Similarly, none of these differences seems to result in any serious "miscommunication." In fact, their difference in sexuality actually gives them a common topic to talk about: boys.

One difference that does cause some confusion, at least for Ho Man, is the fact that she is a Christian and her American friend is a Buddhist. What is interesting about this is that

Intercultural Communication: A Discourse Approach, Third Edition. Ron Scollon, Suzanne Wong Scollon, Rodney H. Jones.
© 2012 John Wiley & Sons, Inc. Published 2012 by John Wiley & Sons, Inc.

it is the opposite of what one might expect. It is, however, not particularly surprising. Over 80 percent of university students in Hong Kong identify themselves as Christians, and Buddhism has been one of the fastest growing religions in California since the late 1960s. Even though Ho Man considers this strange, it still is not the source of any serious miscommunication between the two of them.

Maybe one reason they do manage to communicate so well is that, for all their differences, they also have a lot of things in common. They are both the same age. They are both university students. They are both members of the Facebook "community" and feel comfortable with computer-mediated communication in general. And they are both fans of a particular animated story, the source of which, ironically, is a culture to which neither of them belongs. And they both speak English. In fact, Ho Man seems to have much more in common with her gay American friend than she does with her own grandmother, who is also Chinese. At the same time, Steven has something in common with Ho Man's grandmother that she doesn't: they are both Buddhists.

This example is meant to illustrate the fact that intercultural communication is often more complicated than we might think, especially in today's "wired," globalized world.

Usually when we think of intercultural communication, we think of people from two different countries such as China and the United States communicating with each other and proceed to search for problems in their communication as a result of their different nationalities.

But "North American culture" and "Chinese culture" are not the only two cultures that we are dealing with in this situation. We are also dealing with Japanese culture, gay culture, university student culture, Hong Kong Christian culture and North American Buddhist culture, gender cultures and generational cultures, the cultures of various internet websites and of the affinity groups that develop around particular products of popular culture.

There is nothing at all unusual about this situation. In fact, all situations involve communication between people who, rather than belonging to only one culture, belong to a whole lot of different cultures at the same time. Some of these cultures they share with the people they are talking to, and some of them they do not. And some of these cultural differences and similarities will affect the way they communicate, and some of them will be totally irrelevant.

The real question, then, is not whether any given moment of communication is an instance of "intercultural communication." All communication is to some degree intercultural, whether it occurs between Ho Man and her Facebook friend, Ho Man and her boyfriend, or Ho Man and her grandmother. The real question is, *what good does it do to see a given moment of communication as a moment of intercultural communication?* What kinds of things can we accomplish by looking at it this way? What kinds of problems can we avoid or solve?

The Problem with Culture

But wait a minute, you may say. While it seems normal to talk about "North American culture" and "Chinese culture" and even "gay culture" and "Christian culture," can we also talk about the "culture" of university students (even when they go to university in different countries), the "culture" of English majors or environmental science majors, the "culture" of fans of a particular Japanese anime, or Facebook "culture"? One problem is that the term "culture" may not be particularly well suited to talk about all of the different groups that we belong to which may affect the way we think, behave, and interact with others. In other words, "culture" may not be a particularly useful word to use when talking about "intercultural communication."

The biggest problem with the word culture is that nobody seems to know exactly what it means, or rather, that it means very different things to different people. Some people speak of culture as if it is a thing that you have, like courage or intelligence, and that some people have more of it and some people less. Others talk about culture as something that people live inside of like a country or a region or a building – they speak, for example, of people leaving their cultures and going to live in other people's cultures. Some consider culture something people think, a set of beliefs or values or mental patterns that people in a particular group share. Still others regard culture more like a set of rules that people follow, rather like the rules of a game, which they can either conform to or break, and others think of it as a set of largely unconscious habits that govern people's behavior without them fully realizing it. There are those who think that culture is something that is rather grand, something one finds in the halls of museums and between the covers of old books, while there are others who believe that true culture is to be found in the everyday lives of everyday people. There are those who cherish culture as the thing that holds us together, and others who deride it as the thing that drives us apart.

All of these views of culture are useful in some way, in that they help to illuminate a different aspect of human behavior by leading us to ask certain very productive questions. Seeing culture as a set of rules, for example, leads us to ask how people learn these rules and how they display competence in them to other members of their culture. Seeing culture as a set of traditions leads us to ask why some aspects of behavior survive to be passed on to later generations and some do not. Seeing culture as a particular way of thinking forces us to consider how the human mind is shaped and the relationship between individual cognition and collective cognition. Each definition of culture can lead us down a different pathway, and all of these pathways are potentially fruitful.

It is best, then, to think of culture not as one thing or another, not as a *thing* at all, but rather as a *heuristic*. A *heuristic* is a "tool for thinking." The word comes from the Greek word meaning "to find" or "to discover." It is rumored that when the Greek mathematician Archimedes realized, after getting into a bath and watching the water overflow, that he could use this method to measure the volume of objects, he ran naked through the streets of Syracuse shouting, "*Heureka!*" (rather than, as is commonly recalled, "Eureka"), meaning "I have found it!" Each of these different views of culture has the potential to lead us to a different kind of "Heureka." At the same time, none of them alone can be considered definitive or complete. The way we will be approaching the problem of culture and the phenomenon of intercultural communication in this book will draw insights from many of these different views of culture, as well as from the ideas of people who never used the word culture at all. At the same time, we will, we hope, come up with ways of helping you to use these various ideas about culture without being "taken in" by them, without falling into the trap of thinking that any particular construction of "culture" is actually something "real."

Perhaps the best definition of culture we can settle on for now, though we will be revisiting and revising the concept throughout this book, is that culture is "a way of dividing people up into groups according to some feature of these people which helps us to understand something about them and how they are different from or similar to other people."

While this definition seems rather innocuous, it really points to what is probably the trickiest aspect of this notion of "culture," and that is, when you are dividing people up, where do you draw the line? You might, for example, want to use geographical boundaries to divide people up, to speak, for example, of French, Brazilians, British, Chinese, or Americans. Putting all the people in China, however, into one category might mask the fact that people in the northern part of China eat different food, celebrate different festivals, and speak a different language than people in the southern part, or that older people living in China, who may have been alive during the time of Mao Zedong, tend to have very different ideas about life than their grandchildren who are growing up in a rapidly expanding consumer economy. It might also mask the many similarities people living in China might have with people living in France, Brazil, the United Kingdom or the United States. This problem gets even worse when we make our categories bigger, when we start talking, for example, of Easterners and Westerners, Latinos and Northerners, Middle Easterners, and Europeans. Even when we try to narrow our categories, however, to speak perhaps of New Yorkers or Parisians, the same kinds of problems arise. Do the Wall Street banker and the taxi driver who drives him to his office really belong to the same culture? In some ways they do, and in some ways they don't.

This is the fundamental problem with all *heuristics*, that while they illuminate or help us to focus on some things, they can distort other things or hide them from our view altogether. Later in this book we will discuss how this aspect of dividing people into groups can lead to two particular kinds of problems: one we call "lumping," thinking that all of the people who belong to one "culture" are the same, and the other we call "binarism," thinking people are different just because they belong to different "cultures."

There are other problems as well with studying intercultural communication, one of which many of us who specialize in this field have experienced: You pick a situation to study as an intercultural situation and then you find that nothing at all seems to have gone wrong. The social interaction proceeds smoothly and you come to feel that there is, after all, nothing to the idea that intercultural communication causes problems of communication. Alternatively, you pick a situation to study and things *do* go wrong, but it is very hard to argue that the problems arise out of cultural differences rather than other more basic differences such as that the participants have different goals. For example, even when a Japanese businessperson fails to sell his product to an Indonesian customer, the reasons are likely to have to do with product quality or suitability, with the pricing or delivery structure, or perhaps with the even more basic problem that the customer did not really seek to buy the product in the first place, and the differences between "being Japanese and "being Indonesian" have nothing to do with it.

Even more fundamental than this problem is the problem of bias in the research. How does a researcher isolate a situation to study as "intercultural communication" in the first place? If you start by picking a conversation between an "American" and a "Chinese," you have started by presupposing that "Americans" and "Chinese" will be different from each other, that this difference will be significant, and that this difference is the most important and defining aspect of that social situation. In most cases, none of these can be assumed to be true and yet if the researcher begins by making this assumption and goes through the long, painstaking work of careful analysis, human nature is likely to lead this researcher to *find* significant differences and to attribute those differences to his or her a priori categories "American" and "Chinese" whether they really fit or not.

Culture is a verb

While throughout this book we will be trying to avoid committing ourselves to one definition of culture or another, mostly by trying to steer clear of the term culture as much as possible, if you were to force us to admit what we really think culture is, chances are we would say something like "culture is a verb." This rather provocative statement is actually the title of an article by an anthropologist named Brian Street who is particularly interested in the idea of literacy. What he means by literacy, however, is a bit different from what most people mean by it. Rather than just the ability to read and write, Street would define literacy as something like the communicative practices that people engage in to show that they are particular kinds of people or belong to particular groups. Thus the ability to sing or shop or dress in certain ways or operate certain kinds of machines, along with the ability to read and write certain kinds of texts, would all be seen as kinds of literacy. The most important thing, though, is that these "abilities" are not just a matter of individual learning or intelligence, but a matter of living together with other people and interacting with them in certain ways.

What we mean when we say "culture is a verb" is that culture is not something that you think or possess or live inside of. It is something that you *do*. And the way that you do it might be different at different times and in different circumstances. The way Ho Man "does" "Chinese culture," for example, is likely to be very different when she is talking to her grandmother and when she is posting comments on her friend's Facebook wall, which brings us back to Street's idea of literacy – talking to grandmothers and writing on Facebook walls involve very different sets of knowledge and abilities.

To say "culture is a verb" has some important implications for the study of intercultural communication. It means that if we want to understand intercultural communication we should not focus so much on the people and try to figure out something about them based on the "culture" they belong to. Rather we should focus on what they are *doing* and try to understand what kinds of tools they have at their disposal to do it. Most cross-cultural research takes as its unit of analysis cultural systems of meaning or behaving or thinking, and these systems are also important in our approach. But they are only important in so far as they affect how people do things with other people. Thus, our unit of analysis will not be just systems of culture by themselves nor just the individual person by herself or himself, but rather "people doing things" using these systems of culture.

In order to do anything, we need to use certain tools. To convey ideas to another person, for example, we need language or some other system of communication. To cook a meal, we need certain kinds of pots and pans and other implements. To a large extent the kinds of ideas we can convey and the way we can convey them depend on the kinds of communication systems we have available to us. Similarly, the kinds of meals that we can cook depend on the equipment that we have in our kitchen. Not everybody has the same tools available to them, and even when they do, not everybody uses them in exactly the same way. These tools come from the different groups that we belong to – families, communities, institutions like schools and workplaces – and when we use them we are not only getting a certain job done in a certain way, we are also showing that we are members, to one degree or another, of the social groups that provided us with these tools. At the risk of overusing the word "culture," we will be calling these tools "cultural tools." They include physical things like forks and chopsticks, articles of clothing, and technologies like mobile telephones, but also more abstract things like languages, certain kinds of texts, conventional ways of treating people, social institutions and structures, and even concepts like "freedom" and "justice."

All tools have histories, which means that any particular person is not free to use them in an arbitrary way, but must use them within some range of restricted or shared meanings. And so these tools bring with them to any action a pre-established set of limitations. At the same time, these tools are also altered through their use and thus no use of any cultural tool is absolutely determinant of the social action that it can be used to perform. Put another way, all cultural tools bring into social action a set of contradictions and complications, which are the sources of both limitations and of ambiguity, novelty, and creation.

Since, as we noted before, all of us belong to lots of different cultures at once, we also have lots of different cultural tools available to us to take actions, which we borrow strategically when we are interacting with different people in different situations. Because when we borrow a certain tool we are in some way identifying with the social group from which the tool comes, our decision to use a particular cultural tool (or not use it) may be determined not just by what we want to do, but also by who we want to *be*, the group that we want to claim membership in at any given moment.

Many people in Hong Kong, for example, have access to the tool of English for communication, which they use quite comfortably with one another when they are at school or in the office. It is considered strange, however, to use it in daily conversation. This contrasts sharply with Singapore and India where, since the people around you may be native speakers of a variety of different languages, English is used as a convenient *lingua franca*. Since most Hong Kongers also speak Cantonese, English is not necessary for communication in the same way. At the same time, using English carries with it certain kinds of social meanings based partly on the groups of people that use it such as teachers and other authority figures as well as non-Cantonese speaking "foreigners," and so by appropriating English into casual conversation with another Cantonese speaker, one might be claiming a certain affiliation with those groups of people, or one might be thought by the people to whom one is talking to be claiming such an affiliation, to be "showing off," or, at the very least, to be acting unduly formal. This brings us to another point about which we will have a great deal to say later in this book, the fact that when we appropriate and use particular cultural tools, we are not just claiming that we are particular kinds of people. We are also making claims about other people and the kinds of groups they belong to.

This is not to say we are always conscious of how and why we act in particular ways or appropriate particular cultural tools into those actions. Most of the time we are not consciously aware of the processes that go into appropriating and using cultural tools. We just do what "comes naturally" in the course of social interactions. In fact, when we do become conscious of these processes, it is often because we perceive something to have gone wrong, and when other people point out the processes to us we sometimes feel rather self-conscious. If we have worked hard at learning how to say, "Please take me to Beijing University" so that when we arrive at the airport we can board a taxi and get to our destination without trouble, we are pleased if the taxi driver just takes us there, but if he should launch into some commentary about how we have pronounced it, even if it is entirely complimentary, we may feel that the focus has shifted ground unpleasantly. British and North Americans who have lived in China for some time are equally put off when people quite enthusiastically say, "Oh you know how to use chopsticks!" That is, it is in the nature of much social practice for it to be and to remain out of conscious awareness.

Most of what we know and do, we know and do without knowing how. We have just "picked up" how to walk like our parents, how to talk like them, how to *be* a certain sort of person within a certain type of group. Of course, children growing up in the same family or the same community, members of the same social class, members of the same gender groups and generations and so forth, will have very similar experiences and so similar sets of cultural tools available to them and similar ways of using them.

Cultural tools evolve in social groups and change over time as they are passed down from generation to generation. They also might be taken up by other social groups and adapted to fit their needs. English, for example, is a tool that has changed considerably over the years. The way it was used by writers in the eighteenth century was rather different than the way it is being used by the authors of this book. Furthermore, although it originated in the British Isles, it has, for various reasons, spread all over the world and, as it has been taken up by new groups of speakers, it has been altered and adapted to fit the particular circumstances of its use. And so the English spoken in India is rather different from that spoken in Australia.

Finally, cultural tools that originate in a particular social group tend to have some relationship with other tools that also originate in the same group. Cultural tools come in "sets," and they reinforce and complement other tools. A carpenter has a toolkit, which includes a hammer, a saw, a screwdriver, and other tools that allow her to do things with wood, because working with wood is something she does all day long. One would not expect to find other tools like a cake mixer or a shovel in her toolkit. This is not to say that she does not have access to these tools or know how to use them. When she is not on the job, she may enjoy baking cakes or tending to her backyard garden. The point is, when she is *being* a carpenter, she is likely to draw from her carpenter's toolkit, and when she is *being* a baker or home gardener, she is likely to draw from different toolkits. We will be calling the "cultural toolkits" which we draw upon to communicate with one another and enact different social identities *discourse systems*.

Discourse

We have chosen to call this book *Intercultural Communication: a discourse approach*, and so we should at the outset explain what we mean by that. The word "discourse" is almost as dangerous as the word "culture" – that is, it means very different things to different people. Perhaps the most common meaning of discourse is language above the level of the sentence. And so, while someone who analyzes the way words are put together to form sentences might be called a grammarian, a person who studies the way sentences are put together to form texts would be called a "discourse analyst." Discourse analysts study all kinds of texts including letters, newspaper articles, conversations, jokes, meetings, interviews, emails, and television programs. To some extent, this book will draw upon this definition of discourse. Our basic interest will be in face-to-face conversation within speech events such as meetings, conversations, or interviews, but we will also concern ourselves with written communication of various kinds as well as with computer mediated communication, which can involve complex mixtures of writing, speaking, pictures, and video.

At the same time, discourse analysis has undergone many changes over the past thirty years, most of which have resulted in researchers taking a much broader view of what discourse itself really is. While our primary analyses are based on what happens in specific social interactions, our long-range goal is to address what the French philosopher Michel Foucault has referred to as "orders of discourse" and the American discourse analyst James Paul Gee has called "Discourses with a capital 'D'." Foucault and others have given a variety of names to these broad discourses such as when we speak of "the discourse of entertainment," "the discourse of medicine," "the discourse of law," or "business discourse." Here the meaning intended is the broad range of everything which can be said or talked about or symbolized within a particular, recognizable domain. Our own term for this is *discourse system*, which we will further explain in the following chapters.

For now, we will simply say that a discourse system is a "cultural toolkit" consisting of four main kinds of things: ideas and beliefs about the world, conventional ways of treating other people, ways of communicating using various kinds of texts, media, and "languages," and methods of learning how to use these other tools.

Discourse systems

On Sundays Rodney Jones likes to go to the beach on the island where he lives to practice yoga with his friends. When he does this, he is participating in a particular discourse system, which we might call the Yoga discourse system. This discourse system has associated with it a complex set of ideas and beliefs about the physical and spiritual world, which can be traced back to the writings of the ancient Indian sage Patanjali and which are intimately connected to Hinduism. Although Rodney has read parts of the Yoga Sutras of Patanjali somewhere along the line, he does not by any means fully understand the complicated system of physiology, psychology, and cosmology behind the physical positions he performs. Neither is he a Hindu. However, by performing yoga positions he is in some way *embodying* this system of beliefs and concepts, whether he understands them or not.

Part of this discourse system has to do with the way people treat one another while they are attending the yoga class. It is customary, for example, to show people respect by putting one's palms together and saying *namaste*. How one treats the teacher is especially important. One might address the teacher (who, in this case, is also not a Hindu) with particular respect, and the teacher is given the right not just to tell students what to do, but even to move about manipulating the bodies of his or her students.

Rodney may also communicate in a rather different way when he is with this group of weekend yogis. He may, for example, use Sanskrit terms like *sirsasana* and *padmasana* to describe certain positions, although his knowledge of the Sanskrit language is limited to these few words. He might also use English terms (which often refer to poses using the names of animals), and when he does he might find himself uttering sentences which, outside of this group, would sound rather odd if not totally incomprehensible, sentences like "Let's do a dog," or "She does a nice cow."

Finally, the method of learning in this particular discourse system is rather unique, involving following along as the teacher performs certain physical actions. Students do not take notes or engage in debates as they sometimes do in university lectures. There is also not much room for creativity or individual expression as one might find in a drawing class.

One reason for going through this example is to illustrate the four main components of what we are calling discourse systems. Any group that has particular ways of thinking, treating other people, communicating and learning can be said to be participating in a particular discourse system. Discourse systems can be associated with very large groups of people – and so we will be talking about, for example, the Confucian discourse system or the Utilitarian discourse system (which can be thought of as the discourse system of international capitalism) – or rather small groups of people like families or affinity groups.

Other scholars have used terms such as "discourse community" and "community of practice" to refer to small groups like yoga enthusiasts, stamp collectors, and Japanese anime fans. The difference between these concepts and the concept of discourse system is that both "discourse communities" and "communities of practice" refer to bounded groups of people (defined respectively by the texts they use and by the practices they engage in together), whereas discourse systems refer to broader systems of communication in which members of communities participate.

Another reason for giving this example is to illustrate that people participate in discourse systems in a variety of ways, some more centrally and some more peripherally. Although Rodney likes doing yoga and has been practicing it for many years, his participation in this discourse system is still rather peripheral compared to say a *sadhu* in India for whom the path of yoga is his total way of life, or even from another member of the same community of yoga practitioners in Hong Kong who may be a Hindu. At the same time, although Rodney and the *sadhu* are, as many people would point out, from very different "cultures," they do, to some extent, share a discourse system.

Discourse systems can also mix with other discourse systems. In the United States, for example, the Yoga discourse system has mixed with what might be called the discourse of fitness, so people attend yoga classes in gyms where people also do things like aerobics and weightlifting, and many of the more spiritual aspects of the practice may be practically absent from the consciousness of the practitioners.

In a way, this concept of discourse systems is our solution to the problems we pointed out with the concept of "culture." We will be using the term in many of the same ways that other people use the word culture, and, instead of talking about communication across cultures we will be talking about communication across discourse systems or *interdiscourse communication*. This is not to say that we believe this to be a perfect solution. As you go through this book, you may find problems with this approach in the same way we found problems with the concept of culture, and indeed we have also noticed some problems with the approach since this book was first published which we will try to point out along the way. Like "cultures," discourse systems are *heuristics* – tools that we will use to help us understand something about how people interact with one another and why. They are maps designed to help us navigate the territory of human communication, not the territory itself.

We will however go out on a limb in proclaiming that we think this particular *heuristic* provides a lot more flexibility and analytical power in understanding how people who belong to different groups communicate with one another than a lot of other more traditional ideas of culture. For one thing it gets us away from the idea that intercultural communication always has something to do with people from different countries or, even worse, people of different ethnicities communicating (or, as is usually assumed, *mis*communicating).

Each of us, as we mentioned above, simultaneously participates in many different discourse systems. We are members of a particular corporate group, a particular professional or occupational group, a generation, a gender, a region, and an ethnicity all associated with different discourse systems. As a result, virtually all communication is communication across some lines which divide us according to the systems of discourse that we participate in.

Ultimately we will argue that what we normally regard as the "cultural" differences between people in communication are likely to be rather less significant than other differences which arise from being participants in a host of other discourse systems not normally considered in treatments of "intercultural communication," discourse systems associated with different genders, sexualities, generations, workplaces, and professions.

The concept of discourse systems also helps to highlight the fact that all of us participate in multiple discourse systems, some of which we participate in more fully than others. All of these multiple discourse systems form intersecting and cross-cutting waves of communicative style and form and values which lead us to argue in later chapters that the idea of culture is mostly too large a concept to really capture the complexity of interdiscourse communication. Just as the values and behavior associated with a discourse system that I participate in may clash with those of a discourse system you participate in, there might also be contradictions between two of the discourse systems that I myself participate in which I will need to reconcile somehow, just as Ho Man whose story with which we began this chapter needs to reconcile the way she acts with her grandmother and the way she acts with her Facebook friends. Approached in this way, interdiscourse communication can be seen not just as something that occurs *between* people, but something that occurs *within* people.

Finally, the notion of discourse systems gets us away from thinking about cultures in a deterministic way. We are not "controlled" by our discourse systems. Although the tools that discourse systems provide tend to severely limit and focus the kinds of actions that we can take, we are also able to adapt those tools as we appropriate them into different kinds of situations. We may not always be completely conscious of how we appropriate and use cultural tools, but there is still an element of choice involved.

What Is Communication?

We take it as axiomatic that social actions are accomplished through various forms of communication. That is, the very meaning of the term "social" in the phrase "social action" implies some common and shared systems of meaning, in the first place, and of communication, in the second place.

But communication is far from simple or straightforward, especially given two rather inconvenient facts: that when people communicate they often don't say what they mean, and they often don't mean what they say.

Imagine Mr Wong, a businessperson living in Hong Kong, and Mr Richardson, a businessperson visiting from the United States, have been having a conversation. Mr Richardson has enjoyed this conversation and when they are ready to part he says to Mr Wong that they really should get together to have lunch sometime. Mr Wong says that he would enjoy that. After a few weeks Mr Wong begins to feel that Mr Richardson has been rather insincere because he has not followed up his invitation to lunch with a specific time and place.

The problem here is that Mr Richardson doesn't mean what he says, which is rather different from being insincere or dishonest. To put it another way, what Mr Richardson means is different from what the sentence that he has uttered means. This may seem strange, but it actually happens all the time. "We must get together and have lunch sometime" is quite a common expression people use near the end of business interactions in North America, and for North Americans it means several different things. First of all, it signals that the person who says it thinks that the encounter will (or should) be ending soon. So it can function as what conversation analysts call a "pre-closing." It is also a way of creating what we will be calling in a later chapter a feeling of "involvement," a way to tell someone that you have enjoyed spending time with them and you would not mind doing it again. While it does contain the vague idea that a subsequent meeting would be desirable, it does not in any way commit the speaker or the hearer to such an arrangement, in the same way "see you later" does not commit someone to a later meeting. It would be very odd, therefore, if, in response to this utterance, the hearer were to take out his or her diary and attempt to set a date.

Of course, Mr Wong, not participating in the same discourse system as Mr Richardson, interprets this utterance rather differently, and one could hardly blame him. After all, "we should get together for lunch" does sound like an invitation. A similar kind of misunder-standing might arise if Mr Wong greets Mr Richardson by asking if he has eaten, a typical greeting in Hong Kong and the rest of China. Here it might be Mr Richardson who assumes he is being invited to lunch, but in reality this is a formulaic utterance in Chinese used as a polite way of saying hello.

The root of both of these problems is that language is fundamentally ambiguous.

The field of conversation analysis has been an active area of research for over three decades now. On the basis of this research Stephen Levinson (1990) has argued that it is possible to draw four quite general conclusions:

1 Language is ambiguous by nature.
2 We *must* draw inferences about meaning.
3 Our inferences tend to be fixed, not tentative.
4 Our inferences are drawn very quickly.

In the sections which follow we will take up each of these conclusions in more specific detail.

Language is ambiguous by nature

When we say that language is always ambiguous, what we mean is that we can never fully control the meanings of the things we say and write. The meanings we exchange by speaking and by writing are not given in the words and sentences alone but are also constructed partly out of what our listeners and our readers interpret them to mean. To put this quite another way, meaning in language is jointly constructed by the participants in communication.

I may say something is blue in color but it is another question altogether what the color blue means to you. There is never complete agreement among speakers of a language about the semantic ranges of such items as color terms. This is just one example.

Word-level ambiguity in language
Such words as the prepositions "in" or "at" are notoriously difficult to teach and to learn, and this is because their meanings reside only partly in the words themselves. Much of their meaning is given by the situations in which they are used.

For example, if we say:

There's a man *at* the front door

the preposition "at" tells us something about where the man is located, but it does not tell us very much. We know that he is outside the door. We even go further in assuming that he is standing within reach of the door where he has probably just knocked or rung the bell.

It is not clear just how much it is safe to read into such a sentence, and that is the whole point. This sentence is quite ambiguous in that we do not know very much about just how this man is "at" the door. If we use what is a very similar sentence:

> There's a taxi *at* the door

we can see that there is a very different way of being "at" the door. In the case of a taxi we would expect the taxi to be at some distance from the door, in a roadway or a driveway, probably waiting with its motor running. Furthermore, the taxi includes a driver.

One could say that the difference in these two sentences lies not in the preposition "at" but in the two subject nouns "man" and "taxi." The difference lies in what we know about men and taxis and how they wait "at" doors. The point we want to make, based on Levinson's argument, is that what is different in meaning between these two sentences is how objects are "at" a location and that the preposition "at" does not give us enough information in itself. In order to understand these sentences we must call upon our knowledge about the world, which does not reside in the sentences or in any of the words of the sentences.

This is what we mean when we say that language is always ambiguous at the word level. The words themselves do not give us enough information to interpret their meaning unequivocally.

To give just one more example, if we say:

> The coffee is *in* the cup

you may draw a number of inferences about just how the coffee is in the cup. You may assume that it is coffee in its brewed, liquid form. You will most likely not assume that we are talking about coffee beans or a jar of frozen coffee powder.

By the same token, if we say:

> The pencil is *in* the cup

it is likely that you could draw a picture of that cup and the pencil. The pencil would be sticking out of the cup but more of it would be inside than outside because otherwise the pencil would fall out of the cup. What you do not understand from that sentence is that we have ground the pencil into fine powder, poured boiling water over it, and made a brew of pencil to drink. But there is nothing in the differences between those two sentences or in the words "in" or "cup" which tell you that. These are assumptions you make on the basis of what you know about the world, and the words and sentences only serve to point you in the direction of what you already know.

Sentence-level ambiguity in language
You might think that if words such as the prepositions "at" or "in" or the names of colors are naturally ambiguous, the ambiguity could be cleared up at the level of sentences. Unfortunately, sentences are equally ambiguous.

Our colleague Ray McDermott (1979) has given the example of the simple sentence, "What time is it?," as an excellent example of the ambiguity of language at the sentence level.

If I am walking down the street and I stop you to ask:

What time is it?

your answer is likely to be something like, "It's two o'clock," or whatever time it is. I will then thank you and go on. Nothing out of the ordinary is understood. But let us change the context to the elementary school classroom. The teacher asks Frankie,

What time is it?

And Frankie answers, "It's two o'clock." In this case the teacher answers,

Very good, Frankie.

Notice the difference here. In the first case the sentence, "What time is it?," is part of the speech act of requesting the time and as such it forms a set with the other sentence, "Thank you." In the second case the same sentence, "What time is it?," is part of the speech act of testing a child for his or her ability to tell the time. As such this sentence forms a pair not with, "Thank you," but with, "Very good."

If you doubt that this is true, you can go along the street after reading this and ask somebody the time. When they tell you the time, you answer by saying, "Very good." We assure you that they will consider this to be very odd in the mildest cases or even hostile behavior in more extreme responses.

There are, of course, also many other meanings for this same sentence. If a husband and a wife are at dinner in the home of friends and she asks him, "What time is it?," this question almost certainly could be better translated as something like, "Don't you think it is time we were leaving?"

The point we are making is simply that the meaning of the sentence, "What time is it?" resides not in the sentence alone but in the situation in which it is used as well. Knowing how to interpret the meaning of this sentence requires knowledge of the world as well as knowledge of words and sentences.

Discourse-level ambiguity in language

As a last resort, it might be hoped that we could find unambiguous meaning in language at the level of discourse. Perhaps we could find some way of being specific about the contexts in which sentences are used, and if enough of that information could be made explicit then we could say that language was not ambiguous at least at the level of discourse. Unfortunately, this approach cannot work either. Language remains inherently ambiguous at the level of discourse as well.

One of the most famous international disagreements of recent times, for example, centered on whether a particular piece of discourse could or could not reasonably be considered "an apology." On April 1, 2001 a U.S. spy plane flying without permission in Chinese airspace collided with a Chinese fighter jet, causing it to crash and killing the pilot. The Chinese authorities detained the crew of the U.S. plane for eleven days while they waited for the United States to "apologize" for illegally entering their airspace and causing the death of the pilot. The incident ended when the U.S. government issued what has come to be known as "the letter of the two sorries." The "two sorries" were:

1 Both President Bush and Secretary of State Powell have expressed their sincere regret over your missing pilot and aircraft. Please convey to the Chinese people and to the family of pilot Wang Wei that we are very sorry for their loss.
2 We are very sorry the entering of Chinese air space and the landing did not have verbal clearance, but are pleased the crew landed safely.

Many on both the U.S. and Chinese sides insisted, however, that the "two sorries" expressed in the letter were not "true apologies." They pointed out, for example, that "expressing regret" is not the same as apologizing, since one can express regret over something he or she is not responsible for. They also pointed out that even when the word "sorry" was used, it was attached to circumstances (the Chinese pilot's family's "loss"; the fact that the landing "did not have verbal clearance") that seemed peripheral to the concerns of the Chinese side, which had more to do with the fact that the U.S. plane had entered Chinese airspace illegally and had caused the death of the Chinese pilot.

Some have taken this as an example of "intercultural miscommunication," suggesting that the conflict had something to do with different conceptions between North Americans and Chinese about what constitutes an apology, and there may be something to this. We prefer to see it, however, as an example of the ambiguity of language, an ambiguity which, in this situation, actually contributed to resolving a potentially explosive diplomatic stalemate. The ambiguity of the "sorries" in this letter allowed the Chinese government to triumphantly declare that it had received the apology it had demanded, and it allowed the Bush administration to assure its domestic constituency, which had been encouraging the President to "stand up to China," that it had not in fact apologized.

The point is, however, not just that the ambiguity in this situation was to some degree intentional, but the parties were exploiting the fact that there is something *inherently* ambiguous about the conditions surrounding all sorts of speech acts from apologies to promises to expressions of love.

The ambiguity of language is not the result of poor learning

In this book, which emphasizes interdiscourse aspects of communication, it is important to emphasize now that the ambiguity of language is not the result of poor learning. In other words you should not think that if people just had better vocabularies, a better grasp of English grammar, or better concepts of the nature of discourse these ambiguities would be cleared up. The point we are making is that ambiguity is inherent in all language use. There is no way to get around the ambiguity of language. What is most important is to recognize that this is the nature of language and to develop strategies for dealing with ambiguity, not to try to prevent it from developing.

We must *draw inferences about meaning*

We hope that by now our position is clear. Language is always inherently, and necessarily, ambiguous. That leads to the second point we want to make about communication: that in order to communicate we *must* always jump to conclusions about what other people mean.

There is no way around this. A crossword puzzle is much like the way language works. The first few entries are somewhat difficult, but where we are not sure, a few guesses seem to fit. These then fill in a couple of squares and help us to make more guesses. If those guesses seem to work, we will consider our first guesses to be fairly reliable. We do not consider them to be right answers until the whole puzzle is done and there are no more squares to fill in. If all of the words we have guessed fit in then we draw the final conclusion that our earliest guesses were correct.

Language works in a comparable way. When someone says something, we must jump to some conclusion about what he or she means. We draw inferences based on two main sources: (1) the language they have used, and (2) our knowledge about the world. That knowledge includes expectations about what people would normally say in such circumstances.

Our inferences tend to be fixed, not tentative

A third conclusion of the past three decades of research on conversational inference and discourse analysis is that the inferences we make tend to become fixed conclusions; they do not remain tentative in our minds.

There is a good reason why it should work this way, otherwise we would be always wandering around in uncertainty about what anything might mean. When someone says, "There's a man at the door," we draw the inference that this means that the man is standing at the door and waiting for someone to go to answer his call. We do not immediately begin to consider all the possibilities of what such a statement might mean. That would lead to complete communicative immobilization.

Many researchers in the field prefer to use the distinction between "marked" and "unmarked" to capture this aspect of communication. When we say that we make certain assumptions about the man at the door, those are the unmarked assumptions we are making. In other words, as long as nothing to the contrary leads us to expect differently, we assume that the world will operate the way we have come to expect it to operate. The unmarked expectation for men at doors is that described above. If the man at the door was dead or injured and lying at the door, we would expect the speaker to say, "There's a man lying at the door," or, perhaps, "There's somebody at the door, and he's in trouble." Something would be said to indicate that the unmarked expectation was not in effect in this case.

In other words, when there is no reason to expect otherwise, we assume the world will behave normally and that our unmarked expectations about it will continue to remain true. These fixed expectations are not tentative but are really the main substance of our concept of the normal, day-to-day world that we take for granted without questioning.

Our inferences are drawn very quickly

The fourth point we want to make, based on the research of the past three decades, is that the inferences we draw in ordinary conversation (as well as in reading written texts) are drawn very quickly. Most researchers suggest that such inferences must be drawn every time it becomes possible for speakers to exchange turns, and that such occasions occur approximately once every second in normal conversation.

The use of the term "inference" might lead to confusion, however. In using this term we do not want to suggest that these processes of conversational inference (or what we would really prefer to call practical inference) are conscious, cognitive operations. It would be better to think of our actions in ongoing social interaction as deriving from our senses of who we are more than from any conscious process of inferential interpretation. We want to avoid thinking, "I have acted this way because she/he said X, Y, or Z" because it is closer to the point to think, "I have acted this way because that's who and what I am." That is to say, the processes of conversational (or practical) inference arise out of our customary ways of being in social situations, not out of any conscious process of self-reflection and analysis. From this point of view it is dangerous to over-emphasize the cognitive or reflective aspects of conversational inference and conversational strategizing.

Inferences in interdiscourse communication

Language is ambiguous. This means that we can never be certain what the other person means – whether in speaking or writing. To put it another way, language can never fully express our meanings. Of course it is not surprising that research should confirm what philosophers in both the east and the west have told us for millennia. But what does this mean for interdiscourse communication?

In the first place it should be clear that communication works better the more the participants share assumptions and knowledge about the world. Where two people have very similar histories, backgrounds, and experiences, that is, where they are participating in the same or similar discourse systems, their communication works fairly easily because the inferences each makes about what the other means will be based on common experience and knowledge. Two people from the same village and the same family are likely to make fewer mistakes in drawing inferences about what the other means than two people from different cities on different sides of the earth.

The ambiguous nature of language is one major source of difficulties in interdiscourse communication. Where any two people differ in their discourse systems because they are of different genders, different ages, different ethnic or cultural groups, different educational backgrounds, different parts of the same country or even city, different income or occupational groups, or with very different personal histories, each will find it more difficult to draw inferences about what the other person means.

In the contemporary world people are in daily contact with people who participate in very different discourse systems. Successful communication is based on sharing as much as possible the assumptions we make about what others mean. When we are communicating with people who have different assumptions, it is very difficult to know how to draw inferences about what they mean, and so it is difficult to depend on shared knowledge and background for confidence in our interpretations.

Interdiscourse communication and English as a global language

More and more interdiscourse communication takes place in the language of English, and this fact is not insignificant. In many cases this communication is between one non-native speaker of English and another. When Chinese from Hong Kong do business in Japan, many aspects of this communication take place in English. When Koreans open an industrial complex in Saudi Arabia, again, English is generally the language in which business is transacted. As a result, the use of English carries with it an almost inevitable load of interdiscourse communication. At first this might seem a good thing – the more people have a "common language" the easier it should be to communicate. This however, as we have learned from our example with Mr Wong and Mr Richardson, is not always the case. In fact, sometimes when somebody demonstrates a high proficiency in your language you are lulled into thinking that they actually have the same expectations about what different kinds of utterances mean, an assumption that may not be at all justified.

Furthermore, languages, like all cultural tools, have various built-in affordances and constraints which limit and focus the kinds of meanings that can be expressed with them. We do not take the extreme deterministic position that a language solely determines the thought patterns of its speakers. We believe that reality is far too complex to allow for such a simple statement. Nevertheless, we believe that many aspects of what some might call "western culture," especially "western" patterns of discourse, which ultimately lead to confusion or to misinterpretation in intercultural discourse, are carried within English as well as transmitted through the process of the teaching and learning of English. Many of these distinctive patterns of discourse will be focused on in this book.

What This Book Is Not

We do not want to dwell on what we are not doing in this book as that is ultimately a very large universe. It is important to make a distinction, however, between studies of cross-cultural communication and intercultural communication. This is never a hard and fast distinction, of course, and a quick review of library and internet sources will show the reader that many people are coming to blur this distinction in their use of the terms. The basic distinction that we are trying to capture is the distinction between comparing communication systems of different groups *when considered abstractly* or *when considered independently of any form of social interaction* and looking at communication *when members of different groups are directly engaged with each other*. We would call the former type of study cross-cultural communication studies and what we are presenting in this book we would call intercultural communication, or better yet, interdiscourse communication. Our emphasis is on *people in social interaction with each other*, not upon abstract or independently conceived differences between members of different groups.

Our reasons for doing this are based in the research literature as well as in practical necessities. There is a very large and ever-growing research literature in anthropology, communication, sociology, education, business, and linguistics – to name just some of the fields – in which differences between different systems are compared. We find this literature fascinating and very useful in deriving preliminary hypotheses for studying social interactions among people who are members of different groups. Ultimately, however, there is a difficulty with that literature in that it does not directly come to grips with what happens when people are actually communicating across the boundaries of social groups.

To give just one example, we could say that it is a widespread practice in China (and Hong Kong and Taiwan) to eat with chopsticks and that it is the practice in North America and Europe and many other places to eat with knives, forks, and spoons. We could very elaborately describe these practices which are often quite complex and have to do with how and when the utensils are picked up, how they are held, how they are placed again on the table or on other utensils, and so forth. None of this would tell us, however, what would happen when a Chinese exchange student eats in a cafeteria in a British university nor what a South African would do on her first visit to Taiwan. Furthermore, as we have often observed, it is quite likely that each might try to adopt the other's custom and many times we have seen the North American eating with chopsticks while his or her Chinese counterpart enjoys the meal with a knife, fork, and spoon, each quite happy engaging in this cultural cross-over.

This rather homely example points up our concern to analyze situations in which members of different groups are in social interaction with each other and the interpretive processes they must bring to bear to understand each other in those highly altered hybrid and culturally mixed intermediate situations which are the common situations of intercultural communication. Further, as such research has established, in many situations some aspects of so-called cultural difference are of no relevance at all whereas other aspects that might be thought extremely minor might assume central importance. As an example of this, it might be the case that religious belief is of central personal and cultural importance to two businesspeople as individuals and as members of their home sociocultural groups. Yet in a business meeting, this might never be a factor in successful communication. At the same time, what might seem a trivial matter – whether you hand something to a person with one or two hands – might turn out to be the basis for one party deciding that the other was treating him rudely and make all the difference in a successful business encounter.

For this reason, in this book we have set aside – not as unimportant but rather as not directly relevant – aspects of cultural, group, or social differences that are not directly involved in social interactions between members from different groups. Our focus is on social interactions, on how they develop an internal logic of their own, and how people read those social interactions in making decisions and in taking actions that have consequences far beyond those situations themselves.

Researching Interdiscourse Communication

We will end each chapter of this book with some advice about how to do research in interdiscourse communication, and in particular how to apply the principles discussed in that particular chapter to studying real life situations. We do this with the assumption that many of the students using this book will be engaging in research projects as part of their coursework or planning to design and conduct some research project at a later date. We also do it with the assumption that doing research is the best way to find out for yourself how people communicate and the first step to solving communication problems whether they exist in your workplace, in your personal life, or in the political affairs of your community. And so, we strongly advise you to take the ideas we have presented here "out for a spin." That way you can understand better what is useful about these ideas and what their limitations are.

The ideas which are presented in this book have been derived over a period of decades of our own research and through the reading of the research literature. The primary methodology upon which this research has been based is most often called ethnography, from "ethno" (people) and "graphy" (to describe). Many books have been written on ethnographic methodologies as used in anthropology, sociology, education, and increasingly in business and government and perhaps the essential point made by all of them is that it is difficult to clearly set out the steps and procedures of ethnographic methodology.

Nevertheless there are four general processes which are common to all ethnographic studies and four types of data which bring to these studies not only concrete and vivid reality but also the validity and reliability of any scientific pursuit.

Four processes of ethnography

Ethnographic research methodology is based on fieldwork, participant observation, "strange making," and contrastive observation. Fieldwork is a quite general term which means that the researcher goes to the place where the phenomenon occurs naturally rather than trying to set up artificial or laboratory conditions for its study. This is one of the main distinctions, actually, between most cross-cultural communication research and intercultural communication research. Whereas most research in cross-cultural communication sets up experimental, survey, or test situations which are normally quite far removed from people actually engaged in social interaction, fieldwork takes the ethnographic researcher to the places where intercultural communication is happening. This means that the research is conducted in offices where job interviews are being conducted, in business meetings, in restaurants, taxis, hotels, and other places where tourists and travelers are encountering people different from themselves, but also in family conversations between members of different genders or generations, in classrooms where expatriate teachers are teaching "local" students, and all the other situations of normal life in our contemporary world where people who are different from each other engage in social interaction.

This leads to the second process, which is normally called participant-observation. This idea follows quite directly from the idea of fieldwork. If we are to study intercultural or interdiscourse communication in situations where it is actually happening as part of a day-to-day reality, the researchers themselves must be or must become participants in those situations. In practice this works in one of two ways:

1   The researcher studies a situation in which he or she is already a legitimate participant, such as his or her own family or office, and brings to that participation the formal observational procedures of the researcher.
2   The researcher studies a new situation and therefore has to work over a period of time to apprentice himself or herself to that situation to become a legitimate participant.

Of course in the first case the observations are rich in nuance and understanding of the situation but might easily be colored by less than objective involvement. In the second case the observations might well be quite objective, but to that extent may not truly represent the lived experience of the actual participants.

This leads to the third process, the process sometimes called "strange making." This is simply a way of talking about what happens when a person takes up the dual stance of participant and of observer. As participants we normally do things without thinking much about them. As observers we must come to see these day-to-day activities as "strange" so that we can isolate them and see them *as if* we did not know exactly what was going on. Either way, whether the researcher comes in as a new participant or brings his or her research project to the familiar, the process "makes strange" what is normally taken for granted and this is an essential aspect of ethnographic research which has made an enormous contribution to studies of intercultural communication.

Finally, perhaps the most crucial aspect of all studies of intercultural or interdiscursive communication is that of contrastive observation. We want to know not only *what people do* but also *how might they have done otherwise*. The surest way to learn how someone might have done otherwise is to contrast their action with the actions of people in other places, at other times, or in other groups. We only come to see the North American practice of handing a business card with one hand as strange when we come to realize that many people in Asia hand out a business card with two hands. In this contrastive observation, both practices are "made strange," and we can see that in both cases a perfectly natural option – one or two hands – is chosen and fixed upon as *the* way to do it.

Four types of data in ethnographic research

Of course ethnographers use a very wide range of technologies for producing their data which include photography, video, film, audio tape recording, hand-written field notes, and the collection of artifactual materials. They conduct interviews and focus groups, they attend significant ceremonies, meetings, and social events, and they also use products and materials produced by the members of the groups under study such as works of film and literature and TV and other media of entertainment. The data which are collected can be divided into four types which provide a kind of triangulation or cross-checking to provide both reliability (the idea that other researchers would find the same thing) and validity (the idea that what is observed and described really corresponds to something in the world and not just the researcher's own preconceptions). These four types of data can be called:

1 Members' generalizations.
2 Neutral (objective) observations.
3 Individual member's experience.
4 Observer's interactions with members.

In the first case, the researcher is concerned with getting an answer to the question: What do people in this group say is the meaning of this action? That is, the idea is to see what people themselves say about what they are doing. Of course, we are aware that people can easily give rationalizations of their actions and behavior that are wide of the mark of reality. Nevertheless, it is crucial in intercultural communication to know how the ingroup, the members of the society or group, themselves characterize their own actions.

These members' generalizations, of course, then have to be checked against more objective observations. This is often accomplished with some objective data recording such as with tape or video recording, photography, or some other means of documenting what actually happens as opposed to what people say *should* happen.

As an example of the difference between these two types of data we have the situation in which the mother of one of the authors was holding our infant child in her lap. We were asking her about her views about baby talk. She said that she felt it was a very bad influence on a child for an adult to use any form of baby talk and that she always insists on speaking properly to infants. That was very nice, of course, but the record we have of that same conversation in which she expressed those opinions was fully larded with baby talk to the infant in her lap. This is a case of the member saying that baby talk is bad and *within the same social interaction* using baby talk to talk to an infant.

Of course we know that people are inconsistent and these two sorts of data help to high-light these inconsistencies. The importance of this for our studies of interdiscourse communication is that the second kind of data keeps us from taking members' generalizations at face value. It protects us from making the same generalizations in our own analysis. After all, it is a person's actual behavior which is of importance in interdiscourse or intercultural communication. At the same time, however, it is important to know what members feel about themselves and their own communication. If the researcher is involved in training, for example, it is of no use to begin a training project by railing against (or for) the use of baby talk to infants if everyone in the training session believes that he or she never uses baby talk. They will simply see your comments as irrelevant. They must first be brought to see the contradictions between their own stated beliefs and their actual behaviors for such analysis to be useful.

The third type of data is also very important in achieving a degree of triangulation. Often a member of a group will say something like, "We always do X; but of course, I'm rather different and don't do that." It is very common for members of groups to state both a general, normative principle of behavior and then to also state an individual departure from that behavior. Michael Bond, for example, has found that in Hong Kong university-aged students are quite ready to describe characteristics of the typical Hong Konger but at the same time are also very unwilling to agree that those characteristics apply to themselves. This third type of observation can best be achieved through such means as case histories or life stories where subjects describe in vivid and concrete detail their own personal experiences. These individual and sometimes idiosyncratic observations give the researcher an idea of the range of variation allowed within a particular cultural group or discourse system and are essential to establishing first, how broadly a generalization can be made, and secondly, to what extent members are willing to accept general descriptions as descriptions of their own personal behavior.

Finally, the fourth type of data, and perhaps the most crucial while at the same time most difficult type of data to get is achieved by returning the analyst's observations and generalizations to the group about which they are made. We often feel that a description of our own behavior is an attempt to discredit or disadvantage us, and so it is very difficult for us to hear the descriptions others make of our own behavior. Nevertheless, when an ethnographer takes his or her analysis of a situation or a type of behavior back to the people about whom it has been observed, it provides an unequalled opportunity to see ourselves as others see us. As ethnographers we begin to understand how those we have studied see our studies and our observations. We know of no ethnographers who do not feel that this is by far the most rewarding part of his or her research, as painful as it sometimes is to have people tell you that the little piece of knowledge you think you have produced is basically all wrong. For the serious ethnographer this is a new starting point – a starting point for a much deeper understanding of the behavior he or she was trying to study in the first place.

Choosing a site of investigation

The gist of intercultural or interdiscourse analysis is not simply to try to describe discourse systems and to theorize about what might happen if participants of two different systems came into contact. The gist is to focus on people taking action in particular and concrete tasks and then to ask, without presupposing, what is the role of discourse systems in their taking these actions. How are these actions productive of "culture" or of participation in particular discourse systems? How are these actions significant in producing "others," that is, out-group members, through practices of inclusion and exclusion?

Your first step, then, in planning a research project in interdiscourse communication is to choose a *site of investigation* in which you can observe *people-in-action* in a rather close-up or intimate way. This might be your workplace, your school or university, your church or temple, or some kind of club or organization that you belong to. It might even be a "virtual" place like an online gaming site.

At first you might be tempted to look for a place where the contact between people of different nationalities occurs, and there is nothing wrong with this, although it is not necessary and may lead you to start off by jumping to the conclusion that this fact is particularly important when it comes to how people communicate – it may not be. In any case, whatever place you choose there are bound to be different discourse systems being used by different people and even different discourse systems being used by the same people.

Do not be distracted by the thought that you will have to make a full or exhaustive description of any of these discourse systems or of the social organization at your site. This is simply impossible, but worse than that, even if it were possible you would still be left not being entirely sure how to apply your knowledge when you were finished. It is better to focus on specific tasks, actions, or practices. In the training we provided for an international electronics manufacturer, for example, the task upon which we focused was the filling of service orders. The company had identified that as a particular bottleneck in overall company performance and so it seemed a suitable place to begin and on which to focus our efforts.

Much work in intercultural communication has focused on such tasks as job interviews, advancement or evaluation interviews, committee meetings, writing a committee report, or making a sale with a client. Organizations organize themselves through their tasks, their philosophies, values, and corporate cultures all manifest themselves in tasks, and so this is the most fruitful place to begin an analysis.

You might want to pay attention to a single action – some moment in the accomplishment of the task – which seems, at least at the outset, to be crucial. If it is a meeting over a contract, perhaps the moment of getting the signature onto the contract is the crucial moment. If it is a committee report, perhaps the moment in which a superior marks in red ink a stylistic correction that must be fixed is crucial. All tasks are made up of chains of actions and it is the study of concrete actions that helps you to sort out what is crucial to your analysis and what is actually only interesting but really quite peripheral.

Alternatively, you might want to focus on a practice. Perhaps it is the practice of answering the telephone in a particular way. One might study a large number of telephone calls, focusing upon just answering, to see what variation in the practice there is, when the practice varies, and why. In this case one is interested in who answers in different ways and why. Is it because of who is calling? And how do particular people come to learn to answer in particular ways?

And so, after you have decided on a site, it's a good idea to conduct a series of preliminary observations and talk to the people who inhabit the site in order to get some idea about what the most important actions, tasks, and practices are that occur in this site. When you enter your site, your first question should be a simple one: "What's going on here?" The way you answer this question will determine the course of the rest of your project.

Whether the focus is on a task or on a specific, concrete action, or on some larger social practice, you will be interested in asking how this action, task, or practice is positioned within what discourse systems? What cultural tools are called upon to accomplish the task or action or practice? What kinds of relationships are involved? What kinds of beliefs and values are displayed? These are some of the questions that we will be helping you to answer throughout this book.

In the next chapter we will introduce a method of analyzing the kinds of cultural tools and cultural competences people need in order to perform certain actions, tasks, or practices in different situations.

Discussion Questions

1   Conceptions of "culture" are *heuristics* – tools for thinking. Different tools make thinking about some aspects of human behavior and communication easier while they might conceal or distort other aspects. Look at the quotations below and discuss the various advantages and disadvantages to the definition of culture they contain.

(a)   A culture is the total way of life of a group of people. It includes everything they think, say, do, believe, and make.

(b)   Culture is a storehouse of pooled learning of a particular group of people.

(c)   Culture is the collective programming of the mind which makes certain kinds of people different from other people.

(d)   Culture is a theory on the part of social scientists about why certain people behave the way they do.

(e)   Culture is communication, and communication is culture.

(f)   Culture is the glue that holds societies together.

(g)   Culture is a tool of the powerful to help them to keep or extend their power.

(h)   Culture is the best that has been thought or said or produced in a particular society.

(i)   Culture is a way of life of a group of people – the behaviors, beliefs, values, and symbols that they accept, generally without thinking about them, and that are passed along by communication and imitation from one generation to the next.

(j)   Culture is a way of dividing people up into groups according to some feature of these people which helps us to understand something about them and how they are different from or similar to other people.

(k)   Culture is an illusion.

(l)   Culture is a verb.

2   Think of two different groups that you belong to and consider how you act, talk, and even think differently when you are participating with these different groups. For each of these groups list a) some of the main beliefs or values members have, b) some of the special ways people treat or interact with other members (e.g. according to their age, gender, rank, or how long they have been members) as well as how they treat people who are not members, c) the ways members of the group use to communicate with one another (e.g. text messages, emails, stories, jokes, lectures, insults), and d) the ways people learn to be members of this group. Discuss the similarities and differences between the two groups and how easy or difficult it is for you to be a member of both of these groups at the same time. You might think about how you might act if you were put into the situation of having to simultaneously interact with people from both of these groups.

References for Further Study

Those interested in the sociocultural theory which has influenced our view of culture will find a highly readable account in James Wertsch's 1991 book *Voices of the Mind*. A more complete treatment of mediated action and mediated discourse analysis can be found in Ron Scollon's 2001 book *Mediated Discourse: the nexus of practice*. Another useful approach to intercultural communication based on social constructionism is Philip Riley's 2007 *Language, Culture and Identity*. For more information about "capital D Discourses" readers should consult James Paul Gee's 2010 *Introduction to Discourse Analysis*, 3rd edition. Shorter readings outlining some of the ideas about culture and action laid out in this chapter are Ron Scollon's 2002 article "Intercultural communication as nexus analysis" and Brian Street's 1993 article "Culture is a verb." The basic framework for interactional sociolinguistics which provides many of the analytical tools we use in this book is outlined in the work of John Gumperz, especially in his 1982 book *Discourse Strategies*. The discussion of the four processes of ethnography is based on Ron Scollon's 1998 *Mediated Discourse as Social Interaction: a study of news discourse*. The analysis of the four kinds of data used in ethnographic triangulation began with Ruesch and Bateson in their 1951 (1968) classic *Communication: the social matrix of psychiatry*, and was further developed by Suzanne Wong Scollon (1995) and by Ron Scollon (1998). Michael Bond's (1993, 1996) work on the paradoxical nature of members' generalizations is particularly insightful. More information on the ambiguity of language and how we make inferences can be found in the work of Steven Levinson, especially his 2000 book *Presumptive Meanings*, as well as in the work of many others working in the fields of pragmatics, conversation analysis, and interactional sociolinguistics.

2

How, When, and Where to Do Things with Language

A: *Bill, that's a great idea. Could you write up a one-page summary for tomorrow's board meeting?*

B: *Of course, Mr Hutchins. Should I have it translated?*

A: *You'd better ask Jane. She'll know just who will be there.*

Such a dialogue seems quite ordinary in business communication and it probably does not require much imagination to understand what these two speakers are talking about. We know, for instance, that Bill has just said something which Mr Hutchins thinks is a good idea. We know that there will be a board meeting on the day following this conversation. We also know that Bill is in some way a subordinate of Mr Hutchins. Their way of addressing each other tells us that. Mr Hutchins feels free to use the first names of others (Bill and Jane) but Bill is apparently in the position of needing to use the designation of "Mr" when speaking to Mr Hutchins. In chapter 1 we said that language is always ambiguous. This dialogue is no exception. In spite of the things we know from this dialogue, there are quite a few things we cannot discover from the words alone. As an example of this ambiguity, even though we know that the board meeting is the next day, we do not know when this dialogue took place. The word "tomorrow" is relative to the time when it is spoken. If we do not know when this dialogue occurred we cannot know when the board meeting occurred.

In this short dialogue both speakers understand what is going on by relying on assumptions they make about the situation they are in, about the person they are speaking to, and about the relationship that exists between them (as well as about many other things). They "read between the lines" of their speech in order to make inferences about what is meant. If language were unambiguous there would be no need to make such inferences. And even if perfectly clear and explicit language were possible, it does not seem all that attractive an option. For example, if we were to take this dialogue and to rewrite it to make explicit just those parts of it that we have mentioned above, it might sound like this:

Intercultural Communication: A Discourse Approach, Third Edition. Ron Scollon, Suzanne Wong Scollon, Rodney H. Jones.

A: William Smith, my subordinate, that which you have just told me is a great idea. Since I
       am your superior I require you to write up a one-page summary for the meeting of this
       company's board meeting which is on Tuesday, December 8, 1994.
B: Of course, Robert Hutchins, my immediate superior. Should I have it translated?
A: You'd better ask Jane Pollard, the vice-president and colleague of equal rank to me.
       She'll know just who will be there.

One reason we would not want to try to be explicit is that we could never entirely succeed.
For each step of increased explicitness we would add new elements, which, to interpret, we
would have to read between the lines. For example, we replaced "board meeting" with "this
company's board meeting," but "this company" would also have to be replaced with the
specific name of the company. The second reason, however, that we could not be entirely
explicit is that in becoming more explicit about these matters we become cloudier about
others. For example, we have changed the terms "Bill" and "Mr Hutchins" to make the
relationship between these two speakers more explicit. But in doing so too much attention
is focused on their relationship and it begins to sound rather distant and hostile. It does not
make it sound more friendly and familiar to turn it into the following:

A: William Smith, my subordinate with whom I feel an easy familiarity . . .
B: Of course, Robert Hutchins, my immediate superior, with whom I also feel an easy,
       though respectful familiarity . . .

Such an explicit statement of the relationships actually makes it seem less familiar and
friendly. In fact, we have a very effective system for saying all of that. We do it the way
these speakers did it in the first place: A calls B by his first name "Bill," and he, in turn,
calls the other "Mr Hutchins." Both of these speakers understand this system in which they
exchange such forms of address, so they can use it as a kind of code for exchanging comments about their relationship while they get on with the business of writing up the summary
for the board meeting.
   Shared knowledge is the basis on which these speakers read between the lines of their
conversation. We will consider two different types of shared knowledge in this chapter and
the chapter which follows:

1   shared knowledge of actions and situations (chapter 2);
2   shared knowledge of relationships and identities (chapter 3).

In this chapter we focus on the scenes or venues in which our communicative actions and
activities occur. These communications can be understood as happening in acts, events, and
situations among participants at certain times and places for particular purposes. The dialogue above can be easily interpreted by both participants partly because they share knowledge about what a board meeting is, when and where it is likely to take place, and what sorts
of things will happen when it occurs. And although they do not themselves know who the
participants will be, they know that who the participants are is a significant question and
that their colleague, Jane, is knowledgeable about who will be participants. Shared knowledge about these components of such communicative situations is the framework in which
successful communicative action takes place.

Sentence Meaning and Speaker's Meaning

A: Can you tell me what time it is?
B: Yes, I can.

If this conversation took place under normal circumstances such as in an office or at a bus stop, A would consider B's answer to be very strange. The answer which B gives in this dialogue is grammatically correct and yet it is completely wrong. A is not asking about B's ability to tell time at all. He or she is asking B to tell him or her the time. The problem with B's answer is that it is responding to the sentence meaning but not to the speaker's meaning.

In chapter 1, we used the similar sentence, "What time is it?," as an example of the way in which the speaker's meaning can change depending on the context in which a sentence is used. When you are asking for the time on the street, "What time is it?" conveys a speaker's meaning very close to the sentence's meaning. But when a teacher uses this same sentence in a classroom the speaker's meaning is very different. The speaker (the teacher) really means, "I want you to tell me the time so that I can see if you know how to do it correctly." When the student responds by saying, "Two o'clock," that also means something different from what it appears to mean. What it means is something like, "I know how to tell the time correctly which I will show you by saying the correct time."

Understanding both sentence meaning and the speaker's meaning requires two kinds of knowledge. Sentence meaning depends on knowledge of grammar; speaker's meaning depends on knowledge of context. Our purpose in this chapter is to examine the concept of context.

Speech Acts, Speech Events, and Speech Situations

When you ask for the time at a bus stop with the sentence, "What time is it?," your meaning (the speaker's meaning) is that you want to know the time. This speech act takes place within a speech event which could be called *asking for the time*. Such an event is very brief and usually has three speech acts: asking the time, giving the time, and thanking. We could outline this speech event as follows:

Asking for the time	(speech event)
What is the time?	(speech act 1)
The time is X.	(speech act 2)
Thanking.	(speech act 3)

Your knowledge of communication in English includes both the sentences you need to accomplish the three speech acts and the knowledge of this three-act speech event.

When a teacher asks an elementary student what the time is, this is a very different speech event. We could call it *testing for the concept of telling the time*. It normally consists of three speech acts as well: asking the time, giving the time, and the teacher's evaluation. We could outline this speech event as follows:

> *Testing for the concept of telling the time*   (speech event)
> (teacher):   *What is the time?*   (speech act 1)
> (student):   *The time is* X.   (speech act 2)
> (teacher):   *Evaluation.*   (speech act 3)

The main difference between these speech events lies in the third speech act. There is also a difference in the participation structure. We could not have the student take the role of the teacher and the teacher take the role of the student in the normal use of this speech event.

Speech acts can be expressed in many different ways. The person on the street could accomplish speech act 1 with quite a few different sentences. Any of the following sentences would accomplish essentially the same speech act:

> What time is it?
> Could you tell me the time?
> Excuse me, do you know the time?
> Pardon me, do you have a watch?

In each case part of the meaning (the sentence meaning) is given by the sentence used and part of the meaning (the speaker's meaning) comes out of the fact that the interlocutors know the speech act of *asking for the time*.

In the example we gave at the beginning, the problem was that the person responded to the literal sentence, not to the speaker's meaning. When A asked B, "Can you tell me what time it is?," B responded not with speech act 2 ("The time is X") but with a literal answer to the sentence. In such a case A might conclude that B is ignorant of the speech event *asking for the time*, B is being uncooperative, or B is, perhaps, joking. Since we do not usually joke with strangers on the street, that explanation can be ruled out.

We can interpret the meaning of sentences by understanding the context of the speech events in which they occur. In the same way, speech events take place within the larger context of speech situations. To give another example taken from a business meeting: within the conduct of a meeting the chairman of the meeting might be asked for a point in reference to a preceding meeting. He might then turn to the secretary of the meeting and begin the following dialogue:

> *Chairman*:   Do you have the minutes?
> *Secretary*:   Yes, here they are. I think 2.4.3 is what you will need.

Within this speech event which we might call a business meeting, the question, "Do you have the minutes?," probably conveys the speaker's meaning, "*Please find the relevant point and indicate that to me.*" Both the chairman of the meeting and the secretary understand their participant roles. His role includes such aspects as to conduct the meeting, to gather in the points of view of the members, and so forth. The secretary's role is to provide an accurate record of the meeting, to provide references to other meetings, and to handle such administrative affairs as are needed by the members of the meeting. This is knowledge of the speech event of the business meeting which all of the members share. As a result the fairly simple sentence, "Do you have the minutes?," conveys in polite language quite a complex set of speech acts. Some of them might be as follows:

Take out the minutes of the last meeting.
Find the relevant point within the minutes.
Show me the relevant point.

We can see that the meaning of this sentence depends upon its placement within a speech event by placing it within a different but very closely related speech event, the pre-meeting informal discussion. We can imagine most of the participants of the meeting have come into the conference room. They are casually chatting with each other while they wait for the chairman of the meeting to call the meeting to order. During that period of casual conversation the chairman turns to the secretary and we have the following dialogue:

Chairman: Do you have the minutes?
Secretary: Yes, here they are.
Chairman: Good. Thanks.

In this case the same sentence, "Do you have the minutes?," would be understood as a much more literal question regarding whether or not the secretary had brought the minutes to the meeting. This speech event, which we could call *pre-meeting preparation*, is very similar to the longer speech event which follows but can also be clearly distinguished from it in various ways. We would expect many of the members to speak to each other casually, often on topics not related to the purpose of the meeting. There would be much simultaneous speaking, in contrast to the meeting, in which we would expect one person to speak at a time. Such differences in topics and in participation structures show that there are really two quite separate events within a larger speech situation. We could outline the structure as follows:

Speech situation: Business meeting
Speech event: Pre-meeting preparation
Speech act: Asking if the secretary has the minutes
Speech act: Confirming that the secretary has the minutes
Speech act: Thanking the secretary

Speech event: Meeting
Speech act: Asking the secretary to find the point under consideration in the minutes
Speech act: Indicating point 2.4.3 in the preceding meeting's minutes
Speech event: Post-meeting discussion

Grammar of Context

We understand the meanings of sentences in part because we know the grammatical rules by which they are constructed. Of course, much of our knowledge of those rules is not conscious. Nevertheless, we follow regular patterns in our use of subjects and predicates and in our selections of vocabulary items, which makes it possible for others to interpret our sentence meaning, even if that interpretation is often very ambiguous. In the same way, we interpret the meanings of speakers because we know the rules by which contexts are constructed. We could call this a kind of "grammar of context," which we use to interpret the meanings of speech acts within speech events which occur within speech situations.

In the example we have given above, a number of the features of this grammar of context have been mentioned. We know about participants and their roles. The chairman has a different role from the secretary and both of them have roles which are again different from the members of the board or committee. We also know that the meeting has specific rules for conduct so that we can tell when it has begun and when it has ended. That, in turn, tells us what belongs in the pre-meeting speech event or in the post-meeting speech event. Both of those events have different rules for participation and topics compared with the meeting itself.

The shared knowledge of grammar is well known to be essential for effective communication, and language teaching has focused primarily on helping students to develop that kind of knowledge. Our purpose is to emphasize the shared knowledge of context which is required for successful communication. There are many different theories of grammar and many different schools of thought about how it should be taught. The same is true of what we are calling the grammar of context. For some researchers the term "sociolinguistics" covers this area of study. For others the preferred term would be the "ethnography of speaking." While we follow the latter scheme, we do so in a non-dogmatic way. For our purposes the most important point is that there are many aspects of context which are relevant in interdiscourse communication, and we need some common vocabulary for talking about them.

The outline which follows summarizes the main components which we believe are necessary for the student of interdiscourse communication to study.

Seven main components for a grammar of context

1 Scene:
   (a) Setting:
      – Time
      – Place
      – Location
      – Use of space
   (b) Purpose (function)
   (c) Topic
   (d) Genre
2 Key
3 Participants:
   (a) Who they are
   (b) Roles they take
4 Message form:
   (a) Speaking
   (b) Writing
   (c) Silence
   (d) Other media:
      – Video
      – Digital images such as PowerPoint slides
      – Amplification
      – Recording
5 Sequence:
   (a) Set agenda
   (b) Open agenda

6   Co-occurrence patterns
7   Manifestation:
    (a)   Tacit
    (b)   Explicit

These seven components of a grammar of context, along with their subcomponents, should not be thought of as fixed categories. Rather, they should be used to stimulate your thinking about the elements of which speech situations and speech events are composed. Some speech situations such as business meetings and university lectures are relatively fixed in the constellation of components which make them up. For example, a business meeting will most often have a regular scene – a conference room in the main office of the company at a regular morning hour, etc. University lectures are speech situations which quite predictably take place in lecture halls. Other speech situations are more notable for the variability of the components of which they consist. A friendly conversation might take place in a range of settings from the hallways of an office to the crowded interior of a commuter train.

To make the distinction between the concept of the speech situation and the components of a grammar of context clear, perhaps we could think of the speech situation as an answer to the question, "What are they doing?" The components of the grammar of context are an answer to the question, "How are they doing it?"

Scene

The most obvious aspect of context is probably the setting in which speech situations and events occur. We will use the word "scene" to include the setting as well as topic, genre, and purpose, since they are all so closely related.

The setting is first of all a physical location. For example, the setting for a business meeting is likely to be a conference room located in the office spaces of the company or the organization holding the meeting. In fact most businesses are set up to have prearranged settings for many of their functions. There are general offices in which clerical staff keep the main records and do the main clerical work of the business. There are conference rooms, offices for various members of the staff, storage rooms, and often lunchrooms or lounges for staff. Many businesses also have separate public spaces such as lobbies or sales or display rooms.

We also know, regarding the spaces in which speech events are held, that position in space is an important aspect of communication. We expect the chair of a meeting to sit in a position which will be seen as the "head" of the table, for example. We know that people of higher authority usually have more freedom to occupy more space and to move about freely within it than those of lesser authority. The president of a company might be seen to walk about a room giving a presentation of a new development plan to which all of his or her subordinates sit quietly at a conference table listening.

Setting includes not just the physical location. Time as well is a crucial aspect of setting. If we know that a meeting has been called to discuss a new personnel policy we can assume that the meeting will be held sometime during normal business hours. The internationalization of business and government over the past few decades has combined with rapid air transportation so that more and more the meaning of "normal business hours" has come into question. For example, it is not unusual for those who trade stock to gear their working hours to the hours in which major stock exchanges are open for trading. The "normal working hours" of stockbrokers in Honolulu correspond with the actual hours during which the New York Stock Exchange operates. Because of the location of Hawaii, that makes their "normal" day begin at four o'clock in the morning. Other businesses such as newspapers or television production operate on schedules that are geared to production deadlines. One major aspect of knowing the setting for speech events within such professional contexts is knowing what "normal working hours" means.

For each kind of speech event or speech situation, then, there are likely to be pre-established norms for the places where they will be held, for the use of space within those places, for the times they will occur and the duration of those events. All of these will be considered to relate to the purposes of the events. Issues regarding time and space, however, can be especially tricky in interdiscourse communication given that participants in different discourse systems may conceptualize and use time and space quite differently. Understanding participants' shared knowledge of scene, therefore, often involves getting at more underlying and fundamental presuppositions about time and space.

It was the American anthropologist Edward T. Hall who first brought to popular consciousness the idea that people in different "cultures" understand time and space differently. In his 1959 book *The Silent Language* he claimed that North Americans tend to view time as a commodity that can be used, wasted, or measured as if it were material. Such a view of time, he argued, based on the implicit assumption that time can be measured by duration between two points (e.g. a day which extends from midnight to midnight), is a common characteristic of western cultures. We might call this view of time "clock time" or *chronos* time, to use a word from the ancient Greeks. People who participate in other discourse systems, however, view time rather differently. Hall pointed out, for example, that for the Hopi time is not a durable, fixed, measurable quantity but rather a process of maturing as in the ripening of corn or the growth of lambs into sheep. This is more like what the Greeks called *kairos*, time that becomes ripe with waiting. There is a time for planting and a time for harvest. Planting before spring rains have softened the ground is not only difficult but unwise.

This difference between scheduled, measured time and time that matures to enhance certain activities can result in different behavior when it comes to things like scheduling and punctuality. This difference, according to Hall, caused much conflict in the 1950s between the Hopi and U.S. government bureaucrats who expected them to construct dams and highways according to a planned schedule. When we specify then, under the component of scene, that a particular event should occur at a certain time, we must also attempt to determine how this fits in with participants' view of time – whether they are operating according to *chronos* time or *kairos* time.

In bringing up Hall's observations about time and "culture," however, we do not wish to suggest that all people from a particular "culture" or who participate in a particular discourse system have the same orientation towards time which they apply universally to all situations in which they find themselves. This is clearly not the case. You are, for example, more likely to orient yourself towards *chronos* time when determining when to send in your tax return, while the decision about when to ask a girl or a boy you fancy out on a date might be more a matter of "the right moment' or *kairos* time. This is what makes the grammar of context such a useful tool since it leads us to consider such issues not in terms of the characteristics of particular groups of people, but rather in terms of the characteristics of particular events or situations in which these people are involved.

Hall made similar observations in *The Silent Language* and later in *The Hidden Dimension* (1966) about the ways people from different "cultures" use space. All of us, he contended, consciously or unconsciously, have the notion of "personal space," the invisible "bubble" around our bodies which we feel uncomfortable when other people intrude into. North Americans, he said, have a sense of personal space which extends roughly 4 feet out from a person's skin. Southern Europeans and South Americans, he said, have a much smaller "bubble" of personal space. When engaged in conversation, individuals maintain a distance between themselves and their interlocutors consonant with what they have internalized in a lifetime of socialization. Hall describes the kind of dance that can be performed between persons whose comfort zone differs, so that one can be literally spurred to walk backwards down a long corridor by an interlocutor who is simply maintaining a comfortable distance for herself.

North Americans' sense of personal space is manifested, Hall argued, in their preference for large vehicles. They feel crowded in European or Japanese automobiles unless there are few enough passengers to preserve space without physical contact with other bodies. Some believe that only a stiff tax on gasoline can prevent Americans from purchasing gas-guzzling SUVs. Though the economic crisis of 2008 depressed sales of these petroleum consuming vehicles, as soon as the economy recovered somewhat sales rose steeply.

Again, it is important to remember that all of us are simultaneous participants in multiple discourse systems and that blanket assumptions about people's use of space based on a single trait like their ethnicity or national origin are not particularly useful. At the same time, these insights do remind us that the use of space in particular speech events and situations is often, at least in part, a reflection of notions about space that are deeply ingrained in the "historical bodies" of participants (see chapter 8).

Along with space and time, purpose, topic, and genre are also part of our consideration of the scene. Our shared knowledge of scene includes knowing which spaces are most appropriate for which purposes, and so purpose can hardly be separated from the knowledge of setting. While there is usually some leeway in the purposes for which physical settings can be used, it would be seen to be strange behavior to conduct a high-level management meeting in the customers' waiting room of a large corporation. Or it would be seen as unusual for administrative staff to be typing up memos while seated at a conference table at which a sales presentation was being made. Generally speaking we have some well-defined idea of how to relate the purposes of speech events to conventionally appropriate locations.

Most communicative events also carry some expectations regarding topics. In a letter of credit issued by a company for the import of foreign-made goods one would expect the topics to include such things as the amount of money concerned, the quantity of goods involved, some indication of effective dates for payment and delivery, and so forth. One would not expect to find a discussion of a movie the author had seen on television the night before. In fact one of the main features that indicate a change in speech event is a change in topic. In shifting from a pre-meeting speech event to the main agenda of the meeting the chair is likely to say something like, "Perhaps we should get down to the business on our agenda." It will be understood by everyone present that from then on casual or irrelevant topics should no longer be introduced and that it is time to focus on the topics introduced by the agenda only.

"Genre" is a term borrowed from the study of literature to refer to different conventional forms of speech events. For example, jokes, lectures, business meetings, textbooks, memoranda of agreement, sales letters, product brochures, tables of organization, contracts, evaluation reports, advertising copy, business lunches, and so forth are all different genres. By genre we mean any speech event, whether it is spoken or in writing, which has fairly predictable sets of speech acts, participants, topics, settings, or other regularly occurring and conventional forms. A focus on the internal content and form of genres is not the whole story, however, since to use any genre of communication effectively requires knowing just when it is appropriate to use it. For many years, for example, it has been an unwritten rule of public speaking in many business environments that the speaker should include a few jokes at the beginning of a talk. By the early 1990s this expectation of public speakers had become so generalized that it came to affect the annual address to Congress given by the president of the United States. In the State of the Union address in 1992, for example, then President George H. W. Bush began this significant and formal ceremonial occasion with a sequence of several jokes:

> Mr Speaker and Mr President, distinguished Members of Congress, honored guests, and fellow citizens:
> Thank you very much for that warm reception. You know, with the big buildup this address has had, I wanted to make sure it would be a big hit, but I couldn't convince Barbara to deliver it for me. (*Laughter*)
> I see the speaker and the vice-president are laughing. They saw what I did in Japan, and they're just happy they're sitting behind me. (*Laughter*)

While at one time the inclusion of this genre in public ceremonial occasions would have been considered a terrible breach of decorum, in the business-dominated environment of that particular administration the jokes seemed to convey sympathy with the conventions and practices of the business world.

Different conceptions of time and space can also affect how people understand things like purpose, topic, and genre. People differ, according to Hall, as to whether they take a *monochronic* view of time or a *polychronic* view of time. People with a *monochronic* orientation towards time prefer to do one thing at a time. People with a *polychronic* orientation are more comfortable multitasking. Thus, when analyzing situations and events in terms of purpose, topic, and genre, it is important to remember that some people feel more comfortable than others engaging in multiple activities at one time, that is, there may be more than one topic, purpose, or genre involved at any given moment. When people use computers, for example, it is quite common for them to simultaneously engage in multiple activities at once: surfing the web, chatting with multiple people, answering email, updating their Facebook status, downloading or uploading files, and listening to a lecture – a fact that regularly causes some consternation for lecturers in college classrooms in which students bring along their laptop computers (ostensibly) in order to take notes.

Key

"Key" is a term borrowed from music to refer to the tone or the mood of a communication. A businessperson the authors know once took her young daughter with her to a business meeting. She had told her daughter that they were going to attend a meeting and that she would have to be quiet and behave herself. As it had turned out the meeting had developed a very relaxed key and there was much free conversation and laughing. Afterwards the child said to her mother, "That wasn't a meeting; it was a party." When she was asked why she said that, her answer was that meetings were to be serious and parties were for laughing. This young child understood a significant aspect of two typical speech situations: that a business meeting and a party normally differ in key.

One very interesting aspect of professional communication, especially when it occurs in an international environment, is that there is so much variability across groups in their expectations about key and about how and when different keys should be expressed. Some people, for example, tend to smile or laugh when they are embarrassed, whereas for others laughing or joking is nearly always associated with comfort and conviviality. Hence there is a serious potential for the misreading of key in communications between people with these differing habits of communication. A key of embarrassment or difficulty might be read as indicating a key of relaxation or enjoyment, or a relaxed, joking tone might be interpreted as hiding embarrassment. In either case the failure to correctly interpret the key being conveyed by one's interlocutors could lead to serious misinterpretation of the speakers' meanings.

Participants

Two aspects of participants need to be taken into consideration in reading the contextual grammar of speech situations: who they are and what roles they are taking. Naturally, of course, the sheer number of participants is a significant aspect of any communicative situation. To begin with number first, any speech event needs to take into consideration the number of participants even if just to know how to prepare the setting. A meeting of 200 people cannot be easily held in a conference room. It is equally true, but for a very different reason, that a meeting of twenty people cannot be held in a large auditorium. In arranging for an event such as a lecture or a sales presentation, most people would prefer to arrange to have a space just a little larger than the number of people would require. If the space is too small, people are made uncomfortable since not everyone will be able to sit well or to see the main speaker or presenter. On the other hand if the space is very much too large, people will tend to be seated widely apart from each other and that will create a sense of isolation and social coldness.

Yet number is a relatively minor aspect of the study of participants. It is much more important to know who the participants are and what roles they take. It is well known, for example, that most governments have protocol offices whose job is to make sure that all participants in government functions will be given just the right treatment. Seating at state dinners, for example, is an important matter of correctly signifying the relative positions of power and authority among the invited guests.

A second aspect, of equal importance, is to understand not just who the participants are but what roles they are taking within the speech event. It is quite common, for example, for someone who is of major importance within a company or some other organization to have what is an apparently insignificant role in an actual speech event. Often major decisions are made behind the scenes and the business which is conducted more openly is only done to legitimate or ratify decisions made elsewhere. We have often seen in companies, for example, cases where a junior company position is occupied by someone who is related to the owner or is, perhaps, held in high esteem by someone much more powerful in the company. In actual business events that person may appear to have a fairly insignificant role but nevertheless be more greatly empowered to make decisions than his or her official role would indicate.

One final point on the question of participant roles is important to make. In some companies there is a tendency to give a great deal of power to the individuals who represent them in international negotiations. In other companies, on the other hand, people are often put in the position of negotiating on behalf of someone else who actually holds the power to make decisions. This is for several reasons. It may be, for example, that people lower in the company structure actually have a more agile command of intercultural communication and of languages (such as English), and so they are given the position of conducting negotiations. The result of this difference in the authority given to negotiators is that employees from the second kind of company are often somewhat more restricted in what they can do or say in such meetings than their counterparts from the first kind of company, who are in the position of making their own decisions right there on the spot. This difference in participant roles is not likely to be known or very well understood by both parties. The result is that each assumes the other party has equivalent status and therefore cannot understand or cannot easily interpret the speakers' meanings of the sentences exchanged. One is likely to speak in terms of "I": "I will offer so much for a certain quantity." The other is likely to speak in terms of "we": "We cannot say immediately whether we can meet that price or that deadline." The role of the first may sound like exaggeration or egocentrism to the second, and the role of the second may sound like resistance or non-cooperation to the first. In either case the problem stems from the lack of understanding of differences in participant role structure.

Message form

One of the most important aspects of communication is to know what is the most effective medium to use for communication. A wily educational administrator in the Yukon Territory of Canada once told one of the authors, "Whoever prints the program determines the content." It is well known in business and in governmental communications that whoever makes the agenda for a meeting has already had the strongest voice in how the meeting will come out before it has even begun.

In every field of communication it is important to choose the form of the message carefully. In marketing there is an enormous range of possibilities including television and radio commercial advertisements, newspaper advertisements, direct mailings, brochures, leaflets, banner ads on websites, word of mouth, "viral" marketing on social networking sites, testimonials of well-known people, bus-side and train placards, and virtually every other form in which messages can be conveyed.

The decision of which medium to use is not just a question of medium; it is also a question of contents and of social structure, even of law. An advertising campaign that prints a paragraph of text in a newspaper advertisement might have only two or three words of text in a television spot but emphasize the use of visual symbolism and sound instead. A radio spot would, of course, have only sound. A web based ad could include text, sound, graphics, video, and even a certain degree of interactivity which could allow potential customers to ask questions and make immediate purchases. The result is that the contents themselves would be considerably different.

To look at the legal question, in most cases agreements made face to face or over the phone have little or no legal status. They become legally binding only when they are written, signed, and in some cases witnessed as well. Faxes apparently have no legal status since they are considered copies of documents, not the documents themselves. Documents are often printed, signed, scanned, then emailed, though some more critical documents may require a witness and a notary, in which case they are sent by post or courier. Although "digital signatures" are becoming more common, at the time of writing their legal status had not yet come to be seen as equal to that of physical signatures.

One result of the more official status accorded original written documents is that it becomes a significant aspect of negotiation whether something is given written status or not. As we will discuss below, one major aspect of the grammar of context is that some things are explicitly known and some things remain tacit or unexpressed. A business conducting questionable business practices, of course, will want to keep as few written records as possible so that legal authorities cannot check up on its activities. But even for completely legal activities it is often felt desirable or necessary to keep some aspects of institutional knowledge tacit.

Almost every organization in which professional communicators work has an official organization chart which shows who holds which position of authority and what the normal lines of communication are to be. At the same time, as we have mentioned above when we were talking about participant status, it is often the case that unofficial lines of authority and of communication exist within that organization. Such lines are virtually always kept out of writing. They remain part of the oral tradition of companies and of institutions. One important aspect of shared knowledge is not only knowing what those lines of communication are, but also knowing that they are not to be made explicit, especially not in written form.

Sequence

Speech situations have important internal structures which determine the order in which events can occur. Knowing this structure is essential to being able to interpret just which speech event is happening. For example, in the pre-meeting speech event we discussed above the sentence, "Do you have the minutes?" was understood to mean that the chair was asking if the secretary had brought them to the meeting. Within the meeting, however, the same sentence was understood to mean that the chair wanted the secretary to consult the minutes. At that time we said that this was because one occurred within the meeting and the other occurred before the meeting, but how did we know that? There were several indications, one of which was participant structure and topic selection – people were freely talking to each other about general topics and then the chair called the meeting to order. That still does not tell us, however, how the participants knew that the meeting had not started. The answer to that question is that part of their shared knowledge, part of their grammars of context, told them that meetings have several events and those events come in a normal sequence. The first is a transitional event that takes place while everyone gathers at the meeting place and prepares for the meeting. Since they knew that sequence of events, they knew they could talk freely until the chair called the meeting to order and started it formally.

Across discourse systems there is a particular problem with understanding events, often because most aspects of the events are similar and only the order will be changed, and this difference in sequencing can cause confusion. The more formal a speech situation is the more likely it is to have a formal agenda. This is because sequence is so important in defining participation in speech events. As we have said above, whoever controls the agenda has a major voice in the outcomes of speech events.

There are two sides of sequencing as part of the grammar of context. On the one hand it is part of our shared knowledge, which helps us to interpret meanings if we know the conventional sequences in which things happen. On the other hand it is part of our ability to create meanings, to be able to manipulate the sequences of events to achieve the greatest effectiveness.

Co-occurrence patterns, marked and unmarked

We have presented these components of a grammar of context as somewhat isolated. Nevertheless, we have had no choice but to mention a number of co-occurrence patterns among them. For example, the genre of jokes in most cases occurs together with the humorous key. That does not mean that it is impossible to use a joke in a non-humorous key. For example, someone might be very offended by a joke and find it not funny at all. In telling a friend about it he or she might tell the joke but in a key of having been affronted.

Such a predictable co-occurrence as a joke in a humorous key would be called "unmarked" whereas a joke told in an affronted way would be considered to be "marked." All that this means is that the unmarked configuration would be thought to be quite unremarkable. It is something nobody would really notice unless they were studying the phenomenon. On the other hand something which was marked would be surprising or unexpected. This does not mean that it does not happen; it just means that when marked events or collocations of these components occur, we notice that something is different and that we have to pay particular attention to interpret them correctly.

We have given a number of examples of unmarked speech events or genres above. A board which meets in a conference room during normal business hours and which has an agenda would be unmarked. There is little unexpected about that. If that same meeting was to be held in an underground vault deep in the basement of corporate headquarters, it would be very marked and we would be looking for an explanation of why something so marked was happening.

Manifestation

To close this presentation of the components of communication events and situations, we want to bring up again a point made above. Some of the components of communication are manifested in very explicit form. Other components remain tacit, that is, unexpressed. In the example we mentioned above, the official authority structure of a business or a corporation is almost always presented in an organizational chart or a table of organization (TOE). This is an explicit manifestation of the structure of the organization. At the same time the unofficial power structure or authority structure by which decisions are often directly taken or at least influenced is normally not explicitly given; it remains tacit. There are at least two reasons why not all components of communication are made explicit. The first reason is simply because that is often very difficult to do, because we do not really know how they work. Much of our activity as human beings remains out of our conscious control and so it is not surprising that much of our communicative activity should also remain out of our conscious awareness.

The second reason that many aspects of communication remain tacit is that we prefer for them to do so. It is a major component by which the grammar of context is constructed for some of them to be tacit and some of them to be explicit. Again, perhaps, we should ask what the reasons are that we prefer for some aspects of communication to remain tacit. Some of the reasons are fairly positive aspects of human communication, others are not usually looked upon so favorably.

In professional communication, for example, when a person comes up for promotion, it will be considered a very strong recommendation to see that this person has "read between the lines" of his or her professional requirements and gone beyond that to do what is best for his or her organization. In fact it could almost be thought of as a negative recommendation to say that a particular person has always done exactly and only what was explicitly required. And so, if it is considered valuable for a person to go beyond what is required, it is necessary to never explicitly say everything that is required.

The negative side of this same aspect of communication is that such unstated and tacit understandings can be held against a person, and that person has no recourse where this happens. To take the idea of promotion again, if it is never stated on what basis a person will be promoted, then it is always very easy to say that person has not done enough to deserve promotion. It is for this latter reason that so many attempts to correct social injustices and inequalities have taken the form of trying to make all the rules completely explicit. While the motives for wanting everything to be explicit are laudable – who could say that they really want injustice? – it is unfortunate that this position shows a great misunderstanding of human communication. Human communication is always ambiguous, as we have said. One way of rephrasing this statement is to say that in human communication it is impossible to make every aspect explicit. For professional communication, the main point is not to fret over the injustices which occur but to try to understand how communication is structured through a grammar of context which gives us the basis for interpreting the speaker's meaning.

Variation in context grammar

In the way that we have presented these seven components of the grammar of context, we may have given the impression that all seven components are equally important in all speech situations. This is not true. In fact, different kinds of speech situations are often distinguished by how important different aspects of the grammar of context are to communication and how the different elements interact with one another. Participant roles and use of space may be much more important in classrooms and courtrooms than they are in cocktail parties. Time and space are much more important in boarding a bus than the topic or key of the conversation you are having with your companion.

"Culture" and Context

The main point of all of this is that people who participate in the same discourse system are likely to use the same grammar of context when engaging in and interpreting particular speech situations, speech events, and speech acts. In fact, competence in the Grammars of

Context of particular speech situations is often an important way of showing that you "belong" to a discourse system. At the same time, just as language grammars can be learned by non-native speakers, so can people who are not regular participants in a discourse system learn the context grammars of that discourse system. In fact, over the past few decades, language teaching professionals have become increasingly sensitive to the importance of context in making and interpreting meaning and to the importance of teaching language in the context of "real life" communication.

High context and low context situations

Another well-known concept of the anthropologist Edward T. Hall is that of "high context" and "low context cultures," a concept which has gained considerable credence in cross-cultural communication studies. What Hall suggests with this distinction is essentially that for some "cultures" (or, in our parlance, some discourse systems) the context is a more important component of communication than in others.

Hall defined "high context cultures" as those in which members are likely to refer to contextual aspects of the communication such as background knowledge, setting, and the relationships among participants more than verbal messages. In such "cultures," he said, ritualized forms of communication, constituting shared experiences and expectations, act to cement group members together. In "low context cultures," on the other hand, people tend to rely more on the information encoded in verbal messages in order to communicate and interpret the communication of others, and relationships and roles may be less fixed. Hall considered Asian, Latin American, and southern European cultures to be high context and North American and northern European cultures to be low context.

Naturally, given our position on the concept of "culture" outlined in the last chapter, we are reluctant to label cultures or discourse systems as high context or low context. Such blanket distinctions rarely hold true. One can very easily, for example, think of situations in which Chinese might be very verbally explicit and North Americans might prefer to leave certain things unsaid, communicating them instead through context. It is more useful, we believe, to speak of high context and low context *situations*, and to say that for participants in particular discourse systems, some situations rely more on context for meaning than others.

In the contrast discussed above between different expectations for negotiators, for example, we said that participants from some companies in international business negotiations are often of a lower rank and so tend to impart and receive information rather than make decisions, while those from other companies make decisions relatively more freely. We might rephrase this contrast by saying that for negotiators from the first kind of company business negotiations are rather high context situations requiring formulaic responses such as "Yes, we understand" rather than considered replies such as "Yes, we agree, and further-more we would also like . . ." Those from the second kind of company, on the other hand, treat the same situation or event as low context occasions on which they are relatively free to make decisions on behalf of their organization and discuss those decisions rather explic-itly. The salient difference is in the participant role structures assumed in each "business culture." The ends are the same, to maximize the advantage for the speaker's organization. While they are doing the same thing with the same goals, the manner in which they go about achieving their goals varies. There may not be major differences in most of the other com-ponents of the grammar of context aside from the difference in participant roles.

Seward, in the book *Japanese in Action*, makes fun of the Japanese in the years after World War II by detailing instances of high context communication. For example, his landlady would say every morning as he left the house, "Dekakimasu ka?" ('Are [you] going out?') He was expected to reply "Hai, dekakimasu" ('Yes, going out'). She would then say, "Itte irashai" ("go and return"). After many days of this routine, he tired of it and started varying his reply. "No, I am not going anywhere," "Yes, I am going to hell and you're welcome to come along," and other outrageous remarks. No matter what he said, her response would be "Itte irashai." While this might be considered an example of interaction in the "high context culture" of post-war Japan, it can be described more economically in terms of the grammar of context.

The setting for this exchange was constant, i.e. the same doorway to the same building at the same hour. The purpose, topic, and genre were leave-taking. Seward's landlady needed to perform the ritual of leave-taking in the same flat key whenever he left the house. The participants were always the same two persons, taking the same roles, one leaving and one staying. The message form was constant, with the landlady saying her piece, then Seward, then the landlady. Neither did the sequence vary, although whatever was said by Seward was treated as though he had uttered the expected message. The utterances co-occurred with bowing to the appropriate level. The act of leave taking, then, was accomplished not just with the words, but with all of these components put together in a "grammatical" way. The "grammatical structure" of the situation was so strong that even when Seward did not give the expected verbal response, the other aspects of context overrode what he said. Thus, this situation can be regarded as a high context situation, and although many daily situations in Japan may be similarly high context, what makes this particular situation high context probably has more to do with the regularity with which it occurred than the fact that one of the participants was Japanese. Such situations as greeting and leave-taking tend to be high context in almost all cultures. Most North Americans, for example, respond to the greeting "How are you?" with an automatic "Fine" regardless of whether they are feeling fine or not.

Telling someone where to get off a subway, bus, or train, even though it seems to rely very heavily on the verbal message, might also be a high context situation. In other words, the same sentence, "It's two stops," may have one person getting off at the second stop, another waiting until two stops have been passed and getting off at the third stop. One of the authors caused a party to wait for hours at a Moscow metro station by getting off at the fourth stop having been told by a fellow North American it was four stops from where she got on. Though both were speaking American English, which they had used all their lives, the speaker giving directions was using the system of meaning for talking about metro stops used by Muscovites. That is, the tacit understanding in some discourse systems is that one counts stops passed, while in others one counts stops made. It can be easier to assume the speaker is mistaken than to notice the systematic pattern by which the counting differs from one's own.

Our purpose in introducing Hall's concept of "high and low context" is that it is useful to remember that in some cases context plays a larger role in the communication of meaning than in other cases. At the same time, we would not want to follow Hall in assigning these labels to people or "cultures." Rather we would prefer to speak of "high context" and "low context" speech events or situations. A hearing in a court of law, for example, in which so much is made verbally explicit, including when people should stand, sit, talk, and remain silent, would be a good example of a "low context" speech event, whereas many social situations such as dinner with your new girlfriend or boyfriend's parents, in which so much is communicated non-verbally through contextual cues, might qualify as a "high context" speech event.

Researching Interdiscourse Communication

Using the "grammar of context" as a preliminary ethnographic audit

In the last chapter you were asked to choose a *site of investigation* in which you are able to observe people engaging in social actions and interactions and to talk to them about what they are doing. You were also asked to attempt to discover the tasks, actions, and practices that seemed particularly important to participants. The grammar of context is a valuable tool for you to use in this preliminary ethnographic audit and to help you to begin the next step of your analysis, which is sorting out the kinds of "cultural knowledge" participants need to have when they do things together.

Social life is made up of a very large number of tasks, actions, and practices, which makes this preliminary ethnographic audit potentially problematic. You might begin studying anywhere, of course, but there is often a difficulty that it is only after a considerable amount of time that the researcher discovers that the task or action he or she is studying is really of very minor importance in the overall life of the organization or group he or she is studying. And by the same token, it is difficult to take at face value the analysis of members. One case in which one of the authors worked as a consultant is illustrative. The management of an organization defined the problem for which he was called in to consult a simple problem of poor trickle-down of information through the system. Management was making decisions and promulgating the decisions, but somehow employees were failing to pick up this information and act appropriately. Separate consultations with the labor organization gave a radically different picture. Their view was not that the information flow was bad – they knew *exactly* what the decisions were and what was expected of them. What was bad in their view were the decisions themselves. They had not been consulted, they said, and they were the ones who held the most relevant information. In their view, the management had simply and arbitrarily made poorly informed decisions. They felt that the problem was that their ideas were not percolating upward to the management level. We conclude that it is always dangerous to take any internal definition of what are the important tasks, actions, and practices at face value. There are always alternative views and often enough the first assessment is not only wrong, but strategically wrong – that is, it is designed, unconsciously or consciously, to hide the real problems of the organization or group.

It is for this reason that we feel that the first step that should be taken is to conduct an ethnographic audit of the site of investigation. The grammar of context is the best way to open up such an audit. After identifying what *seem* to be key situations, tasks, practices, or events, these then can be analyzed at least roughly using the grammar of context so that it becomes clear how these situations or tasks or practices gear into the communicative life of the group. From this it is generally possible to begin to set aside some speech situations and events as less relevant and to direct your focus more closely on events that are more relevant both to the participants' goals and your own interests as a researcher or to identify those situations (usually what we have been referring to as "high context" situations) in which miscommunication is likely to occur.

The grammar of context can also help you to begin assembling an outline of the kinds of communicative competencies that are necessary in various speech situations. "Competencies" are what people in the site need to know or need to be able to do to be considered by others as acting like "normal" members of the group. This knowledge or these abilities may not be the same for every member. That is, they may be unequally distributed among members. Administrative assistants, for example, often possess more complete knowledge of the way organizations operate than their bosses, and, of course, newcomers to a discourse system are rarely as competent as old timers. It might also be the case that different participants in a speech situation want to get different things from the situation, as when labor leaders negotiate with management. The unequal distribution of competencies and the sometimes-conflicting goals of participants are what often lead to instances of miscommunication or communicative friction.

The grammar of context, however, at least at this point, can often only give you a rather superficial understanding of these competencies. Much of the grammar of context may not be a matter of overt behavior or explicit knowledge, but instead may be to some degree hidden, immersed in the memories and beliefs of members or in their histories and relationships with other members. However, this preliminary audit will, at least, provide you with a rough outline which you will later be able to fill in as you come to better understand things like how the people you are studying organize their relationships, the kinds of underlying assumptions they have about human beings, society, and communication itself, the various tools they have at their disposal for interacting and making meaning, and the ways they learn how to use these tools.

Discussion Questions

1   Think of something you do weekly, whether a task, action, or practice. Perhaps you search the internet for information on a particular topic, or book a flight or train journey, or talk by telephone to someone, or engage in a formal or informal meeting with friends or colleagues. How would you describe the competencies needed to engage in this activity using the grammar of context? Would you consider the activity to be high context or low context?

2   Write down a short dialogue from some situation in which you were recently engaged. Discuss the degree to which contextual knowledge is necessary in order to correctly interpret speaker meaning.

3   Think of a sentence you have heard or uttered that meant something different to other participants in the speech event. Explain why you believe the difference in understanding occurred.

4   Think of a situation in which you felt uncomfortable or acted inappropriately because you were not familiar with the grammar of context. Describe your experiences and explain which elements of the grammar of context gave you difficulty in the situation.

References for Further Study

Our outline of the grammar of context is adapted from Dell Hymes's framework for the Ethnography of Communication as discussed in his 1972 article "Models of the interaction of language and social life." For examples of using the grammar of context to research professional communication in different settings, see *Professional Communication in International Settings* (2001) by Yuling Pan, Suzanne Wong Scollon, and Ron Scollon. For exercises in the use of time and space, see Ron Scollon and Suzanne Wong Scollon's 1986 book *Responsive Communication: patterns for making sense*. Muriel Saville-Troike gives an excellent review of the literature in this field in her 1989 book *The Ethnography of Communication: an introduction*. Austin introduced the concept of the speech act in his 1962 book *How to Do Things with Words*, which was later extended by Searle in his 1969 book *Speech Acts: an essay in the philosophy of language*. For a full description of address forms, see Ralph Fasold's *The Sociolinguistics of Language* (1990). Edward T. Hall's examination of the use of time and space in different cultures can be found in his 1959 book *The Silent Language* and his 1966 book *The Hidden Dimension*, and his explanation of high context and low context cultures can be found in his 1976 book *Beyond Culture*. An explanation of the difference between *chronos* time and *kairos* time can be found in Frederick Erickson and Jeffery Shultz's 1982 book *The Counselor as Gatekeeper: social interaction in interviews*.

3

Interpersonal Politeness and Power

Communicative Style or Register

On Nathan Road in Tsim Sha Tsui, one of Hong Kong's most crowded tourist and shopping areas, two men passed by a vendor of imitation Rolex watches.

Vendor (to first man):	Eh! Copy watch?
Vendor (to second man):	Rolex? Sir?

Both of the passers-by were Americans. The first was carrying a backpack and was together with some other people who also appeared to be budget travelers. The second man the vendor of copy Rolexes spoke to was in his mid-fifties and dressed much more formally in a suit coat.

In speaking to these two men the vendor of copy Rolexes made a shift in *register* or communicative style. When he spoke to the first man (who was quite a bit younger than the vendor) he used a very informal or familiar style. He addressed him with, "Eh!," and referred to the item for sale as a "copy watch." When he spoke to the second man (who was quite a bit older than the vendor) he used a more formal or deferential form of address, "Sir!," and referred to the item for sale as a "Rolex."

In this case the vendor used somewhat limited linguistic resources to signal that he had perceived a social difference between these two potential customers. This is very much like the example we gave above at the beginning of chapter 2, when Mr Hutchins referred to his subordinate as Bill.

Linguists have used many different terms to refer to such shifts in linguistic form when those shifts are used to indicate changes in components of speech events or speech situations. Among linguists, the term "register" tends to be associated mostly with particular scenes, and "communicative style" tends to be associated with participants, though these are not

Intercultural Communication: A Discourse Approach, Third Edition. Ron Scollon, Suzanne Wong Scollon, Rodney H. Jones.
© 2012 John Wiley & Sons, Inc. Published 2012 by John Wiley & Sons, Inc.

clear distinctions in many cases. For example, a greeting might be given in a very informal way if you meet a friend casually on the street, but much more formally if the two of you are participating in a board meeting. While the participants remain the same, the greeting will vary in register because of the different setting.

"Communicative style" is the term we prefer for this chapter on interpersonal politeness and power because it is a more general term than "register" used by most sociolinguists to refer to either personal identities or interpersonal relationships among participants. We would not say, for example, that Rebecca has an interesting register but we might say that she has an interesting communicative style. On the other hand we could say that Fiona is very good at choosing the appropriate register or communicative style for any situation. In other words, the term "communicative style" is less restrictive and can include the concept of register.

Face

The question of human psychological identity is a complex issue that goes beyond the study of communication into psychology, sociology, and philosophy. Nevertheless, there is an important aspect of identity that has been recognized as an essential element in all communication. In chapter 2 we said that there were two aspects of participation which are important to consider: who the participants are and what roles they are taking. At that time we were referring mostly to the places that participants occupy in an institutional or a social structure on the one hand, and on the other hand, the particular position they were taking in some speech event. Now we want to take up a third and more deeply personal aspect of this component of participation: the interpersonal identity of the individuals in communication.

The concept of face will not be new to many readers in Asia, who will recognize the term *mianzi* in Mandarin (*minji* in Cantonese, *mentsu* in Japanese, *chae myon* in Korean), where it carries a range of meanings based upon a core concept of "honor," but perhaps the way it is used in contemporary sociolinguistics and sociology is somewhat different. The concept was first introduced to western scholars by the Chinese anthropologist Hu Hsien Chin in 1944, though the term had been used in English for at least several centuries before that. Later, the American sociologist Erving Goffman based much of his work on interpersonal relationships on the concept of face.

One of the most important ways in which we reduce the ambiguity of communication is by making assumptions about the people we are talking to. As the simplest example, when we begin talking to someone we try to speak to them in a language we know they will understand. In a monolingual speech community that is rarely a problem, but in the increasingly multilingual international business community it is becoming a major issue, to be solved right at the outset of communications.

We also make significant assumptions about what kind of a person the other person is and what kind of a person he or she would like us to think of him or her as being. When Mr Hutchins called his subordinate colleague by his first name, Bill, he projected the assumption that there was a difference in status between them and he also projected that they both would agree to that difference in status by simply using the name Bill without further comment. Bill, in turn, projected that he accepted that difference in status and ratified that by calling his employer Mr Hutchins.

Many aspects of linguistic form depend on the speakers making some analysis of the relationships among themselves. The choice of terms of address is one of the first of these recognized by sociolinguists. The watch vendor in Tsim Sha Tsui also recognized that different forms of address, "Eh!" or "Sir!," were appropriate in trying to catch the attention of two different potential customers. The study of face in sociolinguistics arose out of the need to understand how participants decide what their relative statuses are and what language they use to encode their assumptions about such differences in status, as well as their assumptions about the face being presented by participants in communication.

Within sociological and sociolinguistic studies face is usually given the following general definition: "*Face is the negotiated public image, mutually granted each other by participants in a communicative event.*" In this definition and in the work of sociolinguists the emphasis is not so much on shared assumptions as it is on the negotiation of face. For our purposes we want to keep both aspects of face in mind. We believe that while there is much negotiation of face in any form of interpersonal communication, participants must also make assumptions about face before they can begin any communication.

We do not have to figure out everything from the beginning every time we talk to someone. Mr Hutchins and Bill do not need to open up negotiations about their relationship each time they speak to each other. Just the fact that Mr Hutchins is Bill's employer is sufficient information to know that they differ in status. Knowing that difference in status and how it is normally expressed in English, we can predict fairly accurately that Bill will say "Mr Hutchins," and Mr Hutchins will say "Bill."

Participants make certain unmarked assumptions about their relationships and about the face they want to claim for themselves and are willing to give to the other participants in any communicative situation. In addition to these unmarked assumptions, participants also undertake a certain amount of negotiation of their relationships as a natural process of change in human relationships. For example, if a person wants to ask a rather large favor of another person, he or she is likely to begin with the assumed relationship, but then he or she will begin to negotiate a closer or more intimate relationship. If such a closeness is achieved then he or she is likely to feel it is safer to risk asking for the favor than if their negotiations result in more distance between them.

In the field of sociolinguistics this combination of unmarked assumptions about the participants and their relationships with the negotiations about those assumptions is called the study of face. Such study also goes by the name of politeness theory.

The "self" as a communicative identity

One reason the term "face" is attractive in communicative studies is that it leaves open the question of who is the "real" person underneath the face which is presented in communication, a question which we will take up further in chapter 8. For now it is important to point out that there may be significant cultural differences in the assumptions made about the "self" that is involved in communication. The idea of "self" which tends to underlie western studies of communication is highly individualistic, self-motivated, and open to ongoing negotiation. As we discuss below, this concept of the "self" may not always be appropriate as the basis for studying discourse systems that have a more collectivistic view of "self," one which is more connected to membership in basic groups such as the family or one's working group and which is taken to be more strongly under the influence of assumed or unmarked assumptions about roles and responsibilities.

The Paradox of Face: Involvement and Independence

Face is really a paradoxical concept. By this we mean that there are two sides to it which appear to be in contrast. On the one hand, in human interactions we have a need to be involved with other participants and to show them our involvement. On the other hand, we need to maintain some degree of independence from other participants and to show them that we respect their independence. These two sides of face, involvement and independence, produce an inherently paradoxical situation in all communications, in that *both* aspects of face must be projected simultaneously in any communication.

The involvement aspect of face is concerned with the person's right and need to be considered a normal, contributing, or supporting member of society. This involvement is shown through being a normal and contributing participant in communicative events. One shows involvement by taking the point of view of other participants, by supporting them in the views they take, and by any other means that demonstrates that the speaker wishes to uphold a commonly created view of the world.

Involvement is shown by such discourse strategies as paying attention to others, showing a strong interest in their affairs, pointing out common in-group membership or points of view with them, or using first names. As we will indicate below, we might say such things as, "Are you feeling well today?," or, "I know just what you mean, the same thing happened to me yesterday," or, "Yes, I agree, I've always believed that, too." Any indication that the speaker is asserting that he or she is closely connected to the hearer may be considered a strategy of involvement.

Many other terms have been used in the sociolinguistic literature to present this concept. It has been called positive face, for example, on the basis of the idea of the positive and negative poles of magnetism. The positive poles of a magnet attract, and by analogy involvement has been said to be the aspect of communication in which two or more participants show their common attraction to each other.

Involvement has also been called solidarity politeness; again, for the reason that sociolinguists want to emphasize that this aspect of face shows what participants have in common. Any of these terms might be acceptable in some contexts, but we feel that the term "involvement" is clearest and creates the fewest analytical complications for the reader.

The independence aspect of face emphasizes the individuality of the participants. It emphasizes their right not to be completely dominated by group or social values, and to be free from the impositions of others. Independence shows that a person may act with some degree of autonomy and that he or she respects the rights of others to their own autonomy and freedom of movement or choice.

Independence is shown by such discourse strategies as making minimal assumptions about the needs or interests of others, by not "putting words into their mouths," by giving others the widest range of options, or by using more formal names and titles. For example, in ordering in a restaurant we might say, "I don't know if you will want to have rice or noodles," or in making the initial suggestion to go out for coffee we might say, "I'd enjoy going out for coffee, but I imagine you are very busy." The key to independence face strategies is that they give or grant independence to the hearer.

Independence has also been given various other names by researchers in sociolinguistics. It has been called negative politeness, as an analogy with the negative pole of a magnet, which repels. We prefer not to use this term, because technical or formal contrast between "positive" and "negative" can easily be forgotten and readers can too easily begin to think of "positive politeness" as good and "negative politeness" as bad.

Another term which has been used as an attempt to get around the potential negative aspects of "positive" and "negative" politeness has been "deference politeness." We have used "solidarity" and "deference" in earlier writings, but find that some readers have a strong preference for one type of strategy or the other and, again, miss the point that *both* aspects of face must be projected simultaneously in any communication.

As we said above, the most important concept to remember about face is that it is paradoxical. By that we mean the concept of face has built into it *both* aspects; involvement *and* independence must be projected simultaneously in any communication. It is always a matter of more or less, not absolute expression of just one or the other. A speaker must find just the right way of saying something which shows the degree to which he or she is involving the other participants and the degree to which he or she is granting independence to them.

The reason involvement and independence are in conflict is that emphasizing one of them risks a threat to the other. If I show you too much involvement, you are likely to feel that your independence is being threatened. On the other hand if I grant you too much independence, you are likely to feel that I have limited your involvement.

Any communication is a risk to face; it is a risk to one's own face at the same time it is a risk to the other person's. We have to carefully project a face for ourselves and to respect the face rights and claims of other participants. We risk our own involvement face if we do not include other participants in our relationship. That is, if we exclude others, while that may increase our own independence, it at the same time decreases our own involvement. At the same time, if we include others, we risk our own independence face.

Looking at it from the other person's point of view, if we give too much involvement to the other person, we risk their independence face. On the other hand if we give them too much independence, we risk their involvement.

The result of the double risk, the risk to involvement face and the risk to independence face of both the speaker and the hearer, means, therefore, that all communication has to be carefully phrased to respect face, both involvement face and independence face. This could be said another way: "*There is no faceless communication.*"

Politeness strategies of involvement and independence

Now that we have given you a general introduction to the concept of face in interpersonal communication, we hope that we can make this discussion clearer by giving a number of examples of actual linguistic strategies which are used to communicate these different face strategies.

The most extreme contrast between involvement and independence is the difference between speaking (or communicating) and silence (or non-communication). Any form of communication at all is somewhat on the side of involvement. In order to communicate at all, the participants must share some aspects of symbolic systems which they can interpret in shared ways. If I speak to you and you are able to answer me, we have already shared some small degree of involvement. As a result we would classify speech on the side of involvement, and silence (or better still, non-communication) on the side of independence.

Perhaps it is important to clarify that there are silences which can be interpreted as high involvement as well. We know that two people who share a very intimate situation can communicate to each other a high degree of involvement while remaining completely silent. That is why we have rephrased "silence" as "non-communication" above. It is the silence of non-communication to which we refer when we say it is at the independence end of the continuum. One grants (and claims for oneself) the highest level of independence by having no communication with the other.

Taciturnity and volubility are somewhat lesser extremes of non-communication and communication. Taciturnity means, simply, not talking very much. Volubility is the other side of the coin, "talking a lot." Both of these are highly relative terms. There is no absolute amount of speech which can be classed as taciturn or as voluble. The same is true for individuals; there are no absolutely taciturn or voluble individuals. Likewise there are no absolutely taciturn or voluble groups, or societies, or "cultures."

Nevertheless, one aspect of the grammar of context is expectations of the amount of speech. For example, many religious rites or ceremonies are very restricted in the amount of incidental conversational or non-formal speech expected. In such a situation, a person who was speaking at all might be perceived as being very voluble. On the other hand, at a friendly dinner party among close friends, a person who was speaking, but not to any great extent, might be considered to be taciturn, because the expectations are for a good bit of conversational exchange.

Psychological studies of conversational exchanges and formal interviews have shown that the more talk there is, the more these exchanges are perceived as "warm" or "affiliative." In contrast, the less talk there is, the more they are perceived as "cold" or "non-affiliative." On the basis of this designation of "affiliative," we believe that it is best to consider more talk, volubility, to be an involvement strategy, and less talk, taciturnity, to be an independence strategy.

From the point of view of face relationships, we have said above that any communication is based on sharing a symbolic system, and that such a sharing is already to some degree an expression of involvement. Therefore, the question of what language to use is a crucial one in international business and government relationships as well as within bilingual or multilingual speech communities. If negotiations are conducted among participants using different languages (but, of course, with translators), this is a situation of lesser involvement or of higher independence than if negotiations are conducted using the same language. Therefore, it is a question of face relationships to decide whether discussions should go on in separate languages mediated by translators or whether they should go on in a common language. Naturally, of course, if the negotiations go on in the native language of one of the participants (or group of participants) that will tip the balance of involvement toward their side. It will give the other participants a sense of having their own independence limited, perhaps even unduly. At the same time, an insistence on the use of separate languages to overcome this problem can produce a sense of too great an independence, which can be felt as hostility or unwillingness to come to a common ground of agreement. The choice of language in discourse is not simply a matter of practical choice governed by efficiency of communication of information. Every such choice is also a matter of the negotiation of the face of the participants.

Linguistic strategies of involvement: some examples

There are many ways in which involvement can be shown through linguistic form. The examples which follow are just ten types which have been selected from English. While there is some disagreement among researchers about exactly which linguistic forms will be used in different languages to indicate these strategies, the examples here will give you a general idea of what we mean by linguistic strategies of involvement. (In these examples the letter "H" represents the "Hearer" to whom one is speaking, and "S" represents the "Speaker.")

1 Notice or attend to H:
   - "I like your jacket."
   - "Are you feeling better today?"
2 Exaggerate (interest, approval, sympathy with H):
   - "Please be careful on the steps, they're very slippery."
   - "You always do so well in school."
3 Claim in-group membership with H:
   - "All of *us here* at City University . . ."
4 Claim common point of view, opinions, attitudes, knowledge, empathy:
   - "I know *just* how you feel. I had a cold like that last week."
5 Be optimistic:
   - "I think we should be able to finish that annual report very quickly."
6 Indicate S knows H's wants and is taking them into account:
   - "I'm sure you will all want to know when this meeting will be over."
7 Assume or assert reciprocity:
   - "I know you want to do well in sales this year as much as I want you to do well."
8 Use given names and nicknames:
   - "Bill, can you get that report to me by tomorrow?"
9 Be voluble.
10 Use H's language or dialect.

Linguistic strategies of independence: some examples

As in the case of involvement, there are many ways in which independence can be reflected linguistically. The ten types below have been selected from among the most common used in English. Again, "H" refers to the "Hearer" and "S" to the "Speaker."

1 Make minimal assumptions about H's wants:
   - "I don't know if you will want to send this by air mail or by speedpost."
2 Give H the option not to do the act:
   - "It would be nice to have tea together, but I am sure you are very busy."
3 Minimize threat:
   - "I just need to borrow a little piece of paper, any scrap will do."

4　Apologize:
   - "I'm sorry to trouble you, could you tell me the time?"
5　Be pessimistic:
   - "I don't suppose you'd know the time, would you?"
6　Dissociate S, H from the discourse:
   - "This is to inform our employees that . . ."
7　State a general rule:
   - "Company regulations require an examination . . ."
8　Use family names and titles:
   - "Mr Lee, there's a phone call for you."
9　Be taciturn.
10　Use own language or dialect.

Face Systems

We have said above that face relationships between and among participants consist of two elements: an unmarked set of initial assumptions and a series of negotiations in which those unmarked assumptions are either ratified or altered in some way. Under normal circumstances, face relationships remain fairly stable and negotiation of the overriding relationship is relatively minor. When the assistant manager of a sales department meets with his or her manager, the relationship is not likely to change from meeting to meeting. Once it has been established at the beginning of employment in that position, it is likely to remain the same until one or the other moves to a different position.

We could describe such general and persistent regularities in face relationships as face systems. For example, Mr Hutchins can be expected to always address Bill by his first name and Bill is likely to always say "Mr" when speaking to Mr Hutchins. Such a regular relationship indicates what we would call a politeness system, because both speakers in the system would use a certain fairly regular set of face strategies in speaking to each other.

There are three main factors involved which bring such a politeness (or face) system into being: power, distance, and the weight of the imposition.

Power (+P, −P)

In discussions of face or politeness systems, "power" refers to the vertical disparity between the participants in a hierarchical structure. In other words, Mr Hutchins is above Bill in the hierarchical structure of their company. We would describe their relationship as +P (plus power) because Mr Hutchins has special privileges (and, of course, responsibilities) over Bill and Bill owes certain duties to Mr Hutchins. In most business and governmental structures, the organization chart shows quite explicitly what the +P relationships are. As a result the language used between such participants is relatively predictable.

In contrast to such a situation, where there is little or no hierarchical difference between participants, we would consider that to be −P or an egalitarian system. Close friends generally share a −P relationship, since neither one is considered above the other. But the relationship does not have to be among close friends. Two people who have equivalent ranks in their own companies or their own organizations might have a −P relationship even though they do not know each other at all. In international protocols in both business and government, most communications are attempted at the same level so that −P relationships can be achieved.

Company presidents talk to company presidents, assistant sales managers deal with other assistant sales managers, ambassadors talk to ambassadors, and clerks talk to clerks.

Distance (+D, −D)

The distance between two participants should not be confused with the power difference between them. Distance can be seen most easily in egalitarian relationships (−P). For example, two close friends would be classified as −D because of the closeness of their relationship. On the other hand, two governmental officials of different nations are likely to be of equal power within their systems but distant, +D.

Even within a single business organization, power (P) is not the same as distance (D). The head of the personnel office and his or her staff will have a hierarchical relationship (+P), but most likely will have a close (−D) relationship because they work together daily. Those same employees will have a hierarchical difference *and* a distance between them and the head of, say, the quality control department within the same company (+D, +P), because they rarely have contact with each other.

Weight of imposition (+W, −W)

The third factor that will influence face strategies is the weight of the imposition. Even if two participants in a speech event have a very fixed relationship between them, the face strategies they will use will vary depending on how important the topic of discussion is for them. For example, if Bill is talking to Mr Hutchins about a routine daily business matter, their face strategies will be quite predictable. On the other hand, if Bill has decided that today is the day to approach Mr Hutchins about getting a promotion, he is likely to take on an extra-deferential tone and use a much higher level of independence strategies than he normally uses. Or on the other side of it, if Mr Hutchins has to approach Bill with some rather bad news, perhaps that his position is going to be eliminated, he will use a much lower level of involvement than he customarily uses.

In other words, when the weight of imposition increases, there will be an increased use of independence strategies. When the weight of imposition decreases, there will be an increased use of involvement strategies.

From this you should be able to see that in relatively fixed interpersonal relationships, such as those within a business or some other organization, power (P) and distance (D) are not likely to change very rapidly or very frequently, and what is mostly under negotiation will have to do with the weight of imposition (W).

Because our focus is now on politeness or face systems and not on individual situational relationships, weight of imposition will not be a major factor in the discussion which follows. We will focus primarily on systems which develop through the variations in power and distance.

Three Face Systems: Deference, Solidarity, and Hierarchy

Three main types of politeness system can be observed in many different contexts. These are based primarily on whether there is a power difference (+P or −P) and on the distance between participants (+D or −D). We have called them the deference politeness system, the solidarity politeness system, and the hierarchical politeness system.

Deference face system (−P, +D)

If a university professor named Dr Wong from Hong Kong meets a university professor from Tokyo named Dr Hamada, they are likely to refer to each other as "Professor Wong" and "Professor Hamada." In such a system they would treat each other as equals and use a relatively high concentration of independence politeness strategies out of respect for each other and for their academic positions. Such a system of mutual but distant independence is what we mean by a deference politeness system.

A deference politeness system is one in which participants are considered to be equals or near equals but treat each other at a distance. Relationships among professional colleagues who do not know each other well is one example.

The characteristics of this system are that it is:

1   symmetrical (−P), that is, the participants see themselves as being at the same social level;
2   distant (+D), that is, each uses independence strategies speaking to the other.

Such a face system can be sketched as in figure 3.1.

One could find deference politeness anywhere the system is egalitarian but participants maintain a deferential distance from each other. Much international political protocol is based on this system, where equals from each government meet but are cautious about forming unnecessarily close ties.

Solidarity face system (−P, −D)

When two close friends have a conversation with each other they exemplify a solidarity face system. There is a high level of involvement politeness strategies. There is no feeling of either a power difference (−P) or distance (−D) between them.

The characteristics of this solidarity face system are that it is:

1   symmetrical (−P), that is, the participants see themselves as being in equal social position;
2   close (−D), that is, the participants both use politeness strategies of involvement.

Such a face system can be sketched as in figure 3.2.

Speaker 1 < ==================== Independence   ==================== > Speaker 2

[+D = Distance between the speakers]

Figure 3.1   Deference face system.

Speaker 1 < = involvement = > Speaker 2

[−D = Minimal distance between speakers]

Figure 3.2   Solidarity face system.

One could find solidarity politeness anywhere the system is egalitarian and participants feel or express closeness to each other. Friendships among close colleagues are often solidarity systems. For example, Professor Wong, who calls Professor Hamada "Professor" or "Doctor," might call a colleague in his own department with whom he works every day by some much more familiar name. Those familiar with North American business will recognize this pattern as one that many people in the United States adopt very quickly in business relationships, especially in sales and marketing.

Hierarchical face system (+P, +/–D)

The third politeness system is hierarchical. In such a system the participants recognize and respect the social differences that place one in a super-ordinate position and the other in a subordinate position. This is the system of face in which Mr Hutchins speaks "down" to his employee Bill and Bill speaks "up" to his superior, Mr Hutchins. The main characteristic of this system is the recognized difference in status, for which we are using the designation +P. It may be of much less significance whether or not there is distance between the participants. For our purposes we have considered this system to be either close or distant, +P or –P.

In such a face system the relationships are asymmetrical. By that we mean that the participants do not use the same face politeness strategies in speaking to each other. The person in the superordinate or upper position uses involvement strategies in speaking "down." The person in the subordinate or lower position uses independence strategies in speaking "up." Calling someone by his or her surname and title (Mr Hutchins) is an independence strategy. Calling someone by his or her given name without a title (Bill) is an involvement strategy.

The characteristics of this hierarchical face system are that it is:

1 asymmetrical (+P), that is, the participants see themselves as being in unequal social position;
2 asymmetrical in face strategies, that is, the "higher" uses involvement face strategies and the "lower" uses independence face strategies.

Such a face system can be sketched as in figure 3.3.

This sort of hierarchical face system is quite familiar in business, governmental, and educational organizations. In fact, it could be said to be the most common sort of organizational relationship, as indicated in tables of organization.

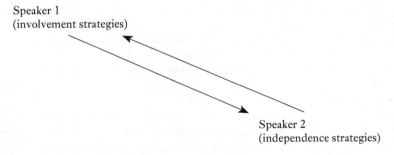

Speaker 1
(involvement strategies)

Speaker 2
(independence strategies)

Figure 3.3 Hierarchical face system.

A sociolinguistic survey of many different communicative systems shows that the factors of power (or hierarchy) and distance may arise for many different reasons. In some societies or at some times in history, power differences (+P) arise based on differences in age, gender, wealth, hunting prowess, ability to entertain, education, physical strength, or beauty, membership in particular families, or color of hair or skin. In fact, almost any element of human life which can be easily perceived by others has at some time or other been the basis for making hierarchical distinctions.

In the same way, distance (+D) can arise for perhaps all of the same factors. Members of one's family might be close (−D) while all others are distant (+D), or family members of one gender are close while those of the other gender might be distant. It has been said that Alpinists in Germany switch from the distant forms of the pronouns for "you" (the so-called V-forms) to the close forms (the so-called T-forms) of the pronouns when their climb brings them above the tree line. In some Asian business circles, late-night entertainment might bring out strategies of involvement indicating little distance (−D) which will then be reversed to the more normal distant (+D) strategies of independence in the next working day in the office.

We are most concerned that the reader understand the main properties of these three systems of face. Two of them are symmetrical: the deference system and the solidarity system. One of them is asymmetrical: the hierarchical system. In the first, all participants use on balance a greater proportion of independence face strategies. In the second, all participants use on balance a greater proportion of involvement face strategies. In the hierarchical face system, however, because it is asymmetrical, the participants use *different* face strategies; involvement strategies are used "downward" and independence strategies are used "upward."

Miscommunication

Although these systems provide basic rules of thumb for which politeness strategies are appropriate in different situations, people participating in different discourse systems might have different ideas about what constitutes power, distance, or imposition and so have different expectations about whether independence or involvement strategies should be used. The mother of one of the authors visited England for the first time some years ago and came back with the opinion that British people are "rude." When asked why she thought so, she offered the following story as an example: One afternoon she was in a crowded café in London. There were no free tables, and she was sitting alone at a table with an empty chair across from her. Suddenly a woman came up and asked if she could sit in the empty seat. Although the author's mother was slightly taken aback – it is less common in the United States for a stranger to impose themselves on your table in a restaurant – she assented. When the woman sat down, the author's mother smiled and began to formulate some polite remark about the weather, but before she could get the remark out of her mouth, the woman took a book out of her bag and began reading, which struck the author's mother as extremely impolite. "If she was going to sit there," she said, "she might have at least been willing to have a conversation."

This example illustrates rather well the difficulties that arise because there are two rather different ways for people to show politeness towards one another and different people may have different expectations about how they should be applied. We contend that neither of these women was trying to be impolite, but rather that they had different expectations about how to be polite. The British woman's gesture of taking out a book, rather than a snub, might well have been a signal to the author's mother that, although she was sitting at the same table, she had no intention of imposing any further. From the author's mother's point of view – no doubt partially derived from her experience of living in the American South – when one finds that they cannot help but impose on a stranger in public by, for example, sitting next to them on long distance bus rides, one is expected to make the best of the situation by striking up a conversation. In other words, in her experience, when two strangers are thrown together by circumstances in which initial attempts at independence fail, the default behavior is to switch to involvement by, for example, talking about the weather or showing each other pictures of their grandchildren. This deviation from the basic rules described above is sometimes disconcerting for visitors to North America, especially those from northern Europe and Asia, often causing some people to stereotype people from the United States as "overly friendly," "pushy," or "loud." Similarly, when the author's mother encountered independence strategies in this situation, she was quick to misinterpret them as evidence that British people are "cool" or "haughty."

Often at the core of misunderstandings like this is the fact that politeness strategies are so intimately linked to our ideas about power and our ways of negotiating what kind of conversational rights different people have in different situations. We have a friend who in learning Spanish could never get right the differences between the familiar set of pronouns and the formal set of pronouns. He found it difficult to remember when he should say, "*Usted*" ("you" formally), and when he should say, "*Tu*" ("you" informally). He simplified the whole system by just insisting on using the T-forms.

This, of course, presented a major problem for Spanish speakers in Mexico, where he was living at that time. As a new acquaintance he was expected to use the formal terms, the "*Usted*" forms of politeness. In other words, he was expected to use independence strategies of politeness. But he was not using them; he was using the T-forms, the involvement forms. In Mexican social terms there were only two contexts in which he could use the involvement forms: either if he was a very good friend or if he was trying to pick a fight (that is, if it was an attempt to assert power over the other). In other words, the solidarity system is used only among intimates.

Remember that when one participant uses involvement face strategies and the other uses independence strategies, the one using the involvement strategies is the *higher* of the two. When someone addresses you as Mr Schneider and you answer back, "Juan," whatever your intentions might be, what he hears is that you are taking a higher position. In the interpersonal world of Mexican conversations this sounded like trying to put someone down or insulting him or her by taking a superior position.

Our friend had thus presented our Mexican friends with a problem. Within their interpretation of these face strategies, they expected a deference politeness system. When he used an involvement strategy, they had only two choices: (1) they could hear it as an insult, or (2) they could hear it as an expression of close and longstanding friendship. It should be noted that within that segment of Mexican society, at least at that time, it was quite normal for people to be relatively good friends for quite a few years before moving on to the stage of using the familiar pronouns or other involvement strategies. Those were reserved for close and old friends.

It is not surprising that our friend ran into both solutions to this problem. Many people befriended him, taking into consideration that his poor ability with the language was the cause of his misuse of pronouns and understanding that he only intended to show warmth and friendship. On the other hand, from time to time someone he did not know well took offense.

The point we wish to make with this anecdote is that miscommunication often arises, especially across the boundaries of discourse systems, because it is difficult to know in a new group, in a new language, or in a new situation how to express these rather subtle differences in face values. This analysis of face also tells us what sort of miscommunication arises. We can state it as a general rule: "*When two participants* differ *in their assessment of face strategies, it will tend to be perceived as difference in* power." If I use involvement strategies I expect to hear either reciprocal involvement (if I think it is a solidarity system, that is, −P−D) or independence (if I think it is a hierarchical system and I think I am in the higher position). If I think it is a solidarity system, and you use independence strategies, it sounds to me like you are putting yourself in a lower position and giving power over to me (if I'm expecting a deference system) or that you are refusing my overtures of friendship, thus putting yourself in a higher position than me (if I am expecting a solidarity system).

If I use independence strategies, I expect to hear reciprocal independence strategies (if I think it is a deference system and we have a level of mutual respect). But if you use involvement strategies back, what I hear is that you are trying to exert power over me.

To put it in the terms of our dialogue between Mr Hutchins and Bill, if Bill answers back to Mr Hutchins, "Sure, Jack, I can have it ready," we are certain that Mr Hutchins will feel that something has gone wrong. And it is not just "something" that has gone wrong. He will feel that Bill is being insulting, trying to rise above his position, trying to usurp authority, or in some way trying to deny the authority structure.

We have said that face relationships consist of two elements: the initial unmarked assumptions and the ongoing negotiation in the interaction. Now we can say that where two or more participants fail to agree on what sort of face system they are using, they will feel the negotiation to be one over the dimension of power (P). This could also be worded conversely: where two or more participants fail to agree on the initial system of hierarchy (P), they will find it difficult to set a comfortable level of face strategies in their communications. Or to put it one final way: the calculation of the appropriate level of face strategies (or the appropriate face system) is always inextricably tied to the expression of the hierarchical system of relationship between or among the participants. We said earlier that there is no faceless communication. Now we would like to add to that there is no *non-hierarchical* communication. That is because any difference in sense of hierarchy gives rise to difficulties in selecting face strategies, and any miscalculation in face strategies gives rise to feelings of power differences.

It is for this reason that we have entitled this chapter "Interpersonal Politeness and Power." The characteristics of the communication of face make it inevitable that power (that is, hierarchy) is interrelated to politeness levels. Having said this we would like to make clear that we do not see power as existing only in face-to-face social interactions, nor do we see power as only a matter of interpersonal hierarchy. Power is also exercised between social groups, classes, and discourse systems. As we will see in chapter 6, whole discourse systems have become naturalized as the normal or natural way to behave and by becoming naturalized exert their power over those who are not participants in those discourse systems as well as over those who are participants. In chapter 6 we show that a broad discourse system which we refer to as the Utilitarian Discourse System, which has spread as both carrier and producer of the contemporary globalizing business and commercial discourse, emphasizes certain characteristics such as clarity, brevity, and sincerity in language as if these were simply the natural state of communication. From this point of view, departures from this "C-B-S" style ("clarity," "brevity," and "sincerity") are seen as problems to be fixed, not simply as different ways of speaking to produce membership in different groups or to achieve different purposes. While we have focused primarily on interpersonal power in this chapter, here we want to remind the reader that, overall, our goal is to show how differences in discourse systems are not only differences in membership and identity, but also differences in relative positions of power.

Variations in Face Systems

We have been presenting these three face systems – deference, solidarity, and hierarchy – and the three factors people take into account when determining what face strategies to use – power, distance, and weight of imposition – as universal aspects of politeness applicable to all discourse systems, and, for the most part, we would argue that they are. At the same time, we have also shown how people participating in different discourse systems might have different ideas about how to judge power, distance, and weight of imposition and what kinds of face systems are appropriate for different occasions. Ideas about distance and when it might be appropriate to move from deference to solidarity, for example, might be different for people who have grown up in North America and people who have grown up in Great Britain, and factors such as age, which may be very important in some discourse systems in determining how much power someone has, may be less important in other discourse systems.

A number of scholars working in the area of politeness research, however, have pointed out that the model we have described above may not be wholly adequate for describing the kinds of behavior they have observed in certain contexts. The problem is, they say, that, like many "western" studies of communication which rely on the concept of the autonomous "self," this model arises from a "western cultural perspective" that emphasizes the face needs and face wants of the individual, and so is less useful in situations in which face is defined in terms of the group and seen to some degree as "public property." It has also been pointed out that the conception of "face" in some contexts has certain moral connotations which are not accounted for in the treatment of face we have given. According to Mao Luming (1994), for example, the Chinese notion of face contains two separate but complementary concepts embodied in the two terms *lian* and *mian-zi*. *Mian-zi*, he says, refers more to an individual's standing in the eyes of others, one's superficial prestige or feeling of being liked or respected. Thus, *mian-zi* can be "granted" by others independently of the individual's actions. *Lian*, on the other hand, is more of a moral concept, implying a social judgment of character dependent upon the individual's actions in relation to the group. *Lian* cannot be "granted"; it must be "earned."

While we acknowledge the variety of ways in which politeness can be understood and realized across different discourse systems, we would also like to approach with caution linking such variability too broadly to national or regional cultures (e.g. "Asian" or "western," "Chinese" or "American"). Whether one's orientation towards face is individualistic or collectivistic may have to do with one's age, gender, profession, or the contingences of a particular situation as much as with one's regional or national culture, and people who share regional and national cultures may exhibit considerable variation in their politeness behavior. Like most of the principles introduced in this book, the principles of politeness we laid out above are not intended as a description of reality but rather a framework for helping us analyze reality. In the course of such analysis, you will more than likely find that reality is much more complex than these principles. Not only do people in different discourse systems have different ways of judging things like power, distance, and weight of imposition, and of communicating and interpreting politeness, but people in the same discourse system may exhibit similar differences depending on the kinds of situations in which they find themselves.

In her book *Politeness in Chinese Face-to-Face Interaction* (2000), Yuling Pan illustrates this complexity and at the same time sheds some light on why visitors to China sometimes have the contradictory perception that the Chinese are very polite on the one hand but very rude on the other, as in when one tries to use official services. In her book Pan analyzes politeness in formal meetings, in family settings, and in service encounters such as the sale of stamps in the Post Office or the sale of clothing in a fashionable women's boutique. She shows that in formal meetings it is official rank which is the dominant consideration, not gender or age. "Politeness" in these circumstances translates to careful consideration of rank and position within the organization. In family settings it is the more traditional "Confucian" values which control the situation, giving prior conversational rights to older over younger, or to men over women. Thus, in family situations "politeness" means showing "traditional Chinese" respect. This contrasts, again, with service encounters in which there is a division between state-run businesses and private business. In the state-run businesses there is a kind of "rudeness" which is so often noticed by both locals and visitors alike because such service encounters are seen as egalitarian and purely pragmatic. In the new private businesses such as the women's clothing boutique she studied, on the other hand, salespeople use the language of kinship to try to establish very close and familiar, almost family-like ties to customers as a "polite" way of encouraging the obligation to buy.

In the beginning of this chapter we defined *Face* as "*the negotiated public image, mutually granted each other by participants in a communicative event,*" and here we would like to reassert that definition while at the same time admitting that there is considerable variation among different discourse systems, and even *within* discourse systems, regarding what might constitute a desirable image or an undesirable one, about the proper ways to conduct this negotiation, about how to grant people face and on what grounds it is to be granted, and even about how to define "public."

Social Organization and Face Systems

What, then, are the factors which determine how a particular discourse system answers such questions as what constitutes a desirable self image and when, where, how, and to whom face should be granted? The answers to these questions depend a great deal on the ways participants in the discourse system organize relationships among themselves and with participants in other discourse systems. Here we will take up four aspects of this organization: kinship, the concept of the self, ingroup–outgroup relationships, and what sociologists have called *Gemeinschaft* and *Gesellschaft*.

Kinship

In Korea, mothers set up temporary shrines outside the university and pray all day while their children inside write their examinations. In the fervor of the Cultural Revolution in China, children were encouraged to criticize their parents. Throughout Asia these and many similar examples indicate that the ancient Confucian kinship relationships are an extremely powerful force in East Asian cultural relationships, whether they are being enthusiastically upheld or fervently resisted. On the one hand, such relationships may be seen as the glue holding together these ancient societies. On the other hand, such relationships may be seen as the great barrier to modernization and development. Our point is that either position indicates the centrality of kinship in the thinking of many people in these countries.

In contrast to this, a recent United States census accepted fourteen different family types, from the traditional extended family to the single parent with adopted child. For many in the United States, kinship relationships are seen as significant barriers to individual self-realization and progress. Children tend to move away from their parents at a relatively early age, and adult children living together with their parents without some extenuating circumstances is considered rather unusual.

There are two aspects of kinship which are of direct importance to interdiscourse communication: hierarchy and collectivistic relationships. Kinship relationships emphasize that people are connected to each other by having descended from common ancestors. In doing so, kinship relationships emphasize, first of all, that ascending generations are before, prior to, and even superior to descending generations. This hierarchy of relationship is emphasized by Confucius and reiterated in such teaching materials as the *San Zi Jing* (Xu Chuiyang 1990) or even the public school workbooks used today in Hong Kong, Taiwan, Japan, and Korea, and throughout the rest of East Asia. The primary relationships are not lateral relationships, those between brothers and sisters, for example, but hierarchical, those between fathers and sons, mothers and daughters.

In any society in which such traditional kinship relationships are emphasized, individuals are acutely aware of their obligations and responsibilities to those who have come before as well as to those who come after. From birth one is made conscious of the debt owed to one's own parents, which is largely carried out in the form of duty and obedience. Often as well one is also made acutely conscious of the debt owed to one's own children and other descendants, which is largely carried out through nurture, responsibility, and benevolence.

This emphasis on hierarchical relationships has a twofold consequence for discourse: from very early in life one becomes subtly practiced in the discourse forms of hierarchical relationships. One learns first to show respect to those above, then, in due time, one learns the forms of guidance and leadership of those who come after. The second consequence is that one comes to expect all relationships to be hierarchical to some extent. If hierarchy is not based on kinship relationship, then it is seen to be based on age, experience, education, gender, geographical region, political affiliation, or one of the many other dimensions of social organization within a society.

The second aspect of kinship which is significant for discourse is that individual members of a culture are not perceived as independently acting individuals but, rather, they are seen as acting within hierarchies of kinship and other such relationships. A son's primary motivation for action is thought to be to bring credit to his parents and to provide security for his own descendants. He is not thought of as acting on his own behalf or for his own purposes. Indeed, such individual action is seen as an aberrant or possibly pathological form.

This emphasis on kinship relationships stands in contrast to the emphasis on individualism and egalitarianism that is practiced in other societies. This assertion of individualism and egalitarianism may reach its extreme in North America, but it has been at the center of political values since the eighteenth century in European political philosophy.

This difference in egalitarianism and hierarchy will, then, most likely play out in the choice of strategies of interpersonal politeness, with the person socialized into more egalitarian face systems using strategies of involvement as a way of emphasizing egalitarianism and the person socialized into more hierarchical face systems using strategies of independence as a way of showing respect.

This cursory sketch of the relative importance of kinship in different discourse systems is just that – a kind of thumbnail depiction of what is actually an extremely complex and contingent set of relationships. To say all Chinese value kinship or all North Americans try to promote egalitarian relationships in their discourse would be very far from the truth.

The concept of the self

A second aspect of social organization concerns the concept of the person or of the self as a unit within that group's organization. Individualism has its roots going back to Socrates or to Jesus. In societies influenced by this tradition of thought there is a tendency to emphasize the separation of the individual from any other social commitments, especially in the pursuit of social or political goals. The Chinese psychological anthropologist Francis L. K. Hsu believes that the excessive individualism of the western sense of the self has led to a general inability or unwillingness among the psychological sciences to consider the social aspects of the development of human behavior. He goes on to say that even in the anthropological and sociological sciences, culture and society are seen as being built up out of the association of individuals, not as primary realities in themselves. In an essay on intercultural understanding in his collection of essays entitled *Rugged Individualism Reconsidered* (Hsu 1983), he says, "The major key (though never the only key) as to why we behave like human beings as well as to why we behave like Americans or Japanese is to be found in our relationships with our fellow human beings" (p. 414). Hsu considers human relationships to be the fundamental unit of analysis, not a secondary, constructed category. He argues that, "the concept of personality is an expression of the western ideal of individualism. It does not correspond even to the reality of how the western man lives in western culture, far less any man in any other culture" (Hsu 1985: 24).

In place of the idea of the individual self, Hsu suggests a concept based on the Chinese concept of person (*ren*), which includes in his analysis not only interior unconscious or preconscious ("Freudian") levels and inexpressible and expressible conscious levels of the person but also one's intimate society and culture. In this analysis of the self, such relationships as those with one's parents and children are considered inseparable aspects of the self. Where an individualistic conception of the self places the major boundary which defines the self between the biological individual and that individual's intimates, Hsu argues that the Chinese concept of person (*ren*) places the major boundary of the person on the outside of those intimate relationships, as we show in figure 3.4, which is based on Hsu's original

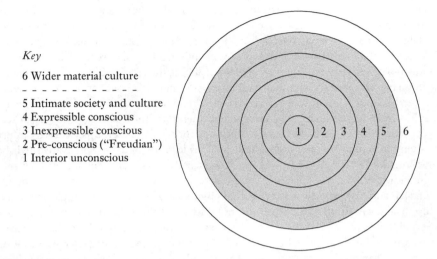

Key

6 Wider material culture
- - - - - - - - - - -
5 Intimate society and culture
4 Expressible conscious
3 Inexpressible conscious
2 Pre-conscious ("Freudian")
1 Interior unconscious

Figure 3.4 The Chinese concept of the self. *Source*: Adapted from Hsu 1983.

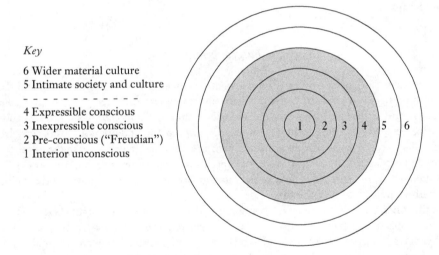

Key

6 Wider material culture
5 Intimate society and culture
- - - - - - - - - - - -
4 Expressible conscious
3 Inexpressible conscious
2 Pre-conscious ("Freudian")
1 Interior unconscious

Figure 3.5 The western concept of the self. *Source*: Adapted from Hsu 1983.

diagram. The western concept of the biological self can be diagrammed using Hsu's categories as indicated in figure 3.5, also based upon Hsu's diagram.

Hsu's point in making this analysis is not just to propose an alternative to the individualistic concept of the self. He argues that the biologically isolated individual is neither culturally nor, in fact, biologically viable. Because intimate human relationships are "literally as important as [a person's] requirement for food, water, and air" (1985: 34), it is a dangerous analytical fiction to believe that the individual is the source of all social reality.

As we argued above, in any society human individuals must have close relationships with other humans as well as the freedom to operate independently. It is hard to imagine a human society in which either one of these extremes was practiced to the exclusion of the other. What is important in studying interdiscourse communication is not so much whether a society is individualistic or collectivistic in itself, but what that society upholds as its ideal, even when we all recognize that we must all have some independence as well as some place in society.

For our purposes, the question we want to consider is the relative difference between two people in their concept of the self as an individual or as part of a larger social group. In many respects on this dimension people in some societies tend to be more aware of the connections they have as members of their social groups, and therefore, they tend to be more conscious of the consequences of their actions on other members of their groups, whereas in other societies tend to emphasize their independence. This leads them to be more concerned about their own freedom of activity than with their connections to other members of their group.

Again, however, we must enter a caveat here, stressing that the distinction between individualism and collectivism we have staked out above is not nearly as simple as it is made out to be. As we will discuss in chapter 10, not only are there many different kinds of individualism in, for example, North American society and many different kinds of collectivism in, for example, Chinese society, but there are also strong strands of collectivism in societies that are often characterized as "individualistic" and of individualism in societies that are often characterized as collectivistic. In fact, in many ways we would consider our current students from China to be much more individualistic than their counterparts from the United States.

Ingroup–outgroup relationships

The third aspect of social organization we want to consider is the problem of establishing relationships between members of the group and members of other groups. One consequence of the difference between individualism and collectivism has to do with the difference between speaking to members of one's own group and speaking to others. In an individualistic context, groups do not form with the same degree of permanence as they do in a collectivist one. As a result, the ways of speaking to others are much more similar from situation to situation, since in each case the relationships are being negotiated and developed right within the situation of the discourse.

On the other hand, in a collectivist context, many relationships are established from one's birth into a particular family in a particular segment of society in a particular place. These memberships in particular groups tend to take on a permanent, ingroup character along with special forms of discourse which carefully preserve the boundaries between those who are inside members of the group and all others who are not members of the group.

People claim and impute ingroup identity in many different ways, mostly associated with the involvement face strategies we have described above. In some cases even the language or the register within that language one uses will be associated with the distinction between ingroup and outgroup communication. In the late 1980s a study was made of the Japanese used for speaking to Japanese as compared to the Japanese used for speaking to non-Japanese (Ross and Shortreed 1990). Even when speaking to non-Japanese with a very high level of competence in the Japanese language, the Japanese in the study considered it more appropriate to use a simplified "foreigner talk" register when speaking outside of their own group. Those who used a complex register of Japanese when speaking to non-Japanese were given more negative ratings by other Japanese in the study.

In this case, as in others, members of an ingroup feel that it is a kind of ingroup betrayal to use ingroup forms of language to non-members. In societies and groups where the distinction between ingroup and outgroup is a significant distinction, this is often paralleled by the use of different forms of discourse such as a special set of personal names or the use of particular registers for ingroup and outgroup communication.

Gemeinschaft *and* Gesellschaft

One of the major and foundational insights of the field of sociology was that there are different ways in which society can be organized. In 1887, in a book called *Gemeinschaft und Gesellschaft* (Community and Society) the German Ferdinand Tönnies (1971) argued that the problems of modern society have arisen because of a split with the traditional, community-based social organization of the Middle Ages. He argued that such an organic, community form of social solidarity, which he called *Gemeinschaft*, was based on the fact that individuals shared a common history and common traditions.

In contrast to the *Gemeinschaft* or community organization of social relationships, in modern society relationships are more contractual, rational, or instrumental. This form of society by mutual agreement and to protect mutual interests – one might say corporate society – which developed as part of the industrialization of Europe, Tönnies called *Gesellschaft*. Sociologists such as Emile Durkheim, Max Weber, and Georg Simmel have developed this concept in their own foundational works.

There are two major types of discourse system: those in which one participates based on one's birth and growth within a family and a community (one's gender and one's generation, for example), and those in which one chooses to participate for utilitarian purposes such as one's professional specialization or the company for which one works. The social structure of the first kind of discourse system is more like what the sociologists would call *Gemeinschaft*, and the goal-directed discourse systems such as corporations are rather strong examples of the *Gesellschaft* form of social organization.

This distinction between *Gemeinschaft* and *Gesellschaft* is thus useful for talking about how people come to be participants in discourse systems. One learns one's community, one's gender, and one's generational place in life through processes of informal, non-institutional forms of learning. On the other hand, participation in goal-directed discourse systems such as the academic discourse system or a corporate structure comes more often through formal education, training, and institutionalized learning.

In interdiscourse communication many problems arise, particularly in professional contexts, when people make different assumptions about whether *Gemeinschaft* or *Gesellschaft* forms of organization are most appropriate. A relatively *Gesellschaft* company doing business in a more *Gemeinschaft* context, for example, might want to set up a subsidiary production facility. From their point of view the most important issue would be to produce the product efficiently, with the lowest possible cost at a predictable flow of production and with a small range of variability in the quality. To do this they would most likely emphasize finding "the right person" for each job. They would be concerned about selecting individual employees on the basis of their training and experience. In other words, they would be most likely to create a social structure along *Gesellschaft* lines of rational, utilitarian purpose.

In contrast to the owners of such a project, their counterparts in the *Gemeinschaft* context might well have in mind aspects of community which they would want to emphasize. It might well be important that the new project would employ certain persons who were well placed in the local community structure, even where they might not have the initial training and experience. From the point of view of *Gemeinschaft*, these would be the best people, because employing them would enhance the community social structure.

No modern "culture" or discourse system, of course, is purely organized as either *Gemeinschaft* or *Gesellschaft* alone. In any social structure we will see a mixture of elements of both forms of organization. What is important in understanding interdiscourse communication is to understand in which contexts one of these forms of organization is preferred over the other. It is also important to understand that conflicts and misinterpretations may arise where participants in a negotiation do not come to agreement over which mode of organization should predominate.

Researching Interdiscourse Communication

Exploring the interaction order

Studying face systems and strategies in your chosen site of investigation is part of a broader concern with what we might call *the interaction order*, which includes both the physical and social relationships of people in particular situations. In many ways, how people are physically arranged – whether they are alone or with other people, whether they are interacting face-to-face or over the telephone or computer, and how they are arranged in space and in relation to the built environment (e.g. sitting across a desk from each other or seated in rows of chairs) – has important effects on the ways their social relationships are managed. Sometimes physical configurations are a reflection of face systems, as when a teacher stands in front of a classroom, and sometimes they can encourage participants to see themselves in a particular kind of relationship, as when a business person moves from behind his or her desk to greet a potential client in order to enhance the feeling of involvement.

Studying face systems and strategies can be extremely complicated and subject to all kinds of pitfalls, especially if you engage in it before gaining a good understanding of the grammar of context at work in particular situations. Even then, it is easy to misinterpret the degree to which people are using either independence or involvement strategies if you are not familiar with the norms of communication of a particular group of people or the kinds of interaction rituals they are accustomed to. Remember, independence and involvement are not absolute qualities, but rather points on a continuum. Whether or not an utterance communicates independence or involvement is relative and dependent on the expectations, past experiences of participants and their previous history of interaction.

The kinds of questions you will need to ask in approaching the phenomenon of politeness include: What are the key relationships in this site? How are these relationships defined in terms of power and social distance? Are these definitions fixed, or are they in some way negotiated with every interaction? How are these relationships implicated in the important social actions which you identified before? Specifically, do these actions involve matters of sufficient import (weight of imposition) as to affect the ways relationships are managed? How are independence and involvement communicated and interpreted in interaction? How are relationships communicated in other ways (for example through dress, furniture)? And do the people involved have the same understanding of the relative power/distance of one another and the appropriate degree of independence and involvement to use with particular people in particular situations?

Obviously it will be impossible to answer these questions simply by observing people interact. Remember, the key issue in face and politeness is not so much the way people treat each other as it is how they *interpret* how they treat each other. Your observations will almost certainly need to be supplemented with interviews in which you elicit from people their expectations about proper behavior. One way to do this is to ask them to relate stories of past encounters of the "polite" or "impolite" variety. Another way is to present them with hypothetical situations and either ask them how they would behave or ask them to judge the hypothetical behavior of others. It is important in such interviews to give participants the opportunity to talk both about their own personal behavior and about their perceptions of how participants in their discourse system *usually* behave or *ought to* behave. You may find that these are not always the same.

Discussion Questions

1   Consider the following situations. First fill in the chart based on whether you think the situation described involves +D or −D, +P or −P, and +W or −W. Then describe the kinds of face strategies the people involved might use and whether both parties are likely to use the same strategies or different strategies. You may discuss these strategies in broad terms (e.g. involvement and independence) or you may suggest more specific conversational strategies. Remember, it is likely in most situations that a combination of both independence and involvement strategies would be used, and people sometimes change strategies based on moment-by-moment conditions in the conversation (e.g. how people have reacted or something they said). Discuss the conditions that might result in shifts from one kind of strategy to another.

	P +/−	D +/−	W +/−	Probable face strategies
You need to ask your teacher for an extension on the due date for an assignment.				
You need to borrow a large amount of money from a good friend or relative.				
You need to ask a stranger for a small amount of money because you are short of your bus fare.				
You want to ask your boyfriend or girlfriend to marry you.				
You are a boss and you need to tell an employee that he or she is being laid off.				

2   Talk about a situation you have experienced in which you believe someone has acted
    impolitely or inappropriately. Discuss what you think polite or appropriate behavior
    would have been in this situation and examine why you hold this opinion. Think about
    the ways the expectations about politeness or appropriateness held by the offending
    party might have been different from your own.

3   Compare and contrast the different ways people treat one another in two different dis-
    course systems that you participate in. Discuss the kinds of strategies people use to show
    friendliness and/or respect and how issues of power, social distance, and the relative
    import of topics being discussed affect decisions about when and how these strategies
    are used.

References for Further Study

The framework for politeness described in this chapter comes from Penelope Brown and
Stephen Levinson's 1987 classic *Politeness: some universals in language usage*. Brown and
Levinson largely derive their concept of "face" from Goffman's 1959 classic *The Presentation
of Self in Everyday Life* as well as in his article "On face-work: an analysis of ritual elements
in social interaction" (reprinted in *Interaction Ritual*, pp. 5–46). The use of the terms
"involvement" and "independence" to refer to what Brown and Levinson call "positive"
and "negative" politeness comes from the work of Deborah Tannen (1984, 1989, 1990a).
Although many aspects of Brown and Levinson's model have been criticized or revised by
later scholars, especially in the area of cross-cultural politeness studies, it remains the foundation of much scholarly work on politeness. Scollon and Scollon (1981, 1983, 1994) have
extended Brown and Levinson's theory to include the concept of global face systems. Other
influential approaches can be found in Geoffrey Leech's 1983 *Principles of Pragmatics* (especially chapters 5 and 6) and Robin Lakoff's 1973 paper "The logic of politeness; or, Minding
your P's and Q's." More recent research on face and politeness can be found in the pages
of the *Journal of Politeness Studies*. For insights into face in Chinese culture readers are
directed to Yuling Pan's 2000 *Politeness in Chinese Face-to-Face Interaction*, Yuling Pan and
Daniel Z. Kadar's 2011 *Politeness in Historical Chinese and Contemporary Chinese*, and Yueguo
Gu's 1990 article "Politeness phenomena in modern Chinese," as well as the work of Francis
Hu (1944) and Stella Ting-Toomey (1988).

4

Conversational Inference: Interpretation in Spoken Discourse

We began by saying that language is always ambiguous. Language has at least two major kinds of ambiguity, which we might call external and internal. External ambiguity has to do with knowing the contexts in which meanings are to be interpreted. In the preceding chapters we have showed two of the means we have to interpret the speaker's meaning through an analysis of context: sharing knowledge of actions and situations (chapter 2), and knowledge of relationships and identities (chapter 3). The second problem of ambiguity in communication is not entirely or exclusively a question of context, however. It is the more internal problem of knowing which pieces go together to form a continuous whole, and how we signal that to each other. This is the study which was originally called discourse analysis, though as we have said, the idea of discourse analysis has been considerably extended in recent years.

The original focus of discourse analysis was on how we form units of communication that are larger wholes than just words or sentences. Nowadays, however, "discourse" is studied in many different ways. For some analysts the main focus is on the logical relations among sentences in texts (or, of course, conversations). For others the focus is more on the processes of interpretation we use in understanding discourse – that is, discourse as communication. We might call the object of study of these approaches "small d discourse." A third group is concerned with what we have called "capital D Discourses" or "discourse systems" such as the discourse of modern western medicine or the discourse of international finance.

Our interest is in communication (small d discourse) between people who participate in different discourse systems (capital D Discourses), and in pursuing this interest we must bring in ideas, terms, and methods from all of these different approaches to discourse.

We begin by asking how we understand discourses of a conversational nature. Even though written communications are also a major aspect of communication, especially in corporate and professional discourse systems relevant to many of those reading this book, we believe that spoken communication is more fundamental. For example, we know that in applying for a position in a company there is almost always some form of a written résumé, an application form with significant details of a person's life, education, and experience, and even examples of a person's work. Nevertheless, in most cases these written materials serve

Intercultural Communication: A Discourse Approach, Third Edition. Ron Scollon, Suzanne Wong Scollon, Rodney H. Jones.
© 2012 John Wiley & Sons, Inc. Published 2012 by John Wiley & Sons, Inc.

a preliminary screening function to select the most likely candidates for a position. Then the crucial decisions about hiring are usually made based upon an oral interview and, perhaps, also an oral presentation. Along with those formal oral presentations will also be informal conversations, which often seem quite incidental and yet create a major impression of one's abilities, competence, and likelihood of success in the position. As we will argue, the processes of inference we use in ordinary conversation are an essential aspect of how we interpret the communications of others.

How Do We Understand Discourse?

First speaker: Should I have it translated?
Second speaker: Yes, here they are.

Most readers should find the "dialogue" above impossible. We also think that most readers can understand perfectly well what each of the separate sentences means. In fact, both of these sentences come from samples in preceding chapters and, in that context, we believe that the speaker's meaning in each of these sentences was made clear by the context.

The problem that we are trying to understand in this chapter is: how do we know that these two sentences do not belong together in this case and how did we know that they did fit into the preceding dialogues? The word most often used for this aspect of discourse is "coherence," which is the characteristic of having cohesion. Coherence in discourse can be loosely defined as whatever tells the participants that all of the pieces go together.

In the first case the original dialogue was as follows:

A: Bill, that's a great idea. Could you write up a one-page summary for tomorrow's board meeting?
B: Of course, Mr Hutchins. Should I have it translated?

Even if we know nothing more about the speech event within which this dialogue took place, we can infer that the word "it" in Bill's sentence refers back to "one-page summary" in Mr Hutchins's sentence. This property of reference is one form of cohesion in discourse. Some analysts would call reference a cohesive device. This is a general term to cover any aspect of language or context that a speaker (or, of course, writer) can use to indicate a connection among elements. The use of pronouns such as "it" as a replacement for the longer, full noun phrase "one-page summary" shows the listener or reader that what one is saying is connected to what has just been said. That is one reason why the second sentence in our false dialogue does not feel like it is connected to the first speaker's sentence. The pronoun used is "they." It is very difficult to imagine any situation in which "they" could refer to the same thing as "it" in the preceding turn in the dialogue.

In that case the original dialogue was as follows:

Chairman: Do you have the minutes?
Secretary: Yes, here they are. I think 2.4.3 is what you will need.

"Yes" indicates a response to the preceding question. The word "minutes" is plural and so it seems quite natural that it would be replaced with the pronoun "they" as a cohesive device to link the dialogue together into a piece of a longer discourse.

And so to return to our original question, "How do we understand discourse?," we can say that at least part of the answer lies in the use of such lexical and grammatical cohesive devices.

A second aspect of our ability to give discourse coherence has already been discussed to some extent in chapter 2 as part of the grammar of context. The same sentence, "What time is it?," took on different speaker meanings depending on the speech event in which it was used. In both *asking for the time* and in *testing for the concept of telling the time* the first two turns are very similar. They could be identical. What is different is the third turn. In *asking for the time*, the first speaker is expected to thank the second speaker. In *testing for the concept of telling the time*, the first speaker is expected to evaluate the second speaker's response to the question.

Such regular, recurring sequences of expected turns have been named "adjacency sequences." Adjacency sequences are one form of learned, predictable, or regular expectations of patterns which bring coherence to discourse. Such regular patterns have been considered one form of schema or script. Together they form a second major source of coherence in discourse.

The third source of coherence in oral discourse is really what makes oral discourse oral; it is what we call prosodic patterning. By that we mean to include such aspects of the discourse as are, in fact, oral: intonation and timing. For example, let us look at the following dialogue:

A: Can you have the report on overseas sales ready for the meeting this afternoon?
B: *This afternoon?* I thought that wasn't due until Thursday.

B says *this afternoon* in a higher pitch and perhaps also draws it out a bit. By this (as well as by the cohesive device of repetition) he shows a connection to the preceding speaker's turn as well as calling into question speaker A's assumption that the report can be finished. We include such emphatic uses of intonation as well as timing under the general category of prosodic patterning.

The fourth major source of coherence in discourse is neither a learned form nor a logical or cognitive structure. It is what John Gumperz (1977) has called conversational inference. This process works one turn at a time as participants move through a face-to-face interaction. At each turn they simultaneously interpret the preceding discourse, give an indication of their own inferences drawn from that discourse, and make their contribution toward the continuation of the discourse. This complex process of inference is both an essential aspect of communication and a major source of miscommunication.

Taken together, cohesive devices, schemata, prosodic patterning, and conversational inference make up the four major means by which we produce and interpret coherence in spoken discourse.

Cohesive Devices: Lexical and Grammatical

No linguist or sociolinguist would attempt to make a complete list of all the possible lexical and grammatical cohesive devices in any one language, let alone as a general statement intended to cover all languages, and it is not our goal to try to do this either. Our goal is just to indicate the means participants have for giving coherence to discourse, not to explicate all of the ways this is done. Halliday and Hasan's *Cohesion in English* (1976) is a full, book-length treatment to which the reader may refer for an extended discussion.

For our purposes it will be sufficient if the reader understands that there are many different kinds of cohesive device available for participants in discourse. We will give a few examples of just two, reference and verb forms, and a somewhat longer discussion of just one other formal cohesive device: conjunction.

Reference

Reference is one of the most frequently used cohesive devices. Perhaps it is impossible to imagine a sentence which does not make reference in some form, and in most cases those references will perform a function of providing discourse cohesion. In addition to pronouns, the use of the definite article "the" is frequently used for discourse cohesion. For example, in the sentence above, "Do you have the minutes?," "the" makes reference back to the minutes both participants know they have been talking about. Of course, the chair could have said, "Do you have the minutes of the last meeting?" In that case, the reference is forward to the words "the last meeting?" In either case, "the" is used to make a connection within the discourse.

Verb forms

All languages have some differences in verb forms which are used to produce cohesion. In English, it is the tense system which most often carries out this function. The dialogue about the minutes takes place in the present and this use of tense is maintained across the turns of the two speakers. It would make an odd contrast and a violation of cohesion if the speakers had used different tenses, as in the following:

Chairman: Do you have the minutes?
Secretary: Yes, here they were. I thought 2.4.3 is what you will need.

On the other hand, a shift in tense could indicate a cohesive discourse but with a somewhat different meaning. It might have been as follows:

Chairman: Do you have the minutes?
Secretary: Yes, here they are. I thought 2.4.3 is what you would need.

In this latter case, the secretary's shift to "I thought" from "I think" indicates a cohesion or continuity with his or her planning for the meeting which took place *before* this speech event. By using these verb forms the secretary is able to indicate to the chairman that it is not any accident that those minutes were available just at that moment.

Conjunction

We have chosen to focus more closely on conjunctions for two reasons: conjunctions are rather widely taught as a part of formal instruction in English as a second language and so our readers are likely to be somewhat more familiar with these cohesive devices, and in addition to that, conjunctions have been found in a number of research studies to be particularly problematical for non-native speakers and writers of English. For example, in one study researchers found that conjunctions such as "but" and "and" were used in such a way that the result was a sense of general confusion and incoherence in the overall structure of the lectures given by Korean, Japanese, and Chinese speakers of English. Very similar findings have been reported for Cantonese writers of English in Hong Kong. Cantonese writers of English in one study used conjunctions more frequently than native speakers and writers of English, and they used those conjunctions more frequently in the marked sentence-initial position.

Conjunctions are lexical items (or words) which are normally placed between two clauses and which show the relationships between those two clauses. Halliday and Hasan (1976) analyze four major kinds of conjunction of clauses in English:

1   additive (typically marked with "and");
2   adversative (marked with words such as "but");
3   causal (marked with "because" or "so," etc.);
4   temporal (markers such as "and" or "and then").

An additive conjunction indicates that the following clause adds to or completes what came before.

> Harvey is good at making oral presentations and he also writes very well.

An adversative conjunction shows that the following clause opposes in some way the idea presented in the preceding discourse.

> Harvey is good at making oral presentations, but he is terrible with written reports.

A causal conjunction indicates that the second clause is in some way a logical cause or a result of the preceding clause.

> Harvey is good at making oral presentations, because he took a training program in presentations last year. (*Cause*)
> Harvey is good at making oral presentations, so the boss always asks him to do them when we have foreign clients. (*Result*)

Finally, a temporal conjunction relates two clauses in time.

> Harvey gave a good oral presentation, then he ruined his chances with a badly written report.

The causal conjunction "because"

We said above that conjunctions normally stand between clauses and show the relationship between them. While this is generally true, and therefore forms the unmarked structure in English, some conjunctions may also occur at the beginning of the two clauses which they relate. The conjunction "because" is a common example of this. The problems begin with deciding whether or not to take the conjunction "because" to be relating the sentence before it to the sentence following it.

There are two main structures in which "because" is used in English. In the most common or unmarked structure it is as follows:

X because Y

where Y is taken to be the cause of X or the explanation of X. That is to say, X is what you are saying, and Y is the explanation.

X = Harvey is good at making oral presentations
because
Y = he took a training program in presentations last year.

In the marked structure the order of the clauses is reversed as follows:

Because Y, X

That is to say, Y is what you are saying and X is the result.

Because Harvey took a training program in presentations last year, he is good at making oral presentations.

It is important to realize that the causal or explanatory relationship is the same in both cases; in either case it is the training program which is the cause of Harvey's skill in making oral presentations. What is different is the focus on Harvey's skill in oral presentations in the unmarked order and the focus on the training program in the marked order.

We will return to this particular conjunction, "because," in our discussion of conversational inference which follows, since it is one which causes particularly acute problems in real-time processing. This is especially so where there is any ambiguity in the use of the conjunction. For now we only wish to point out that conjunctions are among the more significant of the formal, lexical cohesive devices which speakers can use to give coherence to their discourse.

Cognitive Schemata and Scripts

In many North American restaurants there is a regular pattern of activities which with minor variations is like the following:

1   You find a seat.
2   You determine your order.
3   You place your order with the waiter or waitress.
4   You receive your food.
5   When you finish eating, you pay your bill at the cashier's.

Part of normal life and normal knowledge for many North Americans is this expected sequence of activities, which has been called a schema or a script.

The role of such patterns in interpreting discourse is that, even where not all of the details are mentioned, a listener who knows the script can reconstruct the event from a combination of what is said and his or her knowledge of the script.

For example, we might tell a short narrative like this:

> Yesterday I saw Eleanor at the restaurant, but since I had just paid and she was just ordering I told her we'd get together tomorrow.

Those who know this script will know that the speaker was just leaving the restaurant and that Eleanor had just taken her seat, though the narrator has not actually mentioned either of these details.

One of the authors on his first trip to Japan discovered that in at least some cases the restaurant script is somewhat different, even when the restaurant resembles in many other ways the kind of restaurant described above. In that case the script was as follows:

1   You determine your order.
2   You pay for your order at the cashier's.
3   You find a seat.
4   You place your order with the waiter or waitress.
5   You receive your food.
6   You eat, and leave when you have finished.

Although many of the elements are the same, a direct translation of the little narrative about meeting Eleanor above would not carry the same meaning against the background of this script, in which if the narrator had just paid and Eleanor was just ordering, the two participants would be very near each other in their progress through this script. There would be little reason why they could not sit together and talk. His or her justification for not speaking just then to Eleanor, which is clear in the "North American script," would be less justified in the "Japanese script" and need further clarification.

The concept of cognitive schemata or scripts is very useful in coming to understand how people interpret meanings in discourse. Unfortunately, the concept is generally rather vague as it has been used and often covers several quite different phenomena. A fuller study than we are able to present here would require a much more detailed account of the many different kinds of schema. For our purposes we have decided to put together into this category three general types of knowledge which people use to interpret discourse: scripts, world knowledge, and adjacency sequences.

World knowledge

By "world knowledge" we mean something that is vaguer than scripts as such. An example of the sort of thing we mean was given earlier, in chapter 1. When we say, "There's a taxi at the door," our knowledge of the world includes knowing that the taxi will have a driver. As a result there is nothing odd about using the definite article in making reference to this driver, as in the following discourse:

> There's a taxi at the door. Shall I ask the driver to wait a few minutes?

It is from our general world knowledge that we are able to interpret to whom this "the" refers quite unambiguously in this case.

A friend of the authors has told them of his friend who went into business largely because when he was in college he did not know what it meant to have a major. As some readers will know, in U.S. colleges and universities one takes a group of general courses which are required for all degree programs, and then, in addition to those, one specializes with a concentration in one particular discipline. That specialization is called one's major.

Our friend's friend did not know this when he first went away to college. From time to time people asked him what his major was, but he was unsure about how to answer. As a solution, he listened to what others said when that question was asked. The next time he heard the question asked of someone, that person answered that his major was "business." Not too long after that when he was discussing his program with his counselor, the counselor asked him what he planned to have as a major. He answered that it was business. The result was that he was directed into a concentration in business courses and remains in business today.

In such a case, the knowledge of the world is knowledge of the general procedures of an institution like a college or the general requirements of completing a degree program. Unlike a script, it does not form any particular sequence of elements necessarily. This sort of "encyclopedic" knowledge of one's world is the sort that often causes confusion or miscommunication.

Adjacency sequences

The speech events *asking for the time* and *testing for the concept of telling the time* are examples of a kind of schema that occurs very frequently in day-to-day discourse. If someone initiates one of these sequences with the first turn, "What time is it?," it is very predictable that the second turn and then the third will follow. Such predictable sequences have been called adjacency sequences by discourse analysts.

Adjacency sequences have been quite intensively studied by discourse analysts. There are greetings of many kinds, such as face-to-face or by telephone; such greetings may be different depending on the time of day – morning, mid-day, and afternoon or evening – and they may vary in key from lighthearted morning greetings among colleagues in an office to somber greetings at ritual events such as weddings and funerals. Departures also depend on such things as the time of day (with special last departure of-the-day formulas – the difference between "Good evening" and "Good night"), situation, and key. Many textbooks for language learners have been written which focus on just such adjacency sequences, or as they have sometimes been called, "gambits."

There are several questions relating to the interpretation of meaning in discourse which arise in thinking about adjacency sequences. The first of them is that they definitely ease communication by giving a regular and predictable order to the discourse. Even if you do not know English well, when you hear, "Good morning, how are you?," you can feel quite safe in giving the discourse cohesion by saying, "Fine, thank you." In short, adjacency sequences are formulas for cohesion.

It should not be surprising, then, that the great majority of adjacency sequences are used at transitional points in discourse. They are used at the beginnings (greetings), ends (departures), topic changes (such as "by the way," "not to change the subject"), and other points where a change in the participant roles is potentially disruptive of cohesion.

On the other hand, adjacency sequences present two problems, one to the participants in a discourse and the other to the analyst of discourse. The problem for participants shows up quite acutely for learners of a language.

It is not too difficult to master a small set of quite efficient adjacency sequences. One can learn how to greet people, how to depart from them; one can learn how to ask for clarification or for repetition – "What does X mean?," or, "Could you please say that again?" These adjacency sequences can give to non-native speakers a certain level of fluency which can easily give an exaggerated impression of their overall ability in discourse. The authors have often had this experience in learning a new language. You actually become hesitant to use adjacency sequences because once you have engaged the attention of a speaker of the language you find that you are out of your depth and have little ability to continue the conversation once it has begun.

While we have phrased this as a problem, we should point out that we do not mean that learners of a language should not try to learn adjacency sequences. They remain one of the more important aspects of achieving discourse competence.

The problem that adjacency sequences pose for us in our analysis of discourse is that in several decades of study, analysts have now come to agreement that there are virtually no such sequences of more than a few turns. Perhaps four or five turns are the outer limit of regular adjacency sequences. That means that although these sequences are of considerable importance in achieving discourse cohesion and in knowing how to interpret meaning in discourse, they cannot be used to account for any aspects of discourse cohesion beyond just a few turns.

Prosodic Patterning: Intonation and Timing

Prosody is a general term for the study of speech rhythms. In our analysis of conversational inference we feel it is most useful to divide the subject into two main sub-topics: intonation and timing. Naturally, in practice it is very difficult to separate these two aspects in the ongoing flow of a conversation.

Intonation

Spoken English makes relatively little use of pitch alone to make meaningful differences. Usually it is more useful to talk about stress, which is a combination of factors such as higher pitch, louder volume, lengthening, and even a difference in the vowel quality. For example, the difference between the two words, *con*tent ("what is inside") and con*tent* ("satisfied") is ordinarily described as a difference in stress with a higher pitch on the stressed syllable, a slight lengthening of the stressed syllable, and, perhaps, an increase in volume, as well as differences in the two vowels in the words. In other words, stress is a phenomenon which applies to single syllables on the whole, even though other syllables in the vicinity of the stressed syllable might be affected in secondary ways.

Tone contour is the result of the pattern of stressed and non-stressed syllables, the indication of declarative, emphatic, or question function, as well as of the termination or non-termination of a speaker's turn. In practice, it has proved to be anything but simple to accurately describe tone contours in English, and any single analysis has had to be modified for dialectal, regional, and register differences.

In order to understand cohesion in professional discourse it is probably not essential to know and understand all of these aspects of intonation in English. We believe that as long as the reader has a clear conception of how stress is used (or misinterpreted) and how tone contours are used (or misinterpreted), it will be clear how these aspects of discourse are used in achieving coherence in discourse.

Imagine this conversation:

A: Have you paid these invoices yet?
B: Yes, I've paid *those* invoices.

The use of the word "those" tells us several things. For one thing it indicates a reference back to "these invoices" in the preceding turn. That is simply a matter of the choice of the pronoun and indicates cohesion of the sort we discussed above under reference. The emphasis on "those" tells us something additional. It suggests that while "those" invoices have been paid, there are others which have not been paid.

This sort of stress has generally been called contrastive stress; it is used to indicate that something other than the expected situation is being alluded to. In other words, one of the most important aspects of contrastive stress is to indicate that the speaker recognizes the unmarked assumptions being made, and that those unmarked assumptions do not entirely hold true.

All of the following sentences could be used to indicate somewhat different questions about the unmarked assumptions:

Yes, *I've* paid those invoices. (That is, I've filled out the proper forms, but, perhaps, payroll hasn't put them through their process yet.)

Yes, I've *paid* those invoices. (But, perhaps, I haven't finished with recording them or filing them properly. Or, in a second interpretation: And don't tell me I haven't paid them!)

Yes, I've paid those *invoices*. (But I haven't gotten around to paying other bills in the same pile.)

Naturally, we could not be writing about this if it were not possible to transform this aspect of oral discourse somehow into written discourse. In this case, we have used *italics* to indicate emphasis, and we expect the reader to fill in the correct actual pronunciation on the basis of his or her knowledge.

What will be most important for our analysis, however, is to remember that while we are able to use typography in written English to transcribe stress from oral English, normally we would use a different linguistic form to accomplish the same task. For example, in written form the question might be put in a memo as follows:

Have the attached invoices been paid?

The answer would most likely be written back something like:

Yes, I've done the attached invoices, but the others are yet to be completed.

In other words, the written form is likely to be more explicit about the attention being called to the unmarked assumptions and to the fact that there is some variance from those assumptions. In oral discourse, contrastive stress is more likely to be used, partly because it is available in speaking and it is not so easily available in writing, and partly because oral discourse tends to work one turn at a time. If a question does arise from the use of contrastive stress, the other speaker is likely to check it out in the next turn.

Since writing does not allow such rapid feedback between participants, there is usually a greater degree of explicitness, especially where there is likely to be some question about assumptions. Suppose a secretary would like to know if his or her boss has completed drafting up an important report. He or she might ask, "Finish that report?" or perhaps the same secretary is telling the boss the list of things he or she planned to do next. He or she might say, "Call Frankfurt. Write the memo to Purchasing. Finish that report." Now, perhaps, the secretary is talking to his or her assistant who is word processing this same report. He or she might say, "Finish that report."

In all three cases, this same string of words, *Finish that report*, would be said with quite different overall tone contours. In the first case, it would be given a questioning intonation; in the second case, it would be said with a non-emphatic final intonation contour; and in the third case, it would be said with an emphatic intonation contour indicating an imperative. Any native speaker of English would recognize the difference in meaning among these three intonation patterns, though the exact description of such contours is far from being a simple matter.

If we go back to the second example, we can isolate the most important of these contours for conversational inference. In the list of things the secretary planned to do, he or she gave three activities: Call Frankfurt. Write the memo to Purchasing. Finish that report.

We have said that the third of these sentences will have final intonation contour. Here we want to notice that the other two will have non-final intonation contour. It is difficult to describe this contour exactly because there are several different patterns for it used by English speakers. In one pattern, the non-final contour has a slight rise in pitch on the last syllable. In another pattern, the non-final contour has a slight fall in pitch on the last syllable. In either case, what makes it different from the final contour is that it does not fall away to a low and very soft pitch. The reason intonation contour is so important to spoken discourse cohesion is that participants use their reading of intonation contours in deciding whether or not it is their turn to take over the floor. In the example above, if the boss had intervened after the sentence *Write the memo to Purchasing*, with its non-final contour, we would expect that he would make some apology for interrupting and the conversation might be more like this:

Secretary: Call Frankfurt. Write the memo to Purchasing . . .
Boss: Excuse me a moment. Is that the one I dictated this morning?
Secretary: Yes, that one.
Boss: OK, go on.
Secretary: Finish that report.

As we will see below, the interpretation of when it is one's turn to speak is one of the most crucial aspects of conversational discourse, and much of that interpretation depends on a correct understanding of final and non-final intonation contours.

Timing

In the short dialogues we have used as examples, we have usually written the speech of one participant and then put a space between that person's speech and the next person's speech. This is a way of representing typographically the small pause that occurs between turns as one speaker gives up the floor and another takes over the right to speak. Much has been written about these interturn pauses. Our own research interest in them comes from their role in giving rise to interpersonal judgments of competence. We have found that even very small differences in the timing of interturn pauses can lead conversationalists to develop negative attitudes toward each other.

Disfluencies in discourse often produce an apology. This is because we have a strong feeling that conducting a smooth discourse which both is coherent and changes smoothly from one speaker to another is an important aspect of how we conduct our social affairs. The problem of negative attitudes arises because interturn pauses are not just simple silences between turns; they are points at which each speaker must make a quick judgment about what to do next, and that judgment must be based on what he or she assumes the other is likely to do.

This is how it happens: when a person finishes a turn at speaking, he or she pauses a moment for the response of the other speaker. The end of the turn is actually a rather complex phenomenon to analyze, but it is indicated by such things as changes in tempo, intonational contours (often a drop in pitch), and the completion of syntactic units. With these and other gestural clues one speaker shows another that he or she is finishing a point and expects the other speaker to respond. Normally, then, the other speaker may take the floor to comment, to extend the point, or even to change the subject. At the very least a feedback response, such as saying, "Uh huh," or even a simple nod, is required to confirm that the point has been taken.

If the first speaker reaches one of these turn exchange points and the second speaker responds as expected, everything progresses smoothly. If, on the other hand, the second speaker does not respond, the first speaker has a problem. There are many reasons why the second might not have responded.

He or she may not have noticed the cues or may have been daydreaming. Whatever the reasons, the first speaker is left holding the conversational bag. He or she needs to decide whether or not to continue and assume the point was taken, or back up and repeat the point either literally or in paraphrase.

These conversational disfluencies are actually quite rare, even though in ordinary conversations such transitional points come up as often as once a second. This comment masks a considerable analytical difficulty. One issue is the typology of pauses. There are at least four kinds of pause: those taken for time to think (cognitive), those taken so that the other conversationalist may take over the floor (interactive), those taken so that the other may give feedback without actually taking the floor (backchannel), and those caused by other factors such as a cough. In actual conversation it is never entirely certain what sort of pause any particular pause is until it is over, that is, retrospectively. For instance, if one speaker pauses for feedback but the other speaker takes the floor, a feedback pause has been transmuted into an interactive pause. Or, if one pauses to think a moment and the other takes the floor, a cognitive pause has become an interactional pause. The pauses in a conversation are as much in need of ongoing interpretation and reaction as the words, clauses, and sentences. Our comment here is meant to imply only that such points of ambiguity arise typically about once a second.

In fact as we speak we are constantly monitoring our listeners for signs of their response to our speech, and when these responses are absent or disfluent we are thrown out of our rhythm. The results are repetition, paraphrasing, stuttering, and usually embarrassment, if not a sense of some hostility toward the other person. Unfortunately, there are many non-grammatical factors which can influence our timing in such points of transition in a conversation. While our timing varies widely during a single day and one person varies widely in his or her timing from one day to the next, if any two conversationalists are different in their expectations about the appropriate length of these interturn pauses, the results can be disastrous. When the faster person is speaking, he or she will get to a turn exchange point and pause a moment for the response of the other. Since he or she expects a shorter pause than the other, he or she will decide to either move on or repeat before the other person has had a chance to respond. This pattern will be repeated again and again, until cumulatively the result will be that the faster speaker is doing all of the talking, constantly repeating himself or herself, paraphrasing, and finally coming to the conclusion that the other person either has nothing to say or is linguistically incompetent.

On the other side of the interaction, the person who moves through the encounter at a somewhat slower pace will find himself or herself constantly frustrated in trying to get the floor to speak. After waiting a slightly longer time to take a turn, he or she will begin to speak, only to realize that the other has already begun to rephrase a prior comment or is now going on to something new. In any event, the slower of the two now will feel somewhat confused and begin to develop a sense that he or she is being conversationally bullied. It does not take long for this person to develop a defensive or even hostile reaction to the conversation, if not to the other person as well.

There are many factors which contribute to a person taking longer or shorter interturn pauses. Interpersonal face relationships, as we discussed them in chapter 3, are among the most important. Generally, longer pauses are associated with independence politeness strategies, while shorter pauses are associated with involvement politeness strategies. As a result, in a solidarity face system, the pauses tend to be shorter; in a deference face system, the pauses tend to be longer; and in a hierarchical face system, there is a difference in the use of pauses by the person in the higher position and the person in the lower position.

This latter point is quite significant, as we will see below. The situation can be described in the opposite manner: we can also say that where one speaker uses shorter pauses and the other uses longer pauses, there will be a tendency for the system to develop into a hierarchical system, whether the participants intend that outcome or not. In other words, if one speaker takes shorter interturn pauses than another, there will be a tendency for that first speaker to come to dominate the interaction, if not to dominate the other person as well.

The issue for interdiscourse professional communication is that there are differences in expectations about pauses both within and across different groups. There are also significant differences in expectations about face relationships. Asians appear to be among the world's quicker speakers when speaking in their own languages: such as Chinese, Japanese, and Korean. Hayashi (1988), for example, has written about the rapid and elegant conversational dance of the Japanese, which foreigners can hear but so rarely join. It is, of course, impossible to judge such things impressionistically, and a more accurate, research-based comparison would immediately run foul of the problem that the linguistic means of indicating turn transitions differ importantly from language to language.

In communications which take place in English between less proficient non-native speakers and native speakers, the non-native speaker faces many barriers in the way of turn exchange fluency. The most obvious one is simply that he or she is using a second language and may still be a language learner. That almost by definition slows one down. Compounded with a second-language user's lower levels of ability in the language, however, may be other factors, such as the factors having to do with politeness we outlined in the last chapter; the non-native speaker, for instance, may be accustomed to a discourse system in which deference is the proper attitude to take in relation to a stranger, and deference is normally associated with longer turn exchange pauses, if not complete silence. The native speaker, on the other hand, does not just have a better command of the language, but might also be accustomed to a discourse system in which it is assumed that interpersonal relationships should progress to a system of symmetrical solidarity as quickly as possible, and so is likely to emphasize involvement politeness strategies, including shorter interturn pauses. Consequently, in this example, everything conspires to produce a significant difference in the length of interturn pauses between these two speakers.

Unfortunately, if everything else conspires to produce a difference in pause length, that difference will lead the faster speaker to dominate the conversation, even if it is his or her intention to create highly fluent, interactive discussions. Quite unconsciously, they find themselves repeating things, paraphrasing prior statements, simplifying, and linguistically backing and filling to compensate for the conversational gaps and arrhythmia. Where they possess much energy and great goodwill they will press on; where this is not the case, unfortunately, they may come to the conclusion that their interlocutors are less competent linguistically (and intellectually) than they really are.

Metacommunication

We can now come back to the question with which we started: how do we understand discourse? This may not be a crucial question in ordinary, day-to-day life, since we just go about communicating without paying undue attention to how we do it. For professional communicators, on the other hand, it is a crucial question. Professional communication depends on being able to understand not just when and where to communicate what, but also how it is done. Only by explicitly analyzing the process of communication can a professional come to communicate effectively.

In trying to answer the question, "How do we understand discourse?," we have introduced the idea of cohesive devices and cognitive schemata. We could think of the first as the resources we use in bringing cohesion to discourse and to our interpretations of discourse. We could think of the second as the broader conceptual frameworks within which discourse is set.

Nevertheless, knowing both cohesive devices and cognitive schemata is not sufficient to come to an understanding of how we understand discourse. We need to also understand the process of interpretation itself. This process is called conversational inference.

The anthropologist Gregory Bateson (1972) pointed out some years ago that every communication must simultaneously communicate two messages, the basic message and the metamessage. The idea of the basic message we are familiar with. The metamessage is a second message, encoded and superimposed upon the basic, which indicates how we want someone to take our basic message. The prefix "meta" is from Greek and carries the meaning of higher or more general. Bateson also pointed out that this was not just a question of human communication. When we play with a dog, the dog may pretend to bite us. We can tell from the basic message that the dog is biting. The metamessage is conveyed by the dog making its bite quite gentle and at the same time wagging its tail and other such gestures.

Human communication is no different. According to the anthropologist John Gumperz, each successful message carries with it a second metamessage which tells the listener how to interpret the basic message. A basic message by itself cannot be interpreted. Gumperz (1977, 1982, 1992) uses the term "contextualization cues" for the ways in which we convey metamessages in ordinary conversational discourse.

As it stands, this way of talking about communication is simply another way of saying what we have said repeatedly throughout this book: to interpret not just the sentence meaning but also the speaker's meaning, we must make reference to the context. The problem with this statement as it stands is that it does not take into consideration real-time processing. The process of making inferences about spoken discourse is an ongoing process, in which we must be constantly interpreting the immediately preceding discourse at the same time as we are moving on to subsequent stages of the discourse.

The consequence of real-time processing is that every communication that takes place in real time must simultaneously deal with at least three forms of coherence:

1   the basic message (what the speaker is saying);
2   the metamessage (how the message is to be taken);
3   the discourse contextualization (confirmation of the preceding metamessage).

To put it in a more ordinary way, to maintain coherent discourse, each speaker needs to keep the discourse going while at the same time confirming to the others that he or she has followed what has gone on up to that point. Sometimes a conversation can go on a bit with both (or all) participants not knowing that they have gone off the track. For example, we can look at the short dialogue we used above:

A: Bill, that's a great idea. Could you write up a one-page summary for tomorrow's board meeting?
B: Of course, Mr Hutchins. Should I have it translated?

We can imagine this as a somewhat different dialogue as follows:

A: Bill, that's a great idea. Could you write up a one-page summary for tomorrow's board meeting? And could you also be sure the agenda is printed?
B: Of course, Mr Hutchins. Should I have it translated?
A: No, I don't think we usually translate them.
B: Oh, I'm sorry. I meant the summary; should I have it translated?
A: Oh, I see. You'd better ask Jane about that.

When Bill says, "it," there is an unclear reference. Mr Hutchins takes the pronoun to mean the agenda but Bill had intended the summary. He only discovers his error when Mr Hutchins uses "usually" and "them." The summary is a unique event whereas the agenda is a regular, recurring aspect of board meetings. From this world knowledge of meetings and from the use of these cohesive devices of reference, Bill is able to guess that Mr Hutchins has misunderstood his question and they undertake the adjacency sequence usually called a repair sequence, where they go back to straighten out the mistake.

This shows the real-time nature of the structure of coherence in spoken discourse. It is worked out as it goes, and requires constant confirmation among the participants that they are understanding the same things and in the same way. When Bill and Mr Hutchins discover their mistake in the example we have just discussed, they simply go back and make the necessary correction.

There are two things to be observed in this rather simple case. The first is that it is quite simple and does not involve a major misinterpretation of meaning. The second is that even though it is simple, Bill feels obliged to apologize. Successful conversational discourse requires that the participants not only maintain cohesion or relevance, but that where there are breaks in the cohesion they go back and repair them. Cohesion in discourse is not only a convenience or even a simple communicative necessity, it is also a social and interpersonal obligation. One has and feels the obligation to maintain a smooth and coherent discourse, and if one has been responsible for a break it is taken as a disruption of good interpersonal relationships.

Smooth discourse depends so strongly on shared knowledge that when there is a break or disruption, the most immediate reaction is that the culprit must be a member of a different group. To put this another way, smooth discourse is one of the most significant means humans have of demonstrating who is an insider in any particular group and who is an outsider. Most of us are quite conscious of different pronunciations or of different words used by members of other groups, but in day-to-day practice it is cohesion in discourse which provides the strongest and most emblematic forces for group identity.

Non-sequential processing

Most conversational repairs can be handled as the one shown above was, with a brief side-sequence of two or three turns. The participants go off to one side conversationally while they straighten out their confusion, and then return to the main path of their topic. This is because oral discourse tends to be structured one turn at a time. Even within turns, oral discourse tends to be structured a sentence at a time or even a clause at a time.

Cohesive devices tend to be placed between two clauses or sentences to show the relationship between the clauses on the two sides. The reason for this is that real-time processing requires not only the forward movement of saying the next combined basic message plus metamessage, but also the backward-looking confirmation of what has gone before in the preceding turns. It becomes a rather complex problem of processing to load too many messages together into the same utterance.

Nevertheless, there is a sort of conversational overloading when confusion arises for some reason. To give a specific example, let us go back to the conjunction "because." We said earlier in this chapter that the unmarked use of this causal conjunction was:

X because Y

This is the order in which oral discourse normally indicates a logical relationship between two clauses or sentences. There is also the marked usage in which the form is:

Because Y, X

While there is nothing grammatically incorrect about this usage, in real-time discourse it can present a problem. We might think of an ordinary stretch of one speaker's turn as having a sequence of sentences, $E\ F\ G$. Without any further indication, we would take each of them to stand alone. Of course, in actual discourse we would want to analyze the prosodic features of these clauses. That would include the features we have mentioned above, such as their intonation or timing, which would give significant clues about how to interpret the sequence. We will return to the question of the prosodic patterning below.

The logical or sequential problem arises with a cohesive device like "because," since it can stand either in between the two clauses it relates, or *before* the two clauses it relates. In that case, the logical relationship is also taken to be in the reverse order. In other words, we might have the following sequence:

E because F G

If we do not have any further information to clarify this, we would expect the speaker to mean

$[E$ because $F]$ G

This is because the unmarked order assumes that "because" is relating the clauses between which it stands. On the other hand, it is possible that the speaker means

E $[$because $F, G]$

The point we are making is that it is difficult for a listener to know until the speaker gets to G which of these orders is the one he or she intends.

Imagine the sequence, E F G, corresponds with the following three sentences:

He had lunch.
He was so hungry.
He ate at the staff canteen.

It would be difficult to know if the speaker meant to say: He had lunch, because he was so hungry. He ate at the staff canteen. Or if the speaker actually meant: He had lunch. Because he was so hungry, he ate at the staff canteen.

The meanings of these sequences would be quite different. In the first case, the focus is on the hunger and on having lunch. The business about eating at the staff canteen seems quite incidental. In the second case, having lunch seems almost a background detail, whereas the focus seems to have shifted to eating at the staff canteen. We would expect the speaker to go on and talk about the staff canteen. In the first case, we would expect the speaker to go on to talk about the hunger of the person in the story.

As we have said, inferences which are drawn in discourse are drawn as definite conclusions and they are drawn very quickly. By the time the listener, the potential second speaker, had heard the third clause he or she would have come down on the side of one or the other of these interpretations and settled that that was what the first speaker was talking about. The problem is that it has not yet been confirmed by the first speaker which of these two inferences is the correct one, and the second speaker has not spoken yet.

One can easily imagine, somewhat later in the conversation, hearing the second speaker saying, "But I thought you said he went to the staff canteen because he was hungry." And one can imagine the first saying, "No, I didn't say that."

It is what happens at this point that becomes a problem in cumulative ambiguity. It is likely that neither of the participants in this discourse could say exactly what had been said so that it could be clarified. What would most likely happen is that the listener would begin to feel that the first speaker was vague or confused, or did not tell a clear story. It is also likely that the storyteller would come to think that the listener had not been paying attention. His or her attention would begin to shift away from the communication of the story, and come to focus more on the conversational partner's discourse capacity. In extreme cases, it is likely that he or she would begin to accuse his or her conversational partner of failing to cooperate, or even of illogicality.

What happens in this case is that the difference in these two possible interpretations of *E because F G* has not been confirmed at the time it came up in the discourse, because neither participant realized there was any problem. They have simply carried this ambiguity forward and acted as if each of their separate interpretations were the correct one.

Studies of the use of conjunctions by Chinese speakers of English have shown that there is a tendency for such speakers to use more conjunctions than native speakers of English. Other studies have shown that this particular construction, *because Y, X*, (a correlate of which occurs very frequently in spoken Chinese) is very commonly used by Chinese speakers when they speak English, indeed, at a much higher frequency compared with native speakers of English. This fact gives an indication of how processes of conversational inference can function in real time to produce miscommunication between speakers of different languages.

Before going on, we want to make one final note on how this sort of confusion arises even in oral discourse, where prosodic patterning would normally be sufficient to make it clear which of the interpretations was the correct one. In spoken discourse, prosody is often the most ambiguous feature. Even among native speakers of English, for example, there is much disagreement about just how final intonation should be indicated. Since sentence and clause boundaries are indicated by such prosodic contours, it is sometimes quite unclear just where the sentence and clause boundaries are intended to be placed.

If a non-native speaker of English uses the ordinary, unmarked structure we have described above, there is not much of a problem because that is the structure expected by the native speaker. On the other hand, if he or she uses the marked structure and places "because" before the two clauses, it is likely that the native English speaker will be unsure whether this has been done for two reasons, not just one. It both will be the marked form and might be prosodically not entirely clear that this is the speaker's intention. Consequently, there is no solution but to wait until the next clause is finished, balance the two possibilities against each other as to which might be the most convincing interpretation, and then go on to the next point in the conversation.

Interactive Intelligence

The term "conversational inference" was introduced to sociolinguistic studies by John Gumperz in a 1977 paper to capture the fact that as people communicate with each other, the process of interpretation moves through real time from utterance to utterance in an ongoing process of interpretation. As we have indicated above, participants in ordinary conversation are constantly in a state of uncertainty, which is normally resolved through making tentative inferences and then acting upon them until further notice. The most important sources of these inferences beyond the grammatical system of the language itself have been outlined above, namely, cohesive devices, cognitive schemata, and prosodic patterning. As we have said, communication is fundamentally ambiguous. Nevertheless, it is central to all human activity. Therefore, we can begin to understand that it is the fundamental nature of the human interpretive process to seek resolutions to this ambiguity. This interpretive process is what the sociolinguist Stephen Levinson (1990) calls interactive intelligence – the innate human capacity to draw inferences from ambiguous information.

This interactive intelligence is an essential aspect of human intelligence. As such it is brought to bear upon any communicative interpretation. This process seems to work very successfully, in fact, when conversationalists share common histories, cultures, and life experiences. The inferences they draw by assuming others think just as they do are generally safe. Problems are encountered, however, especially in the complex environment of international communication in English, when participants in a conversation have different experiences and conversational habits.

Later we will turn to the discussion of communication among people who participate in different discourse systems. As we will see, conversational inference is a fundamental aspect of interactive intelligence and should be thought of not as a problem to be eliminated in communication, but rather as one of the most fundamental of human cognitive processes. In conclusion we would like to emphasize that we should not think of this as a conscious process or intellectual strategy. The terms "interactive intelligence" and "inference" as found in the research literature we have used in developing this chapter might suggest that people are actively and consciously aware of these processes as they move through social interactions.

We would prefer to argue that, on the whole, these processes arise out of social practice, the basis in what Bourdieu calls *habitus* for the largely unconscious and non-objective actions which we take in day-to-day life. While the analyst can describe the process as working inferentially as we have done, and to some extent participants in social interaction can *in retrospect* also see how the process has developed, at the time of interacting the complexity of the situation is far too great for participants to have any more than a weak grasp of how they are proceeding through the social interaction.

The fact that the processes of conversational inference are largely unconscious in normal social interaction means that it is quite difficult to alter these processes through conscious reflection and action. To give a concluding example, we once were giving an extended training session in the problem of the timing of turn exchanges. Participants in the group were to use the information they received in the training to try to alter their own behavior. They were to return to their workplaces and make videotape recordings of their own communication, and then in a follow-up session we debriefed them on how well they had done.

One of the participants was particularly concerned that he was not allowing others enough time to respond to his questions and comments in business meetings which he was chairing. He had decided that he needed to leave more time for others to respond, but when he returned to the debriefing session he complained that even though he had left large gaps and pauses in his speech, it had not worked to produce more active turn exchanges.

We looked at the videotape he brought and this is what we found:

Does . . . anyone . . . have something . . . you'd . . . like to . . . ask, well if not we'll move onto the next item on the agenda which is the date . . .

He had certainly left very long (and disturbing) pauses, but he had not left them at the crucial points where others might take the floor. Something along the lines of the following might have worked better:

Does anyone have something you'd like to ask? . . . Are you sure? . . . Well if not, etc.

It would be easy to think of this person as a bit obtuse, but we assure the reader that he was overall very astute in matters of communication, and also was genuinely concerned to change his communicative behavior. As soon as we played the videotape and discussed it in the training debriefing session he was able to identify the difficulty. The problem was simply that *in the situation of actual communication* he was so concerned with the meeting itself that he was unable to simultaneously monitor his own communicative processes.

We introduce this example at this point to clarify that even though as analysts it is not so difficult to see what is happening in these processes of practical or conversational inference, as participants in actual situations it is very difficult to split our attention between the practical concerns of the situation and the analytical concerns we are discussing here. By using terms such as conversational inference and interactive intelligence we do not want to mislead the reader into thinking that understanding communication is simply a matter of thinking about it a bit more as you go along. The processes we are describing are much deeper than that and are shot through with concerns of social identity and power that cannot easily be altered by a bit of conscious effort and good will. By the same token, we do not intend to be discouraging, and we hope that the suggestions we provide will be useful to readers in thinking about how to analyze and to improve interdiscourse communication.

Researching Interdiscourse Communication

Collecting and analyzing spoken data

As we have seen, it is not always easy to fully grasp what is happening when participating in conversational interaction, but audio and video recordings of meetings or interviews can provide an invaluable resource for more neutral or objective observations. Because language is always ambiguous, it often takes discussing communicative behavior with participants to discover or resolve what happened or what was meant.

We said above that differences in rhythm between individuals often lead to one-sided conversations in which each person misjudges the intentions and capabilities of the other. Recording such interactions and playing them back offers participants the opportunity to see how uncomfortable moments arise and escalate. Of course, it is not always easy to get people's permission to record interaction, especially in corporate settings, and it is unethical (and in some cases illegal) to record people without their knowledge and permission. In this regard, the practice of playing recorded interactions back for participants can help them to see the value of such recording, and make them more actively involved in the research and more willing to permit future recording.

Another issue in analyzing spoken discourse is what method to use to transcribe it. Transcriptions are not always necessary. Sometimes simply listening to recordings can achieve your purposes. But for closer analysis and more formal academic work, accurate transcriptions are needed. There are many transcription methods that you could use, but we suggest you choose one that is as simple as possible. The method you choose should include ways to represent all of the features you think might be important such as key intonation contours and the length of pauses. Of course, it is possible to render such features with extreme precision or more broadly. For the kind of analysis we described above, it is usually not necessary to mark every intonation contour and measure every pause to the tenth of a second. A good transcription is not judged by how detailed it is, but rather by how useful it is and how relevant it is to what the analyst is trying to find out.

Questions you should ask yourself as you are examining your transcripts or listening to your recordings include: What makes this conversation coherent? Does it contain any cohesive devices that participants need to refer to in order to make sense of what is going on? Do participants have to refer to anything outside of the conversation to make sense of what is going on? What are the roles of interpretative frames and metamessages in this conversation? How is prosody used to make the conversation coherent and express meaning? How do participants manage turn taking with things like rhythm, pausing, and intonation? Do people encounter problems in communicating or understanding each other or in managing the conversation smoothly? If so, are they able to repair these problems? How are repairs carried out?

Reconfiguring default settings

In analyzing with your participants their successes and difficulties in communication it is often useful to consider the degree to which people are able to revise their expectations about conversations as they are progressing. In the last chapter, for example, we discussed politeness strategies and how they constitute face systems. Face systems of deference and solidarity have default settings of symmetrical independence and involvement respectively, while hierarchical face systems are set with asymmetrical strategies of deference in one direction and solidarity in the other. People usually run into problems when the default settings they bring to interactions are not met with the kinds of responses they expect. The author's mother who was annoyed with the woman she shared a table with in a restaurant in London was able to adjust her default practice of conversing with strangers when sharing a table, though it did not feel right and she interpreted the other woman's behavior as rude. The gentleman who used the wrong forms of address in Mexico, on the other hand, retained his default setting of solidarity and faced the consequences.

For Alaska Natives whose default setting is to defer to power with silence, the consequences of failure to reset the deference setting and to engage in conversation with probation officers, in other words to submit to interrogation, are more serious. Small differences in timing are sometimes magnified and misinterpreted as hostility by the officers, who report negative attitudes, which result in longer sentences.

As we have seen in this chapter, we also have default settings when it comes to things like conversational coherence, the ways we form inferences, the ways we use stress and intonation to express ourselves, and how we manage turn taking in conversations using pauses and other devices.

Changing default settings is never easy, as these settings are lifelong habits that are out of conscious awareness. The historical body, or *habitus*, formed by all the experiences of life, conscious and unconscious, resists change. Through careful attention, however, we can learn to become more conscious of our own default settings and more sensitive to those of others. Then with much diligence, intention, and patience we can try to alter selected habits we have been practicing for decades. We can learn not to struggle when subject to rough handling by security guards, for example, though we have been taught not to let strangers touch us. We can learn not to use foul language in the presence of toddlers. We can learn to fall asleep on our feet or stay awake in church. We can even learn to be silent for days on end, whether on a hunt or at a meditation retreat. And we can learn to hold our tongue for a split second before speaking to avoid being interpreted as rude.

Discussion Questions

1   Either by transcribing sections of your recordings or by listening closely to people's interaction, note differences in use of cohesive devices such as reference, verb forms, or conjunction. Discuss these different usages with participants. Are there disparate usages that speakers are reluctant to give up? Is this due to lack of awareness or perhaps to identification with a group that speaks this way?

2   In Korea tea is served at tea houses, while restaurants serve beer, carbonated beverages, or barley tea with meals. Coffee is served at fast food outlets. Foreigners accustomed to having tea with meals must either do without it or go to another venue for another event. If they want coffee with breakfast they may have to leave their hotel and settle for doughnuts. The authors attended an international conference in Beijing at which coffee and bottled water were provided. When they asked for tea, they were informed that "foreigners drank coffee but not tea." Think of a situation in which you were confronted with a schema consisting of familiar elements combined with unfamiliar ones. How did you react?

3   Greetings employ different adjacency sequences in different societies. Speakers of Thai or Chinese might, for example, ask if one has eaten by way of greeting. For speakers of English, "How are you?" may be interpreted either as a routine greeting or an inquiry into one's health. Discuss instances when you experienced confusion with adjacency sequences for greeting or leave taking.

4   Try to recall a situation in which you felt a conversation was one-sided, when either you did most of the talking or you could not get a word in edgewise. How would you describe the person you were interacting with in relation to yourself? Imagine how the course of the interaction would have been different if you had adjusted the timing of turn exchanges, and how your attitude or interpretation might have been different.

References for Further Study

Gillian Brown and George Yule's 1983 book *Discourse Analysis* is a classic and comprehensive introduction to discourse analysis. Guy Cook's 1989 *Discourse* is a briefer, more accessible account. Michael McCarthy's 1991 book is directed to readers whose field is language education, but has much that is useful to general readers. More recent introductions to discourse analysis include James Paul Gee's revised *Introduction to Discourse Analysis* (2010), which focuses on how the concept of discourse analysis has been extended to encompass studies of ideology, Brian Paltridge's *Discourse Analysis* (2006), and the collection *Advances in Discourse Studies* (2007), edited by Vijay Bhatia, John Flowerdew, and Rodney Jones. The seminal concept of conversational inference is laid out in a number of works by John Gumperz including his 1982 book *Discourse Strategies*. Halliday and Hasan's 1976 book is the most comprehensive study of cohesion in English. Scollon (1993a), Tyler et al. (1988), and Field and Yip (1992) are studies of conjunction in the English of speakers of Chinese and Korean. Schema theory is discussed in Kintsch (1977), Kintsch and Greene (1978), Carrell (1983, 1984a, 1984b, 1989), and Scollon and Scollon (1984). Rhythm and timing are discussed in Scollon (1981), and a comparative study of Chinese English and Canadian English is in Feldstein and Crown (1990). Gregory Bateson describes the concept of meta-communication in his 1972 *Steps to an Ecology of Mind*. The concept of interactive intelligence is developed by Stephen Levinson in his 1990 paper "Interactional biases in human thinking." Scollon and Scollon (1986) offer suggestions for modifying communicative patterns.

5

Topic and Face: Inductive and Deductive Patterns in Discourse

What Are You Talking About?

Successful discourse depends on knowing what your discourse partner is talking about and making sure your discourse partner knows what you are talking about. Whether it is professional discourse or ordinary conversation with friends, discourse can hardly proceed without some idea of what the topic under discussion is.

In a meeting between a businessperson from Hong Kong and one from North America, the participant from Hong Kong might say the following:

> Because most of our production is done in China now, and uh, it's not really certain how the government will react in to the debt situation in the United States, and since . . . uh . . . I think a certain amount of caution in committing to TV advertisement is necessary because of the expense. So, I . . . um . . . suggest that we delay making our decision until after the New Year.

This short excerpt is like many others which occur when native speakers of Chinese speak in English. In most cases there is little difficulty in understanding at the level of the words and sentences. There is the normal amount of "uhs" and other disfluencies found in any section of authentic, real-life language use whether the speakers are native or non-native speakers of the language. Nevertheless, even though the words and sentences of the speaker are quite clear, there may be a feeling by the English speaking participant from North America that it is not quite clear what the speaker's main point is.

Research on discourse shows that this confusion in goals or in interpreting the main point of another's speech is caused by the fact that each side is using different principles of discourse to organize its presentations. In this case the speaker of Chinese uses a "topic–comment" order of presentation in which the main point (or comment) is deferred until sufficient backgrounding of the topic has been done. We call this line of argument inductive, because it places the minor points of the argument first and then derives the main point as a conclusion from those arguments. The structure could be sketched out as:

Intercultural Communication: A Discourse Approach, Third Edition. Ron Scollon, Suzanne Wong Scollon, Rodney H. Jones.
© 2012 John Wiley & Sons, Inc. Published 2012 by John Wiley & Sons, Inc.

because of
Y (topic, background, or reasons)
X (comment, main point, or action suggested)

In fact, this kind of structure is commonly found in the speech of Chinese speakers when they speak or write English, mostly because it is typical of the way Chinese discourse is usually organized. This pattern has been observed by many researchers. That is not to say that it is the only pattern speakers of Chinese use. It is, however, particularly common. Speakers of English from the United States or the United Kingdom, on the other hand, tend to expect a discourse strategy of opening the discussion with the introduction of the speaker's main point so that other speakers may react to it and so that he or she can develop arguments in support as they are needed. We call this pattern, in which a topic is introduced at the beginning of a discourse and then the minor or supporting arguments are presented afterwards, the deductive pattern. That form would be as follows:

X (comment, main point, or action suggested)
because of
Y (topic, background, or reasons)

In the case given above a listener from the United States might expect something more like the following:

> I suggest we delay making our decision until after the New Year. That's because I think a certain amount of caution in committing to TV advertisement is necessary because of the expense, and because most of our production is done in China now, and it's not really certain how the government will react to the debt situation in the United States.

This would put the suggestion to delay the decision right at the beginning and then follow this with the speaker's reasons for doing so. The speaker less familiar with this pattern feels uncomfortable putting his or her suggestion first before he or she has given his reasoning. This difference in discourse patterns might lead one to focus on the opening stages of the discourse as the most crucial while the other might look for the crucial points to occur somewhat later.

One result of these different discourse strategies is that they sometimes give rise to the unfair and prejudicial stereotypes of the "inscrutable Chinese" or of the "frank and rude American."

A businessperson from the United States was asked what he thought was the most important aspect of business communication. His answer was, "All you need is the five Ws and one H: what, who, where, when, why and how. Nothing else. If it's too long, you lose money." This U.S. businessperson would certainly favor the deductive discourse pattern. In this discourse style of "five Ws and one H," the idea is to get the topic out onto the conversational floor right away so that you know what you are discussing. Details can then be worked out deductively as they are needed. This pattern forms a strong contrast with the pattern used in the first example above, and this contrast can easily lead to confusion about what the topic under discussion is.

It is important to reiterate that both of these patterns are available to all speakers, no matter what discourse systems they participate in. That is to say, there is nothing inherently "Chinese" or "American" about these patterns. Nevertheless, if two (or more) people in a discourse approach the discourse with different assumptions about which pattern will be used, they are likely to have the problems of misinterpretation we have mentioned above.

Both the inductive (topic-delayed) and the deductive (topic-first) patterns of discourse are used for the same main purpose. That purpose is to reduce the overall ambiguity of the discourse. In the inductive pattern, the point is to make it quite clear why the speaker is coming to that particular conclusion. This is done by outlining the arguments and by testing the other participants for potential acceptance of the topic before introducing it. In the deductive pattern, the topic is introduced at the beginning so that it will be clear what the relevance of the supporting arguments is. While the intent is the same, the strategies are starkly contrasted.

Having said above that there is nothing inherently "Chinese" or "American" in either of these patterns, since both patterns are used in all societies, nevertheless there is a possibility that differences in how discourse patterns are managed in different languages can emerge as a source of miscommunication and even stereotyping. The purpose of this chapter is to resolve these questions: what are some causes of these fixed patterns in discourse; and, more specifically, what causes the differences between the inductive and deductive patterns for the introduction of topics in discourse?

We begin with a discussion of the factors of interpersonal relationships which lead to the choice of one or the other of these rhetorical strategies. Since the introduction of a topic is in itself a politeness strategy of involvement, this question is ultimately a question of interpersonal politeness and face.

Topic, Turn Exchange, and Timing

For those accustomed to the conventions of international business communication, the deductive pattern of introducing the topic at the beginning of a discourse seems quite natural, at least to westerners in professional communication. One can imagine a businessperson saying, "Introduce your topic. Nothing else. If it's too long, you lose money." We believe, however, that the situation is somewhat more complex than this businessperson is ready to recognize or understand. As we will argue below, we do not believe this to be a generalized pattern or a schema for discourse even in the business world. The deductive discourse pattern arises as a result of a complex interplay among many factors. The most basic factor is face. This factor we will take up last. The other factor which produces this typical discourse pattern is an interaction among adjacency, turn exchange, and timing.

The call–answer–topic adjacency sequence

In a bookstore we might hear a telephone call which would begin as follows:

    A: (Telephone rings)
    B: Hello, Scollon Books.
    A: Yes, do you have a copy of *Intercultural Communication*?

There is nothing very remarkable about such a conversation. When the telephone rings, you pick it up and say something like, "Hello." In some cases, you might identify yourself. The caller will ask to speak to a particular person, or, perhaps, he or she recognizes from your voice that you are the person being called for. In any case, once it has been established you are the right person, the caller says why he or she has called. The rest of the conversation follows from there.

One of the best established adjacency sequences was first noted four decades ago in research on telephone calls. This sequence has three main turns (though there are possible side-sequences) in which the caller and the answerer are identified:

1 the call, accomplished through the ringing of the telephone;
2 the answer;
3 the introduction of the caller's topic.

As is the case with other adjacency sequences, there are strong expectations governing each of these turns, and we will take them up in order.

The call

On the telephone this turn is accomplished mechanically through the ringing of the telephone. As this research has been extended, the call has come to be understood as any form in which one person calls for the attention of another. This may be accomplished by knocking on a door or by pushing a doorbell or buzzer, or by sending an instant message to somebody on your "buddy list." We may call someone by saying such things as, "Excuse me," or, "Say, Bill," or, in the case of the instant message, "hi!" or "busy?" In any event, the call consists of any means we might use for indicating that we intend to start a conversation.

The answer

Observations of answers in many situations, not just in telephone calls, show that the most important characteristic of the answer is that it is open-ended. By that we mean that the person who answers does not limit the caller's freedom to introduce the topic. The caller is granted freedom to introduce the topic in his or her next turn. The most important aspect of this limitation on the answer is that the answerer may not introduce a topic, but he or she must show openness for the topic of the caller.

In the phone conversation example we have given just above, it is not possible for the answerer to answer as follows:

A: (Telephone rings)
B: Hello, Scollon Books. We would like you to buy a copy of *Intercultural Communication*.

In other words, the answerer may not introduce a topic, but must say something quite noncommittal, such as, "Hello," or "Good morning." In normal business or office environments the answer is usually the name of the company or office and the person answering: "Scollon Books, order department, Ron speaking."

The introduction of the caller's topic

The third move in this adjacency sequence is the caller's move, and this is to introduce the topic. In recent years, the rapid development of direct telephone marketing has shown that there are almost no limits on what topics may be introduced by the caller. The only way the answerer can really avoid the caller's topic is to avoid answering at all. This is, perhaps, the main reason that people often avoid answering calls from unidentified or "blocked" numbers. Although the original research on the "call-answer-topic" sequence was based on telephone calls, this pattern (with only minor variations) has been shown to be the basis of communication in many societies.

It should be obvious that this adjacency sequence is the sequence by which a deductive discourse pattern is started. This does not mean, however, that the answerer may never introduce a topic. Once the original caller's topic has been developed, the answerer may then bring up a topic of his or her own. There are many formulae or gambits with which the answerer may introduce a topic. These are all of the "by the way" sort, in which explicit mention is made of changing of the topic which is currently on the floor.

One might even go so far as to say that the deductive topic belongs to the caller and the answerer must then resort to an inductive pattern of topic introduction. In other words, the second speaker (the answerer) must follow along with the topic of the first speaker while looking for the means to introduce his or her own topic. It is preferable for this topic to appear to arise inductively out of the caller's topic. The gambits to cover such inductive introductions are ones like, "You know, that brings to mind something I wanted to tell you."

To summarize, the most important aspect of the "call–answer–topic" sequence is that the topic belongs to the caller, and therefore, the conversation will be started on the first speaker's topical home ground.

Deductive Monologues

One phenomenon associated with deductive discourse patterns is that they often lead to extended monologues from the person who has introduced the topic. There is no inherent reason why a person who is granted the right to introduce his or her topic at the start of a conversation should be granted the additional right to produce a long-winded monologue, and yet, this has often been observed to be the result.

For the answer to this, we need to recall our discussion in the last chapter of interturn pausing. There we said that if two speakers (or more) differ in the length of the pauses they take between turns, the speaker with the shorter pauses will come to dominate the conversation. This is because at each point where turns might be exchanged, the faster speaker recaptures the conversational floor. While there are many reasons why one person might have shorter turn exchange pauses than another, some of which are non-linguistic, shorter interturn pauses are an involvement politeness strategy; longer interturn pauses are an independence politeness strategy. Introducing one's topic is also an involvement politeness strategy. As a consequence, the person whose topic is being discussed will have at least some slight tendency to use shorter turn exchange pauses in consonance with their control of the topic.

The combination of these factors is what produces the monologues or dominated discourses so often associated with the deductive discourse pattern. One person speaks first and thereby gains the right to introduce his or her topic. Then that same person tends to use shorter turn exchange pauses. As a consequence, he or she continually regains the floor at each point of possible transition. The combined result is that one speaker will tend to continue to speak about his or her own topic for an extended sequence of turns. The net effect of these combined factors amounts to practically a monologue, even though it is constructed one turn at a time as the participants move through the conversation.

The Inductive Pattern

One problem we are trying to resolve in this chapter is why a deductive pattern for the introduction of topics appears to be favored by some people and in some situations and an inductive pattern for the introduction of topics appears to be favored by other people and in other situations. We have now detailed how the deductive pattern arises as a combination of the "call–answer–topic" adjacency sequence coupled with such factors as turn exchange patterns and timing. We now want to turn to the inductive pattern to see what factors can account for its prevalence.

The problem this pattern poses for discourse analysis is that we usually do not consider adjacency sequences for turn exchanges extending beyond, at most, a few turns. It is doubtful that a person using this pattern will have in mind a fixed point for the later introduction of a topic such as, say, turn 57 or turn 23. All we can say is that the topic will be introduced later, but, until it is introduced, neither participant can say when it will be introduced.

In this it is quite unlike the "call–answer–topic" sequence, in which all participants know that whoever has initiated the interaction has the right (and, in fact, the obligation) to introduce the main topic with which the discourse begins. In the "call–answer–facework–topic" pattern, the only thing we can be sure of saying is that the person who initiates the communication has the right to introduce the topic, but we cannot say when that will be on the basis of this adjacency sequence alone.

In order to clarify the elements of the inductive pattern, we will need to look more closely at the ethnographic description we made of the inductive pattern among Chinese speakers back in the 1980s. We ask the reader to remember that we do not wish to give the impression that this pattern is either restricted to Chinese speakers (or other Asians) or that it is the only pattern available in Chinese (or other Asian) discourse.

When we first described this inductive pattern we observed in Taiwan, we described it, as we did above, as the "call–answer–facework–topic" pattern. By this we meant that, just as in the "call-answer-topic" pattern, the first speaker introduces the topic, but the topic will be delayed until after a period of facework. People around us often expressed agreement with this description. They said that delaying the topic was somehow necessary so that they could get a chance to feel the mood or the position of the other participants. We called this period of getting warmed up to each other "facework," loosely following Goffman's (1967) concept of facework. The point we wanted to make was that a person in this context, even if that person had the right to introduce the topic, might want to be rather sensitive to other participants by delaying the introduction of the topic until the moment was right for it.

This description, however, does not square with two frequent exceptions. Our informants said, for example, that this was not the case at all when they talked among themselves. They said that they felt entirely free to just call up a friend and say, "Let's go to a movie," or to come across a friend on the street and say, "Let's go have coffee." This quick introduction of the topic seemed very much like the deductive pattern of immediate topic introduction.

The second exception to the pattern was in situations such as calling a taxi, paying an electric bill, or buying a bus ticket. In such cases, there was, if anything, even less preliminary communication than in typical deductive exchanges. In such cases, the pattern appears to be simply topic, without any preliminary call or answer. This latter exception has often been noticed by foreigners visiting East Asia, who are confused by the contrast between the elaborate facework and deferential delay of topics in some situations and the very abrupt introduction of topics in other cases.

Inside and outside encounters

To deal with the latter pattern first, we found that the cases of very abrupt topic introduction were often of a kind we came to describe as outside or service encounters. In these encounters, such as buying tickets for a museum, depositing money in a bank, getting a seat in a restaurant, or buying vegetables in a market, the relationship between the participants is considered to be an outside relationship. By that we mean that the participants have no dealings with each other besides in this single transaction.

In an outside encounter the topic is really already known; you are going to buy a ticket or you would not be standing at the ticket window. All that remains to be learned is just which ticket you want. In this sense, outside encounters are highly conventionalized, culturally established encounters which require very little interpersonal negotiation. This would be true in most cultural settings. In some societies there is a quite strong sense of division between outside and inside interactions. The outside interactions receive little attention or interest.

Inside relationships, in contrast, were much more important for our participants, perhaps partly because of the persistent influence of Confucianism in interpersonal relationships in Taiwan. There was a feeling among those we talked to that such relationships as those within the family or between people who have frequent and longstanding relations with each other should be governed by careful propriety. That careful propriety in inside relationships includes careful concern for face relationships among participants in speech events.

Hierarchical relationships and topic introduction

It has been said by some anthropologists that relationships in Asia tend to be hierarchical. From our point of view, that statement is too much of an overgeneralization, especially in such highly modernized international centers as Tokyo, Taipei, Hong Kong, or Singapore. Nevertheless, it is certainly accurate to say that hierarchy in relationships is very much part of the communicative traditions of these societies. The carry-over from Confucianism means that, even today, many people in places like China, Japan, Thailand, and Vietnam are quite conscious in any interaction of who is older and who is younger, who has a higher level of education, who has a lower level, who is in a higher institutional or economic position and who is lower, or who is teacher and who is student. There is often a particularly strong consciousness of such relationships within extended family structures, with each person carefully placed with a kinship term which tells all participants to which generation they belong in relation to others. In other words, such hierarchal relationships are often encoded in the languages themselves.

Under these circumstances, regarding the issue of topic introduction, the crucial question is not so much who speaks first; the crucial question is who is in the higher position and who is in the lower position. Within clearly hierarchal relationships, the person in the higher position has the right to introduce the topic and that right supersedes the question of who speaks first in the interaction.

We were then faced with a further question: if the person in the higher position has the right to speak first, and he or she also has the right to introduce the topic, why does that person not simply introduce his or her topic at the beginning of the conversation? Why is the topic delayed?

One answer we received to this question is that in many, perhaps most cases, the person in the lower position was required to greet the person in the higher position. Schoolchildren in Taiwan, for example, are expected to chime in with, "*Lao shi hao*" ("How are you, teacher?"), when the teacher comes into the classroom. Nevertheless, when asked, many said that they could not always freely greet their superiors, especially when their superiors were clearly occupied.

This leads us to recognize that the first turn, the call, may not be speech at all in hierarchical relationships, but rather, some gesture or facial expression that shows an openness to being greeted. The call is then answered with a greeting, followed by a pause in which the person in the lower position waits to see if he or she is expected to continue in the discourse.

While there is much more which could be said on this topic, it is clear when people are operating within hierarchical face systems it is quite unusual for a person in the lower position to introduce his or her own topic without first receiving the right to do so from the person in the higher position.

The false east–west dichotomy

Because of observations like those we made above, some anthropologists and linguists have come to associate the inductive pattern with "Asians" or "easterners" and the deductive pattern with "westerners." We believe that this is quite wrong since *both* inductive and deductive patterns are used in all societies, and which pattern is chosen is highly context specific, often dependent, as we have shown above, on face systems and relationships.

If we take up the Asian side of this false dichotomy first, we can return to the observation made by our informants in Taiwan and Hong Kong. In ordinary conversations among friends, the deductive pattern is most commonly used. One calls up a friend and says, "Let's go shopping," or when you come across a friend on the street you can easily say, "Let's go have a cup of coffee." In other words, where people are in a close relationship to each other and of relatively equal status, in both east and west the normal pattern is the deductive pattern.

Some commentators have felt that this use of the deductive pattern for the introduction of topics is an adoption of "westernization" in the conversational styles of the younger generation of Asians. Of course, influence from other countries is not unlikely, given the globalization of the media and the circulation of cultural products from places like the United States. Nevertheless, the deductive pattern has been in use in Asia for as long as we have records. For example, it would be very hard to classify the dialogues between Confucius and his students as anything but deductively organized, though often sections show inductive organization. Most frequently, in fact, the dialogues are introduced by a topic which is raised by a student.

As for the use of the inductive pattern in the "west," all we have to consider is the situation in which one is going to a friend with the intention of borrowing some large sum of money or asking for some other big or embarrassing favor. In such a situation the person would understandably be reluctant to come out with his or her topic at the outset of the conversation. We can be certain there would be an extended period of facework in which the would-be borrower would feel out the situation for the right moment in which to introduce his or her topic.

We believe, then, that even though a superficial observation indicates a strong preference for the inductive pattern in Asia and for the deductive pattern in the "west," this apparent "cultural difference" lies not in any inherent "cultural" template for the introduction of topics in discourse, but in differences in the structuring of situations and participant roles.

Face: Inductive and Deductive Rhetorical Strategies

In speaking of the practice of introducing the topic at the beginning of a conversation and comparing that with delaying the introduction, we have used a somewhat vague language. We have called these two ways of introducing topics "patterns," "discourse patterns," or "patterns of discourse." We have been intentionally vague, because we have been concerned not to create the idea that there was behind these patterns anything as formal as a schema or a script as we have used these terms in chapter 4. It is true that the deductive pattern is closely associated with a particular adjacency sequence, the "call–answer–topic sequence." Nevertheless, we are inclined to believe that the sequence is derived from some deeper aspects of discourse, such as expectations about face or the purposes and functions of discourse, and should not be treated as causal in itself.

Now we are prepared to argue that a more accurate way of speaking of these two phenomena is to refer to them as rhetorical strategies, which, therefore, are more appropriate in some situations than others to achieve particular purposes, as we will discuss below. We will show that the use of these strategies is directly related to the three systems of face which we presented in chapter 3. For our purposes now, the most important aspect of the three systems of face which we discussed in chapter 3 is the distribution of the strategies of involvement and of independence.

Readers who have studied Euclidean geometry may remember that the proofs you studied were presented deductively. That is to say, first you had a theorem, in other words, you had a conclusion; then you set about to prove that conclusion, starting from what was well known and obvious and moving on through logical steps until the conclusion with which you started seemed inevitable. In rhetoric, deductive strategies are usually used in cases of proofs or logical arguments where the goal is to show the reader or listener how one has arrived at a foregone conclusion.

In ordinary discourse, the deductive rhetorical strategy is used for basically the same purposes. It is the unmarked way in which one presents an idea that is taken for granted, or if the idea is not taken for granted, it is taken for granted that the speaker has every right to hold or to advance that idea and does not need to convince the listener of that right. In other words, when the speaker assumes that he or she has the right to advance an idea or when he or she believes that what is being said is true and only needs to be demonstrated to be understood, or when there is less emphasis on the listener taking action than there is on the listener understanding and acknowledging the truth of one's proposition, the most effective choice is the deductive rhetorical strategy.

A handbook on effective rhetorical skills points out that the inductive rhetorical strategy works by presenting the evidence one has first, and progressively leading the listener (or reader) to the conclusion one would like him or her to accept. This strategy works best, this handbook says, when your conclusion is one which you believe your listener (or your reader) is likely to resist.

In other words, the inductive rhetorical strategy works in the situation opposite that for the deductive rhetorical strategy. It is best to use the inductive approach when it is not clear that the speaker has the right to advance a particular topic, when it is unclear that the listener will accept the speaker's conclusion, or when the purpose of the discourse is to exhort the listener to action.

Earlier research on face strategies has made no mention of these rhetorical strategies in light of the two types of face strategy. Here we would like to argue that the deductive rhetorical strategy is, in fact, a face strategy of involvement, whereas the inductive rhetorical strategy is a face strategy of independence. We believe this follows from the descriptions we have given above of their respective roles in discourse.

Involvement strategies emphasize what the participants have in common; they assert the speaker's right to advance his or her own position on the grounds that the listener will be equally interested in that position and in advancing his or her own position. The most extreme strategy of involvement has been called "bald on record," in other words, simply stating one's position. This is, we believe, simply another wording for advancing one's own topic. Such strategies of involvement are particularly effective where the other participants do not wish to assert their independence from the speaker and show themselves quite willing to be accepted within a group of common membership.

Independence strategies emphasize the independence of the participants in a discourse from each other. They are particularly effective when the speaker wishes to show that he or she does not wish to impose on the other participants. We argue that the inductive rhetorical strategy is most effective in just such a case, where the speaker is being careful to avoid assuming that his or her listener will automatically agree with his or her position.

Topics and face systems

The conclusions follow quite naturally from this description. In a symmetrical deference face system, both speakers (or all participants) prefer strategies of independence. What this means is that all speakers will use inductive rhetorical strategies. To put this in plain terms, all speakers will avoid the direct introduction of their own topics. They will prefer to let their own points of view arise out of the ongoing discourse as inevitable conclusions from what has been said. Discourses will consist of indirect points which lay the foundation for conclusions (the topics of speakers). Such conclusions may, in fact, never need to be directly stated, because they will follow inevitably from what has been said.

This description of topic avoidance in discourse, by the way, matches almost exactly the ethnographic observations we have made of the discourse of the Athabaskan people in Alaska (Scollon and Scollon 1981). The extreme of "good" Athabaskan conversation is, in fact, silence. People truly enjoy having a nice, quiet sit together with no topics being raised at all. While such an extreme is rare among the people of the world, of course, it does match our experience of the discourse of foreign diplomats, for example, in which each word is carefully chosen (we hope) and new topics are broached with great care.

In a symmetrical solidarity face system, on the other hand, both (or all) speakers will prefer face strategies of involvement. As a result, each participant will feel quite free to introduce topics on the assumption that both speakers and hearers share membership in the same social, or at least discourse, group. If we remember that shorter turn exchange pauses are also a strategy of involvement, we can see that in extreme examples of such symmetrical solidarity there will be a very rapid set of exchanges with many topics being introduced.

This is the sort of system of conversational interaction which Tannen (1984) described for the New Yorkers she observed. She described not only rapid introduction of topics, but much conversational overlapping, finishing of the sentences of other speakers, and other such forms of involvement.

Finally, an asymmetrical (hierarchical) face system will show a rather complex set of possibilities. As we have said above, the person in the higher social position would use involvement strategies of politeness. This would mean that it would be most appropriate to use the deductive rhetorical strategy and for this speaker to introduce his or her own topic. On the other side of the interaction, the person in the lower position would follow an inductive strategy, and avoid introducing a topic in the first case, or put off bringing up his or her topic until it followed naturally from the preceding discourse.

To stand this analysis on its head, we can now ask how we interpret these rhetorical strategies as they occur in discourse. If we do not know in advance what the relationship is between ourselves and others, we will hear the inductive rhetorical strategy as one of two things: expression of mutual deference among equal but distant participants, or expression of subordination to our own superior position. As we have argued above in our discussion of conversational inference, we cannot, in fact, be certain what the other participant's intentions are until we have confirmed them. Nevertheless, in order to proceed we must choose some position from which to continue the discourse. If we have interpreted the inductive rhetorical strategy as equality with distance, we will reciprocate by also avoiding the assertion of our own topics. In other words, we too will use the inductive strategy.

On the other hand, if we have interpreted the other speaker as intending to show deference to our higher position, we will respond to the inductive rhetorical strategy with the deductive rhetorical strategy. In other words, we will introduce our own topic. The other participant, then, will have to respond to our own interpretation. If his or her intention was, indeed, deference to our higher position, there will be no problem. On the other hand, if he or she has assumed mutual deference, our introduction of our own topic will sound like an assertion of authority or power or as an attempt to take control of the discourse inappropriately.

This is what the philosopher Nietzsche had in mind when he wrote, "The familiarity of the superior embitters, because it may not be returned" (1990: 494). The mismatch of inductive and deductive strategies is a major source of miscommunication about what the topic of the discourse is, but it is not only that; it can also be the source of bitterness and other negative attitudes when participants fail to come to agreement about their interpersonal relationship.

We started this chapter by saying, "discourse can hardly proceed without some idea of what the topic under discussion is." Now we can see that our original statement is really too simple. It is not just a matter of stating what the topic under discussion is, because which rhetorical strategy you should use for stating the topic is also undergoing negotiation. The businessperson's strategy of the five Ws and the one H (what, who, where, when, why, and how) is the most effective rhetorical strategy if you are either in a close and equal personal relationship with the other participants, or in a position of power over others to whom you are communicating. If you are not equals, not close, and you are not in power, his advice is bad advice indeed. The result of such a deductive rhetorical strategy in those latter circumstances would be to sound aggressive, domineering, or inconsiderate.

The businessperson who emphasized this deductive rhetorical strategy to the authors is, in fact, in a position of considerable power. He may well be in the situation of the boss who tells his staff a joke and thinks he has been very funny because everyone laughs. They have hardly any other choice but to laugh. He forgets that the acceptance of his discourse strategies is the result of his position, not the result of his own personal merits or stylistic skill.

Face Relationships in Written Discourse

We have based our analysis of the structures of discourse on the idea of conversational inference. We have argued that when people talk to each other, they have the continual ongoing problem of interpreting what other participants are saying at the level of the information, but also they must interpret what face positions other participants are taking in the relationship. Even such aspects of discourse as when, where, and how you introduce a topic are based on this process of conversational inference and face relationships.

On the surface of it, none of this is true when the discourse takes place in writing. In writing, one person (or perhaps a group of people) composes a text which is then read by its reader or readers at another time and most likely in another place. There is limited feedback overall, and no feedback at all in the composition of the text. In other words, a spoken discourse represents the joint product of all of the participants in the situation, but a written discourse represents the one-sided product of a discourse by the participants who compose the text. The other participants, the readers, can more or less take it or leave it in their interpretation of the text, but they cannot manage an alteration in the basic structure of the text.

Of course, there are many variations in the nature of written texts and we could not possibly take them all into consideration at this time. For example, some texts are really much more like individual turns in a face-to-face interaction. Around an office, for example, many short notes are exchanged. The following three notes are actual notes in an office which were written on small memo pads, but they are not very different from three successive turns in a face-to-face conversation:

> *A*: Would it be possible for us to meet sometime to discuss my project? I need to get on to the next step and could use your advice. I am free Tuesday any time after 11 or after 3 on Wednesday.
> *B*: Would 12 o'clock Tuesday be OK?
> *A*: Tuesday at 12 is fine. See you then.

Nowadays, of course, interaction like this would doubtless be accomplished through email or instant messaging. Where the discourse is like this series of exchanges, it is relatively easy to see that processes of interpretation which are very much like those of conversational inference come into play in interpreting these messages. We can see from the first message that A is in a lower institutional position than B. A is introducing the topic somewhat inductively by saying that she would like to meet to discuss it, leaving open the possibility that B might not have the time or the interest to do so. She gives a wide range of options for a time to meet so that B is not unduly restricted in setting up an appointment. B, in turn, confirms that he is willing to let her introduce her topic, but narrows the range of options open quite considerably.

We could compare this with what it might look like if A and B were in the opposite institutional positions. Such an exchange might look like this:

A: I need to talk to you about my project. Would you be free at 12 o'clock Tuesday?
       Otherwise, let me know what other time might work.
B: Tuesday at 12 is fine. I look forward to learning about your project.

In this case the person in the higher position is much more direct and much more limiting in the options available for an appointment. B, on the other hand, is a bit more expansive about his interest in A's project. In other words, this written exchange could be quite easily understood within the framework of interpersonal face relations as we have described it above. The person in the higher position uses strategies of involvement including the deductive rhetorical strategy for introducing his or her topic, while the person in the lower position uses strategies of independence.

The problem we want to discuss here is this: what happens when the written discourse is either quite extended in length or spans a large distance of either space or time between the participants of the writer and the reader? In such a case, is it still possible to talk about face relationships between the writer and the reader, even where little or no feedback is possible between them?

Essays and press releases

We could approach the problem of face relationships in written discourse from one of two directions; either we could analyze the face relationships between writers and readers, and then ask how topics have been introduced and which patterns of politeness and which rhetorical strategies have been used, or we could analyze texts asking which rhetorical strategies and face politeness strategies have been used, and then ask what the face relationships are in such cases.

Since texts are easier to get our hands on than face relationships, we prefer to start with two typical types of text, the essay and the press release. We have chosen these two because both of them are highly salient types of text in the lives of professional communicators; many professional communicators find that writing press releases is a major part of their work, and there is hardly a professional communicator in existence who has not achieved his or her position at least partly through writing successful essays in school and on examinations.

The businessperson we have now quoted so often was actually speaking of how you write a successful press release, though later he went on to say this applied to all business communications. He was only stating what is widely understood in professional communication as the most direct rhetorical strategy: "Say what you have to say and quit; nothing more."

We have said that this rhetorical strategy is the deductive rhetorical strategy and as such implies either a face system of symmetrical solidarity (in which both speakers use strategies of involvement) or a face system of hierarchy in which only the person in the dominant position uses such an involvement strategy. Of course, there are many different types of press release. In some cases, such as when a government issues a press release, it is clear that the writer is, at least officially, in a superior position to the reader.

The press release: implied writers and implied readers

Let us take up this case first. In actual fact, it is not the writer himself or herself who is superior to the reader, since the reader is actually unknown in any specific case and includes everyone who might read the press release. In fact, the actual writer is likely to be someone in a very inferior bureaucratic position compared to the person or the office which has issued the information in the press release. And, furthermore, many of the readers of the press release will be people much higher in the official bureaucracy.

The point this brings out is that the relationship expressed in a press release is not between the actual writer of the press release and any particular reader. The relationship is more abstract than that. It is between the voice of the institution or organization responsible for the press release (such as the government) and the people who will read it. In other words, the use of the deductive strategy is appropriate since it is an institution or organization speaking, not the particular writer of the text.

To put this another way, in written discourse there are really two kinds of relationship we need to consider: the relationship between the actual writer of a text and the actual reader of a text on the one hand, and the relationship between the implied writer and the implied reader on the other hand. The actual writer of a governmental press release may have any of the possible face relationships with some of the actual readers of the press release. The writer may find that his or her text is read by friends, children, parents, work colleagues, strangers, members of the legislature or parliament, or almost any other imaginable real person. Nevertheless, as the writer writes the press release, he or she takes on a role, the role of the implied writer, speaking with the voice of the government in whose name the document is issued. Therefore, the actual writer ignores his or her own social position and composes texts from the point of view of the implied writer, the government.

The same applies to the reader of this text. The governmental press release may be published in a newspaper which might be read by people of many different social positions and statuses. The text does not alter its face relationships with each of those readers separately. It takes one kind of reader as the standard or the model for its implied reader. In the example of a governmental press release, the implied reader is assumed to be a law-abiding, interested, dutiful citizen.

In business environments, press releases are somewhat different in fact, though not any different in principle. When a business sends out a press release about a new product or service, for example, it makes certain assumptions about the implied reader of the press release, whether or not actual readers fit those characteristics. Naturally, in business, one wants to come as close as possible to the actual characteristics of those readers. In any event, a business press release takes the position that its readers are busy, active, interested co-participants in the enterprise of the business. It assumes that they are interested in engaging in commerce with the business which is making the press release, whether as co-partners, as customers of the product or service, or as stockholders in the enterprise.

In other words, the relationship assumed between the implied writer and the implied reader of a business press release is one of symmetrical solidarity, whether or not the actual writer and the actual reader are in that relationship to each other. Again, there is really no telling with written discourse who will read it and when or where. One must assume an implied reader, and that, in turn, means one must also assume an implied writer.

The essay: a deductive structure

We can probably assume that almost any reader of this book will be familiar with the preferred structure for an essay within the deductive rhetorical tradition, since being asked to read many such essays as well as to write them is part of secondary and university education in many parts of the world. The structure of such an essay has been laid out in many textbooks on composition. The general structure is as thoroughly deductive as one might find anywhere.

Textbooks on composition tell us that an essay should have a thesis. A thesis is a straightforward statement of the main point the essay has been written to advance. Such textbooks tell us that the thesis should be presented very early in the text. In a short essay of several paragraphs or several pages, that thesis should appear in the first paragraph. In a longer essay or in a book, the thesis might be delayed until after a bit of preliminary material, but in any event, the reader should be able to determine the main point within the first formal section of the text.

In the same way, each section of the essay is expected to be treated deductively as well. Each paragraph, according to standard composition textbooks, should have a topic sentence, and that sentence should be the first sentence in the paragraph. Of course, in some cases a transition will be required; in those cases the topic sentence might be the second sentence. In any event, the main topic of the paragraph is generally said to be required at the beginning of each paragraph.

There is little question that the essay, as it is presented in standard composition textbooks, is a completely deductive rhetorical structure. What follows from this is that the relationship between the implied writer and the implied reader of the essay is one of symmetrical solidarity, as it is in the press release. In fact, you will find many examples of involvement politeness strategies in the language of essays within this particular tradition of essays. In addition to the deductive introduction of topics, there are many phrases such as, "it will come as no surprise," "as we have seen above," and "it is obvious that," which express that the implied writer and the implied reader have the same point of view in approaching the text.

Just as in the case of the press release, in the essay it is assumed that the crucial face relationship is one of solidarity between the implied writer and the implied reader. It makes little difference, actually, what the real relationships might be between the real writer and the real reader. Within the enclosed world of the essay text, it is assumed that a close, familiar relationship exists in which both parties are commonly pursuing a common goal. In most cases, of course, this unstated goal is the establishment of truth.

Limiting Ambiguity: Power in Discourse

Since language is inherently ambiguous, our main concern is with understanding how participants in communication are able to interpret each other. One main form of ambiguity in discourse is determining the topic. We began this chapter with a study of this question of topics in face-to-face discourse. We argued that even though conversational inference is the primary means by which we interpret each other in face-to-face discourse, conversation analysis alone cannot account for the structures which arise in discourse. In order to understand those structures, we have to take into account not only processes of conversational inference, including timing, schemata, adjacency sequences, and the rest, but also the face relationships among participants.

In order to understand how topics are introduced, given certain face relationships, we borrowed from studies of rhetoric the idea of two different and opposing rhetorical strategies, the deductive rhetorical strategy and the inductive rhetorical strategy. The first strategy, the deductive, is most effective when the topic is understood as given or when the authority of the speaker is unquestioned; the second strategy, the inductive, is most effective when the listener may question either the conclusion one wants to draw or the authority of the speaker to make such a statement.

Then we argued that the differences one might observe between "Asian" and "western" patterns for the introduction of topics were not really a matter of "culture," since both patterns are used widely in both societies. We argued that the use of these strategies depends most on the face relationships which exist between or among the participants in a discourse.

Finally, we have raised the question of how such interpersonal relationships are expressed in written communications, since in most cases there is little or no back-and-forth negotiation among the participants, the writer(s) and the reader(s). The conclusion we have drawn is that in some forms of written discourse, such as the press release and the essay, the relationships under consideration are not those between the real writer and the real reader, but those between the implied writer and the implied reader.

Researching Interdiscourse Communication

Collecting and analyzing written data

In the last chapter we gave some advice on how to collect spoken data and how to analyze it using tools from discourse analysis. You will also want to apply some of the ideas we have introduced in this chapter to the analysis of the spoken data you collected, paying attention, for example, to how people manage the introduction of topics in conversations. Now we will turn to the collection of written texts as data and discuss how you might apply some of the ideas about rhetorical strategies we have introduced here to analyzing it. Of course, there are many other discourse-based approaches to the analysis of written texts, some of which we will cover in later chapters.

Written texts may come in many forms in the context of your site of investigation. They may include business letters, memos, press releases, emails, instant messages, "tweets," books, magazines, train schedules, street signs, logos, and brand names, and directions for use on packages and other objects. In fact, one thing that might surprise you as you set about looking for texts to collect is how many written texts surround us in our everyday lives. The first step, then, is determining which texts are worthy of collection and analysis.

In making this determination we can return to the focus on actions and practices we began with in the first chapter, focusing on those texts which are somehow implicated in the actions and practices in which we are interested. If, for example, we are interested in meetings, we may collect agendas, minutes, presentation notes, and the like. This, however, may not be entirely sufficient, since there might be other texts which, while not foregrounded in the meeting itself, might somehow be connected to the meeting, texts like emails, reports, and newspaper articles. This difficulty points to two important qualities of texts. This first is what some have referred to as "intertextuality" – the fact that texts tend to be connected to other texts in rather complex ways so that when you start looking at one text you are invariably led to questions about other texts that might somehow be connected to it. The second is that texts are not just tools with which people take actions, they are also themselves the result of often very involved chains of actions. The agenda for a meeting, for example, is normally the result of numerous informal discussions and the exchange of other texts like memos and emails among key managers and administrators as well as of the discussions and texts produced at numerous previous meetings. Our colleague Sigrid Norris calls texts "frozen actions," and we believe this is a useful way to think of them because it reminds us to ask not just what actions texts are being used to take, but also what actions resulted in the creation of these texts in the first place.

We'll return to this issue later when we consider forms of discourse, but for now it is important to point out that those actions almost always involve more than one person. That is, the traditional notion that many have of texts being the result of a single person holding a pen or tapping on a keyboard is often not the case. Many texts involve the collaboration of many different people at different stages of their creation.

Another important thing to remember about texts is that different kinds of written texts can involve very different relationships between writers and readers in terms of their placement in time and space. An instant message, for example, is, as its name implies, instant, that is the time between the moment it is written and the moment it is read is usually very short. The same is true of text messages sent from mobile phones. The time between writing and reading is relatively longer for emails, still longer for letters, and even longer for proposals, reports, essays, novels, and poems. Similarly, readers' understanding of the identity of writers and writers' understanding of the identity of the reader varies greatly for different kinds of texts. The author of a personal email, for example, is reasonably sure at whom his or her discourse is directed, and the reader of such an email is reasonably sure who wrote it. For other texts, however, such as government documents or nutritional labels, it is much less clear to the author or authors who will read the text and why, and the people who authored such texts for the most part remain totally anonymous to their readers. In any case, however, as we pointed out above, all texts create implied readers and implied writers, and for now trying to understand how they do this should be the focus of your analysis.

In order to understand this you might start out by asking the following questions: What seems to be the purpose of the text? Does it have multiple purposes or different purposes for different people? Is the structure of the text inductive or deductive, that is, does the writer begin with his or her main idea(s) and then give supporting reasons, or does the writer begin with background information that leads up to his or her main idea? What does the rhetorical structure of the text tell you about the kind of relationship the text sets up between the writer and the reader (is it hierarchical or symmetrical, close or distant?). Such questions will at least give you a start in understanding how texts can function to create identities and relationships in the group or groups you are studying. In later chapters we will delve deeper into how people use texts and the concept of literacy itself to construct social practices and enforce ideologies.

Discussion Questions

1   Think of some different situations in speech and/or writing in which you think you might use deductive or inductive rhetorical strategies. Discuss the people you would be addressing and the topics you would be talking about and how these might influence your choice of rhetorical patterns.

2   Think of the different discourse systems you participate in. Are either inductive or deductive patterns prevalent in any of these discourse systems? Why do you think this is?

3   Compare a text that you have written for a school assignment to a text you have written for some other purpose outside of school. How do these texts differ in structure and style? Account for these differences.

References for Further Study

There are a number of books that discuss inductive and deductive rhetorical patterns in communication between "Asians" and "westerners," among the best known being Linda Young's 1995 *Crosstalk and Culture in Sino-American Communication*. For a comparison of the rhetorical structure of business letters written by Chinese and New Zealanders see Zhu Yunxia's 2005 *Written Communication across Cultures: a sociocognitive perspective*. For a fuller treatment of the relationship between topic introduction and face see *Narrative Literacy and Face in Interethnic Communication* by Ron and Suzanne B. K. Scollon (1981). Differences between spoken and written discourse are discussed in Ochs (1979), Tannen (1982), and Scollon and Scollon (1981), especially as these differences relate to essays.

6

Ideologies in Discourse

Three Concepts of Discourse

As we have mentioned before, the word "discourse" has been used in talking about language in three somewhat different ways. In the most technically narrow definition of the word, the study of discourse has been the study of grammatical and other relationships between sentences. These relationships are often discussed as a problem of cohesion. This is the study of discourse which we developed in chapter 4. The purpose of such studies of discourse is to come to understand the inferential processes by which speakers communicate their meanings and by which hearers interpret what is said.

A more general use of the word "discourse" has been to study broader functional uses of language in social contexts. Most of our book up to this point has been given over to this broader definition of the concept of discourse, especially chapters 2, 3, and 5. In such studies, the purpose is to come to understand how the language we use is based on the social environments in which we use that language. As we argued in the last chapter, for example, the placement of topics in conversations depends on social relationships among the participants.

Now we consider the broadest concept of discourse, which is the study of whole systems of communication, what the discourse analyst James Paul Gee has called "discourse with a capital D." For example, we might study the language of dealers in foreign exchange, of public school teachers, or of members of the North American "Baby Boom" generation. Such broad systems of discourse form a kind of self-contained system of communication with a shared language or jargon, with particular ways in which people learn what they need to know to become participants, with a particular ideological position, and with quite specific forms of interpersonal relationships among participants in these groups.

To give a simple example to help to clarify this concept of a discourse system, we could consider what happens when a young person right out of school takes a position in a corporation. Liu Ka Man has just taken a job in an international corporation in Hong Kong.

Intercultural Communication: A Discourse Approach, Third Edition. Ron Scollon, Suzanne Wong Scollon, Rodney H. Jones.
© 2012 John Wiley & Sons, Inc. Published 2012 by John Wiley & Sons, Inc.

At first she feels somewhat out of place. This new company has many forms to be filled out, memos to be circulated, and locations of offices and people who are all new to her. In order to fit into the new situation she needs to start to learn this language (the forms of discourse), which is quite specific to this company.

There are two ways in which Ms Liu goes about learning her way through these new forms of discourse as she becomes socialized to this new work environment. On the one hand, the company provides various kinds of training. There are orientation classes for new employees as well as handbooks which outline company or office forms and procedures. On the other hand, Liu Ka Man is already beginning to learn a great deal from other members of the staff, who tell her just what is needed in particular circumstances. These forms of socialization to the new company, both formal and informal, have the result that over a period of time she starts to become more at ease and to sense greater confidence that she is beginning to fit into the new position.

Along with Liu Ka Man's socialization into the new company comes a sense of the company's "culture" or ideology. While in corporate circles this company ideology is now often referred to as the corporation's "culture," to avoid the kinds of connotations and confusions associated with the word "culture" we discussed in chapter 1, we prefer to use the word "ideology." By ideology we mean the worldview or governing philosophy of a group of people or of a discourse system. The concept of power usually lies behind this word. That is to say, one aspect of the ideology of a group is whether or not it sees itself as more powerful or less powerful than some other relevant group.

The word "ideology" is a difficult one to use, because it has been used in so many different ways in the two hundred years or so of its existence. We can summarize what we use it to mean as follows: a system of thinking, social practice, and communication, which is used either to bring a particular group to social power or to legitimate their position of social power, especially when the discourse system itself is not the actual source of that group's power.

At the core of ideologies are certain sets of *assumptions* held by people regarding such things as what is true and false (epistemology), what is good and bad (values), what is right and wrong (ethics), and what is normal and abnormal (norms). These assumptions usually focus on such fundamental aspects of human life and social interaction as "What is the definition of 'good'?" "What is 'human nature'?" "What are the basis and goals of human society?" and "What are the best means for determining the right course of action for individuals and societies?" We use the word *assumptions* rather than *beliefs* because, unlike most beliefs, ideologies often go unquestioned and uncontested. They are the fundamental assumptions upon which more conscious and debatable beliefs are built. That is not to say that ideologies are always unconscious and unquestioned. Throughout history there have been times of vigorous and often violent debate over ideologies (e.g. Christianity, Communism). We are simply saying that one characteristic of an ideology is that it is often seen as synonymous with "truth" or "common sense." While there have at various points in the history of the United States, for example, been debates about the meanings of "freedom" and "democracy" and the methods by which these ideals might be realized, to question the fundamental value of these ideals, that is, to come out against "freedom" and "democracy" would simply be to exclude oneself from participating in the political conversation in any meaningful way, so sacred are these ideals to the ideology of this society.

As noted before, however, these assumptions can never really be seen as independent from the power relationships that exist within a group and the kinds of resources (material, symbolic, and communicative) that are available to different people in the group. Ideologies always serve the interests of certain people, and it is inevitable that those people who have access to the resources with which to promote their ideology and make it seem "normal" to other people will be able to maintain their power.

Another way to see ideology is as a kind of orientation a group of people takes towards itself as a whole and its individual members, towards people outside of the group, towards the group's history and heritage, and towards the group's future. As Liu Ka Man becomes socialized into the ideology of her new company, she gradually comes to identify with the attitude the company takes to its clients, its own history, and its future. Whether or not she really believes this position, there will be little doubt that her success within the company will come with projecting the corporate ideology when dealing with others, which brings us to a very important point: it is by no means necessary for one to "buy in" to an ideology completely for one to become an agent in the spread of the ideology.

This governing ideology will, in turn, have a considerable effect on interpersonal relationships (face systems) both within the company and between members of the company and their clients. Ms Liu begins to learn through subtle cues from older company members how to take the right attitude toward suppliers, toward various subsidiary companies, and toward the parent company of which her own company is a subsidiary. She learns very quickly which of the office employees should be addressed by their given name, which by their family name, which she might go out with for lunch, and which she should avoid in anything but strictly business matters.

Finally, these clusters of interpersonal relationships or face systems have a very strong effect on the forms of discourse which Ms Liu comes to use. Letters or emails to subsidiary companies are likely to be written somewhat more directively than letters or emails to the parent company, which will show a certain amount of deference. In telephone calls and instant messages to colleagues she learns to nurture friendly relationships, but with clients she comes quite directly to the point.

There are four basic elements to this system of discourse into which Liu Ka Man has been introduced: the forms of discourse, the socialization, the ideology, and the face systems. Each of these four elements mutually influences the others, and so they come to form a rather tight system of communication or a "discourse system," within which she becomes increasingly enclosed. The more neatly she fits into this discourse system, the more she comes to feel identified with it and the more others come to treat her as a full-fledged member. A discourse system could be represented as in figure 6.1.

When Liu Ka Man enters into this new company, of course, she does not think of it as entering into a new discourse system and she would certainly not think of her experience as dividing up into these four elements or categories. We will use the conceptual construct of the discourse system as a way of talking about what some other researchers have called simply "discourses," or following Gee, "Discourses with a capital D." Our purpose in using this construct is to bring to attention the various elements or components of our experience of becoming a member of a discourse system. Although we could present them in any order, the four characteristics which will define a discourse system are as follows:

1   Members will hold a common ideological position and recognize a set of extra-discourse features which will be taken to define them as a group (*ideology*).
2   A set of preferred forms of discourse serves as banners or symbols of participation and identity (*forms of discourse*).

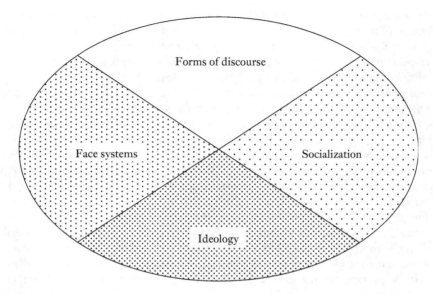

Figure 6.1 Discourse system.

3   Socialization is accomplished primarily through these preferred forms of discourse (*socialization*).
4   Face relationships are prescribed for discourse among participants or between participants and outsiders (*face systems*).

It should be clear by now that, although we are treating these components as separate, they are at the same time fundamentally interrelated and interdependent upon one another. The assumptions that make up the ideology of Liu Ka Man's new company are enshrined in and expressed, sometimes explicitly and sometimes rather subtly, in the forms of discourse the company makes use of, in the expectations people have about how certain people are to be treated, and in the processes the company has in place for the training and induction of new employees. By the same token, the forms of discourse used in the company are designed, either explicitly or subtly, to construct certain kinds of implied readers or listeners and implied writers or speakers, and so to construct certain kinds of social relationships. Finally, the social relationships that take place on a day to day basis in the company constantly reinforce and reproduce certain identities, patterns of communication, and assumptions about what is good and bad, true and false, right and wrong, and normal and abnormal.

The Utilitarian Discourse System

As we noted in the first chapter of this book, one of the advantages to using the concept of discourse systems rather than the more "loaded" notion of culture is that this concept gives us a tool for analyzing systems of social organization of various sizes and scopes. A discourse system can be rather small or very large. That is, any group that can be said to have a unique ideology, unique forms of discourse, unique patterns of relating, and unique systems for the socialization of its members that somehow distinguish it from other groups can be said to have its own discourse system. And so, insofar as Liu Ka Man's company is different in these respects from other companies in Hong Kong, as any company invariably is, we can speak of the discourse system of that particular company.

In many respects, however, this company is not unique. It shares many characteristics with other companies not just in Hong Kong, but in the world. It shares, for example, certain assumptions about the economic system and how it is supposed to work, about the kinds of things it can expect from its employees and the kinds of obligations it has to them, and about the responsibilities it has towards its clients or customers and towards its stockholders. It also makes use of many of the same forms of discourse that are common in business communication worldwide: emails, memos, reports, meetings, presentations, etc. It shares a kind of hierarchical organizational structure with various layers of authority and expectations about how people at different points in this hierarchy are to be treated, and it shares a variety of practices for socializing new workers including training programs, employee manuals, as well as more informal practices like coffee break conversations, lunches, and company picnics and dinners. In fact, as much as Liu Ka Man's company has its own unique discourse system, it also participates in a much larger discourse system, one which we will be referring to as the Utilitarian discourse system.

The Utilitarian discourse system is a discourse system whose influence is felt in nearly every corner of the world. Another name for it might be the discourse system of "global capitalism." Its influence, in fact, is so powerful that many of its assumptions as well as the patterns of social organization it reproduces are taken for granted, considered by many people as "just the way things are." All discourse systems, however, have histories, and understanding those histories can be very helpful in understanding the ideology of a discourse system and the kinds of social and material circumstances which contributed to its development.

The Enlightenment: reason and freedom

The Enlightenment or the Age of Reason reached its high point in the eighteenth century. This movement arose as part of the reorganization of European thinking as the authority of the Christian church was declining. The central philosophers in their essays emphasized the rise of science as the new authority, and in doing so set the course for western and world development for the next two or three centuries.

We are certainly still under the primary influence of these writers. For example, Adam Smith's (1723–90) *An Inquiry into the Nature and Causes of the Wealth of Nations* (1990) laid the foundations for the modern concept of capitalist economic exchange. This book introduced the notion of the free exchange of goods within an open, unregulated market, which is still being argued in reference to such entities as the WTO, the European Union, NAFTA, ASEAN, and a number of others.

The concept of free economic market exchange cannot be separated from the concept of government by laws, which was first clearly articulated in the writings of Montesquieu (1689–1755). His book, *The Spirit of Laws* (1990), laid the cornerstone for the major state papers on which the new American government was founded: the Declaration of Independence, the Articles of Confederation, and the Constitution (*American State Papers*, 1990).

Immanuel Kant (1724–1804) was also a major figure in the development of Enlightenment thought. One essay, *The Science of Right* (1990), laid down the principles upon which the idea of intellectual copyright was established. This concept remains a hot point of dispute between nations in international negotiations, as well as among individuals, corporations, and courts of law, especially with the development of digital technology, which makes the copying and distribution of "intellectual property" such as texts, images, videos, and music recordings extremely easy.

All of these writings were based on the flowering of scientific and philosophical writing of the immediately preceding period. Sir Isaac Newton (1642–1727), for example, had laid down the principles for a completely rational concept of the physical universe. In Newton's science, the physical universe could be explained entirely through the application of physical laws and mathematics.

Writers such as John Locke (1632–1704) extended such studies of the physical universe by placing human beings within that universe as equally physical entities. For example, Locke (1990) described the human being as being born a *tabula rasa*, a blank slate, upon which the experience of the universe wrote a life.

This concept of the human being was a radical departure from the concept of the person upheld until that time in Europe, and, indeed, throughout most of the world. Before this, and elsewhere, humans have been thought of as deeply connected participants in a larger social and spiritual structure of society. The new Enlightenment concept of the human was to isolate each person as a completely independent, rational, autonomous entity who moves about through society according to society's laws, just like Newtonian physical entities move about according to natural laws. Newton argued that the universe could be understood entirely with just two concepts, entities and natural laws (including, of course, mathematics). Locke, Smith, Montesquieu, Kant, and the other Enlightenment thinkers reduced humans and human life to the same simple principles: isolated entities and social laws.

Bentham and Mill's Utilitarianism

Jeremy Bentham (1748–1832) is an enigmatic figure in western thought. His writings were extremely influential in the development of contemporary economic, political, and social life, and yet his name is not widely known outside the circle of historians and scholars who have studied the roots of modern politics and economics.

Bentham coined the term "Utilitarianism," which was what he called his philosophy. Utilitarianism grew out of the Enlightenment, and simplified even that rather oversimplified line of thought. Bentham's problem was to find an ethical principle to replace the idea that good was defined by the authority of God or the Christian church. Bentham argued that we should consider good whatever followed the "principle of utility":

> By utility is meant that property in any object, whereby it tends to produce benefit, advantage, pleasure, good, or happiness, (all this in the present case comes to the same thing) or (what comes again to the same thing) to prevent the happening of mischief, pain, evil, or unhappiness to the party whose interest is considered. (Bentham 1962: 34)

This led to the most basic ideological concept of Utilitarianism – that something was good if it produced happiness, and therefore, the best society was the one which provided the greatest happiness for the greatest number of people.

This Utilitarianism was further developed by John Stuart Mill (1806–73) and has become the philosophical basis of the core of contemporary western social and economic life. While most people might never have heard of Jeremy Bentham or of J. S. Mill, if one asks an American, for example, what the purpose of government or of society is, one will most likely hear a statement which embodies almost the exact words of these two political philosophers.

A second central concept of Utilitarianism is that progress is the goal of society. Of course, by "progress" is meant an ever-increasing amount of happiness and wealth. Underlying this is an orientation towards time which we can call a Utopian view of time. A belief in progress sees human life and human culture on a time line that points towards the future and away from the past.

As J. S. Mill understood it, progress was to be achieved by overcoming tradition and through the exercise of individual freedom of expression.

> The despotism of custom is everywhere the standing hindrance to human advancement, being in unceasing antagonism to that disposition to aim at something better than customary, which is called, according to circumstances, the spirit of liberty, or that of progress or improvement. The spirit of improvement is not always a spirit of liberty . . . but the only unfailing and permanent source of improvement is liberty, since by it there are as many possible independent centres of improvement as there are individuals. The progressive principle, however, in either shape, whether as the love of liberty or of improvement, is antagonistic to the sway of Custom, involving at least emancipation from that yoke; and the contest between the two constitutes the chief interest of the history of mankind. The greater part of the world has, properly speaking, no history, because the despotism of Custom is complete. This is the case over the whole East. Custom is there, in all things, the final appeal; justice and right mean conformity to custom; the argument of custom no one, unless some tyrant intoxicated with power thinks of resisting. And we see the result. Those nations must once have had originality; they did not start out of the ground populous, lettered, and versed in many of the arts of life; they made themselves all this, and were then the greatest and most powerful nations of the world. What are they now? The subjects or dependents of tribes whose forefathers wandered in the forests when theirs had magnificent palaces and gorgeous temples, but over whom custom exercised only a divided rule with liberty and progress.
>
> A people, it appears, may be progressive for a certain length of time, and then stop: when does it stop? When it ceases to possess individuality. (J. S. Mill 1990: 300–1)

For the Utilitarians, free individual expression was the keystone of the development of their ideology. This freedom of expression was based on the third principle of Utilitarianism – their idea that the individual, not the community, was the basis of society. "The community is a fictitious *body*, composed of the individual persons who are considered as constituting as it were its *members*. The interest of the community then is, what? – the sum of the interest of the several members who compose it" (Bentham 1962: 35).

Of course, basing their concept of society on the individual, the Utilitarians needed to develop their concept of the individual. The fourth principle in this system is that humans are defined as logical, rational, economic entities. By that they meant that they assumed that humans would always choose their own greater happiness and wealth over all other considerations and that social action could be analyzed in terms of the value placed on goods and on human actions.

This emphasis on rational, individualistic, economic behavior led the Utilitarians to believe that technology and invention would be the key to the greatest happiness of the greatest number, as the fifth principle. The newly developing sciences as well as the discoveries in other parts of the world of major sources of raw resources for exploitation led them to believe that the society they imagined could actually be achieved.

From this set of ideological principles, it is not difficult to see that within the Utilitarian ideology, the creative, inventive (wealth-producing) individuals are thought of as the most valuable for society, since such individuals produce most of what the ideology considers its most valuable assets. This sixth principle provides justification for the sometimes greatly exaggerated social and economic differences found between members of what is otherwise supposed to be an egalitarian society.

Finally, one aspect of Benthamism or Utilitarianism which is not well known today is its emphasis on numerical calculations. The problem Bentham faced was how he could determine the greatest happiness for the greatest number of people. He developed what he called the "Felicific Calculus" or the "Hedonistic Calculus," which was a system by which he believed every pleasure and every pain could be given a numerical value and then, through a complex calculus, the relative value of all human actions could be determined.

In this Felicific Calculus, everything, he imagined, could be given a numerical value, from the value of dinner to the value of parliament. Then if your arithmetic was good enough you could just run the calculations and find out what decision to take. This calculus was rejected by others as quite an impractical suggestion. At the time Bentham and Mill developed their Utilitarian thinking, there were no computers for them to use in doing their numbers. Nevertheless, methods were developed, which look very crude today, for taking massive counts of large populations of people. The idea of the census developed straight out of Utilitarianism, for example, and since the modern computer arose out of census taking, it is no stretch of the historical fabric to say that contemporary uses of computers for such functions as public opinion polls and market surveys are a direct realization of the thinking and the Utilitarian philosophy of Jeremy Bentham. This emphasis on quantitative measures of value forms the seventh principle of the Utilitarian ideology.

We can summarize the ideological position of the Utilitarian discourse system as follows:

1 "Good" is defined as what will give the greatest happiness for the greatest number.
2 Progress (toward greater happiness, wealth, and individuality) is the goal of society.
3 The free and equal individual is the basis of society.
4 Humans are defined as rational, economic entities.
5 Technology and invention are the sources of societal wealth.
6 Creative, inventive (wealth-producing) individuals are the most valuable for society.
7 Quantitative measures such as statistics are the best means of determining values.

Forms of discourse in the Utilitarian discourse system

The next chapter will be given over completely to the role of various forms of discourse and attitudes towards communication in discourse systems, including a full account of the forms of discourse associated with the Utilitarian discourse system. For now we would like to discuss in a rather general way the style and philosophy of communication associated with the ideology we described above and raise a number of issues about this style of communication that we will take up in more detail in the next chapter.

We have, over the course of many years of teaching professional communication in various countries, had occasion to review many textbooks, professional tradebooks, and popular books on communication in business and professional environments. When these books directly express their philosophy of communication, it is never much different from the five Ws and one H of the American businessperson we quoted in the last chapter. In most cases these books explicitly state that the purpose of professional communication is to convey information, and the philosophy of communication which is explicitly stated is that information should be conveyed as clearly, briefly, directly, and sincerely as possible. Richard Lanham (1983), an English and rhetoric teacher at the University of Los Angeles, California, has called this the C–B–S style, for "clarity," "brevity," and "sincerity."

Western European writers did not always prefer clarity, brevity, and sincerity in their writing and speaking. In the Middle Ages, for example, the preferred mode of presenting one's ideas was very inductive. One was to begin with all of the objections which might be raised to the position one planned to take; then, one moved on to the arguments in favor of the position; finally, one arrived at a statement of one's conclusion.

The historical question is this: when did we come to assume that communication should be analytic, original, move rapidly forward, have a unified thesis, avoid unnecessary digressions, and, in essence present only the most essential information? Most likely this preference for the C–B–S style began in the seventeenth century, and the Royal Society was most likely the leader. In 1667 Thomas Sprat, Bishop of Rochester, in writing his *History of the Royal Society*, commented on the approach to language taken by the Royal Society. He wrote,

> They have therefore been more rigorous in putting in Execution the only Remedy, that can be found for this *Extravagance*; and that has been a constant Resolution, to reject all the Amplifications, Digressions, and Swellings of Style; to return back to the primitive Purity and Shortness, when Men deliver'd so many *Things*, almost in an equal Number of *Words*. They have exacted from all their Members, a close, naked, natural way of Speaking; positive Expressions, clear Senses; a native Easiness; bringing all Things as near the mathematicall Plainness as they can; and preferring the Language of Artizans, Countrymen, and Merchants, before that of Wits, or Scholars. (quoted in Kenner 1987: 117)

It seems clear enough that the preferred C–B–S style, or, as Sprat puts it, "close," "naked," and "natural" style, which is put forward in so many textbooks on business communication, is a style taken on quite self-consciously by the Royal Society as the preferred style for scientific deliberations. As science and technology have risen in the west to their current central position, business has risen together with them, and this preferred style has been carried with it into near total dominance in our thinking about effective communication. The businessperson who urges the style of five Ws and one H was, without knowing it, giving a twentieth-century version of Thomas Sprat's warning against extravagance.

The Panopticon of Bentham

Any account of the Utilitarian discourse system would not be complete without a discussion of Bentham's notion of the "Panopticon," an idea which the French philosopher Michel

Foucault and other cultural critics have taken as a metaphor for the way governments and institutions control individuals in modern societies.

Bentham was excessively concerned with efficiency, including efficiency in settings for discourses of the broadest kind. In one case he turned his attention to the structure of buildings, such as the newly developing factories and the rapidly increasing number of prisons. He invented the concept of what he called the Panopticon. This was a structure in which one person could survey and control the work or activities of many individuals. In his ideal Panopticon the observer would be located in the center and surrounded by a ring of cells in which each individual could be seen by the observer in the center, but no individual could see the person on either side. Each individual's vision was limited to the observer in the centre, as indicated in figure 6.2. "P" in the figure represents the prisoner in Bentham's original Panopticon. In more recent configurations such as the lecture, however, it might be understood to represent the participants.

In actual usage, the most common form of Panopticon we know is the lecture theater. The speaker is elevated and stands alone where he or she can easily see everyone else in the room, and they can see him or her easily, but none of the participants has any communication except with those on either side. That structure is illustrated in figure 6.3.

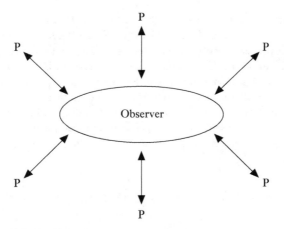

Figure 6.2   Bentham's Panopticon.

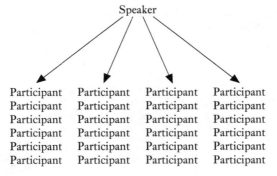

Figure 6.3   The lecture theater Panopticon.

Anyone who has taken a class in a school knows this structure. Although in recent years it has been modified, with circles, centers, and other small-group distributions of students, the Panopticon remains the favorite structure for larger lectures, for after-dinner speeches, for sales presentations, for political conventions, and for so many other public and professional events that we hardly see that there is anything unusual or historical about it.

Our point in bringing up the Panopticon here is to show that even in the layout of the participant structures of communicative events, Utilitarianism has placed its stamp upon contemporary life. In every case, it is the same form. Communication should be highly focused with one or a few participants controlling the activities of the many; topics should be introduced deductively in a style that is clear, brief, and sincere; and all participants should participate as "public" entities subject to the constraints that that implies. In other words, one should in all communications be able and willing to take on this highly historical and highly constrained communicative role. In the next chapter on *forms of discourse* we will have more to say about what it means to be a "public" communicator in the Utilitarian discourse system.

Face systems in the Utilitarian discourse system

We have already pointed out that the predominating ideology of the Utilitarian discourse system is one of individualism and egalitarianism. Now we need to clarify that while that ideology is widely expressed and practiced, nevertheless, there are two major exceptions which must be understood. In the first place, a distinction needs to be made between communication within the Utilitarian discourse system – that is, among participants – and communication outside of the discourse system – communication with non-participants. Then, with that consideration in mind, we will need to understand that within the discourse system there is also a major distinction between communications in "public discourse" and communications within institutional or bureaucratic structures. These multiple systems may be sketched as in figure 6.4.

Internal face systems: liberté, égalité, fraternité

There were two political revolutions which arose out of Enlightenment philosophy: the French Revolution and the American Revolution. Without going into these histories in detail, we only want to point out that the motto of the French Revolution, "*liberté, égalité, fraternité*," captures the essence of the concept of the person as well as the concept of interpersonal face relationships. As it was essential for the Enlightenment and the Utilitarian

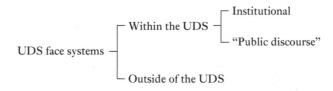

UDS = Utilitarian discourse system

Figure 6.4 Utilitarian discourse face systems.

concept of society for each individual to make free choices, it was also essential for each member to be considered an equal. The greatest happiness could not be achieved for the greatest number if some members of society were allowed to have a somewhat larger portion of happiness than others.

The U.S. Constitution also established the legal basis for social equality, though, of course, it should be clear to the reader that over two hundred years later the details of this social equality remain to be worked out in practice. The point we are making is that the Enlightenment established that a hierarchical system of social relationships was not consistent with its philosophy of free choice and rational, individual decision-making. Over the two hundred years since then, this philosophical ideal has been transformed into a popular concept of universal symmetrical solidarity. In the most extreme forms, such as in various sub-cultures in North America and elsewhere, it is now taken as a major point of social development to eliminate any and all suggestions of hierarchy in any interpersonal or social relationships.

From talk shows on television to press conferences with political leaders, there is a reinforced emphasis on direct talk, on avoiding elaboration and extravagance, and on promoting close, egalitarian social relationships. The Utilitarian discourse system has little tolerance for the appearance of hierarchical social relationships, and even where they exist, it is assumed they should be set aside in contexts of public communication. Within this system, everyone from presidents and prime ministers to corporate executives is expected to seem in their public communications just like "one of us." There is a great emphasis on popular appeal and commonness, even where these figures are known to live and move in social and financial circles to which the ordinary person would never have any form of access.

However, as we have already pointed out, such egalitarian discourse is really only considered appropriate within the Utilitarian discourse system when, as J. S. Mill has said, one does not "make himself a nuisance to other people" (1990: 293). In other words, the face system of symmetrical solidarity is taken to be appropriate only within contexts of socially and institutionally sanctioned public discourse. This, of course, is a much more narrowly restricted domain than it might at first have seemed to be. It is certainly a much narrower domain than is usually spoken of when people argue that their right to freedom of speech has been infringed.

The institutions of the Utilitarian discourse system

The institutions of the Utilitarian discourse system are many. They include most governments of industrialized democracies, virtually all multinational corporations, many schools, private manufacturing and service businesses, professional associations, and so on. Despite the egalitarian face system of public discourse discussed above, communication within such institutions is almost always hierarchical – the face system we called asymmetrical or hierarchical in chapter 5. Virtually all such institutions have an organizational chart which shows the hierarchy of position, power, and decision making. From the time of Taylor's *Scientific Management* (1911) with its "span of control," it has widely been accepted that the most efficient organization or institution will operate along such hierarchical lines of the flow of power and communication. Despite the more recent emphasis in international business organizations on "flatter hierarchies" and "self-managing teams," managers and leaders of organization still retain considerable control over operations and the overall direction of the organization, and we believe it will be some time yet before any internal face system other than this asymmetrical or hierarchical system will come to dominate in the institutions of the Utilitarian discourse system.

Outside discourse

This would be a good place to point out that J. S. Mill was not simply a political philosopher. He, like his father before him, was an officer of the British East India Company and, in his view, the major role of Europeans in relationships with the colonies was one of exploitation of resources on the one hand and of justified despotic leadership on the other. In this, J. S. Mill expressed the belief widely held within the Utilitarian discourse system that none of its principles of equality, individuality, freedom of expression, or rational thought need be applied to anyone who is not a participant in the discourse system.

Mill put it as follows:

> Over himself, over his own body and mind, the individual is sovereign.

> It is, perhaps, hardly necessary to say that this doctrine is meant to apply only to human beings in the maturity of their faculties. We are not speaking of children, or of young persons below the age which the law may fix as that of manhood or womanhood. Those who are still in a state to require being taken care of by others, must be protected against their own actions as well as against external injury. For the same reason, we may leave out of consideration those backward states of society in which the race itself may be considered as in its nonage. The early difficulties in the way of spontaneous progress are so great, that there is seldom any choice of means for over-coming them; and a ruler full of the spirit of improvement is warranted in the use of any expedients that will attain an end, perhaps otherwise unattainable. Despotism is a legitimate mode of government in dealing with barbarians, provided the end be their improvement, and the means justified by actually effecting that end. Liberty, as a principle, has no application to any state of things anterior to the time when mankind have become capable of being improved by free and equal discussion. (1990: 271–2)

This aspect of the Utilitarian discourse system recapitulates an old theme in many societies in which members are treated as real, normal, and worthy of "civilized" treatment, and non-members are treated as "ethnics," "barbarians," and "pagans." In more recent terminology, participants in the Utilitarian discourse system are judged to be "progressive," "democratic," "free," and "developed," and non-participants or more peripheral participants are judged to lack these assumed qualities. One has only to consult the 1948 Universal Declaration of Human Rights to see that the ideology of the Utilitarian discourse system has been taken for granted as the natural and rightful state of human life on earth, though it includes many aspects which had never or rarely been observed in human culture before the seventeenth century, except by the aristocracy, such as freedom of individuals, the right to own property, or the right to travel individually and freely throughout the world.

This is not a book on political philosophy and so it is not the place to develop further the theme of whether or not the ideology of the Utilitarian discourse system is or is not an adequate expression of universal human conditions and rights. The point we are making is that for members of this discourse system, the discourse system prescribes a face system of asymmetry and hierarchy with any and all non-members. The Utilitarian discourse system, while advocating equal rights for all members, quite specifically denies those rights of equality to those who do not show themselves willing to participate in the ideology of this discourse system. This is a point first made in J. S. Mill's essay *On Liberty*, quoted above, it is reiterated in the Universal Declaration of Human Rights, and it continues to be a major issue, in international discussions of such issues as the protection of intellectual copyright and international free trade agreements.

Multiple discourse systems

For professional communicators, this Utilitarian discourse system has become the system which is taken for granted as the natural way to communicate among those who work in fields related to business or government. Since international business and government circles have generally taken the political and economic philosophies of the Enlightenment as self-evident, they have also taken this discourse system as self-evident. Virtually any textbook one might pick up on business or professional communication will emphasize this discourse system. The task of these textbooks is taken to be to explicate the system, make it clear how to participate in it, and show how to produce most successfully the spoken and written forms of the Utilitarian discourse system.

If there were really no other competing discourse system, there would be no problem with this approach. Unfortunately, there are a number of other, different, and competing discourse systems. Communications in the home, communications between men and women, communications of members of different generations, and communications among members of many ethnic groups all show major departures from the patterns of this discourse system. The self-evident nature of a particular discourse system tends to make those other discourse systems invisible. Within a particular discourse system, communications which are framed within another discourse system simply appear faulty or inefficient. One either does not interpret them or one interprets them within the discourse system one is using oneself. This latter problem is the central one of intercultural communication. Intercultural communication is interdiscourse system communication. Communications which cross discourse system lines are subject to being either not heard or misinterpreted.

The Confucian discourse system

One of the main discourse systems competing with the Utilitarian discourse system is one which we might call the Confucian discourse system, a discourse system whose ideology derives chiefly from the philosophy of the Chinese sage Confucius, who lived from around 551 to 459 BC and whose ideas have come to influence nearly all aspects of social and political life throughout East Asia. As Asian nations become increasingly dominant players in the global economy, which is firmly based on Utilitarian principles, the points of contrast and friction between these two major discourse systems – the Utilitarian discourse system and the Confucian discourse system – have become more and more evident. Sometimes these tensions manifest themselves on the level of the individual as Asian workers for multinational corporations find they have to negotiate the competing values and norms of behavior that they encounter at their workplaces and in their day-to-day lives with their friends and family members. Sometimes they manifest at the level of institutions as traditional practices of doing business based on family ties and personal connections are seen as at odds with new laws and regulations based on Utilitarian principles. And sometimes these tensions manifest on the level of international relations as the political and economic policies of Asian nations fail sometimes to meet the Utilitarian expectations of global trade organizations or of large trading partners like the United States regarding issues like "fairness," transparency, intellectual property, and "human rights."

It is useful to briefly contrast the ideological assumptions of this discourse system with those of the Utilitarian discourse system, partly by way of emphasizing that the assumptions of the Utilitarian discourse system which so many take for granted are far from universal. Confucian ideas, in fact, have been around more than two thousand years longer than Utilitarianism.

As we stated above, Utilitarians like Jeremy Bentham and John Stuart Mill defined "good" as the greatest amount of "happiness" for the greatest number of people. In other words, goodness in this perspective is primarily seen as related to the physical and mental state of the individual: the more individuals that are happy, the more "goodness" exists. For Confucius and his followers, in contrast, goodness was seen not so much as a function of the individual as a matter of the relationships among individuals and between people and nature. Goodness in this perspective is not a matter of "happiness," but a matter of "harmony." What is meant by "harmony" is essentially balance and order, which is considered the foundation of everything from the internal workings of the human body to the external workings of astronomy and meteorology. In his commentary on the *Book of Rites* called the *Doctrine of the Mean*, Confucius states,

> This equilibrium is the great root of the world and this *harmony* is its universal path. What is here called the "state of equilibrium" is the same as the nature given by Heaven, considered absolutely in itself, without deflection or inclination. This nature acted on from without and responding to the various emotions so as always "to hit" the mark with the entire correctness produces the state of harmony, and such harmonious response is the path along which all human activities should proceed. (Legge trans. 1971: 45–6)

Order in social relationships in the Confucian worldview is related to order in nature, so that storms, earthquakes, famines, and other natural disasters have often been seen throughout the history of China and other east Asian countries as reflections of disorder in the social world. While this view is in many ways quite different from that of the Utilitarians, one important similarity is the notion that the natural world is in some sense *naturally orderly* and that society and the individuals that compose it should endeavor to somehow imitate this natural order.

The chief way harmony is to be achieved in society according to Confucius, interestingly enough, is through discourse. Disorder is seen as the result of a failure to perceive, understand, and speak about reality in an accurate way, and at the root of this is a failure to call things by their proper names. The solution to this was what Confucius referred to as "the rectification of names" (*zhèngmíng*). He explained this in the *Analects* as follows:

> If names be not correct, language is not in accordance with the truth of things.

> If language be not in accordance with the truth of things, affairs cannot be carried on to success. When affairs cannot be carried on to success, proprieties and music do not flourish. When proprieties and music do not flourish, punishments will not be properly awarded. When punishments are not properly awarded, the people do not know how to move hand or foot. Therefore a superior man considers it necessary that the names he uses may be spoken appropriately, and also that what he speaks may be carried out appropriately. What the superior man requires is just that in his words there may be nothing incorrect. (Legge trans. 1971: 264)

As we said above, the central goal of society in the Utilitarian discourse system is progress, by which is meant an ever-increasing amount of material wealth, and therefore, happiness for individuals. The idea of progress, at a very basic level, presupposes a linear Utopian view of time in which the future is necessarily better than the past by virtue of the inevitable advance in scientific knowledge and technical innovation driven by human reason and individual freedom. Custom and tradition are seen, from this perspective, as barriers to progress, as reflected in the passage from J. S. Mill quoted above. Confucianism, in contrast, does not see time in terms of a linear forward movement, but rather in a more cyclical way, and does not see tradition as an encumbrance to progress, but rather as something to be revered. Confucius himself looked back to the sage-kings of the early Chou dynasty who ruled more than 500 years before his birth for models to which society should aspire.

Such a view is predicated on what we can call a Golden Age orientation towards time. In the China of Confucius, and continuing down to very recently, it was felt that the present time was worse than the times of the past, in which human society was more reasonably ordered, justice and benevolence prevailed, and benevolent rulers concerned themselves with the good of their subjects. Changes in society were justified from the point of view of restoring the better conditions of the past, not with moving toward new conditions in the future. This same Golden-Age concept of the past was held in Europe up until and through the Renaissance. The thinkers of the Renaissance looked back at their immediate predecessors and considered them to have degenerated from the much higher state of culture of the Roman and Greek ancients, and it was their goal to restore Europe to this former condition.

This is not to say that the Confucian philosophy should be regarded as "regressive," eschewing the notion that things can get better over time. Progress, however, in the Confucian sense, has less to do with the material advancement of the society and more to do with learning and moral cultivation, which leads to the realization of the human potential of which the ancestors are held up as exemplars.

The focus for the realization of such potential is not the free, equal individual, as in the Utilitarian formulation, but rather the individual as he or she exists in a web of social relationships. Society, according to Confucius, is built upon five primary relationships: those between the ruler and the ruled, the father and the son, the husband and the wife, the elder brother and the younger brother, and finally, the relationship between friends. All but the last of these is based upon hierarchical face systems, and respecting the authority of those in the superior position in these hierarchical relationships is seen as central to both cultivating personal virtue and maintaining social harmony.

Obviously, the self-interested, economically minded inhabitants of a Utilitarian society would not be regarded favorably in this system in which people are counted on *not* to pursue their own interests, but rather to subvert their interests in the interest of the group. Rather than "rational, economic entities," then, humans in the Confucian system are defined as *moral* entities, characterized by what Confucius referred to as *ren* or "humanity." "Humanity" is perhaps best defined as the potential for human goodness and compassion that all people innately possess. In some sense, Confucianism shares with Utilitarianism a belief in the power of society to shape human consciousness and behavior, and hence emphasized the importance of education and the cultivation of good citizens. On the other hand, while according to Utilitarianism humans begin life as *tabula rasa* or "blank slates," in Confucianism humans start out possessing a basic goodness which later may be corrupted through contact with less than virtuous people.

It should be clear by now that learning and self-cultivation, rather than technology and invention, are regarded as the sources of societal wealth in the Confucian view of things, and that wealth itself is seen less in material terms and more in terms of honor and right-eousness. It then follows that society's most valuable members would not be creative, inventive individuals but rather moral individuals who respect their superiors and cultivate their natural humanity and benevolence. Confucius referred to such people as *junzi*, sometimes translated as "gentlemen" or "superior men." Finally, the idea that values or virtue could be determined based on some mathematical equation would doubtless have been an anathema to Confucius, for whom wisdom born from learning is the only legitimate means for determining what is valuable and what is not.

"Conversations"

From the above comparison one might be led to believe that the Confucian ideology, which developed in China around 500 BCE, and the ideology of Utilitarianism, which developed in Europe more than two thousand years later, are so different as to be totally incompatible with each other. This belief, reasonable as it might seem, however, would have to contend not only with the fact that today in much of East Asia these two ideologies exist side by side, but also with the lesser known fact that the Utilitarian philosophy itself along with much intellectual and scientific thought in eighteenth-century Europe was influenced by Confucian ideas. Not only were accounts of Asia written by missionaries, merchants, sailors, soldiers, and independent travelers wildly popular in Europe at the time of the Enlightenment, but a number of European philosophers of the time explicitly professed admiration for the work of Confucius to the point that, in his book *China and Europe* (1968), Adolf Reichwein calls Confucius "the patron saint of [the] eighteenth century Enlightenment." As early as 1687, a book on Confucius compiled by a team of Jesuit monks led by Philippe Couplet and Prosper Intorcetta entitled *Confucius Sinarum Philosophus* asserted that:

> One might say that the moral system of this philosopher is infinitely sublime, but that it is at the same time simple, sensible and drawn from the purest sources of natural reason . . . Never has Reason, deprived of divine Revelation, appeared so well developed nor with so much power. (quoted in Hobson 2004: 194)

One of Europe's chief admirers of Confucius at the time was Voltaire, who wrote of him in his *Dictionnaire Philosophique* (1764): "What more beautiful rule of conduct has ever been given man since the world began? Let us admit that there has been no legislator more useful to the human race" (quoted in Brown and Ly 2003: 9). What Voltaire and other European philosophers of the eighteenth century admired about Confucius was, first, the reliance of his moral system on principles of reason rather than on articles of faith or superstition, and second, the notion of meritocracy implicit in his philosophy, the idea, revolutionary by European standards of the day, that nobility should be based on virtue rather than on blood. In fact, both in his *L'Orphelin de la Chine* (1755), and *Zadig* (1748), Voltaire drew on what he viewed as the rational principles of Confucianism in order to attack the European preference for hereditary aristocracy.

Among the other Enlightenment thinkers who were heavily influenced by eastern philosophy was François Quesnay, who credited the Chinese for the codification of laws for ethical conduct and economic policy derived directly from Natural Law and coined the term "Enlightened Despotism" to describe China's feudalistic system of government. He also took from Daoism the idea of *wu wei* ("non-doing") which he translated into the economic principle of *laissez-faire*, a principle which later became a central tenet in Adam Smith's model of free market capitalism.

China's influence on eighteenth-century Europe was felt not just in the realms of politics and philosophy, but also in the domains of science and technology, with many of the major inventions that spurred the agricultural and industrial revolutions of the time – for instance the iron moldboard plough, the rotary winnowing machine, and the steam engine – having their antecedents in earlier Chinese inventions. Among the most significant of these technological advances was the introduction of ships with bulkheads and watertight compartments based on technology imported from China by the naval architect Samuel Bentham (1757–1831), none other than the brother of the chief architect of Utilitarianism Jeremy Bentham. Ironically this borrowing was probably the single most important contributor to the development of the naval capacity which in the two centuries that followed allowed Britain to exert imperial domination over much of Asia.

Of course, the greatest paradox of this brief history of China and Europe in the eighteenth century is that while Europe was borrowing and assimilating many Chinese ideas, these same ideas became part of an ideology which imagined the people of the east to be barbaric, uncivilized, and unworthy of the rights and freedoms that the Utilitarian discourse system reserved for its own participants. We do not wish to belabor the injustice of this nor to overly exaggerate the role of Chinese philosophy in the development of European modernity. What we would like to emphasize, however, is this paradoxical nature of ideology. All ideologies develop in dialogue with other ideologies, what Gee, extending his idea of "capital D Discourses" calls "capital C Conversations," and these Conversations are rarely as neat and sharply delineated as we might expect as people strategically appropriate and adapt the ideas and practices of others for their own advantage. No ideology is purely practiced. You would be hard pressed to find any pure Confucians or any pure Utilitarians outside of classical Chinese literature or the pages of a Dickens novel. Instead, what you will find, both in the past and now, are individuals who draw upon the variety of ideas and social practices that surround them in the societies in which they live as they claim and impute membership in various, sometimes competing discourse systems.

This chapter has considered in some detail the characteristics of ideology in systems of discourse, with a focus on the Utilitarian discourse system. We have three reasons why we have gone into this particular discourse system in such detail: it is the system most frequently presented as self-evident to practitioners of international business and commerce, it is the self-proclaimed "standard" of international discourse, and it can be shown not to be all that it claims to be. The Utilitarian discourse system, in spite of its merits in commerce and in international affairs, represents a particular ideology and as such needs to be carefully analyzed, especially from the point of view of asking what is *not* self-evident within it.

As a way of putting the sometimes unquestioned assumptions of the Utilitarian discourse system in relief, we have introduced some principles of a competing discourse system, what we have called the Confucian discourse system. This discussion has brought us to the problem which will be taken up in the following chapters: the problem of communication between different systems of discourse, the complexity of which we have touched on briefly above.

Of course, there is no telling just how many such systems might be analyzed. As we will see, the Utilitarian discourse system, while it may dominate in business, government, academic, or organizational affairs, does not occupy the entire field of discourse, even within a single society. One needs to look at different systems and sub-systems of discourse used across ethnic lines, across generational lines, between genders, and between corporate, professional, and affinity groups. The crucial point upon which to focus, however, is not how many discourse systems there are or on either their internal, defining characteristics or the ways in which boundaries between them and others are made and maintained. The crucial point is to realize that all communication arises from within some discourse system or complex "Conversation" between or among discourse systems. We speak simultaneously as men or women, as older or younger members of our groups, as professionals or independents, as expatriates or locals. We cannot say anything without positioning ourselves within some discourse system(s).

We do not wish to take the extreme position of saying that everything we say is determined by the discourse systems within which we act because each discourse system has internal contradictions and, as we have said and will say again later, we always function simultaneously from within multiple discourse systems and this produces points of conflict and contradiction around which we construct speaking positions. From the point of view of the analysis of interdiscourse communication, the relevant issue is that we need to see in any situation what discursive resources a particular set of participants have, how those resources enable saying some things and taking some positions while at the same time restricting or limiting the participants' ability to say or do other things.

We take the position that successful interdiscourse communication depends on learning to move with both pragmatic effectiveness and interactional sensitivity across the lines which divide discourse systems and within the contours of the "Conversations" between them. Successful communication relies on two factors: increasing shared knowledge and dealing with miscommunication. Pragmatic effectiveness in communication means participating as fully as possible in the discourse systems of those with whom one is wishing to communicate, while never taking their requirements as simply self-evident. Interactional sensitivity means being conscious of the ways in which one's own communications may be perceived and also accepting the fact that one is never likely to be considered a full member of most of the discourse systems in which one will participate.

What "Counts" as an Ideology?

Before leaving the subject of ideology in discourse systems it is necessary for us to clarify in a more practical way what "counts" as a discourse system and what "counts" as an ideology.

As we said above, one of the advantages of the concept of discourses systems is that it can allow us to study both rather large and rather small systems of communication and social organization. That is, we can speak of smaller discourse systems like the discourse system of Liu Ka Man's company as well as larger discourse systems like the Utilitarian discourse system and the Confucian discourse system. We have also talked about how smaller discourse systems can participate in or be embedded in larger discourse systems. Here, then, it is important to say that not all discourse systems are created equal and that not all belief systems can be considered ideologies.

What we mean by this is that some discourse systems are what we might call "hegemonic" in that many smaller discourse systems participate in or draw from them and their influence is felt in nearly all aspects of the societies in which they operate. In fact, such discourse systems exercise leadership precisely by co-opting smaller discourse systems and gaining control over what Foucault (1972) calls the "archive" of a society, the set of statements and texts that govern a society's view of reality, statements which have for participants self-evident status and which cast those who do not agree into the pariah class of infidel or non-believer. It is when statements take on the ability to cast the people who accept them or reject them as either belonging or not that these statements take on the status of ideologies.

We can think of a fairly small number of truly hegemonic discourse systems worldwide in the sense of systems which exercise leadership through controlling the archive. The Utilitarian discourse system is one obvious example. Naturally there will be a greater number of contesting or counter-hegemonic discourse systems, and there are of course discourses systems within discourse systems, but often it is difficult to understand these smaller discourse systems without reference to the larger, more powerful discourse systems operating in a given place and time.

We have spoken of the historical or philosophical basis of the Utilitarian discourse system as the Utilitarian ideology. The concept of ideology arises when a discourse system, such as the Utilitarian one, comes to assert itself as a complete communicative system. That is, it becomes ideological when it denies or devalues other forms of discourse or communication. In reference to the Utilitarian discourse system, we would call this discourse system ideological because the system takes itself as the cause of its worldwide political, economic, and communicative domination. In other words, within this discourse system it is widely believed that personal economic power can be achieved through direct, deductive expression of information. It is also believed that as a general system of communication, it is this system which has given free market capitalism the worldwide base it now enjoys.

We are neither economists nor political philosophers, and so it would be inappropriate for us to undertake here a discussion of the forces behind the rise of a worldwide market economy and the political structures of law that accompany this system. Any knowledgeable reader knows that this is an extremely complex subject which is, perhaps, not really completely understood by anybody. And that is our point: the actual reality of the international market economy and political structure is far too complex to be attributed to any single cause. One thing we can say for certain is that the Utilitarian discourse system is not the single or even the primary cause. Nevertheless, within that system it is widely believed that this discourse system is the key to success for this international political and economic system. We consider this an ideological position. It is a belief structure which is maintained in the face of a contrary and much more complex reality.

Within the Utilitarian discourse system, it is believed that this discourse system is the reason for its own ascendancy in the world. Nevertheless, within that same system it is widely said that such matters are far too complex to be reduced to such single-factor analyses. The question then arises, "Why would such a discourse system promote itself so vigorously when it flies in the face of real-world analysis?" To get an answer to this, we need to look at the self-reinforcing aspect of a discourse system. Not only is a discourse system self-evident to its users, it is very difficult to break into from outside. A discourse system rejects communications and participants who do not play the full game.

Let us look at this from the point of view of education, since this book itself may be used in teaching students in programs in professional or business communication. We can imagine that one major reason someone would be studying in such a field is because he or she plans to work in the field of professional communication upon graduation. The Utilitarian ideology would say to you, "The Utilitarian discourse system is both the means of communication and the source of the success of the worldwide market economy. Learn this system and you will thereby become a full participant in this political and economic world." What this ideology does not say is that the actual sources of power do not lie within the discourse system as such, but within more traditional concepts of connections among significant players, inherited position, and the exploitation of non-member participants. To put this another way, the C–B–S style of this discourse system appears to favor telling you everything you need to know in a direct, straightforward way. This can easily lead one into thinking that this is actually what people who participate in this system *do*, which is clearly not the case.

The main point we are trying to make here is that an examination of ideology itself is not enough to fully understand a discourse system and, in fact, what participants in the discourse system actually do sometimes runs counter to the ideology they profess. Therefore, along with ideology, we also have to account for the *social practices* engaged in by members, the forms of discourse they favor, the kinds of relationships that exist between participants and between participants and outsiders, and the ways people learn to be participants and how they are eventually accepted as such by others. It is these aspects of discourse systems that we will focus on in the following two chapters.

Researching Interdiscourse Communication

The relationship between small d discourse and big D Discourses

Over the course of this book we have shifted our understanding of the word "discourse" as we have moved in our discussion from a very limited concept with a concentration on the basic forms used for cohesion, such as conjunctions, to a meaning which now seems to enclose a very large portion of society and culture. This is not just a personal whim of the authors, but reflects a shift in the topics which discourse analysts have studied in the past three decades.

At first the focus of discourse analysis was cohesion, mainly within and between clauses in sentences. As analysts began to see that it was difficult, if not impossible, to understand how discourse cohesion works through such a close lens, they began to take context into consideration in their studies. Of course, once context came into view, it was difficult to say just what should be included and what should not be included. One recent textbook on discourse has said that actually anything that humans communicate has been called discourse and analyzed by discourse analysts now at one time or another.

In this chapter we have arrived at the conceptualization of discourse or "Discourses" as rather large and somewhat unwieldy things which include not just language but also, in Gee's words "language *plus* 'other stuff'." This "other stuff" includes "thinking, valuing, acting, and interacting, in the 'right' places and at the 'right' times with the 'right' objects" (Gee 2010: 34).

While we do not wish to take the view that *everything* is a matter of discourse, we would argue that "Discourses" like the Utilitarian discourse system play a major role in our ability to interpret (and fail to interpret) the communications of others. As we have pointed out in relation to the Utilitarian discourse system, such a system contains within it a self-reinforcing circle: a complete view of the person as a communicator, the person as a member of society, assumptions about proper socialization and educational practices, and norms governing the ways in which communication should be done. Such a self-legitimating circle of discourse, because it constrains the ways in which things can be said, consequently also constrains *what* can be said.

Of course the danger with concepts like Discourses and discourse system is that we focus so much on these larger entities (which themselves are really only *heuristics*) and become so concerned with such big issues as ideology that we pay less attention to what people actually say and do in their daily lives. Successfully researching ideologies in discourse (or ideologies in Discourses), then, requires to some degree that we attempt to reconcile and integrate these three different levels of analysis, to understand how the ways words and sentences are put together to form texts with tools like grammar are related to the ways people actually use these texts to perform actions in their social worlds, and the ways these social worlds are themselves governed by larger self-reinforcing systems in which what gets said (or fails to get said) is tied up with notions of what it means to be a legitimate member of a particular group. In other words, the goal we should have as analysts is to explain how "small d discourse" reproduces "big D Discourses," and how "big D Discourses" create and constrain "small d discourse."

Looking for or, as critical discourse analysts say, "uncovering" ideology in the "small d" discourse of texts is particularly tricky since ideological positions are more often than not expressed by what is *not* said in texts rather than what is. One good place to begin, however, is to consider the way that reality is being represented in the text. All texts present representations of reality through participants (people, places, things, or ideas) and processes (actions which participants take part in in some way). How these participants and processes are expressed and arranged grammatically can give some indication of the version of reality the authors of texts are trying to get us to believe in and sometimes even the underlying ideological basis for this version of reality. It is quite different, for example, to say "The army pacified the agitators" and "The army pacified the demonstrators," and still different if we use a less abstract word for the process and say, "The army shot the demonstrators." In each of these three versions we are invited to form very different opinions about the army and the demonstrators and what went on. Which participant is portrayed as the "doer" or agent of the action can also be very important, and in English and most other languages we have quite a number of ways in which "agency" can be expressed. If I say, "John kissed Mary," I am giving John responsibility for the action, whereas if I say, "Mary kissed John," Mary is portrayed as the active participant. Such sentences are not in themselves ideological, but when they are embedded in larger texts and social practices they often belie ideological assumptions. In North America, for example, it used to be the case (and still may be in some places) that after a couple exchanged wedding vows the person officiating over the wedding would say to the man, "You may now kiss the bride." What ensued afterwards was usually a mutual practice of kissing, but this mutual practice was construed in the words uttered as something that the man was doing to the woman, reflecting a whole set of assumptions about the roles and proper conduct of men and women both in the context of marriage and in society as a whole.

The kinds of questions you should ask when looking at texts in this way are: (1) What kinds of participants are being included and how are they portrayed? (2) What kinds of participants might have been included but have instead been excluded? (3) What kinds of verbs are used and which participants are portrayed as performing these verbs? and (4) Are there other

possible ways of portraying what happened using different verbs or making different participants agents, and how would this alter the "world" being represented by the text?

Another important thing to consider in looking for the ideological foundations of texts
is the kinds of assumptions upon which the text depends. Very often texts present various
aspects of the world they are portraying as "given" or "taken for granted," when in truth,
these presuppositions themselves are highly debatable. By presenting them as presuppositions, however, authors preempt any debate about them. One example of this that Fairclough
and other critical discourse analysts have observed is the rhetorical strategy of proponents
of the Utilitarian discourse system to portray globalization as inevitable, and thus rendering
moot any debate on whether or not it is desirable. In a pragmatic sense, presuppositions are
meanings which have been made implicit through being embedded in sentences or utterances whose interpretation depends upon tacit acceptance of these meanings. So, for
example, asking someone if he brought his girlfriend to the party presupposes both that he
attended a party and that he has a girlfriend. Presupposition often involves certain grammatical constructions, and being alert to these constructions can aid you in detecting it.
These constructions include: (1) verbs which portray what follows as a fact, such as to regret,
to know, and to be aware of (for example, "He regretted arriving late." "Are you aware of
the impact this will have on the environment?"), (2) verbs followed by infinitive comple-
ments (to + Verb constructions) (e.g. "He managed to get their support." "They struggled
to get their voices heard"), (3) verbs showing some kind of change in state (e.g. "Have you
quit smoking?" "The government should stop giving handouts to lazy people"), and (4)
words which imply that some action has occurred more than once ("There you go again!").

Another important grammatical tool through which ideology is often expressed is that
of modality, the way we talk about probability and obligation in our language. Modality is
often expressed through modal verbs like "should," "would," "will," "might," "may," etc.,
but it can also be expressed thorough adverbs (for example, "probably" and "definitely")
and through other constructions like "It is certain that . . ."

In his 2008 book *Analyzing Public Discourse*, Ron Scollon related the story of whistle-
blower Rick S. Piltz, Senior Associate of the Climate Change Science Program Office of the
U.S. government, who alerted the media to the fact that scientific reports on climate change
were regularly edited by White House staffers in the Bush administration in a way that
portrayed it as much more uncertain and contingent than it was portrayed by the scientist
who had originally submitted the reports. The example Scollon gives provides an illustration
of how remodalization can change not just the meaning but the ideological positioning of a
text. An excerpt of an original draft text submitted to the White House in October of 2002
reads as follows:

> Warming will also cause reductions in mountain glaciers and advance the timing of the melt of
> mountain snow packs in polar regions. In turn runoff rates will change and flood potential will
> be altered in ways that are currently not well understood. (quoted in Scollon 2008: 138)

In response to this draft the White House editor suggested the following revisions, presented
in bold type:

> Warming **would** also cause reductions in mountain glaciers and advance the timing of the melt
> of mountain snow packs in polar regions. In turn runoff rates **would** change and flood potential
> **would** be altered in ways that are currently not well understood. (quoted in Scollon 2008: 139)

In this example, the transformation of the modal verb "will" to the conditional "would" creates a portrayal of these events as much less certain, as dependent upon other conditions which are not stated.

Later in November of 2002 when the public review draft was made available, the lead sentence had been further changed to read:

> Warming **could** also **lead to changes in the water cycle in polar regions.** (quoted in Scollon 2008: 139)

The implied conditional "would," then, had been reduced still further to the merely probabilistic "could," and the specific "cause reductions" had been changed to the more general "lead to changes." Finally, when the report was published in July of 2003, the entire paragraph had been deleted by the White House editor on the grounds that it was too "speculative."

What this example illustrates is not just the ways small grammatical features like modal verbs can affect how we understand reality as it is mediated through texts, but how, in a more fundamental way, our understanding of truth and reality as it is mediated by texts is at the very heart of our ability to take action in the world. The editors in the anecdote above were not just able to change texts. They were able to affect policy. Another important lesson from this example has to do with the relationship between the Utilitarian discourse system and science. It is important to remember that to say that the Utilitarian ideology adopts the language of science as a preferred form of discourse does not necessarily mean that it is necessarily scientific. In fact, part of the success of this discourse system in exercising hegemony has been its ability to portray ideas, policies, and states of affairs as grounded somehow in scientific facts when very often this grounding has been at best questionable. While public communication and decision making in cases such as this may be carried out on a surface level of scientific discourse, underlying this discourse is a definite ideological position.

It is important when looking at texts in this manner, however, not to stop with the texts, but also to consider the actions these texts are being used to carry out. In fact, the ideology expressed in any given text is heavily dependent on the context in which that text occurs and the actions which it is being used to take. The slogan "Serve the People" serves a very different ideology if it is printed on a "big character poster" at a political rally in the China of the 1960s (see chapter 10) and if it is printed on a tee-shirt being sold at a trendy boutique in Hong Kong in 2010.

The question for the analyst, then, is not just what actions are possible with a given text, but what actions are actually being taken with it by which people in which specific place and time and to what effect. This question focuses on the second level of discourse analysis, the analysis of discourse *in use*, and without answering it, it is really impossible to say anything meaningful about ideology in texts. And so here is a good place to return to the site survey you conducted earlier and to link the texts you are analyzing to particular actions and social practices, to the people who are carrying them out, and, sometimes most importantly, to the people who are being affected by them.

Here it is also important to consider not just which texts make which kinds of actions and social relationships possible, but how they make them possible. In other words, the analyst has to consider how the kinds of textual features that we discussed above affect not just what the text means but what people are able to do with the text. This also involves looking at aspects of the text beyond its grammatical and lexical features such as who has access to the text and who doesn't, how the text is produced, what kind of authority people in this context are likely to lend to a particular text, and what kind of social organization accompanies the production or consumption of the text. The ideological positioning of a text may be very different depending on whether it is read alone at someone's desk or recited publicly, and whether it is read as part of institutionally sanctioned activity or as part of a more informal kind of interaction.

The kinds of questions one should ask at this level of analysis are: What actions are enabled, constrained, prohibited, or required by this text? What actions is this text actually being used to mediate? Who is taking action with this text and what kind of authority do they have? Who is addressed in this text and acted upon by it and what must or may they do because of it?

Discussion Questions

1   Think of a group that you belong to and discuss its ideology based on the following seven questions:
    (a)   How is "good" defined in this group?
    (b)   What are the main goals of the group?
    (c)   What is the "basis" of the group (e.g. autonomous individuals or social relationships)?
    (d)   How does the group define humans?
    (e)   What is the main source of wealth, strength, power for the group?
    (f)   What kinds of people are considered most valuable for the group?
    (g)   What are considered the best methods for determining what is valuable for the group?
    Which of the answers to these questions would be considered "self-evident" by group members? And which might be subject to debate among them?

2   Discuss how the ideology and social organization of your school or workplace is or is not influenced by the principles of the Utilitarian discourse system described above.

3   Discuss your own "philosophy of life" and how much it conforms to or deviates from the principles of the two large discourse systems discussed above (the Utilitarian discourse system and the Confucian discourse system). Can you describe other ideologies that have influenced you?

References for Further Study

For a more detailed discussion of "capital D Discourses" and "capital C Conversations" see James Paul Gee's 2010 *An Introduction to Discourse Analysis*, 3rd edition. The related concepts of "orders of discourse" and "archives" can be found in Michel Foucault's 1969 (1972) *The Archaeology of Knowledge*. There are a number of books in addition to Gee's book cited above that deal with ideology from a discourse analytical point of view including Theo van Leeuwen's 2008 *Discourse and Practice: new tools for critical discourse analysis*, Norman Fairclough's 1992 classic *Discourse and Social Change*, and Teun van Dijk's *Ideology: a multidisciplinary approach*. More details on the analysis of ideology in texts can be found in Ron Scollon's *Analyzing Public Discourse* (2008). Richard Lanham (1983) suggested the term "C–B–S style," and Kenner (1987) quotes Bishop Thomas Sprat. Sources on the thinking of the Enlightenment are Adam Smith (1990), Montesquieu (1990), American State Papers (1990), Kant (1990), Locke (1990), and Bentham (1962, 1988). Kant's view on public and private is in Behler (1986); his essay regarding authorship is in Kant (1990). Mill (1990) is the foundation of Utilitarianism and includes a discussion of the ideas of Bentham.

Lakoff and Johnson (1980) discuss the anti-rhetorical nature of Utilitarian discourse, though not using this terminology. Foucault, in his 1977 *Discipline and Punish*, brought Bentham's Panopticon to the attention of contemporary readers. Those interested in the influence of Confucian thought on the Enlightenment and Industrial Revolution Europe can consult John Hobson's 2004 *The Eastern Origins of Western Civilization*.

7

Forms of Discourse

Functions of Language

When we use the term "forms of discourse" we mean to include all of the different ways in which discourse might take form – specific genres and events and preferred styles and registers – as well as the fundamental conceptions about communication, its value, and its purpose that underlie these preferences. Participation in a discourse system necessarily entails mastery of a number of forms of discourse that are closely tied up with the kinds of social practices people in that discourse system engage in and the kinds of social relationships they are trying to maintain. Doctors must be able to conduct medical examinations; professors must be able to write academic papers; comedians must be able to tell jokes. At the same time, through these forms of discourse, discourse systems tend to promote more fundamental sets of theories about what kind of discourse is most desirable and what kind of people should make use of such discourse, for what purposes, and in what circumstances.

Information and relationship

Communication theorists, linguists, psychologists, and anthropologists all agree that language has many functions. In previous chapters we have showed how all language must be used simultaneously in a communicative function as well as in a metacommunicative function. Of course, there is much discussion among researchers about how many functions there are and just which functions take priority in any particular case. One dimension on which there is complete agreement, however, is that virtually any communication will have both an information function and a relationship function. In other words, when we communicate with others we simultaneously communicate some amount of information and indicate our current expectations about the relationship between or among participants.

At the two extremes of information and relationship, there are often cases in which one or the other function appears to be minimized. For example, in those daily greetings such

Intercultural Communication: A Discourse Approach, Third Edition. Ron Scollon, Suzanne Wong Scollon, Rodney H. Jones.

as, "How are you? I'm just fine," there is often a minimum of actual information. After all, we do not really expect the other person in most cases to answer about how they actually are. Nor do we expect them to believe that we are literally "fine." Such exchanges are nearly, but not quite exclusively, relational. The meaning of such exchanges is simply to acknowledge recognition and to affirm that the relationship you have established remains in effect. At the other extreme, such discourses as weather reports may seem almost completely devoid of relationship, focusing only on information about the weather.

What is of concern for us is not to establish whether or not the purpose of language is to convey information or relationship; the use of language always accomplishes both functions to some extent. From a communication point of view, we can see that discourse systems often are different from each other in how much importance they give to one function of language over the other. For example, international business culture, what we have been calling the Utilitarian discourse system places a very high value on the communication of information and less value on the communication of relationship, whereas the Confucian discourse system puts much more emphasis on the communication of relationship.

In regular conditions of interdiscourse communication, this difference between a focus on information and a focus on relationship often leads to a misunderstanding of the purposes of specific communicative events. From the point of view of the functions of language, a participant in the Utilitarian discourse system may well want to get to the bargaining table as quickly as possible because he or she believes that it is in direct talk that information is exchanged and that any other form of communication is quite beside the point. His or her counterpart, on the other hand, more influenced by the Confucian discourse system, may want to set up a series of social events in which the participants can more indirectly approach each other and begin to feel more subtle aspects of their relationship.

Negotiation and ratification

Having said that there is often a difference among discourse systems in the belief about whether language is primarily used for the purposes of conveying information or expressing relationships, we now need to complicate the picture somewhat further. There is also a difference among discourse systems in the extent to which relationships are thought to be freely negotiated on the one hand, or given by society in a fixed form on the other. This is the second aspect of the functions of language we will need to consider.

As we noted in chapter 3, kinship is a major source of structure within many discourse systems. In many societies, human relationships are thought of as being largely vertical relationships between preceding and following generations. Whether it is family relationships such as those between parents and their children or relationships outside of the family such as those between a teacher and a student, the significant point is that most of the relationships are understood to be given by the society, not newly negotiated by the participants in the situation. One is born the son or daughter of particular parents, the descendant of particular ancestors, a member of a particular village. These characteristics of one's personal identity are not negotiable; they are given by the circumstances into which one is born.

In contrast to this, in societies in which the Utilitarian discourse system prevails, the word "relationship" has come to mean almost exclusively horizontal or lateral and often, in fact, sexual, relationships made between people who freely choose to enter into them. Thus, one would not be likely to advertise on Facebook that one is "in a relationship" with one's mother or father, one's siblings, or one's boss, despite the fact that one's ties to all of these people constitute "relationships." The primary concern in what are called relationships is with the establishment of equality and freedom. In fact, one could safely say that one of the greatest concerns one finds in the popular press in places where the Utilitarian discourse system dominates is about how to keep relationships from taking on hierarchical characteristics.

If we return, then, to the question of forms of discourse and the functions of communication, we can see that a major difference between these two points of view lies in the question of negotiation or ratification. Within a traditional concept of vertical and generational relationships, discourse is thought of as being used for the purposes of ratifying or affirming relationships which have already been given. On the other hand, in the concept of relationships influenced by the Utilitarian discourse system, discourse is seen as a major aspect of the ongoing negotiation of the relationship. Particular care is taken not to merely ratify existing relationships, but to seek continual change, or as it is more favorably put, "growth."

The difference is that in one view the stable condition is seen as the favorable condition and in the other it is the changing condition that is thought of as being preferable. Sometimes people who participate in discourse systems that privilege hierarchical face systems continue to call each other quite formally by their last names and titles even after they have known each other for many years and engaged in mutually profitable business arrangements. On the other hand, sometimes people who are heavily influenced by the Utilitarian discourse system feel that their attempts to develop a better relationship with those prioritizing hierarchical relationships have not succeeded because after a long series of encounters with them they have not been able to establish themselves on a first-name "friendly" basis.

Group harmony and individual welfare

The third way in which we can see that discourse systems differ in their view of the functions of language is to mention the research of Japanese psychologist Yutaka Sayeki, who studied group processes in solving problems. In this research project, subjects were given individual problems to solve in some cases and in other cases they were asked to solve the problems in groups. He found that when there was a conflict within the group about how to solve a problem, group harmony was always the greatest consideration, even if it meant that the group had to select a worse solution. In other words, his conclusion was that members of a group much preferred to say they would go along with the group than to express their own, individual solutions, if those solutions would produce disharmony in the group.

Other scholars have pointed out that one major difference between Ancient Chinese and Ancient Greek rhetoric was on this dimension of group harmony versus individual welfare. Ancient Chinese rhetoric emphasized the means by which one could phrase one's position without causing any feeling of disruption or disharmony. Ancient Greek rhetoric, on the other hand, emphasized the means of winning one's point through skillful argument, short of, Aristotle says, the use of torture.

We do not suppose that contemporary international business circles would approve of the use of torture to achieve a good contract on the one hand, or that people would scuttle the possibility of a good contract just for the sake of a harmonious group feeling on the other. Nevertheless, we do believe that this difference in assumptions made about the functions of language will often have some effect on interdiscourse communication involving people from different discourse systems. At the same time, we caution against stereotyping all people from particular countries or cultural contexts as "individualistic" and all people from other cultural contexts as "collectivistic." Whether or not someone focuses on individual goals or group harmony depends very much on what they are doing and to whom they are talking. We will take up this issue of individualism and collectivism more fully in chapter 10.

Clarity, Brevity, and Sincerity Revisited

In the last chapter we introduced the idea of the C–B–S style of discourse and discussed how in books on management and business communication as well as in college and university composition courses this style is put forth as the best way of communicating, especially in business and professional contexts. As we said above, when we speak of forms of discourse, we are not just interested in the external form that texts take (in terms of, for example, genre and style), but also in the theories of communication that lie behind these forms. In this section we will attempt to elaborate on the set of theories about communication that are part of the Utilitarian discourse system along the three dimensions discussed above: *information and relationship, negotiation and ratification*, and *group harmony and individual welfare*. We will also discuss how these theories and the forms of discourse associated with them both reflect and advance the ideology, face systems, and processes of socialization associated with this discourse system. Along the way we will contrast these theories and the forms of discourse they promote to theories about communication found in other discourse systems.

Theories of communication in the Utilitarian discourse system

There are essentially six main characteristics of the forms of discourse preferred within the Utilitarian discourse system, or, as we might put it, six primary "theories" regarding what communication should be like and what it should accomplish. These forms of discourse, as we have said before, have become the preferred ones for the expression of the ideology of the Utilitarian discourse system and are among the main ways in which new members are socialized into this discourse system. Naturally, not all of the characteristics which we will give below will be found to the same extent in all of the forms one might analyze. Formal business letters and contracts, for example, will vary widely from such genres as emails and instant messaging conversations. However, these theories of discourse by which the system conveys its ideology will be found to a greater or lesser extent in most instances of Utilitarian discourse. The six theories are that the discourse should be:

1 anti-rhetorical;
2 positivist-empirical;
3 deductive;
4 individualistic;
5 egalitarian;
6 public (institutionally sanctioned).

Anti-rhetorical

In the last chapter we quoted the *History of the Royal Society* by the Bishop of Rochester, Thomas Sprat. The Royal Society took a strongly anti-rhetorical position. By that we mean two things: speakers and writers tried to avoid obvious uses of rhetoric, and a new rhetoric with the appearance of using no rhetoric began to develop.

Jeremy Bentham himself was a strong opponent of the use of such rhetorical figures as metaphor. He wrote, "Systems which attempt to question it [the principle of utility], deal in sounds instead of senses, in caprice instead of reason, in darkness instead of light. But enough of metaphor and declamation: it is not by such means that moral science is to be improved" (1988: 34). Quite typically for Bentham, after using a series of metaphors – "sounds," "senses," "caprice," "reason," "darkness," "light" – he then turns and denounces the use of metaphor and declamation.

In a study of academic writing, which we would consider a sub-system of the Utilitarian discourse system, Swales (1990) has pointed to this apparent non-rhetoric of Utilitarian discourse forms. "The art of the matter, as far as the creation of facts is concerned, lies in deceiving the reader into thinking that there is no rhetoric . . . that the facts are indeed speaking for themselves" (p. 112). A bit later in his discussion of research writing he writes: "We find the research article, this key product of the knowledge-manufacturing industry, to be a remarkable phenomenon, so cunningly engineered by rhetorical machining that it somehow still gives an *impression* of being but a simple description of relatively untransmuted raw material" (p. 125). The essence of this anti-rhetorical characteristic is that Utilitarian discourse forms should appear to give nothing but information, that they should appear to be making no attempt to influence the listener or the reader except through his or her exercise of rational judgement. This anti-rhetorical feature reflects ideological opposition to the use of authority while at the same time emphasizing the rational, scientific nature of human discourse.

Many other rhetorical traditions do not begin with this assumption that rational argument should eschew rhetoric and deal only in hard facts and plain language. In her analysis of Arabic arguments, for example, Barbara Johnstone (1991) points out that what is regarded as effective writing in this tradition is characterized by elaborate rhetorical and prosodic devices and frequent repetition. What makes such texts persuasive for readers, she says, is not that assertions are "proven" in the kind of syllogistic manner we are familiar with in academic and scientific writing, but that they are presented in ways that resonate with readers and establish the authority of the writer as knowledgeable and articulate.

This rhetorical tradition constructs a very different set of face relationships between writers and readers than the egalitarian relationships constructed by the plain, unadorned writing of the Utilitarian discourse system. Johnstone, in fact, points out that such modes of argumentation are more common in societies which value hierarchical face systems and gives as examples early Judeo-Christian communities as well as Victorian England where, despite the pervasiveness of Utilitarian ideas in commerce and industry, highly rhetorical styles of argumentation flourished in the works of such respected figures as Arnold, Carlyle, and Disraeli. In such traditions, it is the very form of the words and the identity of those who write or utter them rather than the reasons they express that are considered persuasive. In other words, the establishment of a certain kind of relationship through the use of rhetoric is considered more important than simply conveying information in a clear and accurate way.

It is important to acknowledge here, however, that persuasion through repetition and other rhetorical devices is a technique not totally foreign to the Utilitarian discourse system. While it may be relatively rare in academic and scientific writing, it is extremely pervasive in political discourse and commercial advertising.

Positivist-empirical

Utilitarian discourse considers scientific thinking to be the best model for all human thinking and for human discourse. Therefore, as its second characteristic, it emphasizes the features of positivist-empirical psychology while at the same time it plays down the contingent factors of human relationships. When the scientific community began to establish its procedures and practices in the sixteenth and seventeenth centuries, one problem the early scientists faced was how they might "prove" their findings to others. Traditionally, proof was based upon quoting authorities such as Aristotle, but the new scientists insisted that one should reject any evidence but the empirical and positive evidence of his (or her – though women were expected to play little or no role in science during this period) own observations.

Swales (1990) describes the problem faced by Robert Boyle. His experiments with gases required elaborate pumps and other equipment which could not be afforded by very many other observers. Therefore, it was unlikely that anybody else would be able to observe and replicate the experiments which he believed demonstrated the truth of his scientific findings. His solution was to donate the equipment to the Royal Society and to carry out his experiments there under the close observation of his scientific colleagues. He then asked them to sign a roster saying that they agreed with him in his observations.

At the beginning, then, it was assumed that anybody who underwent the same procedures would find the same results, because it was believed that all reality was simply the interaction of the physical universe and universal laws of logic. It was assumed that the role of discourse was to simply state these observations and these results as clearly and directly as possible.

Nevertheless, it was only a short time before the practice which came to be called *virtual witnessing* came into play. In the first place, scientists had cut out the step of having separate individual researchers do the research themselves. Now scientists of the Royal Society and others cut out the step of conducting their experiments before other witnesses. They felt that if they simply narrated the experiment clearly, the logic of the narration would lead inevitably to the same conclusions one would reach if one had gone to the trouble of conducting the experiment oneself. Thus it began to develop that, in fact, the C–B–S style of discourse came to replace actual scientific experimentation.

The important aspect of this positivist-empirical characteristic is that the authority of the person or of personal relationships is played down and is replaced by the authority of the text itself. One believes what is said not because of who is saying or writing it but because of how the text is written. The positivist-empirical text came to replace the authority of even the scientist.

Another important aspect is the underlying assumption that there is an objective reality independent of the way we talk about it and that the purpose of discourse is to reflect that reality as accurately as possible. While for many readers this may seem an uncontroversial assumption, it is at odds both with many traditional non-western views of language and with contemporary postmodernist perspectives which highlight the role of discourse in constructing rather than reflecting reality.

In the Confucian notion of "rectification of names" which we discussed in the last chapter, for instance, this notion that discourse should reflect reality is in fact reversed: it is rather reality which is seen as a reflection of discourse. Disorderly discourse results in disorderly reality. This view of discourse as constituting reality rather than the other way around is not just a matter of ancient Chinese philosophy. It is, in fact, one of the ironies of Chinese intellectual history that the discourse system most strongly opposed to Confucianism, the revolutionary discourse of Mao Zedong, promoted a very similar view of the relationship between discourse and reality. During the revolutionary period in China, and especially during the Great Proletariat Cultural Revolution, a view of discourse was promoted which equated the words of Mao with absolute truth, and where mismatches occurred between this truth and "reality," it was "reality" that was seen to be in need of correction, in the same way that for Confucius the key to remedying a disharmonious political and social reality was to attempt to bring that reality more in line with the fundamental principles and relationships embodied in language.

Gu Yueguo, in his comparison of the discourse of Mao with that of his successor Deng Xiaoping, who instituted the reforms which began contemporary China's increased integration into the Utilitarian discourse system, argues that the greatest difference between these two leaders was that Mao urged the Chinese to match the world to his discourse whereas Deng urged them to match their discourse to the world. Deng saw as essential to China's modernization a reversal of this view of discourse as constituting reality. Rather than attempting to change the world to conform to discourse, Deng urged people to "seek truth from facts" and to rely on "practice" as the "sole criterion of truth" (Deng 1993: 10). While there are important differences between Dengist Utilitarianism and the Utilitarianism of Bentham and Mill, especially in their views of individualism and authority, both share this positivist orientation towards discourse and its relationship to reality.

Finally, associated with this positivist orientation towards discourse is the idea that discourse is, by its nature, a rather neutral and transparent "container" through which ideas can be conveyed from one person to another with a minimum amount of distortion, and, following from this idea, a rather optimistic view of discourse as an appropriate tool for communicating the "truth" and solving problems, whether those problems are scientific, political, economic, interpersonal, or psychological.

The notion that discourse is a kind of container for thought is, as Reddy has pointed out, strongly reflected in the metaphors for communication common in the English language. The most pervasive is what he refers to as the "conduit metaphor" in which ideas are treated as objects and communication is seen as a process of packaging these ideas (in discourse) and sending these packages from one person to another. We speak, for example, of the *contents* of an article, of *putting our ideas into words*, of *trying to get an idea across to someone*, and of someone's words seeming *hollow*.

Related to this deep seated conceptual orientation towards communication is an attitude that regards this traffic of ideas along the conduits of communication between speakers and hearers as an invariably positive phenomenon, in the same way the Utilitarian ideology sees the unencumbered flow of goods and capital among free markets as positive. Communication is not just a way to communicate scientific discoveries: it is a way to solve problems of all kinds, and in so many corners of the Utilitarian discourse system, from politics to business to medicine, the idea that problems are "caused" by poor communication is taken as more or less axiomatic.

Other discourse systems, however, exhibit very different orientations towards communication. In the early 1990s, Suzanne Wong Scollon conducted a study of the metaphors for communication and the self in Cantonese, and found them to differ in many ways from those found in English. Rather than as a "container for ideas," discourse (particularly speech) is often compared to bodily secretions (saliva, excrement), and is not considered a reliable reflection of what a person actually thinks. Discourse is just as likely (if not more likely) to be a carrier of falsehood as it is to be a carrier of truth, and the only way to really understand somebody's thoughts is through direct, non-linguist intuition based on common experiences.

Neither is discourse regarded as a means of solving problems, but rather as the *cause* of problems. In chapter XIX of *The Analects*, Confucius tells his disciples that he prefers not speaking to speaking. When they ask him what they will have to record if he does not speak, he replies, "Does Heaven speak? The four seasons pursue their courses and all things are continually being produced, but does Heaven *say* anything?" (Legge trans.: 326).

The tradition of communication without language which the Japanese call "direct transmission" (*ishin denshin*) has also been strongly influenced by Zen Buddhism. This influence originated in China in the early Tang period (AD 618–907) and has had a major impact on Chinese, Korean, and Japanese societies, even in the modern period. In this tradition of thinking about communication, it is believed that the most important things cannot be communicated in language, that language is only useful for somewhat secondary or trivial messages.

Such differences in attitudes towards communication have also been observed in social psychological studies. Howard Giles and his colleagues (Giles, Coupland, and Wiemann 1992), for example, in a survey of Chinese and U.S. beliefs about talk, found that U.S. respondents were more likely to see talk as pleasant, important, and as a way of controlling what goes on, and reported being uncomfortable with silence, whereas Chinese respondents were more likely to feel less comfortable with talk and more comfortable with silence, characterizing quietness as a way of controlling what goes on.

We must caution, however, against assigning these different orientations towards communication uncritically to particular ethnic groups, nationalities, or the speakers of particular languages. Other discourse systems such as gender and sexuality discourse systems, generational discourse systems, and professional discourse systems may also affect an individual's attitude towards communication, and the kinds of values one associates with discourse may be dramatically different at different times and in different circumstances. A therapist, for example, is likely to have a very different orientation towards talk than a diplomat. In a study of attitudes towards communication and disclosure of Chinese HIV-infected patients in Hong Kong and the Chinese doctors who were attending to them Rodney Jones found that the doctors viewed communication as a way of solving problems and ensuring their patients' emotional well-being, and often complained that their patients did not talk enough, whereas the patients regarded communication as highly problematic, more likely to jeopardize their emotional well-being than enhance it, and often complained that their doctors wanted them to talk too much.

Deductive

We said in chapter 5 that the use of deductive and inductive strategies for the introduction of topics depends on factors having to do with relationships between speaker and listener, or between implied writer and implied reader. When no relationship needs to be established or when the person speaking (or writing) does not need to call upon authority or does not need to establish his or her own authority, then a deductive strategy will be used.

Utilitarian discourse is fundamentally anti-authoritarian as well as anti-rhetorical. As a result, the relationships between participants in this discourse system are played down and the text of the discourse itself comes to have primary authority, as we have just argued. The result of this third characteristic of Utilitarian forms of discourse is that there is an overall preference for the deductive rhetorical strategy for the introduction of topics. There is something anti-rhetorical in this in that the deductive strategy is used whether or not relationships are really an issue. In other words, Utilitarian discourse prefers to act as if human relationships are of little or no consequence. The use of the deductive rhetorical strategy is one effective way in which this apparent (though not necessarily real) situation can be communicated.

As we have already shown, this deductive rhetorical pattern is by no means the preferred pattern outside the Utilitarian discourse system. In chapter 5, for example, we talked about the preference speakers sometimes have for delaying the introduction of the main idea and how this can be seen as a function of the relationship between speaker and hearer or between reader and writer in particular situations. Studies in what has come to be known as contrastive rhetoric have found similar patterns of inductive topic introduction in a range of genres from business letters to school essays written by writers from Chinese, Korean, Japanese, Arabic, Finnish, Spanish, and Czech backgrounds.

At the same time, we should also mention that such studies have been criticized on many of the same grounds we used in the first chapter of this book to problematize the notion of "culture." Assigning particular rhetorical patterns to particular groups of people or to particular languages, it has been pointed out, exhibits a view of languages and cultures as static, homogenous entities and of rhetoric as divorced from politics and power relations between people. Some have even suggested that the whole project of contrastive rhetoric, originating as it did in the West and based on the desire to assign particular rhetorical patterns to "foreign" languages and cultures, is itself a reflection of the ideology of the Utilitarian discourse system, which seeks to construct practices different from its own deductive rhetorical patterns as somehow deviant or deficient.

If studies in contrastive rhetoric have shown anything, they have shown that no language or cultural group can be reduced to a set number of diagrammatic rhetorical patterns that can be applied across the board. While there might be generically or stylistically preferred forms that vary from discourse system to discourse system, these forms also vary from situation to situation within discourse systems. What this means is that sometimes features that are characteristic of one genre in one discourse system may show up as well in another discourse system, but in an altogether different genre, or that certain genres in one discourse system might serve functions that are served by altogether different genres in another. Spence (1992), for example, has noted that some Tang Dynasty poems might best be compared to some twentieth-century British memos which function also as officially placed critiques of the policies of authorities in higher positions. The main point to remember is that claims about contrastive rhetorical patterns always need to take into account the ways various genres are placed in social practice and the ways they are produced, re-produced, and transformed by competing discourse systems.

Individualistic

The fourth characteristic of Utilitarian discourse derives from the emphasis in Utilitarian ideology on the creative individual. J. S. Mill wrote that, "Over himself, over his own body and mind, the individual is sovereign" (1990: 271). A major aspect of this sovereignty of the individual is that it should be demonstrated in discourse. This not only means that the function of language is to aid the individual in reaching his or her own goals (as opposed to helping to create group harmony), but also that the function of language is to allow the individual to enact his or her own unique identity. Thus, in forms of discourse promoted in the Utilitarian discourse system, speakers and writers are meant to avoid set phrases, metaphors, proverbs, and clichés, and strive to make their statements fresh and original. Obelkevich (1987) described this aspect of Utilitarian thought as a reaction to "a culture in which intertextuality was rampant; in which the notion of plagiarism (and the word itself) did not yet exist; in which there was no author's copyright, no property in ideas and no footnotes" (1987: 56). We will have more to say about this issue below. What we want to emphasize here is that there are two sides to this notion of individual creativity: on the one hand there is the insistence that communication must be free – that an individual may say whatever he or she wants – on the other hand there is the dictum that individual expression *must* be original. That is, not only may one be free from the restrictions of social discourse, one must continually show oneself to be free, or *perform* freedom by producing original phrasings and statements.

Donal Carbaugh, in his study of cultural conceptions of discourse and communication in the United States, argues that for many people in that country the whole point of discourse is to publicly enact a unique and individual "self." Not only is there the Utilitarian notion discussed above that communication is an efficient means of self-expression, but there is also the idea that self-expression is a communicative imperative. The *main purpose* of communicating is to constantly re-create the self and to assist others in their task of re-creation. In his analysis of the U.S. talk show *Donahue*, he found that participants consistently spoke of the "self" as a kind of abstract entity separate from the body (including the constraints of things like race, age, and gender) as well as from social structures and institutions, and constructed the act of talking as a means by which to discover one's individual identity, to negotiate one's role in interaction, and to liberate the self from physical or social limitations through expressing unique opinions.

This impetus in discourse to show that one is constantly seeking freedom from the limitations of physical circumstances and social roles contrasts with discourse systems in which the role of discourse is more to ratify one's status as a biological and social being placed within a network of social relationships. In the Confucian discourse system discussed in the last chapter, for example, one's identity as a male or female, as an old person or a young person, as a son or daughter, husband or wife, teacher or student, is not seen as necessarily a threat to the realization or expression of any "true self." In fact, one's role in society *is* one's "true self," rather than some abstract entity which needs to be discovered, reinvented, negotiated, or expressed.

In such discourse systems, there is little of the insistence on discursive originality one finds in the Utilitarian discourse system. Rather, there is often a heavy reliance on set phrases, formulaic language, and commonplace rhetorical devices. Such set phrases have multiple functions in discourse including reinforcing common values in a discourse system, providing writers with opportunities to demonstrate learning or erudition, and providing them with the opportunity to *downplay* their role as individual authors.

Egalitarian

One consequence of the ideological position that individuals are the basis of society is that these individuals must be considered to be equal to each other. As we discussed in the previous chapter and will take up further in the next, this egalitarianism of Utilitarian discourse is not applied to all human beings but only to "those capable of being improved by free and equal discussion" (Mill 1990: 271–2). That is to say this egalitarianism is applied only to members of the Utilitarian discourse system. Within this discourse system, while actual speakers and hearers or writers and readers may have rather unequal positions in their organizations or in society, from the point of view of discourse, they are expected to take the stance of equals.

Such expectations have a profound impact on the style writers are expected to use in their writing. Not only are deductive rhetorical patterns favored, but the burden of understanding is seen to fall to the writer rather than to the reader, compelling the writer to express things as clearly and transparently as possible. Scholars in contrastive rhetoric have long labeled whole "cultures" (or speakers of particular languages) as "reader responsible" and others as "writer responsible," and, although this distinction obscures the fact that there can be substantial variation in the way the burden of understanding is distributed in different genres within the same discourse system (compare, for example, the expectations regarding clarity for a poet as opposed to for the writer of a business letter), there are clear trends within different rhetorical traditions.

It was probably Hinds who first made this distinction in his study of Japanese newspaper discourse, showing that the Japanese texts that he studied made more demands on the reader with respect to coherence than corresponding texts from English publications. Scholars working with Chinese discourse have similarly found a tendency to employ fewer explicit cohesive devices, to use more covert structural clues which require readers to contribute more to establishing connections among different ideas in texts, and to appeal more to history, tradition, and authority, requiring readers to activate certain background knowledge. Studies of Finnish academic writing have also found a more "reader responsible" rhetorical style. In her study of papers by Finnish economists, for example, Mauranen (1993) found that writers used relatively little of the kind of metalanguage typically used by English writers to organize their texts and orient their readers, to the extent that some might consider Finnish academic prose to be "aloof and uncaring toward the reader" (Connor 1996: 51).

Just as with other studies in contrastive rhetoric, it is best to take with a grain of salt studies which associate particular relationships between readers and writers with particular "cultures" or "language groups," remembering that rhetoric is always produced at the nexus of multiple discourse systems. At the same time, such work does give us some indication as to the kinds of factors that might affect whether or not writers construct more egalitarian "writer-responsible" relationships with their readers or more hierarchical "reader-responsible" relationships. One factor has to do with the notion of context, which we discussed in chapter 2. In situations in which there is a strong presumption of shared knowledge, and especially in which such knowledge is seen as a marker of membership within a discourse system, more "reader-responsible" practices might be expected. Such is the case, for example, when writers of literary Chinese make frequent use of "four character expressions" or *cheng yu* which require readers to be familiar not just with the conventional meanings of such expressions but also with the elaborate historical or mythological stories behind them in order to fully grasp the nuances of meaning expressed in their use. Another possible factor is related to the desire or need for a writer to construct a relationship of mutual respect with his or her reader (as opposed to the relationship of solidarity implied by more egalitarian discourse). Mauranen, for example, sees the "reader-responsible" style of Finnish academic prose as a way of not patronizing the reader and of constructing him or her as intelligent, knowledgeable, and patient.

Public (institutionally sanctioned)

Finally, the sixth characteristic of Utilitarian forms of discourse is that they are largely seen as forms of *public* discourse. The consequence is that constant checks have been placed upon discourse, so that only institutionally authorized discourses may get through the filter and become "free speech." Letters to the editor of a newspaper are screened by the editorial staff before publishing, and then only in edited form. Academic articles and books are screened through a process of peer review so that only articles which meet the standards of colleagues will come to actual publication. Most institutions from schools to supermarkets have some process by which notices which are to be put up for display are first screened by some authority for appropriateness. Even on the internet, which is often celebrated as a bastion of free speech, chat rooms, blogs, and internet discussion boards typically have moderators who filter out inappropriate contributions.

This characteristic of the Utilitarian discourse system is often ignored in the enthusiasm for freedom of speech. It should be borne in mind, however, that from the beginning in the seventeenth century down to the present, freedom of speech has meant and continues to mean not absolute freedom for any individual to speak or write to the public at large. It has meant that any individual has the right to submit his or her communications to the scrutiny of this very large array of institutionalized boards and review panels, and that where those communications are judged to meet the standards for "public discourse" they are then allowed to pass on to the public.

In other words, the freedom of expression of the individual depends upon the status of the discourse produced: whether or not that discourse is public or private, and whether or not it is *regarded* as public discourse by the various authorities empowered to make such decisions. To understand this apparent contradiction, we need to revisit the ideas of Immanuel Kant, mentioned briefly in the last chapter.

Kant's view of the "public" writer

In an essay entitled "What is Enlightenment?" (1983), Immanuel Kant took up the problem of what it means for a person to have freedom of expression. His view was that a writer had freedom of expression only in his (or her) public self. By that Kant meant what we have called the implied writer. It is the implied writer who is the public person and who has freedom of expression, not the real writer. This is a very important point when it comes to discussing the notion of freedom in the Utilitarian discourse system. When, in Utilitarian discourse, people refer to "free and equal individuals," they mean free equal individuals in the public sphere. In the private sphere, people may not have the same freedoms and certainly are not equal. As Kant put it, "The public use of one's Reason must always be free, and it alone can bring enlightenment into being among men. The private employment of Reason, however, may often be quite narrowly restricted without posing any special obstacle to the progress of enlightenment" (Kant 1991: 55).

J. S. Mill also put forward the same restriction on where the concept of freedom of speech should apply. In his essay *On Liberty* he wrote:

> No one pretends that actions should be as free as opinions. On the contrary, even opinions lose their immunity when the circumstances in which they are expressed are such as to constitute

their expression a positive instigation to some mischievous act. An opinion that corn-dealers are starvers of the poor, or that private property is robbery, ought to be unmolested when simply circulated through the press, but may justly incur punishment when delivered orally to an excited mob assembled before the house of a corn-dealer, or when handed about among the same mob in the form of a placard. Acts, of whatever kind, which, without justifiable cause, do harm to others, may be, and in the more important cases absolutely require to be, controlled by the unfavourable sentiments, and, when needful, by the active interference of mankind. The liberty of the individual must be thus far limited; he must not make himself a nuisance to other people. (1990: 293)

Whether or not one's discourse is public or private affects not only what one can say or write, but also the kinds of claims one can later make about what one has said or written. In his essay on *The Science of Right*, Kant (1990) describes written discourse as a kind of intellectual property which is owned by the original author (real writer), much in the same way as money is used as an abstract form of exchange. A real writer through an implied writer creates discourse, which can then be sold in the form of a book. The physical book is not the discourse any more than the physical object of the bank note is the wealth it represents. At the same time, the discourse only becomes intellectual property when it is published as a book, that is, when it enters the public sphere. The authors of this book do not own the ideas that they express when they are discussing them casually over coffee, but we can claim ownership of them after these ideas are published. So, even though the "real writers" (Scollon, Scollon, and Jones) are the ones who own the words, this ownership depends on us constructing implied writers (by writing and publishing a text). So, like freedom, ownership of intellectual property in the Utilitarian discourse system depends on the public sphere.

We believe it is important to understand that the connection between the concepts and language of financial exchange and those of communication is not an accidental one. It is not just a matter of convenience that certain styles and forms of discourse have come to symbolize the communication of international business exchanges. Both the communication style and the economic principles were laid out together at the same time in history, and often by the same writers. They are products of exactly the same psychology, philosophy, and worldview.

Plagiarism and ideology

This idea of discourse as a form of property is so central to the Utilitarian discourse system, so unique to it that it is worth spending some time teasing out its implications and contrasting it to the position taken in other discourse systems, particularly since, for most of the readers of this book, students and teachers in universities, questions of the ownership of discourse play an important role in their professional lives. Plagiarism is often cited by professors in universities in the United States and other western countries as a particularly persistent problem of students from abroad, especially from East Asian countries. Furthermore, the internet and digital technology are often blamed for an alleged increase in incidences of plagiarism in universities and the "fact" that "kids today" do not respect intellectual property. The issue of plagiarism, then, provides a useful window on how theories about discourse vary not just between those already in the Utilitarian discourse system and those seeking to enter it from other discourse systems, but also between generational discourse systems within the Utilitarian discourse system.

Most contemporary discussions of plagiarism tend to fall into one of two extremes; they are either overly polemical or overly relativistic. Discussions of the polemical variety usually condemn the plagiarist as either wicked or incompetent, based on the assumption that what is and what is not plagiarism is in some way straightforward and self-evident and that nobody in their right mind would consider defending such a practice. Discussions of the relativistic nature tend to go to the opposite extreme, attributing such practices to "culture" and imply-ing that the plagiarist (especially if he or she is from a country different from our own) is neither wicked nor incompetent, but simply "can't help it." Such arguments inevitably lead to sloppy thinking and stereotypes like, "In Chinese plagiarism is allowed." We believe that neither of these positions takes into account the complexity of the discursive practices that are involved in establishing our relationship with the words that we write or say, no matter what "culture" we belong to, and how dependent these practices are on different kinds of social relationships and different kinds of circumstances of communication.

The concept of plagiarism as it is currently constructed in courts and in classrooms is by no means a universal concept. It is, as we have said above, the result of a particular ideology. At the same time, we do not wish in any way to encourage those reading this book to dis-regard conventions of academic citation or rules governing intellectual property promul-gated by the schools they attend or the legal systems of the countries in which they live. Mastering these conventions and upholding these rules are important ways in which to show one is able to competently participate in the Utilitarian discourse system, and performing such competence will be, for most readers of this book, extremely important for their future careers.

Perhaps the biggest problem with the notion of plagiarism is that it is almost impossible to speak or write without using the words or ideas of others. Communication is characterized much more by the recycling of old ideas and ways of saying things than by the invention of new ones. As the Soviet literary critic Mikhail Bakhtin (1986/1936) has famously pointed out, none of the words we utter are truly our own – whenever we speak or write we neces-sarily borrow the words of others. Every utterance is *heteroglossic*, populated by the voices of numerous others who have used similar phrases and expressed similar ideas before us.

Even Locke himself expressed considerable skepticism regarding the idea of individual originality. In *An Essay Concerning Human Understanding* he wrote:

> Men having been accustomed from their cradles to learn words which are easily got and retained, before they knew or had framed the complex ideas to which they were annexed, or which were to be found in the things they were thought to stand for, they usually continue to do so all their lives; and without taking the pains necessary to settle in their minds determined ideas, they use their words for such unsteady and confused notions as they have, contenting themselves with the same words other people use. . . . Men take the words they find in use amongst their neighbors; and that they may not seem ignorant what they stand for, use them confidently, without much troubling their heads about a certain fixed meaning; whereby, besides as in such discourses they seldom are in the right, so they are as seldom to be convinced that they are in the wrong. ([1690] 1990: 292)

What Bakhtin meant when he said that our utterances are "filled with the words of others" is not that at heart we are all plagiarists or, as Locke implied, that our appropriation of the words of others is a sign of laziness. What he really meant is that communication is always a matter of *dialogue*. Whenever we speak or write, we are, either consciously or uncon-sciously, appropriating the words of others and positioning ourselves in certain kinds of relationships to those words and to the people from whom they were appropriated. From this perspective, the question is not whether or not people in a particular discourse system "respect intellectual property," but rather what the different conventions and expectations within different discourse systems are for enacting these relationships.

The American sociologist Erving Goffman noted that whenever we speak we are in some way juggling three roles, each with a different relationship to the words we are speaking: We may take up the role of *animator*, of *author*, or of *principal*. Although Goffman formulated these roles in relation to speech, they are equally relevant to the written word.

The *animator* is the person who is actually speaking or writing, the person responsible for physically articulating the words. Whether or not one has the right to animate the words of others and how one is meant to do so is complex and highly dependent upon social context. In workplaces, for example, the role of animator is often taken up by rather low-level clerical staff. In the publishing world in most countries the role is legally reserved for publishers with valid contractual agreements with writers, but later delegated to printers who are rarely directly involved with the writers whose words they are printing. Presidents and other political figures often allow their positions to be animated by press secretaries, and the words of corporate leaders may be animated by the writers of press releases, and then reanimated by newspaper reporters who often publish these press releases verbatim as "news" without any attempt to attribute the words to the original animator, much less to the individuals whose thoughts they represent.

Rights to animation, then, are often a matter of institutional and professional practices that may vary widely among corporate and professional discourse systems. Allan Bell (1991), for example, has pointed out that what might be called plagiarism in academic contexts is regarded as common practice among journalists. A large proportion of what is passed off by newspapers as authored by a particular journalist is actually the animation of the words of press officers working for public relations companies, corporations, or government departments. Furthermore, it is common practice in preparing such press releases for public relations professionals to use a press release previously authored for another purpose as a "template" and often to cut and paste information rather liberally from the internet and other sources.

The frequency, even within the Utilitarian discourse system, with which writers are called upon to animate the words of others without attribution, then, highlights the complicated and highly contingent nature of authorial ownership.

While sorting out the relationship of the *animator* to the words he or she is speaking or writing is sometimes tricky, distinguishing between the roles of *author* and *principal* is also highly problematic. Goffman defines the *author* as the person who actually selects and combines the words in a text to express a particular sentiment. At the same time, such persons are not always the originators of the ideas and sentiments that they are expressing and sometimes do not even share these sentiments. One need only think back to the press officers discussed above who often do not personally harbor the same degree of enthusiastic positive regard for the product or the company they are writing about as they express in their press releases. The person whose views are actually being expressed is the *principal*, the person who takes "ultimate responsibility" for what is written, but often this person is difficult to identify, and sometimes it is not a person at all but some complex combination of bureaus and committees, as it is with most governmental discourse. Who is ultimately responsible for the words written in a press release? Is it the public relations company that produced the release or the company that hired the PR company to handle the campaign?

Who in these companies can we point to as principals? Legally the responsible person is the CEO, but it is actually rare in large corporations for CEOs to be involved in such mundane affairs as deciding what ideas and sentiments should be expressed in run of the mill press releases.

In academic discourse within the Utilitarian discourse system it is usually assumed that the principal and the author are the same person unless otherwise stated. When this person expresses ideas that originated with other people, he or she is expected to indicate the *principalship* of these ideas, and especially when the words of others are appropriated, he or she is expected to indicate through various conventions that these words are being animated, and that authorship belongs to another. The academic writer, in the service of constructing an argument by using the ideas and words of other principals and authors, must master various techniques for indicating his or her stance toward these words and ideas, often in very subtle ways such as using different kinds of verbs like *note*, *report*, *claim*, and *allege* to describe what other authors were doing when they wrote their words and how the writer feels about what they were doing.

This system, complicated enough for students and novice academics, becomes even more complicated in cases like the present one where more than one author is involved. In such cases, all sorts of possibilities present themselves. In cases where doctoral students publish with their supervisors, for example, all of the research and much of the writing is usually done by the student, though the article may gain a certain weight of authority through the fact that the supervisor has taken up the role of principal. In the case of this book, the person who is presently writing these words is Rodney Jones. Later, they will pass though the hands of Suzanne Wong Scollon who will no doubt amend them, and after that they may be further amended by colleagues, editors, and proofreaders before finally being published. Many of the ideas being expressed originated with Ron Scollon, who himself derived them from his reading of Erving Goffman. Ron, however, although he might be considered the primary principal, being no longer with us, has no control over how his ideas, previously expressed in lectures, conversations, and other writings, are presently being presented and, in some cases altered and distorted, any more than Erving Goffman had any control over what Ron did with his ideas. Thus, even though the elaborate system of attribution in academic prose is designed to preserve scholars' "ownership" over their words and ideas, one rarely has the same kinds of control over what happens to one's words as one does over other things one owns like cars or houses which one can secure against trespassers or thieves and bequeath intact to one's relatives after death.

These practices, of course, are quite different in other professions like journalism and, even within the profession of journalism, practices may vary from country or country, language to language, medium to medium, and publication to publication. In a comparative study of attribution of authorship across three media (newspaper, radio, and television) conducted by Ron Scollon and his colleagues in Hong Kong in the early 1990s (Li et al. 1993), it was found that while English newspaper accounts were presented under the authorship of specific individuals and English television and radio accounts were often attributed to particular reporters, Chinese versions of the same stories produced under nearly identical conditions were presented as the work of anonymous editors or broadcasting companies. In both cases, principalship of the facts being reported was carefully managed through the same kinds of reporting verbs used by academics.

The point of this rather lengthy discussion has been to emphasize that the concept of plagiarism as articulated by the Utilitarian discourse system actually disguises the complexity that is involved in actual communication by promoting the notion that the unmarked state of affairs is that animator, author, and principal speak as the same person: this is clearly not the case. Who has the right to use discourse and how they are supposed to represent it is highly context specific and embedded within a matrix of overlapping and inter-nested discourse systems and social practices. How the Utilitarian discourse system grants such privileges, therefore, has less to do with protecting the sanctity of individual ideas and more to do with preserving a historically established system for the distribution of social power and privilege, a system which, as we will discuss below, is undergoing profound changes in the modern (or should we say, postmodern) world of word-processing, emails, weblogs, twitter feeds, and massively multiplayer online games.

Modes, Media, and the Materiality of Discourse

It should be obvious from the discussion above that the development of copyright laws within the Utilitarian discourse system cannot be separated from the material economic conditions surrounding it or from the physical materiality of the printed page which made possible the commodification of discourse. The development of the notion of copyright began with the spread of the technology of printing in the late fifteenth century. By the sixteenth century, European governments began regulating what could be printed, and in 1557, The Stationers' Company was established in England, shortly afterwards achieving a practical monopoly over publishing in the country. According to legal historian Lyman Ray Patterson (1968), the word *plagiarism* first came into use in 1701 in the records of this company. The purpose of the concept was to limit competition among members of the company, not to protect the commercial rights of authors. Aside from avarice, what made this possible was the technology of printing itself, and the concentration of this technology in the hands of a few people.

What this story tells us is that the *materiality* of the preferred forms of discourse in a particular discourse system plays a major role in how those forms of discourse can be used to promote the ideology of that discourse system and to regulate its preferred face systems. When we speak of the materiality of discourse, we are chiefly concerned with three things: mode, medium, and the emplacement of discourse in the material world.

Mode

Throughout this book we have emphasized communication in speaking and in writing, and yet we realize that much communication takes place without the use of words. The way a person dresses for a meeting, for example, may suggest to other participants how he or she is prepared to participate in it, and the graphics, layout, and embedded video in a webpage might carry as much if not more meaning than the text. In fact, we can use virtually any aspect of behavior or presentation which others can perceive as a means of communication. This would include our posture, our movements, our attire, our use of space, and our use of time.

The concept of mode as we are using it here should not be confused with the concept of modality in grammar which we briefly touched upon in chapters 4 and 6. What we mean by mode here is any conventionally recognized semiotic system such as speech, writing, color, taste, or the design of images. Some modes, such as speech, posture, gaze, and gesture, can be considered "embodied modes" in that we must use our physical bodies to produce them. Others like images, writing, and architectural layout can be considered "disembodied modes." Different modes allow us to make different kinds of meaning. There are things that we can express in pictures, for instance, that we cannot express in words, and vice versa. In other words, different modes bring to communication different sets of "affordances" and "constraints." From the perspective of interdiscourse communication, the important thing about modes of communication is that different discourse systems might favor different modes or combinations of modes, and that they might use and interpret these modes differently.

The fact that different discourse systems might favor different modes of communication is no small matter. Since the mode we use affects both how we can communicate and what we can communicate, modes of communication can have a profound effect on how we view the world and how we organize our social relationships. Perhaps the best example of this is the distinction between what have been called "oral cultures" and "literate cultures." According to Walter Ong (1982), the shift from oral communication to communication dominated by writing engendered fundamental changes in the way people thought and organized their social relationships. While orality favored the development of faculties of memory and an orientation towards discourse as something social, immediately engaging, and even sacred, literacy allowed people to generate ideas, store them, and retrieve them as needed across time in a highly efficient and accurate way, giving rise to modes of thinking favoring abstract reasoning and problem solving and making possible advances in science, philosophy, history, and politics. New technologies like television and radio, Ong further argues, are promoting a new kind of orality, which he calls "secondary orality" in which some of the immediacy and interactivity of oral modes of communication are again becoming central.

Another example involves the importance accorded to images in particular discourse systems and the relationship that is set up in discourse between pictures and the written word. Before the development of the printing press, texts and images regularly appeared together in illuminated manuscripts prepared by monks. Similarly, ancient China had a strong tradition of integrating painting, poetry, calligraphy, and seals, especially in the Song and Tang Dynasties. With the development of the printing press, however, images and words were, at least until advances in lithography, separated, with words taking on a certain air of authority and seriousness to the extent that in Europe and North America in the nineteenth and early twentieth centuries only books published for children and less proficient readers, or for specialist readers like students of anatomy, could be expected to contain pictures. This situation began to change with the development of photography and the practice of photojournalism, and by the mid-twentieth century, images had taken on a new authority, linked not just to print and broadcast journalism, but also to evidentiary practices of law enforcement agencies. Today, with the rise of the internet and digital media, images have become even more central to texts: for most internet web pages, visual elements like pictures, layout, color, and fonts are just as important if not more important than the propositional content of the words.

Different orientations towards images and words, however, are not just a matter of historical trajectories. The rhetorical traditions of different discourse systems also promote different ways of using words and pictures and different values associated with their use.

The Islamic artistic tradition, for example, tends to favor calligraphy and repetitious floral or vegetal designs over figurative images, which have been interpreted as inherently idolatrous, and prohibitions on the visual depiction of Mohammed remain strong in many Islamic communities.

The non-verbal modes that we use when we are engaged in face to face interaction with people usually go under the label "non-verbal communication." While there are many kinds of non-verbal communication that are important in interdiscourse communication, the three we are most concerned with are: the movements of our bodies (called kinesics), our use of space (called proxemics), and our use of time. We have already dealt with these modes to some degree in chapter 2 when we discussed the grammar of context, and we would like to reiterate the warning we gave then, which applies equally to the analysis of all modes of communication: while participants in different discourse systems might exhibit different patterns in the way they use particular modes of communication, they are also likely to vary their behavior substantially based on the different kinds of communicative situations in which they find themselves. In other words, participation in a discourse system alone is not an accurate way to predict how a person might communicate in any given circumstance.

Media

Modes are clearly distinguished from *media*, which are the physical or material carriers of modes (for example, paper, telephones, television, computers, mobile telephones, and the like). For example, while dress would be considered a mode (a system governing the combination of various semiotic elements involving color, shape, and texture and their placement on a human body), clothing is a medium, the physical means through which this system is expressed. Like modes, media also impose certain affordances and constraints as to the kinds of meanings that can be made with discourse and the forms of social organization it can support. Rather than neutral conduits for messages, media actively shape our perception of phenomena, our relationships with those with whom we communicate, the meanings we can make, and the actions we can take.

In the 1960s, Canadian scholar Marshall McLuhan captured this ability of media to shape our experience of reality in his now famous slogan: "the medium is the message." McLuhan, however, was hardly the first to observe this phenomenon. Back in the early 1950s, the communication scholar Howard Innis noted that all media involve some kind of "bias" in terms of how they affect our perception of space and time.

Despite the popularity of McLuhan's position, we will not go quite so far. While media clearly have an important effect on how we perceive the world and make meaning, the overarching role McLuhan gives to media at the expense of other aspects of communication to us smacks of technological determinism. Furthermore, members of different discourse systems may use media differently and assign different values to it. We would rather, therefore, use the concept of *mediation* developed by Soviet psychologist Lev Vygotsky. For Vygotsky, all action in the world is indirect – mediated by various tools which have the effect of either *amplifying* or *constraining* certain social actions. The use of media is, he says, the hallmark of human consciousness and learning: the emergence of higher mental processes is grounded in the phenomenon of mediation. Therefore, media and media use provide a link between social and cultural processes and individual mental processes. Because mental functioning is carried out by mediational means provided by the society, all thought is essentially social. At the same time, individuals appropriate and adapt mediational means for particular concrete purposes. Therefore, the relationship between individual consciousness and the mediational means provided by society is always dialectical, media acting to both amplify and limit actions, and individuals constantly adapting media to fit the contingencies of particular circumstances and goals.

An example of this tension between what media enable us to do and what we are able to do with them can be seen in the ways the Utilitarian discourse system is dealing with challenges to intellectual property in the age of digital reproduction. As we noted above, the advent of copyright laws really depended on the technology of the printing press which, as Ong (1982) argues, "created a new sense of the private ownership of words" (p. 131). Computers have, in some sense, had the opposite effect. Because they make it so easy to reproduce words and images and distribute them to a large number of people, digital technologies are undermining this sense of the private ownership of discourse. In other words, digital technologies have created a dilemma for the Utilitarian discourse system insofar as forms of discourse are concerned. In some ways the computer, with its roots in Charles Babbage's nineteenth-century "analytical engine," a machine he believed would eliminate "human error" in the calculation of tables of numbers, is the quintessential machine of the Utilitarian discourse system. Not only does it make possible complex calculations, but it also facilitates the free flow of information separated from its physical and social contexts, thus making possible the free flow of economic goods and services at a rate never before seen. Finally, some would argue that the internet and digital technologies have also made possible a kind of vast electronic *panopticon*, allowing governments and corporations to dramatically increase their ability to monitor the activities of citizens and customers. At the same time, however, because it alters the materiality of discourse and the ways it is distributed, the computer disturbs the important Utilitarian boundaries between public and private and individualistic and collective.

First, the internet allows producers of discourse to bypass many of the traditional gatekeeping mechanisms put into place by the Utilitarian discourse system to sanction public discourse – anyone with a computer and an internet connection can create a website or a blog. Second, because it makes the appropriation, altering, and redistribution of texts so easy, it threatens regimes of intellectual property which depended on the materiality of texts and the physical limitations on their exchange. Finally, Web 2.0 technologies that make it possible for readers to comment on and even alter texts they find on the internet, have threatened the status of the autonomous Utilitarian author. Practices of "linking," "embedding," and "remixing" are making it more and more difficult to discern exactly where a particular text (or a particular author) begins and ends.

It remains to be seen exactly how the Utilitarian discourse system will resolve this dilemma. So far two types of solutions have been pursued, both characteristically Utilitarian. First, governments and copyright owners have pursued a legal strategy, passing legislation that dramatically extends the reach of copyright laws in terms of what they cover and how long texts are kept out of the public domain. Second, corporations, governments, and other institutions have pursued technological solutions in the form of software which, for example, facilitates the buying and selling of intellectual property and scans the internet for violations of copyright, and embeds computer code into texts to make them more difficult to copy and redistribute.

One of the best examples of these technological solutions can be seen in the widespread use in colleges and universities of plagiarism detection software, which automatically compares students' writing to a large database of texts in order to detect instances of "copying." What is interesting about this solution is the degree to which it promotes the Utilitarian view of discourse as decontextualized information easily separated from the web of human relationships that have given rise to it. Our earlier discussion of plagiarism and the complexities involved in managing the relationship among principals, authors, and animators of words and ideas in different discourse systems should make readers question the simple yes-or-no framework with which such software approaches the detection of plagiarism. One further difficulty with such systems, however, is that while purporting to instill in students a respect for intellectual property, they may actually be violating students' intellectual property rights by automatically making texts submitted to the system part of the database which they offer to users as a commercial product.

Emplacement

The final aspect of the materiality of forms of discourse we would like to consider has to do with where discourse is located in the material world, what we are calling *emplacement*. All discourse is to some degree *indexical*; that is, it takes its meaning partially from the physical circumstances of its use and its relationship to those circumstances. A stop sign, for example, has a different meaning depending on whether it is placed at a busy intersection, in the warehouse of a municipal highways department or on the wall in a teenager's bedroom. Rules governing indexicality of discourse, the way it derives meaning from its physical emplacement, are far from universal. Different discourse systems have their own rules about when and where certain forms of discourse may appropriately appear and how their appearance in these different places may affect the kinds of meanings that can be made and the kinds of social relationships that are promoted.

In their 2003 book *Discourses in Place: language and the material world*, Ron and Suzie Wong Scollon point out, for example, that while the appearance of writing on mountainsides and rock faces in parks and wilderness areas in North America would doubtless be regarded as transgressive, compromising the natural beauty of the surroundings, scriptural passages and the names of the Buddha and Bodhisattvas carved and painted on hillsides and mountains in China and other Asian countries are not only considered acceptable, but are also regarded as *part of* the natural beauty of the surroundings. Similarly, any first time visitor to Hong Kong cannot help but notice the plethora of shop signs and advertisements which cover the facades of nearly every building and even extend from metal braces out into the street. This urban landscape provides a stark contrast to places like Georgetown in Washington, DC, and many northern European cities where there are strict regulations on the emplacement of discourse in public and signage is kept to a minimum.

Such differences in attitudes about the emplacement of discourse can to some extent be understood with reference to what we have said previously about the different functions of discourse in different discourse systems. For some discourse systems, such as the Utilitarian discourse system, discourse is regarded chiefly as information which can often be easily transported from one context to another without altering its meaning. In fact, for the Utilitarian discourse system, one measure of the *value* of a piece of discourse is the degree to which it can be separated from the context of its creation and "stand alone" in some other context; this was the whole point of the practice of "virtual witnessing" described above. An exception to this is when the piece of discourse provides information about a particular physical locale, as in the case of street signs and traffic signals, and it is the emplacement of such informational forms of discourse in public that is most likely to be considered legitimate in the regime of the Utilitarian discourse system.

In other discourse systems, however, emplacement is much more crucial for certain forms of discourse. That is, these forms of discourse take much of their meaning from their relationship with their surroundings. In the case of scriptural verses inscribed on the rock faces of sacred Buddhist mountains in China, for instance, the meaning and the function of the discourse depends crucially on where it is placed. Furthermore, such discourse is not placed in a particular spot in order to give readers information about that place, but rather to demonstrate a certain relationship among the place, the producers of the discourse, and certain transcendental beings that supposedly reside there.

Just as digital technologies are altering our understanding of the ownership of discourse, they are also dramatically changing the relationship between discourse and the contexts in which it is situated. With the advent of computers, not to mention mobile telephones and computing devices, forms of discourse are becoming increasingly unmoored from the places where they traditionally occurred. With email, instant messaging, and social networking, forms of discourse traditionally associated with work are intruding more and more into the home, and forms of discourse associated with play and social life are intruding into workplaces. With the increased use of mobile telephones, forms of discourse, such as intimate conversations between lovers, which before were restricted to more private places, are migrating into public spaces like buses and shopping malls. At the same time, by introducing forms of discourse into places where they were not previously present, these technologies are also altering the kinds of social interactions and social relationships associated with these places. Rodney Jones, for example, has shown how, when computers are placed in traditional classroom settings, they alter the relationship between teachers and students as well as participants' understanding of what constitutes the context of the interaction. As GPS technology becomes more advanced, to the extent that one's exact location can be transmitted over one's mobile telephone when one sends a message or a contribution to a social networking site, emplacement is becoming not just a matter of the way discourse is embedded into places, but also the way places are embedded into discourse.

Researching Interdiscourse Communication

In previous chapters we have suggested ways that written and spoken texts might be collected and analyzed based on the key social actions the people you are studying engage in at a particular site of investigation. We have explored how texts and talk might be analyzed for the ways they encode social relationships (face systems) and the ways they encode ideologies. In this chapter we have discussed how the ways that people construct and use texts reveals something about their underlying understanding of the role of communication in social life and of the relationship speakers and writers should have to the words they speak and write.

There are a number of ways to go about studying forms of discourse and their role in discourse systems. The most obvious is to simply observe how different kinds of texts are used in different situations by different people. This should begin with a process of cataloguing the different kinds of discourse available to people in your site of investigation and observing in a very concrete way how people engage with these various forms of discourse, which may include printed texts of various kinds such as novels, newspapers, magazines, tickets, certificates, shop signs and other advertisements, transgressive texts such as graffiti, spoken texts like conversations, speeches, debates, and lectures, and technologically mediated forms of discourse such as television shows, movies, radio broadcasts, web pages, YouTube videos, and Facebook newsfeeds. In fact, any situation you analyze is likely to include multiple forms of discourse arranged in what we have elsewhere called "semiotic aggregates." And so one of the first questions the analyst must ask is: which of these forms of discourse are actually significant? Which of them are actually being attended to by participants? Which of them are actually being appropriated to take social actions?

Once you have identified the forms of discourse that seem important to your participants, you can begin asking questions about how these forms of discourse are being used. Are they, for example, individually or collectively produced? Do people read, view, or listen to them in groups or in isolation? Are they only available to some people and not to others? Are they attended to closely or in a more cursory fashion?

Many of these initial observations will focus primarily on the materiality of forms of discourse, the modes they make use of, the media through which they are conveyed, and how they are situated in the physical world. Are the forms of discourse people use primarily verbal or non-verbal? How do verbal and non-verbal modes interact? How do the media through which discourse is transmitted affect the ways meaning can be made? How important are the context and emplacement of these forms of discourse to their meaning? And finally, how do these material aspects of forms of discourse end up enabling or encouraging certain kinds of actions and constraining or discouraging other kinds?

After this initial round of observations, we are ready to consider the role that these various forms of discourse play in social relationships. Do people use them primarily to convey information or to communicate about their social roles, status, or attitude towards each other? Does using these forms of discourse confer certain rights or responsibilities for communication on those who are using them? Are they used to promote the individual goals and interests of particular people or of a wider group of people? In many institutional settings like schools and offices, this stage of the analysis may involve trying to understand the role discourse plays in practices of "gatekeeping" – in other words, how discourse is used as a means to exclude certain people from certain social actions.

Finally you will want to analyze samples of each of these forms of discourse more closely, examining, for example, the rhetorical patterns they exhibit and other clues they might contain as to participants' underlying theories of communication. Is the information presented in an inductive or a deductive way? What kinds of relationships do the texts construct between their producers and their consumers? How is authorship attributed, and how are words, images, or ideas taken from other texts represented? Finally, does the text contain any metaphors or other rhetorical devices that convey something about the stance the producers of the discourse are taking up towards it or towards the act of communicating in general?

Discussion Questions

1   List the different forms of discourse used in a particular setting such as a school, an office, or a shop. Discuss how these forms of discourse reflect the social goals, the social relationships, and the ideologies of the people in these settings.

2 Look at the pieces of discourse below and discuss the degree to which they communicate information or relationship, the kinds of relationship they create between authors and readers (ratified or negotiated), and whether or not they promote individual welfare or group harmony.

(a) This is a Non-Smoking Campus (from a sign on a university campus)
(b) Just Do It! (from a Nike advertisement)
(c) Smoking Kills (from a cigarette package)
(d) A: hihi
    B: hihi
    A: ^_^
    B: :P
    A: kaka~~~ (from an MSN messenger conversation)
(e) Christopher Chan and three others like this (from Facebook)
(f) To the extent permitted by law our aggregate liability to you, whether for breach of these terms or in negligence or in any other tort or for any other common law or statutory cause of action arising in relation to these terms, the Site or the Content is limited to 100 Hong Kong dollars. (from a corporate website)

References for Further Study

Readers interested in studies of contrastive rhetoric are directed to Ulla Connor's 1996 book *Contrastive Rhetoric: cross-cultural aspects of second-language writing* as well as her more recent volume *Contrastive Rhetoric: reaching to intercultural rhetoric* edited with Ed Nagelhout and William Rozycki. For a detailed study of rhetoric in Arabic discourse see Barbara Johnstone's 1991 book *Repetition in Arabic Discourse: paradigms, syntagms and the ecology of language*. Swales' discussion of the evolution of the practice of *virtual witnessing* as well as a wealth of other pertinent information on scientific and academic discourse can be found in his 1990 classic *Genre Analysis: English in academic and research settings*. Jonathan Spence's 1990 *The Search for Modern China* contains a great deal of useful information on forms of discourse in China since the dynastic period, as does his 1992 collection of essays *Chinese Roundabout: essays in history and culture*, and Gu Yueguo's 2001 paper "The changing orders of discourse in a changing China" describes the way forms of discourse in China have changed since the mid-twentieth century. On the difference between Ancient Greek rhetoric and Ancient Chinese rhetoric, see *Thinking through Confucius* by David Hall and Roger Ames (1987). Reddy's 1979 paper "The conduit metaphor – a case of frame conflict in our language about language" is the source of much of the material on western metaphors for communication, and Suzanne Scollon's 1997 article "Metaphors of self and communication in English and Cantonese" is the source of the material on Chinese metaphors. The material on U.S. attitudes towards communication comes from the work of Donal Carbaugh, particularly his 1989 book *Talking American: cultural discourses on Donahue*. The material on plagiarism comes from a number of published works of Ron Scollon, among them his 1995 paper "Plagiarism and ideology," and the distinction among *animator*, *author*, and *principal* which informs this work comes from Goffman's 1981 book *Forms of Talk*. Readers wishing to learn more about ways of analyzing non-verbal modes of communication are directed to the book *Reading Images: the grammar of visual design* by Gunther Kress and Theo van Leeuwen, first published in 1996, and Sigrid Norris's 2004 *Analyzing Multimodal Interaction: a methodological framework*. More on the relationship between discourse and how it is situated in the material world can be found in Ron Scollon and Suzie Wong Scollon's 2003 *Discourses in Place: language in the material world*. An analysis of the effect of computers on the physical contexts of their use can be found in Rodney Jones's 2004 paper "The problem of context in computer mediated communication."

8

Socialization

The Individual and "Culture"

So far we have discussed how people organize their social relationships and display intimacy with or power over each other (*face systems*). We have also talked about various practices of speaking, writing, and non-verbal communication that grow up within groups and the theories of communication that underpin these practices (*forms of discourse*). And we have explored the larger belief systems and assumptions about right and wrong, normal and abnormal, and the role of human beings in the world which these face systems and forms of discourse reflect and reinforce (*ideologies*). In this chapter we will turn our attention to the question of how individuals come to take up and gain mastery over these discursive practices, integrate themselves into their social relationships, and come to believe in, or at least identify with, the ideologies of the discourse systems in which they participate. To what extent do individuals from China or the United States, Korea, Britain, Australia, or Singapore, men or women, teachers or doctors, gays or straights personally represent the beliefs and practices associated with the discourse systems in which they participate, and what difference does this make to their ability to communicate with people who participate in different discourse systems?

As we have indicated before, the question of the relationship between the individual and the "cultures" or discourse systems he or she participates in is perhaps the most difficult issue we have to address in the study of intercultural communication. One reason for this is that none of us are members of only one "culture": throughout our lives we are socialized into multiple discourse systems, and sometimes mastering the face systems and forms of discourse of one of our discourse systems or upholding its ideology creates conflicts with other discourse systems that we participate in. Another reason, related to the first, is that mastery of the face systems and forms of discourse of any particular discourse system can never be complete, and belief in a particular ideology can never be total. In other words, socialization into a particular discourse system is always to some degree partial, and participation in discourse systems is always to some degree peripheral.

Intercultural Communication: A Discourse Approach, Third Edition. Ron Scollon, Suzanne Wong Scollon, Rodney H. Jones.
© 2012 John Wiley & Sons, Inc. Published 2012 by John Wiley & Sons, Inc.

Socialization

It is an oversimplification to say that whereas animals have instinct, human beings have culture. Nevertheless, while the exact proportion of inborn, innate behavior to learned, cultural behavior will probably always be debated, most scholars would agree that human beings are born with fewer preset patterns than other animals. What this means is that human beings must begin at birth what is a life-long process of learning how to be human beings. We will use the general term "socialization" to refer to this process of learning.

Technical definitions of all of the terms relating to learning how to participate in a particular discourse system are difficult to establish, since in different fields, such as psychology, sociology, and anthropology, they are used somewhat differently. For our purposes, four terms in addition to "socialization" will be sufficient for a general understanding of how we learn to be members of particular groups and how we gain mastery over particular systems of discourse: education, enculturation, acculturation, and participation.

Education, enculturation, acculturation

The most important distinction to be made is between what we might call formal and informal means of teaching and learning. While both education and socialization have been used for both forms of learning, we will use the word "education" for formal teaching and learning, and "socialization" (or "enculturation") for informal teaching and learning.

When a person takes up employment in a new company, he or she might be in doubt about the way employees are supposed to dress for work in the office. It is possible that the company would have a handbook in which such things as a code of dress would be specified. In that case we would call that formal education. In the business context it would normally be called training and would probably consist of a formal orientation session, in which the handbook would be introduced, new employees would be guided through the main points, and questions they might have would be answered.

On the other hand, the issue of dress might not be mentioned at all, but when the new employee arrives in the office for the first day of work he or she might notice that there is some difference in the way he or she is dressed and the way others in the office are dressed. It is quite likely that this new employee will take this into consideration and make some changes for the next day at work. Such a process of just looking around to see what others are doing and then trying to match their behavior we would want to call socialization.

It should be obvious that in most cultures the first learning of children is socialization, not education. That is, they are not given explicit training in behavior through rules, guided practice, testing, and other forms of formal assessment. They look around at what others are doing, and others make comments which indicate whether or not they approve.

While in the case of infants there is little to distinguish between the words "socialization" and "enculturation," in most cases the word "enculturation" is restricted just to the early learning of culture. It is what in the next section we will call "primary socialization." When a person learns a new job through observation of the actions of others and through their informal approval or disapproval, it would be best to call that sort of learning socialization rather than enculturation, as it applies largely to adult behavior.

The distinction between education and socialization, then, is based upon whether or not the procedures for teaching and learning are formally worked out by the group or the society and systematically applied to new members (whether those new members are just born into the society or enter it later in life). The concept of education is most often associated with what sociologists have called *Gesellschaft*, whereas socialization is more often associated with *Gemeinschaft*. This is not a hard and fast distinction; many societies which sociologists consider traditional communities have clearly formal practices of education. Nevertheless, historically from eighteenth-century Europe on there has been a clear association of the rapidly increasing *Gesellschaft* structures of the Utilitarian discourse system and the rapid rise of universal formal public education in those societies which have embraced Utilitarian forms of discourse (see below).

Another aspect of the distinction between education and socialization is that education tends to be periodic or formally structured into units of instruction, what educators call "scope and sequence," whereas socialization tends to be continuous. The units of instruction in education tend to have entrance or admission procedures and requirements as well as exit requirements and ceremonies, along with completion credentials. On the other hand, it would be difficult to say in the process of socialization just when one is actually engaged in learning. As a result, there is often a corresponding devaluation of the learning one acquires through socialization and an exaggerated valuation of learning acquired through formal education.

A third point is that education and socialization are often, perhaps nearly always, mixed. For example, in entering a new position, a person might receive specific training as we have mentioned above through handbooks and manuals of company procedures, while at the same time being expected to observe the general practices of older and more experienced employees and to follow their behavior.

Finally, we want to briefly comment on the term "acculturation." Anthropologists and sociologists have used this term to talk about situations in which two different "cultural" or social groups come into contact. When one group is more powerful than the other and therefore produces a strong influence on that second group to forget or put aside its own culture and to adopt that of the more powerful group, that process of enforced "cultural" learning is called acculturation. Generally speaking, acculturation is used as a negative term, since the process of cultural loss is considered by analysts to be an unfortunate one.

Primary and secondary socialization

We have one further terminological complication to add to this picture. Social psychologists have widely used the term "primary socialization" to refer to what anthropologists would be more likely to call "enculturation"; that is, primary socialization consists of the processes a child goes through in the earliest stages of becoming a member of his or her "culture" or society. Generally speaking, this learning takes place within the family and among close intimates. In this same framework, then, secondary socialization refers to those processes of socialization which take place when the child begins to move outside the family, such as when the child first goes to school and begins to interact with other, non-familial children.

One might think it pointless to talk about secondary socialization instead of just calling it education when a child goes to school, but the point being made with these terms is that there are really quite complex processes of learning taking place. Education remains the best term for the formal processes of school learning – the curriculum, if you like; secondary socialization refers to those informal processes of learning which take place in and around or even during the other, more formal processes.

While it goes beyond the purposes of this book to go into primary socialization in detail, it is important to bear in mind what sorts of things a child learns as part of this process. For our purposes, language and social behaviors are the most important. Linguists are in agreement that the great majority of the basic syntactic and phonological structures of one's language are learned (or acquired) as part of one's primary socialization (or during the period of one's primary socialization). For many, probably most humans, the ways one learns to speak during this period of early learning among the family and close intimate relatives place an indelible stamp on one's discourse for the rest of life. This is when one picks up the "accent" one will carry, with relatively few modifications, throughout life. This is when one becomes handy at using the basic syntactic structures and functions commonly used in one's community. Whatever other forms of discourse one might learn later on, for most of us they are largely learned against the background of the language acquired during this period of primary socialization.

Patterns of social behavior are also given a firm cast during the period of primary socialization. The child learns and develops patterns for relating to those of higher and lower status, older and younger and same age, boys and girls, and he or she learns how to be a "boy" or "girl" as well. Beyond these general forms of learning, the child also receives toilet training, and learns how to dress, how to eat, and how to play with others. All of these very fundamental aspects of human behavior are first learned during this period, and while they may undergo changes later in life, those changes are set up against this early learning as modifications and revisions more than simply taking on entirely different behavior patterns. Whatever discourse systems we may come to participate in later in life, the discourse systems which we enter through primary socialization have a weighted advantage over any we enter into later on.

Figure 8.1 summarizes our usage of these first three key terms. Socialization is being used *both* as the term covering all forms of cultural learning *and* as the more specific term to cover informal aspects of cultural learning.

Socialization as legitimate peripheral participation

The final concept we would like to introduce is that of *participation*. Whether we are talking about socialization or education, primary socialization, or secondary socialization, learning how to be a member of a group is not just a matter of mastering a set of knowledge or skills, but also a matter of learning how to work together with the other people in the group according to one's status as a member and the level of expertise one has attained. This aspect of

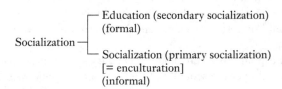

Figure 8.1   Terms for socialization.

learning can only be achieved through participating with other members of the group in joint tasks with shared goals.

It was the educational psychologists Jean Lave and Etienne Wenger who came up with the notion of *legitimate peripheral participation* to describe how people learn in groups. In considering a wide range of different kinds of "communities of practice" from midwives to Alcoholics Anonymous, they came to realize such communities tend to be made up of experts and novices, and people somewhere in between these two poles. Learning in communities, they observed, seems to occur most efficiently when novices are given the chance to participate in tasks with experts as they are "learning the ropes." Such participation is *peripheral* since these novices are not yet qualified or even fully able to perform these tasks on their own. It is *legitimate* because the participation of unqualified members is nevertheless sanctioned by the group. In other words, learning is seen as a process through which novice members gradually become full members by being given the chance to participate *as if they were* members.

Here it would be useful to reiterate the distinction we are making between "groups" or "communities of practice" on the one hand and "discourse systems" on the other. A "discourse system" is not a group of people. Rather, it is a kind of abstract system of communication and behavior that people draw upon as they engage in social life in various groups, rather like a language. At the same time, it is impossible to master discourse systems without to some degree participating in the various groups or "communities of practice" which draw upon these systems of discourse, and it is these communities that form the basis for socialization into discourse systems. At the same time, a given community of practice may draw upon and expect its members to master multiple discourse systems, and individuals, of course, are always members of multiple communities of practice from families, to companies, to volunteer organizations and affinity groups.

The concept of *participation* is important first of all because it reminds us of the rather obvious but sometimes overlooked fact that socialization is a *social* process which depends crucially on the kinds of relationships that exist between experts and novices *in groups* and the kinds of practices they engage in together. This relationship becomes particularly complicated in situations where more than one discourse system overlap within a community of practice. More and more, for example, especially in technology companies, newcomers might be considered to have more expertise in certain areas of their professional discourse system than old-timers, whereas the old-timers have more expertise in the corporate discourse system of the company. Such mismatches in expertise can sometimes cause friction among old and new members and jeopardize the smooth and efficient process of socialization.

Another reason that the concept of participation is important is because it highlights the perpetually "unfinished" nature of socialization: whether one is an expert or a novice in a particular discourse system is always relative since there will always be people in the group with more expertise than they have and people with less. In a sense then, "full membership" in a community of practice is only a kind of abstraction and all participation in discourse systems is to some degree peripheral.

Theories of the person and of learning

It is comfortable to think that all humans are alike in basic human processes, and that is certainly true to a considerable extent. Unfortunately, different discourse systems have quite specific ideas about the nature of the human person and of human society, which it simply takes for granted as the obvious truth and yet which people participating in other discourse systems might find quite surprising or with which they would strongly disagree. We will only consider three of the ways in which discourse systems may differ in their understanding of the nature of humans: their assumptions about whether humans are good or evil, their views about whether the group or the individual is the basic unit, and their understanding of the human life cycle.

The *Three Character Classic* (*San Zi Jing* – Southern Song Dynasty, AD 1127–1279; Xu Chuiyang 1990) has been used in Confucian education in China, Japan, Korea, and Vietnam for as long as eight hundred years as a primer for the learning of both classical Chinese writing and Chinese ethical philosophy. It is based on Confucian classics such as *The Analects* of Confucius and the *Mencius*, and therefore it embodies the ethical position taken by that school of thought that all humans are born good. It begins with the following words:

人之初，性本善。
Ren zhi chu, xing ben shan

性相近，習相遠。
Xing xiang jin, xi xiang yuan

(Man, by nature, is good; people's inborn characters are similar, but learning makes them different.)

This view that human nature is basically good has been held in Confucian ideology from at least the time of Mencius to the present. In contrast to this belief, we could cite a nineteenth-century New Englander who has been quoted by the historian Robert Sunley as saying that all children are born with an evil disposition: "No child has ever been known since the earliest period of the world, destitute of an evil disposition – however sweet it appears" (Sunley 1955: 159). Sunley's view, in fact, is as emblematic of Christian ideology as the opening lines of the *San Zi Jing* are of Confucian ideology.

Of course within Chinese history there have been many arguments put forward for why it would be better to consider humans not to be basically good, and in western history many arguments have been put forward that humans are really good.

The important issue for us is not to try to decide whether or not humans are good or bad; we are more interested in what this issue means for socialization into a discourse system. If you assume humans are basically good, in trying to teach them you will assume that they are trying to do what is right and that what is needed is to show them the right thing to do. Motivation will be based on the learner's own intrinsic desire to do what is right.

On the other hand, if you assume humans are basically evil, in trying to teach them you will assume that they will do everything they can to distort your teaching, to turn it to their own mischievous purposes, or to refuse to cooperate. Motivation of such learners is more likely to be based on punishment and threats than rewards and promises. In other words, the theory of education and socialization which is held by a society or within a discourse system will be based on the more general concept of the good or evil nature of the people who participate in it.

A second factor which will be important is whether the group believes that individuals or collectivities are the basic units of society. As we have discussed above, the anthropologist Francis Hsu and many others have argued that some societies are primarily founded upon a "self" which is larger in scope than the "self" predicated in other societies. This "collectivistic" self includes intimates of the immediate family, whereas the "individualistic" self does not include such intimates.

A society which emphasizes the individual as its basic unit will adopt forms of education and socialization which focus on individual learning and individual success, even where those individuals become competitive with each other and destroy group harmony. On the other hand a society which emphasizes a broader concept of the person that includes familial intimates, will focus education and socialization on the development of that broader unit. The activities and the successes at learning of the individual unit will be seen as part of the activities of the larger units of society, and their successes will be gauged against their contribution to those larger units.

Finally, a third factor in understanding the concept of the person and of learning for a particular group is that group's conception of the human life cycle. In many societies the human life cycle is divided into such phases as infancy, childhood, adolescence, early adulthood, the midlife transition, and so forth. Such terms are so widely used that they are taken as the only imaginable division of the human life span into developmental periods. Nevertheless, many societies make rather different divisions of the human life cycle.

If we take only Europe as an example, we can see that in earlier historical periods there was little recognition of the major divisions between childhood and adulthood we now consider to be so important. Furthermore, we tend to forget in these days of longer life expectancies that for many people now on earth as well as for much of our own earlier history, when an expected life span was closer to fifty years, an "old" person might well have been a person in his or her late forties or early fifties. When child bearing is expected to begin shortly after puberty, a person of the generation of mothers might be in her teens, a grandmother in her thirties. If we compare this to the rather late child bearing of some contemporary mothers who are having their first children even in their forties, we can see that it becomes very difficult to make direct translations of the experience of motherhood and the practices of primary socialization between mothers in such different periods in their lives. A contemporary mother who is a professional woman in her forties approaches the problems of primary socialization very differently from a mother who is in her early teens, whatever else these two women might have in common.

Seen from the point of view of the individual, differences in the society's conception of the life cycle include major differences in the importance ascribed to various periods as well. The prolonged adolescent period, which people in many contemporary industrialized societies enjoy, is in sharp contrast to the plunge into a short lifetime of hard work experienced by the children of the early Industrial Revolution or by many children today in the "developing" world. As lifetimes have increased under industrial development and as the overall complexity of society and its technologies has increased, more and more of the person's total life span is given over to educational preparation. In some societies, direct socialization through apprenticeship into the adulthood tasks is sufficient for most members of the society. In modernized contemporary society or in what some have called "postmodern" society, much of one's life is spent in preparation for fully legitimate "adult" activity.

A childhood friend of one of the authors is now a brain surgeon. In a real sense his period of education and training lasted nearly forty years; he was in his forties before he was sufficiently well prepared to stand on his own feet as a fully legitimated practicing brain surgeon. His life experience may be compared to an Athabaskan hunter also known by the authors who entered into his full adulthood occupation when he was fifteen years old. While there is much to separate the experiences of these two men, the point we wish to make here is that if we want to understand their membership within their cultures and within their discourse systems, it will be important to see that the processes of socialization for each of them are strikingly different, and that difference has as much to do with different conceptions of how the life cycle is to be divided up in their respective discourse systems as it does with the relative time it takes to master brain surgery or caribou hunting (both of which demand considerable skill).

Socialization in the Utilitarian Discourse System

In the last several chapters we have explored the face systems, ideology, and preferred forms of discourse of the Utilitarian discourse system. The question we want to ask now is how one becomes a participant in this discourse system? What are its preferred forms of socialization?

Education vs. socialization

We discussed above the contrast between education and socialization, the former taking place through institutional means and the latter through informal means of bringing members into full participation in society. In Europe, at least, this distinction between education and socialization arose in large part through the activities of the early Utilitarians.

J. S. Mill was one of the first and strongest advocates of the concept of government-supported and controlled public schooling. Up until that time, education for most people consisted of various forms of apprenticeship. Formal education in schools and universities was the privilege of a very few members of European society. For the rest, one picked up the trade of one's father or uncles, or mother or aunts, or one carried on the family farming. It was clear to the Utilitarians that the development of industrial society, upon which they pinned their hopes for the development of greater wealth for all, depended upon producing workers for those factories. These workers would have to be weaned away from their trades and apprenticeships and schooled in the skills and knowledge of the newly developing technologies.

The solution hit upon in both Europe and in North America was to develop government-controlled public schooling. In the period since about 1850, public schools have become the standard throughout all of the world dominated by Utilitarian thinking. These schools have two essential components – they are compulsory on the one hand and they are free (of cost) on the other. That is to say, it has come to be both a privilege and a legal requirement for students to attend these schools. Formal education has become a formal requirement of the Utilitarian discourse system.

In keeping with its view of the individual as a "blank slate" upon which experience writes his or her character or as an empty cabinet which experience comes to furnish, by the late nineteenth century, a child's mind had come to be taken as an empty container which it was the purpose of society and of schools to fill. The very influential book by the psychologist G. Stanley Hall (1844–1924), for example, carried the title *The Contents of Children's Minds* (1883).

This brings up two points regarding socialization: the value placed by the Utilitarians upon education (as opposed to socialization) and the nature of education (formal school) itself. In order to establish the concept of public schooling, formal education was given an exaggerated valuation while at the same time there was a powerful devaluation of non-formal types of learning. Within the Utilitarian discourse system, education through formal procedures has been considered the only really acceptable form of learning.

Education in most public schools in the United States and other societies influenced by the Utilitarian discourse system reflects the ideology of this system. The emphasis in these schools is on the development of inventive and creative individuals who are seen to be in competition with each other. The goal is for them to become "productive members of society," and evaluation is primarily based upon numbers (grades or marks). In 1904 Alfred Binet developed his now famous IQ test, which was further developed at Stanford by Terman as the Stanford–Binet IQ. This test or some variation is widely used to assess the creative or intelligence potential of virtually each individual who falls within the purview of the Utilitarian system. While there are, of course, many local variations, the reader will certainly recognize the Utilitarian theme of standardized testing in most public schools throughout the industrialized world.

Along with the development of public schooling came a major shift in patterns of socialization within the home. The historian Robert Sunley (1955) has argued that in the eighteenth and nineteenth centuries there was a major shift in Britain and the United States from considering the father to be the moral authority for the family to the mother's taking on that role. The reasons underlying this shift in role had to do with the fact that men were increasingly becoming involved in business and other Utilitarian activities outside of the home. Ironically, these outside activities were seen as at least amoral if not immoral and, therefore, damaging to the moral authority of the men who engaged in them. As it was assumed that women would remain isolated within the confines of the household, it was inferred that their moral purity would remain unsullied. Whatever the reality of these assumptions, the major shift is a social fact to be considered when we think of socialization into the Utilitarian discourse system. This discourse system has seen its appropriate place to be outside of the home, in public situations, that is, within business and governmental contexts, and also, at least in the beginning, to be largely the domain of men. As we will see in chapter 11 this polarization of inside and outside (the home) and of women's and men's roles is an ideological position which had important implications on the formation of gender discourse systems within the Utilitarian discourse system.

Socialization and face systems

A key aspect of all socialization is the way people are socialized into the face systems of social relationships of the discourse systems in which they participate. In fact, this aspect of socialization will affect all other aspects of learning. Studies of baby talk to very young infants show that rather than using the simpler pronouns (I, you, we, they) people speak to infants with terms which sketch out for them the key relationships of the people they need to interact with. They say things to them like, "Say hi to Auntie," "There's your Momma over there," "Hold Gramma's hand," and "There's Goong-goong [grandpa]." Through such early interactions, children learn how to navigate the important relationships in their world and how different people are to be addressed and treated.

This socialization into face relationships continues as children engage with adults in various kinds of storytelling practices. Children being socialized into the Utilitarian discourse system typically listen to stories read to them by adults, internalizing deductive rhetorical patterns as well as face strategies of symmetrical solidarity. Children in such situations are expected to be active participants when adults read storybooks to them. It is not unusual in such cases, for example, for the adult to point to pictures and to ask the child to identify the objects portrayed or give comments on them, and children are encouraged to ask questions when they do not understand something. Such practices contrast with those in other discourse systems. Athabaskan children, for example, who grow up listening to oral narratives rather than written stories read aloud learn to abstract themes rather than argue these deductively.

Similarly, socialization to a deference politeness system for young Athabaskans entails having their speech ignored by adults. In both deference politeness and hierarchical politeness systems, children learn to be silent in the presence of their elders, to be seen but not heard. Children are encouraged to engage with adults on a more or less equal footing (with certain limitations). Television programs such as *Sesame Street* model this system of symmetrical solidarity for viewers as well as teach them various cognitive skills. *Sesame Street*, in fact, arose in the United States in the 1970s out of a concern to provide children from "economically disadvantaged" families with the skills so that they could overcome political and economic discrimination. In other words, it was an effort to compensate for what the privileged considered deficient primary socialization delivered by people whose participation in the Utilitarian discourse system was more peripheral.

To put the Utilitarian Discourse System into perspective, Ron Scollon and Suzanne Wong Scollon compared it to the non-literate discourse of First Nations people in Fort Chipewyan, Alberta. They compared a young child, their own, being socialized into the modern literate tradition with a young child being socialized into the vernacular oral tradition with its models of oral narrative performance. What they discovered was a mutually reinforcing circle of causation among discourse patterns, practices of socialization, interpersonal relationships, and face strategies. For the bush community, nonintervention in interpersonal relationships was the primary assumption. This value was reflected in discourse by the traditional oral narrative, where the abstract core of the story is contextualized according to the needs and knowledge of the audience in the current performance. The discourse is structured by the relationships between storyteller and audience, with the text made to fit those relationships. In the literate community, on the other hand, the author and audience are fictionalized into a set of conventional relationships through which it is assumed that the text itself speaks to its reader. The Scollons' child, who typified this discourse pattern, was socialized to significant amounts of what we have called the "fictionalization of the self" through her interactions with her parents, especially around the practice of reading books.

These differences continue when children move on to more formal schooling. Athabaskan children who entered a sort of head start preschool at the age of three in Ft. Chipewyan, Alberta in the mid-1970s could expect to be ignored by teachers if they spoke. Children like the Scollons' whose primary socialization was to solidarity, on the other hand, learned to ask questions of their teachers. In a classroom in which a hierarchical face system prevails, the teacher claims the floor. Students ratify their subordinate position by greeting the teacher. They may listen or appear to listen or signal attention with nods and gaze. If the teacher calls on them to speak they are obliged to comply, at least by saying, "I don't know." He or she may direct them to open their textbooks, to watch a video, to write letters or essays on a topic she supplies. Another classroom may run according to a solidarity face system, with corners and tables for small groups who work together on projects and feel free to offer opinions and tell each other what to do. The teacher's role may be that of a facilitator who offers opinions but does not exercise authority. Students may clamor for his or her attention not so much for approval or direction but simply because they want to include her in the group.

In some schoolrooms in Guangdong during the early Chinese Republic, students recited lessons they learned by rote, each at their own pace in a cacophony of many voices. The teacher sat at his desk (the teacher was always male) at the front of the room helping individual students or explaining passages to small groups. Though all students worked through the same classics, there was no ideology of equality. Individual effort led to diverse results as some persisted until they mastered the set of classics and took the Imperial Exams while others quit and worked in the rice fields. Lateral relationships between students were not regulated and no creativity was expected as each student set about to master the same set of collective texts. There was no need for competition as peers recognized that having one of their village pass the national exams would reflect well on the whole village. Face relationships in such a classroom differed little from those at home, with young students showing deference to parents and teacher as well as older students and siblings or cousins.

Of course, we all know that in taking up a new job, entering into a new school program, or marrying into a new family it is extremely important to get the names of people right and refer to them in the most appropriate way. The theoretical principle here is that whatever we say, we claim ourselves to be members of one community rather than another and to be participants in a particular discourse system or combination of discourse systems; it is the extent to which we succeed in making these claims that we are actually able to move from more peripheral levels of participation to more central levels of participation.

Socialization and the "Historical Body"

When we usually think of learning, whether it is of the formal or informal variety, we think of learning "something," that is, some kind of body of knowledge or skill. Moreover, especially if we participate in the Utilitarian discourse system, we are apt to think that learning primarily takes place in the mind of the learner rather than in his or her body. The discussion above, however, should have already given you the idea that learning is not just about knowing something or being able to do something, but rather of *being someone* within a particular community with its various systems of discourse.

When people spoke of "literacy," for example, they mostly meant the simple ability to recognize and decode marks on a page. Learning how to read was seen as an essentially cognitive exercise, and people who had difficulty learning were seen as cognitively deficient. Now, thanks to the work of "New Literacy" theorists like Brian Street, Shirley Brice Heath, James Paul Gee, and David Barton, we know that learning to read involves all sorts of different kinds of texts and processes and social relationships embedded within particular communities. In other words, reading is not a skill: it is a *social practice*.

Our theoretical position is that, on the whole, not just reading, but all communication arises out of social practice. By that we mean two things. First, that communication within discourse systems requires the mastery of complex sets of relationships and identities and actions that grow up around the concrete circumstances of our social lives. Second, that much of what we mean by social practice we engage in more or less unconsciously; we do not really "know" how we act or communicate, and we do not think of it as something we have "learned." We just do what "comes naturally" in the course of social interactions.

Most of what we know and do, we know and do without knowing how we have learned it. We have just "picked up" how to walk like our parents, how to talk like them, how to *be* a certain sort of person within a certain type of group. The French sociologist Pierre Bourdieu used the word *habitus* to refer to the repository of an individual's life experiences which manifest psychologically as habits, goals, and mental dispositions and physically as bodily features, habitual ways of acting and walking, and various forms of physical dexterity. Bourdieu defines the *habitus* as the "system of durable and transposable dispositions" and "structured propensities to think, feel, and act in determinate ways" (1977: 72) which forms as the individual interacts with his or her society.

This *habitus* is unique to each person. Of course, children growing up in the same family or the same community, members of the same social class, members of the same gender groups and generations, and so forth, will have very similar experiences and so the *habitus* of these people will have much in common.

The idea of the habitus is used to capture the idea that we usually act as we do, not because we want to accomplish X, Y, or Z, but because we are the "sort of person who normally does that sort of thing." Bourdieu (1990) makes a point of arguing that social practice originates outside the individual person and so this entirely "natural" sense of doing things because we are "that sort of person" is a kind of "amnesia." That is, we normally have completely forgotten that at one time our mothers might have said, "We put the fork on the left of the plate because mostly people use the fork in the left hand." Of course it is more likely that when, as children, we were helping to set the table our mothers simply said, "Put it like this . . . no, not like that, like this." Now as adults when we set the table, if we put the fork on the left, we do so simply because that's how it's done.

The way social practices become submerged into our habitus is often quite complex. In a study of one seemingly simple social practice, Ron Scollon followed a child over a period of a year during which she learned how to hand objects to her mother and others in her home in response to the Japanese request "chodai" as well as to make such requests herself. What he found was that the social practice of handing is assembled a piece at a time out of separate actions of listening to requests and making sounds that are interpreted by the mother as requests, and of approaching and grasping, naming objects, and releasing objects, all in interaction with the mother and others in the home environment. In other words, socialization into even a simple practice like handing an object to another person is constructed out of numerous other linked practices such as offering and accepting food, complying with requests, and recognizing key people and key social relationships. In other words, even simple practices submerged within the *habitus* carry with them a whole history of hidden dialogicality, linking them with particular forms of socialization and, ultimately, with particular ideologies.

In our more recent writings, we have preferred to use the term *historical body*, borrowed from the Japanese philosopher Kitaro Nishida (1959), rather than *habitus* to refer to the individual in interaction with the various discourse systems in which he or she participates. We prefer it because Bourdieu's formulation of "durable dispositions" and "structured propensities" seems to us rather rigid, implying that individuals come to internalize the beliefs and rules of the discourse systems they participate in and afterwards are to a large degree controlled by these internalized beliefs and rules. While this may be true in some situations, we believe the process of socialization into discourse systems, especially when it involves the negotiation among multiple discourse systems, is a much more partial and dynamic affair. The notion of the *historical body* represents a more fluid and unstable relationship between the individual and society. For Nishida the historical body is about becoming rather than being, representing a movement "from the formed to the forming."

In the past, Suzanne Scollon (2003) has used an organic metaphor for the historical body, seeing it as "a compost heap of social practices." What is useful about this metaphor is that it allows us to see individuals not just as storehouses of past social practices, but also as the ground for the ontogenesis of new social practices. What resides in the *historical body*, she writes, "is not hard fossil remains nor abstract rules, but humus and detritus, not buried treasure, but compost that prepares the ground for new growth" (2003: 186). A person's primary socialization deposits layers of habit formations and experiences that compost in the unconscious, nourishing similar and compatible habits while filtering out incommensurate ones. If secondary socialization encounters conflicting social practices there is resistance, while compatible practices tend to foster growth.

The point we are trying to make is that the *historical body* is an unstable, dissipative structure in interaction with its environment rather than an objective, regular, or durable set of dispositions, and the environment in which it develops typically consists of multiple discourse systems with multiple cycles of discourse circulating through it, some commensurate and some incommensurate, some new and some already present in the embodied experience of the individual. In other words, socialization is always to some degree dialogical, involving an inevitable negotiation among multiple discourse systems and between what has already been learned and what is about to be learned.

Researching Interdiscourse Communication

The basic concept of the discourse system which we have introduced and elaborated on in the previous chapters involves four elements: a group of ideological norms, distinct socialization practices, a regular set of discourse forms, and a set of assumptions about face relationships within the discourse system. We have chiefly taken as our example the Utilitarian discourse system which first began to develop in the late seventeenth century as part of the Utilitarian economic and political philosophy of the Enlightenment. It continues down to the present day to be the primary discourse system identified with business, both within European-derived cultures and increasingly throughout international business and governmental circles. This is a cross-cutting discourse system which is found widely across cultural boundaries, while at the same time it does not represent more than a portion of the discourse within any particular cultural group. At the same time, we have also introduced other discourse systems, most notably the Confucian discourse system, and discussed how they differ from the Utilitarian discourse system.

So far, then, our use of the term discourse system has mapped on pretty easily to what many people refer to as "culture," the Utilitarian discourse system covering a set of beliefs and practices many people would associate with "western culture" and the Confucian discourse system covering a set of beliefs and practices many people would associate with "eastern" or "Asian" culture. Since both of these discourse systems, and in fact most large, hegemonic systems, cut across geographical boundaries, and these boundary crossings are becoming even more prevalent with the rise of globalization, we believe that such notions as "western culture" and "Asian culture" have outlived their usefulness. The real advantage to the concept of discourse systems, however, is not just that they free us from the temptation to associate "culture" solely with nations or geographical regions, but because it allows us to analyze systems of belief and social practice which do not neatly fit traditional notions of "culture," systems associated, for example, with gender, sexuality, age, profession, and place of work. It is these kinds of discourse systems that we will be considering in the rest of this book. At the same time, it must be remembered that such discourse systems are also affected by the larger, cross-cutting discourse systems we have discussed so far: being a woman in Japan is not the same as being one in Sweden; being a gay man in Beijing is not the same as being one in San Francisco; and being a software engineer in Bangalore is not the same as being one in Silicon Valley.

Before we go on to examine these other kinds of discourse systems, we would like to briefly review the four main aspects of discourse systems we have proposed in the previous chapters and to offer an outline of the main points we have made about each of these aspects.

1   Participants will hold a common ideological position and recognize a set of extra-discourse features which define them as a group.

These extra-discourse factors which define participants in a discourse system may be common experiences (such as those shared by members of the same generation), a common historical background (such as immigration from the same country of origin), a common race or gender, a common language or linguistic variety, or even common treatment by outgroup members. Ideology is often a major factor in guiding people's attitudes toward outgroup members.

2   Socialization is accomplished primarily through these preferred forms of discourse.

A somewhat circular, self-reinforcing system is set for potential participants in discourse systems in that one learns how to be a participant through learning how to use the preferred forms of discourse, and then one shows one's participation through competent use of these forms of discourse. In the case of a voluntary discourse system such as a corporation, one "learns the ropes" by a form of on-the-job training. One learns to write documents in the corporate style by following the formats used by one's predecessors in the corporation. As a special precaution, in many cases voluntary, goal-oriented discourse systems will set up training programs or even credentialing courses. Such courses will often focus on the forms of discourse required for successful participation.

More "involuntary" discourse systems such as those of generation or gender do not normally have formal systems for teaching the preferred forms of discourse. One becomes a participant through socialization or enculturation. One is simply told, "Don't talk like a girl," "Don't talk to your mother like that," "Good girls don't say such things," or "We don't say such things." One is left to work out the system as one progresses toward fuller participation and identity over a period of apprenticeship.

3   A set of preferred forms of discourse serves as banners or symbols of legitimate participation and identity.

These preferred forms of discourse may include the use of involvement or independence face strategies, certain genres (such as proposals and reports in business), certain specialized forms of address, a highly specialized lexicon (such as is used in law, linguistics, or the travel industry), or, in fact, any other aspect of the grammar of context which we have outlined in chapter 2. The crucial point is that these preferred forms of discourse serve to symbolize identity and "membership" for participants in the discourse system.

One consequence of the fact that preferred forms of discourse function as banners of identity and legitimate participation is that a person will be reluctant to shift patterns of discourse, because this will be experienced as a change in identity. In the same way, members will use these forms as a guide to test the participation of others as legitimate or not. As codes or badges of "membership," these preferred discourse forms will come to dominate discourse within these systems.

4   Face relationships are prescribed for discourse among participants or between participants and outsiders.

A discourse system can be identified in part by having regular expectations for how legitimate participants will speak to each other as well as for how they will speak to non-
participants. The Utilitarian discourse system, for example, prescribes a face system of symmetrical solidarity for public discourse among participants. The Confucian discourse system described in the *Li Ji*, as we mentioned in chapter 6, prescribes a system of hierarchy between ruler and ruled, father and son, and elder and younger brothers. It prescribes a system of "difference" (perhaps symmetrical deference) for husband and wife, and a system of symmetrical solidarity between friends. As we will discuss below in looking at other discourse systems, there are also significant expectations for discourse among different kinds of participants.

An outline guide for the study of discourse systems

The outline guide for the study of discourse systems which follows is the basic format around which we have organized our comparative studies of discourse systems. There are four key questions, based upon the four main elements of a discourse system, as well as a number of secondary questions which have been raised in earlier chapters of this book:

1   *Ideology*: what are the historical/social/ideological characteristics of the discourse system?
    (a)   Natural or purposive (that is, involuntary or voluntary)
    (b)   History
    (c)   Worldview
    (d)   Beliefs, values, religion
          –   How is "good" defined?
          –   What is the main goal of society?
          –   What is seen as the basis or foundation of society?
          –   What does it mean to be human?
    (e)   Place in society, stance regarding other discourse systems
2   *Socialization*: how does one learn legitimate participation/identity?
    (a)   Education, enculturation, acculturation
    (b)   Primary and secondary socialization
    (c)   Expert and novice participation

   (d)　Theories of the person and of learning
-   Good and evil
-   Individual and collective
-   Life cycle

3　*Forms of discourse*: what are the preferred forms of communication?
   (a)　Grammar of Context
   (b)　Patterns/types of cohesion
   (c)　Rhetorical strategies
   (d)　Functions of language
-   Information and relationship
-   Negotiation and ratification
-   Group harmony and individual welfare

   (e)　Production formats
-   Principal
-   Author
-   Animator

   (f)　Modes of communication
-   Embodied and disembodied modes
-   Verbal and non-verbal modes
-   Kinesics
-   Proxemics
-   Concept of time

   (g)　Media
-   Participation structures
-   Presence
-   Synchrony

   (h)　Discourse in the material world (emplacement)

4　*Face systems* (social organization): what are the preferred or assumed human relationships?
   (a)　Face systems
-   Deference
-   Solidarity
-   Hierarchical

   (b)　Face strategies
-   Independence
-   Involvement

   (c)　Kinship
   (d)　The concept of the self
   (e)　Ingroup–outgroup relationships

In the three chapters to follow our goal will be to explore how these questions might provide a fruitful analytical guide to begin the analysis of the wide range of different kinds of discourse systems which might affect interdiscourse communication.

Discussion Questions

1　Think about the different ways you were educated in school and socialized at home. What were the similarities and differences in terms of the face systems and forms of discourse you were expected to master? How did the ways you interacted with parents and playmates in your early childhood prepare you for things you later did in school? How did practices you learned in school seem to contradict those you had learned at home?

2   Look at a children's book or a children's television show that is popular where you live. Consider the face systems and ideology this book or television program promotes. How does it do this? How does this book or television program fit with other forms of socialization and education where you live?

3   Think of some everyday practices you do unthinkingly such as tying your shoes, crossing the street, or brushing your teeth. Try to remember how you learned to do these things. How much involved informal socialization and how much involved explicit explanations or instructions? What other social practices, forms of discourse, and face systems were linked to these practices as you learned them?

References for Further Study

In their 1981 book *Narrative, Literacy and Face in Interethnic Communication* Ron and Suzanne Scollon introduced the concept of socialization into particular discourse systems by contrasting the socialization of their daughter as a two year-old into the Utilitarian discourse system with that of a neighbor and playmate in Fort Chipewyan, Alberta being socialized to the discourse common to Athabaskan people in subarctic North America. Their 1984 article "Cooking it up and boiling it down: abstracts in Athabaskan children's story retellings" further contrasts socialization through literacy with socialization through oral narrative. Jenny Cook-Gumperz in her 1986 book *The Social Construction of Literacy* shows how literacy declined during the nineteenth century in England and North America when it went from being learned as part of primary socialization in the home to being taught in compulsory education in schools, and Ruth Cowan presents a sociological-historical study of what she calls the industrialization of the home in her 1983 book *More Work for Mother*. For an excellent introduction to the study of literacy, the reader is directed to David Barton's 2007 book *Literacy: an introduction to the ecology of written language*. Jean Lave and Etienne Wenger introduced the idea that learning entails legitimate peripheral participation in communities of practice in their 1991 book *Situated Learning: legitimate peripheral participation*. Xu (1990) is a recent updating of the ancient *Three Character Classic* (or *San Zi Jing*). The puritan view that children are born with evil dispositions is quoted from Robert Sunley (1955). Further discussion of the relationship between discourse and the historical body can be found in Rodney Jones's 2008 article "Good sex and bad karma: discourse and the historical body" and Suzanne Scollon's 2003 article "Political and somatic alignment: habitus, ideology and social practice."

9

Corporate and Professional Discourse

Voluntary and Involuntary Discourse Systems

It is useful to distinguish between two types of discourse systems: voluntary and involuntary. Voluntary discourse systems are goal-oriented discourse systems such as those that form around corporations or governmental and other institutional structures and which have been formed for specific purposes. These purposes might be to gain a profit for the owners in the case of discourse systems associated with corporations or to educate children in the case of those associated with schools. In the case of discourse systems associated with professional groups or organizations, the goals will be to provide support to other colleagues and to enforce professional practices and codes of conduct.

Involuntary discourse systems are those formed around gender, race, generation, ethnicity, or other such characteristics, in which individual participants have relatively little choice about whether or not they share in the characteristics that most people associate with participation. This does not mean, however, that they have no choice at all about whether or not to participate and their degree of participation. It is not uncommon, in fact, for individuals who share in the characteristics associated with a particular discourse system to reject participation. In such cases there is often a conflict created between participation and identity, since members of the communities which identify with this discourse system are likely to treat this person as a member in spite of his or her attempts to reject identity with the group and the discourse system it promotes.

Participation in a discourse system is often displayed through attention to the goals or the extra-discourse features of a group or groups promoting that discourse system and by expressing or upholding the ideology expressed as part of that discourse system. In a corporation, a member might be criticized for paying too little attention to the goal of gaining a profit. A member of an ethnic group might be criticized for ignoring the oppression his or her group has felt historically in an attempt to achieve better communication with someone from outside the group. In each case, the criticism is based upon some defining

Intercultural Communication: A Discourse Approach, Third Edition. Ron Scollon, Suzanne Wong Scollon, Rodney H. Jones.
© 2012 John Wiley & Sons, Inc. Published 2012 by John Wiley & Sons, Inc.

characteristic of participation in a discourse system, which is then translated into an emblem of group membership or non–membership.

This distinction between voluntary and involuntary discourse systems, however, is far from cut and dried. As we have argued in chapter 6, the Utilitarian discourse system is a broad, overarching ideological system widely spread through international business and governmental organizations. As a kind of background to corporate culture, on the one hand, it could be considered to be a goal-directed, and thus, a voluntary discourse system. On the other hand, most of its members begin their socialization into this system at a very early age with little recognition of its ideological status. It might therefore in some ways be considered an involuntary discourse system for many participants. Similarly, the discourse systems associated with religion in many places, Islam in much of the Middle East, and Catholicism in much of South America, are also so strongly associated with one's birth and one's family to be considered in many ways involuntary discourse systems, although they are goal-directed and participation is not a matter of any outward physical trait. Throughout the next three chapters we will explore further this fuzzy boundary between voluntary and involuntary discourse systems and its relationship to ideology, socialization, forms of discourse, and face systems.

Five key discourse systems in corporate and professional life

We have said above that the concept of culture is too broad to be very useful in the analysis of discourse. In the contemporary world what are usually referred to as cultures can be shown to consist of a number of internal, cross-cutting, and overlapping discourse systems, such as those of generation, ethnicity, and gender. In addition to these discourse systems, virtually all of these "cultures" participate in the worldwide economic system for the extraction of resources and the production and distribution of goods which we have been calling the Utilitarian discourse system, although the amount of this participation may vary considerably.

In a book such as this one it would be impossible to give a comprehensive description of even a single discourse system, let alone adequate descriptions of even the most basic overlapping discourse systems within which we all communicate. On the other hand, we feel it is important to sketch in at least the outlines of a few main discourse systems, while pointing out the major issues which need to be analyzed in order to understand how individual members take up participation within those systems, and to understand how communication between participants in those systems works.

Mr Kim, a mechanical engineer for Kolon company in Seoul, works for a major South Korean corporation, which has branches not only throughout South Korea, but also throughout Southeast Asia, North America, and Europe. He is married and has two young children. His own mother has passed away, but his father lives with him.

Mr Kim is simultaneously a participant in quite an array of discourse systems. As an employee of one of South Korea's largest corporations, he enjoys the prestige of being identified with their "corporate culture." As an engineer, Mr Kim is a member of the discourse system of mechanical engineers; he belongs to their professional association, receives their journal, and has attended training sessions in order to keep up with his specialization. As a member of such a corporation doing international business – Mr Kim has worked on a joint venture team in Frankfurt – he is a member of the Utilitarian discourse system, which predominates in such international business and professional exchanges. At the same time Mr Kim participates in the Confucian discourse system, which is reflected in his attitudes toward education, toward his position in society, and toward his family. Mr Kim is in his early fifties and this means he is a member of the generation of Koreans who were born just after the Korean War. This separates him from his father and mother, who were born during the period of Japanese occupation before World War II, and it also separates him from his own children, who have been born in a period of great affluence and economic development. Mr Kim, as a man, finds himself too a member of a gender discourse system which promotes certain models of speech and behavior for men and certain other models for women. As a result, he finds himself frequently going for drinks after work with fellow male employees and generally finding that most of his social relaxation is in the company of other men and not with his wife or family.

Most professional discourse today takes place at the nexus of these five major types of discourse system:

1   the corporate discourse system;
2   the professional discourse system;
3   the Utilitarian discourse system;
4   the generational discourse system;
5   the gender discourse system.

The first two of these are, for the most part, voluntary or goal-directed discourse systems. That is, the corporate culture and the professional group are motivated by a goal-directed ideology. The Utilitarian discourse system, as we have said, while goal-directed, is so pervasive that it is difficult for people to opt out of and still function in most contemporary workplaces. Finally, the generational discourse system in which one participates as well as one's gender group are largely involuntary discourse systems in that one is to some extent born into them, though, as we will argue in chapter 10, even these so-called involuntary discourse systems often take on goal-directed characteristics.

In the chapters which follow, we will give descriptions of these separate discourse systems. In doing so, we will bring out crucial points which such discourse systems raise for our overall understanding of interdiscourse communication. We hope that this strategy will accomplish two purposes. The first of these is simply to illustrate the complexity of these multiple discourse systems as they operate in our day-to-day lives. Our second purpose is to encourage the reader to undertake his or her own analysis of the discourse systems in which he or she participates.

The Corporate Discourse System (Corporate Culture)

When we use the term "corporate discourse" we have in mind the over-riding discourse system practiced in the sorts of large companies and multinational corporations in which many of our readers will ultimately be employed. Nevertheless, we do not mean to exclude more locally owned businesses or the very wide range of governmental and other institutional organizations. From the point of view of the analysis of discourse systems, there may actually be little difference between the functioning of a hospital and an airline company. A local arts council founded for the purposes of arranging art exhibits and concerts will, in fact, demonstrate many of the same principles of corporate discourse structures as a corporation listed on stock exchanges throughout the world. We are not concerned with examining what is usually known as organizational communication – that would differ considerably from structure to structure. What we want to focus on are the most significant ways in which institutional or corporate discourse systems come to be major factors in the understanding of ordinary discourse among participants. Such understanding is especially important as corporations themselves increasingly regard their "corporate culture" as a kind of "asset" which they spend considerable amounts of time and energy developing and promoting.

Ideology

The corporation, also known as a limited liability company in contrast to sole proprietorships and partnerships, is without question the dominant form of business organization in the modern world. The roots of corporate law extend back to the time of Rome, but it was not until the nineteenth century that the form of the corporation as we know it now really came to be established. By the turn of the twentieth century, the limited liability company or corporation had come to dominate.

As the reader will be aware, this period in which the modern corporation evolved into its present form is the period of the rise of the Utilitarian ideology. It is not an exaggeration to say that the limited liability corporation is the organizational and legal expression in business affairs of the Utilitarian ideology. One of the key concepts is that of the juridical personality, which means that the corporation is taken as a legal person or individual. To put this another way, under corporate law, the corporation is the one person who can best exemplify the Utilitarian ideology, because this person is entirely fictive and can be logically defined as nothing more than or other than an economic entity.

Because we have already presented the Utilitarian ideology in chapter 6, here we will only need to say that the dominant ideology in corporate discourse systems is normally Utilitarian ideology. This matching of ideology and organizational structure is the goal which was pursued by the first generations of Utilitarians, and finally accomplished by the monopolistic American corporations of Rockefeller, J. P. Morgan, and the rest.

Goals
The first consideration is that corporate discourse systems are goal-oriented. That is, they are brought into being to achieve certain purposes and, at least in the beginning, those purposes will dominate the ideology of the discourse system. In most cases the founding purposes will be stated in such documents as articles of incorporation and charters. They will sometimes be restated as "mission statements," which are used internally to produce cohesion in staff ideology and externally for marketing or public relations purposes.

There are two broad classes of purposes for which corporate structures come into existence: (1) to make a profit for the owners and stockholders, and (2) to provide some service to some constituency. A manufacturing company is most likely to be governed by the purpose of making a profit. A school, on the other hand, is more likely to be governed by the second type of purpose, that of providing a service.

One should be alert to the possibility that these two broad motives may well be combined in the basic ideology of the organization. A private school may, indeed, be founded for the purpose of providing an education, but it may also be required to do so, if not at a profit, at least not at a loss. In other words, such private educational institutions as Stanford

University are well known for the fact that along with providing their foundational educational services, they also manage to make profitable returns on their many investments, which constitute a form of ongoing financial support for the educational goal.

A secondary purpose of most corporate discourse systems is to provide employment. Sociologists have often pointed out that while institutions come into existence with certain external goals in mind, it is not long before internal and quite secondary goals come to dominate. American automobile manufacturers, for example, had as their original purpose the production of cars and other motor vehicles in order to earn money for their owners. Nevertheless, after a period of time the employees, through the medium of their organized labor unions, voiced the view that the purpose was to provide them with employment.

This is not the place to engage in an analysis of the past forty years of international automobile production and of the labor market. The point we are making is that a corporation or other organization may begin with one set of stated goals or purposes, but those goals and purposes may change significantly over time and, in fact, come to dominate the operation of the organization. Often that shift in goals is described by sociologists as a change from external motivation to internal motivation. The main purpose of the organization comes to be maintaining the existence of the organization, whether or not the organization serves any external purpose.

A similar kind of shift can be seen from the point of view of workers within a corporation. When one first takes a job in an organization, the main goal is usually to procure gainful employment in order to support oneself and others who might be dependent on one's income. As time goes by, however, employees often take on the organization's goals – goals such as increasing sales, improving productivity, or promoting the ideology of the organization – as their own. In many contemporary workplaces, the line between organizational goals and individual goals has become so blurred that periodic appraisals of performance, in which the employees' contributions to the organization's goals are assessed according to various performance indicators, are often couched in the rhetoric of "self-actualization," with employees being asked to consider things like their "personal growth" and whether or not they are working "to their full potential."

The ideology of most corporate discourse systems, then, is likely to consist of multiple goals which include the stated, foundational purpose and any number of implicit, evolved, internal purposes. In making an analysis of corporate ideology, one should remain alert to the likelihood that the purposes which appear in corporate handbooks, in founding documents, and in corporate training activities may well be only the original, externally motivated purposes of the organization. They are quite likely not to be the more tacit, unstated, or even largely unrecognized internal purposes, and discourse within such a discourse system is often measured against the standard of the more internal goals.

At the same time, it has become common recently for corporations to explicitly put forward as their ideologies secondary goals of, for example, benefiting society or protecting the environment, or, in the case of Google, "doing no evil," under the name of "corporate social responsibility." The extent to which such goals represent the genuine ideologies of these corporations and their members or are simply part of their public relations strategies is often hard to gauge, and one must look carefully at the corporation's actions in circumstances where such secondary goals may interfere with their primary goal of making a profit in order to do so. This is complicated since in many cases being "socially responsible" is closely intertwined with the construction of an image or lifestyle that corporations use to sell their products or services or to recruit new employees. For example, it has been observed that members of the Millennial generation in North America, people born between 1991 and 1995, which we will discuss in the following chapter, place a great deal of value on working for organizations which strongly espouse goals of "social responsibility," and so one often finds that these secondary goals of social responsibility feature prominently in job advertisements and other recruitment materials.

History

At the time Ron Scollon worked for Ford Motor Company, many of the employees of the company who were retiring were the original employees of the company. Like many other of the major automobile corporations and their feeder companies in Detroit, these companies, which were just then being established, had hired new immigrants to the United States in the 1920s. These immigrants, like the elder Mr Scollon, went to work for these new companies, often within days of arriving in the new country, and then worked for the same company until the day they retired some forty years later. As a result, in the 1960s, the history of these companies was virtually inseparable from the history of United States industry in the interwar period (between World War I and World War II) and from the history of European immigration to the Midwest of the United States.

This can be starkly contrasted with those same companies in the decades which have passed since. Two major historical developments had the effect of major restructuring of these corporations. On the one hand, the companies have developed into multinational corporations which can no longer be identified with the regional history of any particular country, and on the other, employees of these companies no longer have the long personal parallel attachments to these companies. In the 1960s, the history of Ford could largely be told in the histories of the individual employees who had lived out their employment lives in the company. By the 1990s, such companies had come to take on much more consciously developed and abstract characteristics. The corporate culture of Ford was once very much the same as the cultural history of downriver Detroit. Now it is carefully crafted by specialists in human resource management and corporate communication.

This, then, is the major question to be considered in analyzing a corporate discourse system from the point of view of its history: to what extent is it grounded in the history of a particular place and time? Generally speaking, the smaller and more local a corporate discourse system, the more it will share in the characteristics of its time and place. Large, multinational systems will often take on rather artificial, consciously designed characteristics, which have as their purpose to provide some sense of history and of corporate culture in the absence of more naturally occurring local or regional history and culture.

With the rise of globalization and increased decentralization of management, many corporations have faced considerable challenges in maintaining a consistent corporate discourse system across diverse workplaces spread throughout the globe. Adding to this challenge is the fact that employees like the elder Mr Scollon, who stayed with the same company for their entire lives, thus helping to maintain a sense of continuity in the culture of the organizations for which they worked, have become a rarity. For a variety of reasons we will explore further below, most workers nowadays are likely to have many jobs throughout their lives and to feel less of a sense of loyalty to any one company.

Worldview

Of course history and "culture" are closely tied to worldview. As we have argued, starting in chapter 6, most international corporations and governmental organizations have taken on as their organizational worldview the ideology of the Utilitarian discourse system. This is so much the case that in recent years it has become a struggle among management analysts to see if such organizations can be restructured along lines that would modify some of the less productive aspects of this dominant discourse system.

As Japanese manufacturers began to dominate U.S. and then world markets in the 1980s, many western corporations began to look at Japanese management for clues to their success. To some management specialists, the individualism of the Utilitarian discourse system was beginning to be seen as unproductive at the level of day-to-day management of work or task groups. Starting perhaps with Ouchi's *Theory Z*, attention began to be focused on aspects of management practices which emphasized consensus rather than individual competition. In the United States these principles translated into the adoption of Total Quality Management (TQM) in many corporations, a system which aims for the continual improvement of products and processes through the greater involvement of workers in team decision-making. Nowadays, these practices are a normal part of most corporations participating in the Utilitarian discourse system. At the same time there is still an ongoing debate in management circles about what is the right combination of individual competitive motivation on the one hand and group or task motivation on the other. Most such discussions come up against the fact that underlying much thinking in management circles is the Utilitarian ideology, which continues to foster concepts of the creative, innovative individual.

In North America, this debate around management principles and practices has been largely driven by the entry into the workforce of employees who have been increasingly skeptical of the goals and principles of the Utilitarian discourse system. Both Generation X (those born between 1965 and 1980) and the more recent Millennial generation grew up in periods when the Utilitarian discourse system had to some degree failed to live up to its promises of prosperity – Generation X witnessing in their childhoods the stagflation and energy shortages of the 1970s, and many Millennials witnessing the bursting of the technology bubble in the year 2000 and the worldwide financial crisis of 2008, which occurred just as many of them were preparing to enter the job market. Partly as a result of this, younger workers in many places are demanding management systems that make accommodations for non-work priorities such as childcare, provide them with opportunities for learning and self-development, and recognize their capacity for self-management.

Beliefs, values, religion

Corporations established for the purposes of doing business generally adopt the Utilitarian ideology. As we have said in chapter 6, one major historical aspect of this ideology is that the authority of the rational, logical, human individual came to replace the authority of the church or of formal religious beliefs. This economic and rational concept of humans tends to take a strongly secularist position in modern corporate discourse systems. In most cases there is a formal policy, or at least an informal understanding, that employees will leave their beliefs, whether political or religious, at home when they report to work. Discourse is organized around the idea that objective facts and logical processes should be sufficient to determine courses of action.

This same ideology of objectivism and rationalism dominates even in organizational structures which are not strictly organized for economic purposes. Schools throughout the western world, for example, typically eschew the explicit treatment of beliefs and values by taking a rationalistic and relativistic stance. In both cases, it should be observed that the ideals of "freedom of belief" and "freedom of expression" are generally proscribed. One is free only to express the Utilitarian ideological position of empiricism and rationalism. This is quite dramatically illustrated by laws in France and other European countries which ban the wearing of conspicuously religious clothing in schools and government offices.

Nevertheless, in some cases there are corporate structures which are organized specifically for the purpose of advancing beliefs, values, or religious principles. Most churches are now organized as not-for-profit corporate structures and have their fundamental beliefs encoded in their articles of incorporation or charters. In these cases as well there is no espousal of freedom of belief or expression. Membership in such discourse systems is tied to the expression and support of the foundational beliefs. In other words, the Utilitarian ideal of freedom of individual expression is rarely to be found within corporate discourse systems, whether they are of the economically motivated type or of the not-for-profit type. Many such discourse systems promote as part of their corporate identity ideas about inclusiveness in decision-making and their desire for creative employees with innovative ideas. Such innovation, however, must always stay within the ideological boundaries of the organization's beliefs and goals.

Despite the variety of "corporate cultures" and the recent changes in workplaces brought on by the increased use of digital technologies, the ways most corporate discourse systems would answer the four questions outlined in chapter 6 has not changed considerably from the ways such organizations would have answered them a century ago. "Happiness" for the greatest number of people, whether that is defined in purely monetary terms or in the new language of "quality of life" (which attempts to measure things like satisfaction, freedom, and the quality of social relationships in economic terms), is still seen as the greatest good. "Progress" is still defined as the goal of society, though now it might also include things like "progress in reducing carbon emissions" or "progress in sustainability." The individual is still seen as the basis of society. Although the role of the individual as a responsible member of a "community" might also be stressed, the function of "communities" in the Utilitarian discourse system is still to serve the goals of individuals rather than the other way around. Finally, the idea of "self-actualization," of finding, developing, and expressing one's unique qualities or talents, is still seen as central to being human.

Place in the larger society
The final aspect of the ideology of corporate discourse systems to be considered is the question of how that discourse system sees itself as part of the larger society within which it functions. Chief executive officers of large corporations have traditionally viewed themselves as major contributors to the welfare and stability of their social environments. In more recent years, multinational corporations have grown to be larger institutional structures with greater resources than all but the largest of the world's nations. In a real sense, some of the world's largest corporations are the defining entities and the world's nations the smaller units which feed into those structures. This constitutes a significant reorganization of the world political structure within the past several decades.

From the point of view of discourse systems, the crucial question is how a particular corporate discourse system views itself in this worldwide complex of nations, societies, and corporations. A meat buyer working for McDonald's will approach a potential supplier knowing that he or she has the structure of one of the world's largest and most popularly known corporations to rely upon. On the other hand, a buyer for a small jewelry shop in Tokyo will have no such internationally known back-up support. While this difference in size or in degree of internationality may not make a direct difference in ideology, it will make a difference in how strongly the employee can put forward the company ideology in his or her dealings with others outside of the company. For a member of one of the world's large multinationals there will be some expectation that part of his or her agenda will, in fact, be to put forward the company ideology. For a member of a small, family-held business, in contrast, the governing ideology is likely to be put into the background or even set aside where necessary.

The point we want to make in taking up this question of the place a corporate discourse system has in the broader picture is that the corporate ideology itself may be a more or less central aspect depending on the relative strength of the corporation. The stronger the position of the corporate discourse system, the more its employees are likely to think that strength derives from corporate ideology and therefore the more likely they are to self-consciously take on that ideology and to bring it to the attention of others.

With the flattening of hierarchies and the increased reliance on self-managing teams in many workplaces, and the trend for members of teams to be geographically dispersed, many corporations have come to see the promotion of the ideology of the organization as an even more important means of managing and inspiring loyalty in their employees, Many organizations, in fact, have embarked on sophisticated programs of marketing their corporate ideology to workers, encouraging them to adopt it as part of an overall "lifestyle" in the same way products are increasingly being marketed as "lifestyle choices" (see below). Digital media are increasingly playing a role in this as organizations set up "Facebook-like" social networks for employees in which they are encouraged to share personal information about themselves and their feelings about working for the organization.

There are, of course, many other aspects of the ideology of corporate discourse systems which we might have considered. Our goal here is simply to introduce the reader to the kinds of issues which must be analyzed if we are to develop an adequate understanding of such discourse systems.

Socialization

Education, enculturation, acculturation

As goal-oriented discourse systems, corporate cultures have a large component of formal institutional learning as part of the means by which members become socialized. As we have said in chapter 6, public schooling in European countries developed right along with industrialization as an inseparable aspect of the Industrial Revolution, and most corporate discourse systems assume that entrance will be limited to appropriately schooled candidates.

Of course, a major distinction is usually made in the qualifications for "white-collar" (or "salaried") and "blue-collar" (or "hourly") employees, with higher levels of formal education required for higher levels of status and pay. As anyone who has worked in such corporations certainly knows, such a distinction bears little comparison with actual distinctions in knowledge, work responsibility, or importance to the company of the work accomplished. In virtually all organizations one can find relatively low-paid hourly workers with little official educational background carrying rather significant loads of decision-making work. One finds, for example, administrative assistants who have worked for years in an office who, through experience and informal socialization into the job, know a good bit more about how to accomplish the work of the office than their newly hired, highly credentialed, and much better-paid supervisors.

In the preceding paragraph we wrote "little official educational background" because we wanted to signal that it is not the actual educational background which matters in most cases, but rather the officially sanctioned educational background. It often happens that a person with rather extensive formal educational credentials ends up working in a job which requires only the minimal educational qualifications. Within corporate or institutional discourse this virtually always means that he or she will be treated according to his or her official status – an "hourly" worker – not his or her actual competence. This experience has, unfortunately, been widely shared among women, immigrants, members of ethnic minority groups, and even majority populations under colonial rule.

In other words, the amount and kinds of formal, schooled education and training are a significant measure used in setting job requirements and in screening potential members of these corporate discourse systems, whether or not those qualifications are actually significant in carrying out the functions for which new members are hired. These formal credentials remain a significant aspect of members' participation in and advancement through such systems of discourse. In fact, with the advancement of technology and the new emphasis on efficiency in human resource management, credentials such as test scores have become much more important in decisions about hiring, not to mention other quantitative measures of the "quality" of recruits ranging from IQ tests to personality inventories to genetic screening and tests for drug use.

James Gee, Glynda Hull, and Colin Lankshear argue that what they call "the new work order" is characterized by an increasingly "techno–rationalist" view of the world in which job performance is more and more broken down into distinct, measurable components (often referred to as "key performance indicators") which can be tracked using technological tools (such as software that tracks the amount of time employees spend doing particular tasks on their computers). In many ways this is the logical extension of Utilitarian ideas formulated more than two hundred years ago such as Bentham's idea of a "Felicific Calculus" and his vision of the "Panopticon," in which prisoners (or workers) could be closely and constantly monitored by central authorities. The paradox of the "new workplace" is that alongside the promotion of less hierarchical management structures and an increased role for employees in decision making has come the proliferation in many workplaces of technologies of control such as standardized tests, sophisticated techniques of employee surveillance, and "key performance indicators."

As we enter an era in which people are likely to change employers much more frequently than ever before, the demand for "portable" forms of certification like test scores will likely increase. At the same time, schools and other training institutions will increasingly be expected to produce graduates who have the ability to adapt quickly and reinvent themselves frequently to respond to changing market conditions. People who are able to effectively create and recreate identities by bringing together evidence of past achievements will be at an advantage. Here skills learned in more informal settings may play a particularly important role. Some have argued, for example, that video games and social networking sites like Facebook give young people practice at taking on new identities and constructing the kinds of flexible "portfolios" they will need to use for employment purposes in the future. At the same time, digital tools ranging from "e-learning packages" to corporate social networking sites are increasingly playing a central role in both formal and informal practices of socialization into corporate discourse systems.

Once a person has passed through the "gates" of a corporate discourse system, that is, once a person has been hired, both education and enculturation are major aspects of that person's learning how to become a full member. As we said in chapter 6, most corporations, businesses, government offices, or other goal-directed discourse systems have prepared materials for the education of new members. There are employee handbooks, policy statements, newsletters, bulletins, corporate social networking sites, and standard operating procedures (SOPs) as well as orientation and training sessions to introduce the new member into the ideology and daily procedures of the company and the job.

There is a longstanding recognition that, even though most organizations require formal educational credentials for most positions, nevertheless new employees will require training for the specific tasks they are expected to do. Such on-the-job training programs recognize that the formal educational credentials are serving some purpose other than directly training future employees for such corporate structures.

At the same time, it is also widely recognized that a great deal of the learning that new members need to do will be done quite informally, by observation and imitation. In other words, there is a widespread recognition that success in taking on corporate identity and in being accepted as a full participant depends upon successful enculturation. This enculturation, oddly enough, is often carried out across the lines of institutional status. Frequently a new "lieutenant" is broken in and shown the corporate ropes by a well-seasoned "first sergeant." Often enough one finds an administrative assistant with meager academic or formal educational background enculturating a highly credentialed supervisor who is struggling through the first stages of becoming a member of a new corporate culture.

Finally, while the terms "enculturation" and especially "acculturation" are normally used in anthropology to refer to cultural processes, there is an important way in which acculturation is significant in studies of professional discourse. As we said in chapter 8, acculturation refers to the process by which a dominant culture comes to supplant the culture of people over which it has come to exercise its power. In recent years throughout the world there has been a marked increase in the consolidation of smaller companies into larger, multinational conglomerate structures. Many employees of the smaller companies which have been involved in these mergers and take-overs have experienced acculturation when the parent company comes to enforce its own corporate culture throughout its merged system. As a problem of learning membership and identity, acculturation shifts the focus from learning a new membership to accepting a membership which is being forced upon one. It is not unusual for continued employment to ride at least partly upon how quickly and how well a member is willing to put aside the former sense of membership and its ideology and to take on the identity of the new corporate discourse system.

Primary and secondary socialization

Since primary and secondary socialization normally refer to processes which are well developed before people come to the age of taking up jobs within corporate cultures, they might seem to be of no particular relevance to the analysis of corporate discourse systems. Nevertheless, in interpersonal communication there are many ways in which participation in a corporate discourse system comes into serious conflict with participation in the discourse systems of one's primary socialization.

For example, remember that the majority of the world's international corporations have adopted the basic ideology of the Utilitarian discourse system, which places a high value on progress, on the creative, free, and equal individual who functions as a rational economic entity, and who seeks first of all his or her own advantage. In many places in the world these are also the basic values into which children receive their primary socialization. From the earliest days of their lives they are enculturated into this Utilitarian individualistic ideology.

One can see, then, that there is a quite natural match between the children who have grown up within this ideology and the corporate ideologies in which they will seek employment as adults. On the other hand, as these corporations extend their operations throughout the world, they seek employees from the countries in which they are operating. In many cases those potential employees have not received primary socialization into the Utilitarian discourse system. At most these potential employees have only come into contact with this ideology through secondary socialization; that is, these potential employees have run across the Utilitarian ideology only in the schools they have attended. Outside of these schools they have been enculturated, for example, into an ideology such as the Confucian one, which places a strong emphasis on interpersonal and familial relationships and which puts the success of the group ahead of the success of the individual. For them the individualistic ideology is foreign, something taken on only for instrumental purposes. It is not something deeply felt as part of their very definition as human beings. It may even feel deeply inhuman and mechanical.

As international corporations which espouse the individualistic Utilitarian ideology take on employees who have been primarily socialized to a very different ideology, conflicts begin to arise. There are no particular problems if employees can maintain clear separations between their purely instrumental corporate identities and their more fundamental, non-corporate identities. In fact, our observations have led us to believe that this is just how most people cope with this potential for conflict between these two ideological systems.

Problems arise, however, when employees are expected to break down the separations between these two discourse systems. This difference in primary socialization and the ideological systems of corporate discourse systems is one of the factors which contribute to the development of separate and quite isolated communities of expatriates in multinational corporations which regularly send their employees abroad to work. Even where people from these different backgrounds are able to maintain very successful and cordial relationships under working conditions, that is, within the corporate discourse system, these relationships sometimes do not carry over into discourses outside of the corporate system.

Participation (apprenticeship)

Despite the formal training sessions and printed manuals that many corporations provide for new employees, socialization into most corporate discourse systems relies heavily on processes of legitimate peripheral participation in which novice employees are gradually given more and more responsibility for undertaking certain tasks supervised by more experienced employees. Decisions about continued employment and advancement are usually made based on employees' performance of such tasks. Thus the relationships between workers and their supervisors and other members of their working teams are perhaps the most important relationships in corporate discourse systems.

In this regard, two important trends can be observed in contemporary organizations. The first is an increasing uncertainty regarding the definition of expertise. With the rapid advancement of digital communication technologies and their increased importance in the workplace, it is often the case that newer employees need to take on the role of experts where the use of such technologies is concerned while older members take on the role of relative novices. Second, in many organizations the sense of hierarchy between supervisors and employees is increasingly being de-emphasized, and one is just as likely to be assessed by one's peers or even one's subordinates as by one's supervisor or manager. What this means is not that the interaction between experts and novices that forms the mechanism of socialization into most groups is breaking down, but that it is operating in much more complex and sometimes unpredictable ways.

Theories of the person and of learning

Good and evil. We have pointed out that in socialization, whether by that one means education or enculturation, motivation depends upon whether or not the person is thought of as being, first, basically good or bad and, second, self-oriented as in individualistic ideologies or other-motivated as in collectivistic ideologies. In fact, there seems to be a good bit of ambivalence within corporate discourses on the first of these conceptions of the person. Most frequently the problem is resolved by employing both incentive and coercive motivations for the learning of the new members of the discourse system. On the one hand there are various incentives for becoming a successful member, such as advances in pay, special privileges, and preferential work assignments. On the other hand there are forms of coercion, such as company policies, disciplinary committees, or the threat of contract terminations. The position taken by most corporate discourse systems is that while one cannot be sure whether people are basically good or bad or whether they are most likely to be motivated by incentives or by punishment, they will leave nothing to chance and use push–pull strategies of socialization into corporate ideology.

Individual and collective. The second point, however, is often quite significant. Most institutional rewards or punishments take the basic position that the person functions as an isolated unit of the sort put forward in Utilitarian ideology. This frequently goes against the actual needs of corporate task organization. A basic conflict is created when motivation for becoming a member of a corporate discourse system is based upon individual performance and yet the accomplishment of corporate tasks depends on successful cooperation among small or large groups of corporate members.

In the past three decades, especially with the development of newer international corporations, there has been much discussion of this sort of paradox in corporate learning. While the issue is far from settled, there now seems to be a recognition that the motivation for performance within a corporate discourse system needs to be brought in line with the assumptions made about how corporate tasks are best accomplished. As an issue of socialization for the new member of a corporate discourse system, there is often a personal conflict over whether he or she should pay most attention to the successful accomplishment of corporate tasks or to individual performance. It still remains the case that integrating oneself into the corporate structure may appear to be what the discourse system is asking of one, while those who do not fit in receive the greatest rewards because they display the individualistic characteristics of the Utilitarian discourse ideology.

There are also important differences in how members of different generational discourse systems orient towards teamwork and individual goals. In North America, for example, members of the Baby Boom generation, people born between 1946 and 1964, are regarded by managers as operating well in teams, despite the polemic individualism of their generation, and members of the generation following them, known as Generation X, are thought to prefer working individually and to be motivated more by individual goals.

Life cycle. From the point of view of corporate discourse, the most important issues regarding socialization and the life cycle within the past four decades have been the entry of more women into corporate careers beginning in the late 1970s, and the aging of the population in many countries, coupled with improved medical technologies, which have in the last two decades resulted in people remaining in the workforce much longer than before and older workers outnumbering younger workers in many workplaces.

Up until the mid-1970s, at least in Europe and North America, management levels of corporations were populated almost entirely by men. Women, when they worked within the corporate structure, tended to hold lower positions in salaried ranks, or work in secretarial or clerical positions. What this meant for education as well as for socialization, as we will discuss in more detail below in our discussion of gender discourse systems, is that men were educated to take these higher-level and higher-status positions and women were educated for the lower-level and lower-status positions or, in most cases, not to enter corporate discourse systems at all. This polarization of the workforce into two discrete classes along gender lines produced frustrations for both men and women, though these frustrations had somewhat different manifestations.

At the end of the twentieth century, two trends were evident in corporations in North America and Europe and other places as well. First, was an increase in career changes among men as they entered into mid-life transition (a period somewhere around forty to fifty years of age). As men began to see that they had reached the top of their potential for advancement, they also tended to shift away from their interest in advancing corporate goals in favor of emphasizing more personal goals. As a result, corporations saw many more men reaching mid-life and, instead of staying on until retirement, moving out of corporate life into some other, often quite unrelated activity. Thus corporations lost the experience and continuity these members of the discourse system had formerly provided them.

The second trend was that more women were seeking professional careers within corporations. At least in the first waves of this development, many of these women were somewhat older than their male peers. They often followed a pattern quite complementary to these males in the same age cohort. Whereas the men moved directly through secondary and tertiary education straight into employment and then in mid-life turned to look for other avenues of self-development, the women often interrupted their educational and professional careers to raise their families. In some cases they did not return for further education or training until their children became teenagers.

The result of this was that multinational corporations in the 1980s and 1990s often had two types of employee, who may have had quite similar formal educational backgrounds and credentials, but among whom the men tended to be much younger and without subsidiary experience, while the women were somewhat older and had considerable world experience. As we have said above, corporations often officially recognize only the formal credentials achieved through education and devalue the experience one gets outside of schools. This pattern of placing a higher value upon formal, schooled credentials and a lower value upon experience made it difficult both for men and for women. For men it was difficult to move outside of the formal structures of corporate discourse systems when at mid-life they sought other avenues of experience. For women it was correspondingly difficult to enter into the formal structures of corporate discourse, even though they brought with them considerable experience.

Today, as men and women in many countries are sharing housekeeping and child rearing tasks more equally, this age and experience disparity in workplaces is becoming less pronounced, but it still exists. In any case, it has now become an important part of corporate discourse systems to accommodate the family related obligations of their employees with things like flexible schedules, paternity leave for men along with maternity leave for women, and the provision of childcare in the workplace in order to accommodate the more egalitarian division of labor in the home.

Another important life cycle related phenomenon in contemporary corporate discourse systems is the marked increase in older workers in many organizations. With the aging of the populations in many nations, including the United States, Japan, China, and most European countries, and with advances in medical technologies that are increasing overall life expectancy in such countries, more and more people are remaining in the workforce longer than before. In North America this trend was further exacerbated by the financial collapse of 2008, which compromised the savings of many people, forcing them to delay their retirement. One consequence of this is that fewer jobs and fewer opportunities for advancement are opening up for younger workers, especially in countries with struggling economies. This, of course, raises important issues regarding socialization into corporate discourse systems: with the rapid advancement of technology, many older workers are finding it necessary to retrain in order to maintain their usefulness to the organizations in which they work. Whereas in the past, continuity and knowledge of the traditions embedded in the corporate discourse system were highly valued, companies today, in order to stay competitive, tend to place greater value on more flexible, mobile (and often more inexpensive) workers.

There is a large research literature on corporate training, on organizational and management structure, and on organizational communication. We have not, of course, been able to do more than to raise a few of what we think are the more important issues regarding socialization into membership in corporate discourse systems. If there is one point we might make in summary, it is that there is much more to socialization into such discourse systems than at first meets the eye. Most of the large literature on these subjects treats the problem as one largely of skill development. As important as professional communication skills are, in themselves we believe they are hardly sufficient to allow participants to "read between the lines" of corporate discourse systems. Our purpose in this chapter is to highlight a few of the areas in which socialization into corporate discourse systems goes beyond the simple approach of learning the skills necessary to do the job.

Forms of discourse

Corporate discourse systems are goal-oriented. Furthermore, as we have said above, the corporation itself is the outcome of the rise of the Utilitarian ideology. It should not be surprising to find, then, that the preferred forms of communication within corporate discourse systems are the most focused, goal-oriented forms of discourse, as they are within the Utilitarian discourse system. To put it quite generally, most corporate discourse systems tend toward the use of anti-rhetorical, positivist empirical, deductive, individualistic, egalitarian, and publicly or institutionally sanctioned forms of discourse.

This close paralleling of the Utilitarian discourse system and corporate discourse systems raises the question of whether or not it is worth making a distinction between them as two different types of discourse system at all. We believe it is worth making this distinction. The Utilitarian discourse system is a very widespread ideological system which is favored in many contexts which go considerably beyond corporate discourse. What sets corporate discourse apart to be treated separately is that it is an almost perfect embodiment of this discourse ideology. Corporate discourse is in some ways the model Utilitarian discourse system.

In the discussion of the forms of discourse of the corporate discourse system which follows, then, we will not recapitulate our discussion of chapter 6, but simply bring up a few points which we believe are useful for further analysis.

Grammar of context

The idea of focused interaction dominates the grammar of context. The corporate ideology is that in discourse nothing should be left to chance. Speech situations and events are carefully orchestrated and controlled. For example, a business meeting may have an agenda which may include open discussion. Within corporate ideology it is necessary to keep open discussion from springing any surprises for the controllers of the agenda. Often such points will be anticipated and then discussed in advance of the meeting, with responses even rehearsed so that what appears to be "open" is, in fact, equally focused.

A second aspect of this control of speech situations and events is that in corporate discourse, outside contextual factors are often expected to be eliminated. Sometimes staff members will be assigned to prepare business meetings, for example, just to ensure perfect uniformity of the setting. Each position will have a chair, a note pad, relevant papers tabled, a glass or cup of refreshment, and so forth. Uniformity and regularity are corporate ideals so that participants can produce a highly regular, scripted, and mechanized performance.

Genres, of course, vary considerably in corporate discourse systems. We have already given in previous chapters multiple examples of situations, events, and genres commonly found in corporate discourse. To extend this list the reader could consult any textbook on professional or business communication. While there are many of them, they all share to a greater or lesser extent the basic features of the forms of Utilitarian discourse.

What we need to ask is: what is missing? One does not find in most corporate discourse the use of lyric poetry, novels, songs (rock, popular, classical, or traditional), folk tales and myths, religious texts, prayers, ritual discourses (weddings, funerals), literary criticism, ethnography, or any of the many, many other genres of discourse used so commonly in other discourse systems. These other forms of discourse are proscribed because they do not fit the ideological characteristics of the five Ws and the one H; they do not carry forward the goal orientation of the corporate ideology.

One caution must be considered here. In the first place, one may find these genres within the discourse of corporate members within the walls of the corporation. Employees may engage in quite a variety of unofficial or non-legitimated behavior while otherwise operating within the corporate discourse system, and sometimes organizations even encourage such discourse up to a point as part of their corporate culture. The crucial point is that if these genres and this behavior begin to interfere with the utilitarian goals of the corporation it is legitimate for corporate members to ask that they be stopped.

Thus within corporations all kinds of underground communications may develop, from instant message gossip to "Facebooking" to the unauthorized photocopying or scanning of jokes or cartoons. Most companies tolerate a fairly large amount of these communications on the principle of allowing their employees to work in a relaxed, more "humanized" environment. Nevertheless, it is understood by all that these non-legitimated forms of discourse are inappropriate in official contexts – they should not show up at business meetings, for example – and that there is some unstated limit on just how much the company will tolerate. Some companies, in fact, are pursuing technological solutions to perceived losses in "productivity" that allegedly result from those practices by, for example, installing surveillance software on their employees' computers. Others are attempting to cordon off such activities in officially sanctioned periods of "creative loafing" or company sponsored parties or junkets.

At the same time, as mentioned above, many corporations are seeing the value of integrating non-goal directed forms of discourse such as social networking into the everyday management of their organizations. The reason for this, however, is not so much that they are moving away from an emphasis on productivity and other corporate goals. Rather, these moves come as the result of a realization that sometimes non-goal directed discourse can play a part in building solidarity among team members, which in turn impacts positively on the realization of corporate goals.

This brings up another important aspect of socialization as far as forms of discourse are concerned: an important aspect of socialization into a corporate discourse system is the need to understand the limits to what one can safely "get away with" when it comes to unauthorized forms of discourse, and, to some degree, learning how to successfully manage or circumvent the surveillance practices of one's superiors.

One further consideration is that we would want to distinguish between corporate forms of discourse and corporate products. We have said that songs are not used in corporate discourse. Nevertheless, many very large media corporations exist for the purpose of producing songs and other forms of music. While these corporations produce music, it would certainly be taken as odd for such a corporation to produce its annual report to stockholders in the form of a rock concert with annual production figures set to music, or for a company that manufactures computer games to conduct meetings through the medium of a massive multiplayer online game.

Finally, concerning the question of genre and of media, advertising raises considerable problems for our analysis. Corporate communications with the world of clients and customers is carried on largely through advertising. We have said that corporate discourse is anti-rhetorical, for example, and yet advertising freely employs virtually any and all rhetorical strategies to accomplish its purposes. We have said that songs are not used in corporate discourse, and yet they are widely used in corporate advertising campaigns.

While we have a partial answer to these questions, we believe that it is really beyond the scope of this book to fully analyze this distinction. We might, for example, argue that advertising is not, in fact, communication within the corporate discourse system, but a product of the corporation. We might argue that the corporate discourse system applies the corporate ideology rigorously only within the boundaries of the discourse system. That, however, seems to us to be stretching a point. It has also been pointed out, for example, that the discourse contemporary organizations need to employ in order to recruit and retain staff is increasingly taking on the discursive features of advertising.

If we look at the history of advertising, as has the sociologist Ruth Cowan in her book *More Work for Mother* (1983), we see that in the first period of advertising, around the turn of the twentieth century, it followed rather closely the principles of Utilitarian and corporate discourse. Advertisements at that time concentrated on two basic themes, descriptions of the product and its manufacture on the one hand, and instructions for the use of the product on the other. In this we could see that advertising at first followed the principles of the five Ws and the one H.

It was in the 1920s and the 1930s that advertising became "psychologized" and advertisers began using themes of guilt and other psychological needs to spur potential consumers into making purchases. Advertisers began to introduce more and more classical rhetorical strategies for the purposes of convincing an audience. Further, as technology develops, advertisers are becoming more and more able to personalize their messages and to target them to smaller and smaller niche markets. Advertising today for many corporations has moved from strategies of widespread rhetorical persuasion to the more interpersonal techniques of social networking in which consumers are invited to participate with corporations as "friends" or even "consultants" rather than customers.

There is evidence that advertising strategies are themselves subject to the ideologies, face systems, and preferred forms of discourse of the larger discourse systems in which they are produced and consumed. Studies by both Rodney Jones in Hong Kong and Richard Schmidt in Hawaii, for example, have shown that Chinese and Hong Kong television advertisements in the 1990s were more likely to take a narrative format, perhaps reflecting the importance of narrative as a persuasive device in the Confucian discourse system, and that television commercials from the United States, for all of their rhetorical flourish, still tended to focus heavily on information.

Functions of language

Corporate discourse, because it is goal oriented, tends to emphasize information over relationship, negotiation over ratification, and individual creativity over group harmony. Having said that, we should be careful to notice that, in the first place, in the preceding section we have pointed out that in collegial relationships, the information function of language is buffered by careful attention to the collegial relationship.

In the same way, there is a stated ideology within corporate discourse of the value of negotiation. From external marketing and sales negotiations to internal brainstorming activities, corporations tend to express a high value on the negotiation of relative positions of power and status. "Anyone can succeed" is the underlying motto within most corporate discourse systems. At the same time, however, it is well known that those who get the institutional rewards of promotion and privileged work assignments are often the ones who clearly, often loudly, ratify the existing structure of power and status.

One major point of contemporary discussion in management circles has to do with the question of group harmony over individual success within corporations. There was a feeling back in the early 1980s that Asian corporations had succeeded to a great extent because they quite naturally or "culturally" adopted patterns of communication which strengthened the group and the ability of the group to work in concert. It was also felt that at least some part of the divisiveness of "western" corporate discourse could be traced to excessive individualism on the part of members of the discourse system. Such conclusions were later, however, called into question when the Japanese economy stagnated in the mid-1990s and, at the end of the decade, the economy of the entire Asian region collapsed. There has also been a dramatic shift in management practices in places like the United States and Europe towards more team-based and collectivistic decision making. In fact, nowadays it is possible to witness more competitive, individualistic management practices in many companies in places like China, and more collectivistic management styles in many companies in the United States.

Forms of discourse in the new service economy

One of the most significant factors affecting forms of discourse in corporate discourse systems in the early twenty-first century is the replacement in many places of the old manufacturing based economy with a new service based economy in which communication plays a central role. In 2009, more than three-quarters of the workers in the United States were

employed in the service sector. Even in countries like China, which rely heavily on manufacturing, the number of people in service jobs is expected to exceed 40 percent of the
workforce in 2015. Many places like India, where the service industry accounts for 57
percent of the country's GDP, have become favorite places for the outsourcing of service
work from the United States and Europe.

One result of this is an increased attention in many corporate discourse systems to what
have come to be known as "communication skills." In her book *Good to Talk?: living and
working in a communication culture* (2000), Deborah Cameron argues that a major preoccupation of corporations in the "new work order" has been the cultivation and policing of the
communicative "styles" of their employees. Furthermore, it is often the lower paid workers
(those for example who work as servers, flight attendants, and operators in call centers) who
tend to be the most subjected to linguistic regulation.

Part of this new emphasis on communication skills in the workplace has been the introduction of what previously was considered "therapeutic discourse" into both workplace and
service encounters. Cameron relates, for example, stories of supermarket checkout staff
learning the techniques of "active listening." There has also been an increased emphasis on
involvement strategies, in particular on the importance in corporate and sales communications of showing interest and concern for one's interlocutor.

Cameron also points out the sometimes gendered nature of this stylized discourse. In her
research on telephone call center operators in the United Kingdom, she points out that the
language these workers are taught to reproduce has a strong similarity to what is popularly
thought of as "woman's language" (whether or not it has much to do with the way women
really talk; see chapter 11). Operators are taught to use expressive intonation, show concern
and interest in their voices, ask questions, and use frequent minimal responses.

The implications of this new stylized discourse of the service worker on corporate discourse systems is still uncertain. In some ways it seems at odds with the anti-rhetorical,
information focused orientation of traditional Utilitarian forms of discourse. On the other
hand, it is often highly scripted and regulated by training manuals and computer protocols
that embody the Utilitarian discourse system's emphasis on uniformity and efficiency.

Non-verbal communication

In chapter 7 we outlined three of the major elements of non-verbal communication which
we believe it is important to consider: kinesics (the movement of our bodies), proxemics
(the use of space), and the concept of time. Each of these is a very broad topic and we can
do no more than to mention here some of the aspects of non-verbal communication which
are of relevance to the corporate discourse system.

It is no accident that corporate life at the end of the twentieth century was often called
"the rat race." Life within corporations had come to be dominated by a fast pace in which
more and more is done in less and less time. If there was one defining kinesic characteristic
of corporate life at that time, and in many respects today, it is this ever increasing rapid
pace.

While the increasingly rapid pace of work within corporate discourse systems has not
abated, two major changes have taken place which in some ways challenge the Utilitarian
view of time discussed in previous chapters, causing corporate discourse systems which have
been unable to adapt to find themselves at a disadvantage. The first is a blurring of the
distinction between *chronos* time and *kairos* time. As we said before, *chronos* time is "clock"
time, whereas *kairos* or "appropriate" time is based more on the contingencies of a given

situation. In the past, corporations tended to do things by clock time. They set production and sales goals to be met and time lines for sub-stages of projects. Hours were kept on employees and, and employees themselves usually had a clear sense of separation between the times they were "on-duty" and the times they were "off-duty." Nowadays, with the rapidly moving global economy, corporations can no longer afford to operate according to rigid schedules, but rather must be flexible and ready to take whatever opportunities come their way. For multinational corporations with offices all over the world, the end of the "workday" in one office may be the beginning of the workday in another. Similarly, for employees who are increasingly working outside of the confines of traditional office walls and tethered to their workplaces through mobile communications devices, the boundary between work and "life" is breaking down. The traditional 9 to 5 work day has given way to an orientation towards time which promotes "anytime anywhere" work.

Another important change is the growing importance of polychronic orientations towards time in cooperate discourse systems as multitasking becomes the norm in many workplaces. Writing back in the late 1960s, Edward T. Hall pointed out that the "polychronic" orientation towards time of many "cultures" (Hall, for example, singled out Asian and South American cultures) stood in direct contradiction to the "monochronic" orientation towards time promoted by most multinational corporate discourse systems. Nowadays, a polychronic orientation towards time is likely to be seen as an advantage in many workplaces, and differences among workers are more likely to be drawn along generational lines rather than "cultural" lines, as younger workers bring to their jobs practices they have learned from digital media and older workers struggle to keep up with them.

Another aspect of non-verbal communication where changes are evident is the use of space. As Hall pointed out, in corporate discourse the use of space is often a major aspect of how we communicate power and status as well as our availability for communication with others (Hall 1969; Hall and Hall 1987). In the 1950s and 1960s when he did his work, he noted that in U.S. corporations, large corner offices are awarded to members of high status while, in contrast, though Japanese corporate officials may have similar offices, they rarely use them for day-to-day operations. Japanese high-ranking officers preferred to work in an open area along with many other employees so that they could be part of the give and take of operational discourse.

With the relative flattening of workplace hierarchies and the increased tendency for many highly paid executives to work from home or from the road, the use of physical space as a symbol of status and power is gradually being replaced by access to virtual spaces. Thus, the provision of an expensive mobile communication device, such as a top of the range Blackberry, to a corporate executive might be considered as important a status symbol as a nice office. Similarly, executives and managers who wish to feel closer to the day to day operations of their companies or their work teams are more and more likely to interact with colleagues in virtual spaces like workplace wikis and corporate social networking sites.

Modes, media, emplacement

As we have already hinted at above, perhaps the most profound changes that are occurring in corporate discourse systems today are occurring as a result of the changes in the material aspects of forms of discourse that we discussed in the last chapter. Rather than sending internal memos, for example, staff in corporations are communicating more and more through instant messaging programs that have the same degree of immediacy as telephone and face to face communication but do not make the same kinds of demands on face. This and other technologies like groupware and teleconferencing have made it easier for organizations to coordinate the activities of work teams situated in disparate locales across the globe.

This same technology is also changing what is meant by "workplace," as more and more companies are finding that it is cheaper to allow employees to work from home via their computers. As a result, working hours have become much more flexible and, as we mentioned above, the boundary between work time and leisure time has become much less clearly demarcated. What this often means is not that people work less, but that they work *more* as the "work week" is no longer defined by temporal boundaries but rather as "however long it takes to get the work done."

This spatial and temporal displacement of work from the workplace has also contributed to the changing relationships people have with corporate discourse systems. Many organizations, for example, are outsourcing work to what have come to be known as "human clouds," armies of on-line part-time workers who may have contracts with a large number of clients or may make their skills available through third-party companies. The managers of the corporate discourse systems to which these workers are temporarily attached have often never met them, may not even know their names, and do not accord them the benefits of full participation in the corporate discourse system, benefits like medical benefits and pension plans.

The biggest changes in the materiality of forms of discourse in corporate discourse in developed nations are really part and parcel of broader changes in the economy in which the manufacture of material goods has for the past several decades been giving way to the production of "knowledge" as the major activity of work. According to Manuel Castells, author of *The Rise of the Network Society*, in the new economy, wealth generation resides in the ability on the part of societies, organizations, and individuals to "create new knowledge and apply it to every realm of human activity by means of enhanced technological and organizational principles of information processing" (Castells 1993: 20).

Other scholars have taken this even further, claiming that not only have material goods been supplanted by information as the source of value in the new economy, but information itself has been supplanted by something that is even in scarcer supply: attention.

The wealth of information brought on by the technological revolution, this theory goes, has created a scarcity of attention, and created an increased need for products, services, and forms of discourse that assist people in allocating their attention more efficiently both in their jobs and in their everyday lives. Such forms of discourse include things like RSS readers, search engines, and social bookmarking sites, forms of discourse that allow individuals and organizations to manipulate information in creative ways, to evaluate it, and to make decisions about it very quickly, and to distribute it efficiently to those who need it. A chief advocate of this view is the scholar Michael H. Goldhaber, who argues that the emerging attention economy "involves a quite different pattern of life than the routine-based, industrial one with its work/home, work/play and production/consumption dichotomies. What matters is seeking, obtaining and paying attention" (Goldhaber 1997: para. 3).

Face systems

Face systems and strategies
As we have said before, while hierarchical face systems are the unstated rule in most corporate discourse systems, Utilitarian ideology often calls for the enactment of egalitarian

relationships in many workplace situations. Thus it is not uncommon for supervisors and even CEOs to encourage their employees to call them by their first names. The value placed on such displays of solidarity, of course, is not shared in corporate discourse systems in places where the influence of the Utilitarian discourse system does not extend beyond the workplace. It is not unusual in multinational corporations, therefore, for there to be some confusion across global offices and work teams as to which systems should be considered the default face systems when people at different levels of the organization interact.

As we noted above, one of the main trends of the "new work order" has been an even greater emphasis on the *performance* of egalitarian face systems in corporate discourse resulting in an apparent, if not always actual, flattening of hierarchies in many workplaces. This is partly a result of changes in the ways work tasks are being organized, with people tending to work more and more in less stable and more diverse work teams which are constituted around particular tasks and break up after those tasks are completed. In such arrangements, monitoring with possible sanctions for non-performance is more likely to come from fellow team members than from a supervisor.

Management theorists, in fact, are now talking less about how to control workers within hierarchical face systems and more about how to "empower" them to manage themselves, and human resources officers are increasingly advertising for recruits who are "self-directed" and exhibit "critical thinking." Of course there is a limit to such critical thinking. As long as it is directed towards innovation and improvement within the parameters of the organization's goals it is rewarded. When it is extended to holding those goals or the larger social, political, economic, or environmental consequences of the organization's actions up to scrutiny, however, it is less likely to be sanctioned.

Another reason for this apparent flattening of hierarchies is that the relationship between corporate discourse systems and the people who work for them is in many cases becoming increasingly temporary and tenuous as many businesses choose to outsource many of their activities rather than hiring new employees. Since these workers have little emotional or financial commitment to the overall goals of the organization, managers can only exert limited authority over them.

Because corporate discourse systems epitomize the Utilitarian discourse system, the face strategies one often finds in corporate discourse are those we have described in chapter 6. Communications within a corporation are generally hierarchical, though, as we have said above, the performance of egalitarian relationships is becoming an important feature in many corporate cultures, and public communications are generally characterized by symmetrical solidarity.

One example of the simultaneous operation of hierarchical face systems within corporate discourse systems and the systems of symmetrical solidarity that they promote in public discourse is the practice at Walmart of requiring retail employees to take an "oath" to smile, make eye contact, and utter a greeting "every time a customer comes within ten feet of me" (Cameron 2000: 57). The irony in this case is that the egalitarian strategies of involvement that employees are meant to use towards customers are enforced by non-egalitarian relationships within the company in which supervisors have the right to require employees to swear "oaths."

Rhetorical strategies
We have said above in corporate discourse there is often a preference for deductive strategies for the introduction of topics. Now we need to clarify that this does not mean that one will

never find inductive rhetorical strategies employed by members of corporate discourse systems.

In the early 1990s Ron Scollon undertook a study of business telephone calls (Scollon 1993b) which showed that the use of these strategies depends on the actual relationships between the people who are communicating with each other. Where the participants are in a client relationship, that is, where their primary purpose is economic exchange, telephone calls take on a deductive structure. In contrast, however, where the relationship is that of colleagues, that is, when information is exchanged without an accompanying economic transaction, a more inductive strategy is used.

The point we want to make is that the choice of inductive and deductive strategies is not simply a matter of the overall discourse system. In chapter 5 we argued that one could not say that deductive or inductive strategies were either "western" or "Asian," since both strategies are used within both cultures. Now we want to say that while there is a clear preference for the deductive strategy for introducing topics in corporate discourse, that does not mean one will not find the inductive pattern. In corporate discourse, one crucial contextual distinction is the type of relationship between or among the participants. Our point is that in the analysis of discourse systems, one needs to be watchful against rigid application of general statements. While deductive strategies may be preferred, they will not be used exclusively. It becomes an important analytical point to ask why other strategies are used and when. Such questions will usually highlight features of the discourse system which might otherwise be missed.

Kinship, the concept of self, and ingroup–outgroup relationships

Here we want to bring up three quite closely related issues which are likely to be important, especially in interdiscourse communication within corporate discourse systems: kinship, the concept of the self, and ingroup–outgroup relationships. The question of their importance arises because within the Utilitarian discourse system there is a strong ideological position that individuals are isolated, autonomous, rational entities. As members of corporate discourse systems, it is felt that they should behave as such, even if that means down-playing relationships with their families or spouses, other groups to which they belong, or members of other discourse systems. The general terms which cover this problem are "nepotism" and "conflict of interest."

A person the authors know is a Native American. Within her family and social group, kinship ties are very strong and lines of authority are drawn along lines of kinship. In other words, in such a system if I want to have somebody employed under me in an institution over whom I want to be sure I can exercise my authority and who I can expect to respect that authority, I will employ a niece or a nephew. By doing so I can bring both institutional authority and kinship authority to bear upon this employee.

This person was the head of a department in a governmental office and, using the cultural practices of her group, hired her nephew for a job. She did this in the interest of advancing the work of her department, knowing that this person was both competent to do the work and quite constrained by her authority to do it as well. Unfortunately, governmental regulations quite specifically proscribed such hiring, on the grounds that she would be likely to show favoritism to her nephew and be unable to expect a normal work performance from him.

This case illustrates a conflict which runs throughout corporate discourse systems from France and Italy to Hong Kong and Singapore. The ideology of the Utilitarian discourse system has it that individuals should set aside personal, cultural, and other group-derived relationships and enter into purely logical relationships in corporate discourse. On the other hand, many, perhaps most, groups emphasize that human beings are deeply connected to each other through their kinship ties. It is rare to find people who assert the Utilitarian ideology of the isolated, autonomous individual in all their affairs. As a problem for corporate discourse systems, then, most members of these systems find themselves in constant conflict between the goals of the corporate system and their own personal goals, which are often group-derived.

What holds true within corporations is even more strongly felt in relationships with people outside of corporate discourse. Should an officer of a corporation take into consideration the opinions of the community in which he or she lives when he or she implements corporate decisions? In most cases, such exercises in community consultation are not for the purposes of making more informed decisions; they are largely marketing and public relations activities designed to get the community to more easily accept decisions already taken internally by the corporation.

The size and scope of corporate discourse systems

Now that we have gone through our outline guide for the analysis of discourse systems with reference to corporate discourse systems, there remains one consideration: the size and scope of such systems. On the one hand we would argue that the very broad, overarching discourse system which we have called the Utilitarian discourse system is too broad, too vague, and not sufficiently institutionally grounded to really do more than provide broad historical and ideological outlines.

If the Utilitarian discourse system is too broad, what is too narrow? Would we want to consider a multinational corporation such as McDonald's or Sony Corporation as a single corporate discourse system? Or, on the other hand, might it be better to consider a regional office of such a corporation to be a single corporate discourse system operating as a subsidiary of another, larger system?

Ultimately, while there might be much interesting discussion in trying to resolve such questions, we do not believe that any clear resolution would ever be achieved. Any discourse system is constantly in the process of evolution and change, and the point is not to try to fix the description of any one system permanently in place. The point, we think, is to open up the questions for analysis, which will allow communicators to analyze the dimensions which will be of the greatest use in coming to understand interdiscourse communication. Our purpose here has been more to raise questions than to provide final answers.

Professional Discourse Systems

The authors have often enough been in conversations which begin as follows:

Q: What do you do?
A: I teach at City University.
Q: Oh, what do you teach?
A: I teach English.

Sometimes, however, this same question-and-answer sequence goes somewhat differently:

Q: What do you do?
A: I teach English.
Q: Oh, where do you teach?
A: At City University.

These two sequences show the underlying problem of membership and identity faced by participants in voluntary discourse systems; in most cases one is simultaneously a participant in a corporate discourse system and a professional or occupational discourse system. In the first sequence, we interpreted the question, "What do you do?," as a question about corporate or institutional membership. Then we have treated our membership in the worldwide professional discourse system of university teachers of English as a secondary membership.

The second sequence goes the other way around. We have first interpreted our primary membership as membership in the professional discourse system. We are first identifying ourselves as English teachers. Secondarily we are presenting ourselves as employees of a particular institution.

Although in this case we are focusing directly on the professional group teachers or academics, the same would apply in many occupations. One might say that he was an electrician (occupational identity) and then later point out that he worked for Kolon Corporation. On the other hand, someone might point out that she works for Singapore Airlines and later clarify that she is an accountant.

Our purpose here is to introduce the concept of cross-cutting voluntary discourse systems such as those of corporation and professional group, and to point out how identity in those two cross-cutting discourse systems may produce conflicts of identity for participants in those systems. These conflicts of identity, in turn, may lead to confusion or misunderstanding in discourse among people who sense such cross-cutting identities. The important point is that such conflicts and multiple identities are not problems which can be solved; they are characteristic of virtually all situations of professional communication. In virtually all goal-directed discourse systems individuals will simultaneously be participants in both corporate and professional discourse systems, and in some cases participation in one system will tend to undercut or call into question full participation in the other system. In the career of a single person there are often periods of greater or lesser identification with professional goals, and of corresponding complementary identification with corporate goals.

This holds true for members of a great variety of professional or occupational discourse systems, such as those of engineers, travel industry managers, bus drivers, traders in foreign exchange, sports journalists, advertising photographers, electricians or carpenters, or symphony orchestra musicians. In each case there is a possible problem: one is simultaneously a member of the discourse system of one's professional or occupational group and of one's institutional, organizational, or corporate discourse system.

These two forms of membership are potentially in conflict because they are goal-directed systems which often have competing goals. The corporate discourse system normally has some primary goal, such as earning a profit, and the secondary goal of self-preservation of the system. The professional discourse system has the goal of supporting its members in the realization of their own career interests. Those individual career interests may well be in competition with the corporate goals. What is important is to recognize that such cross-cutting identities exist and will be operating in most communication which takes place either among professional colleagues or among members of the same corporate structure.

We can summarize the problems which arise from multiple participation in discourse systems as follows:

1 *Conflicting ideologies*: the purposes of the two (or more) systems pull the person toward different goals, and as he or she places a value on both sets of goals, it becomes a recurring problem to decide in any particular case which set of goals to emphasize. A scientist might, for example, work for a government or a corporate entity which requires him or her to compromise his or her commitment to truth or accuracy in order to protect the interests of his or her employers.

2 *Fragmentation of socialization and experience*: often the education or experience which is valued in one system is devalued in one or more of the other systems in which a person participates. A person must select from among his or her total experience as a human just those aspects each discourse system values, and this produces a feeling of fragmentation.

3 *Dilemmas in choosing the most appropriate forms of discourse*: each of the multiple systems favors different forms of discourse, and difficult selections must sometimes be made. The engineering report which would be most useful within the corporation might be considered oversimplified or naive to professional colleagues or, vice versa, the most professional engineering report might seem loaded with jargon or excessively academic for corporate planning purposes.

4 *Multiple faces*: the separate system may require the presentation of a different set of face relationships, and the person may come to feel quite "two-faced" in maintaining both corporate and professional relationships.

As simultaneous members of multiple cross-cutting discourse systems, people must constantly tune and adjust their sense of identity and membership so that the goals of all or most of these systems are at least minimally satisfied. While at times this can be a rewarding challenge, it is often also extremely stressful.

Researching Interdiscourse Communication

One of our main goals in this chapter has been to demonstrate how the outline guide to discourse systems we developed in the last chapter can be practically applied to one kind of discourse system. Another goal was to raise some important questions about voluntary discourse systems into which people tend to be socialized later in their lives and the kinds of relationships such discourse systems have both to larger discourse systems like the Utilitarian discourse system and the Confucian discourse system and more "involuntary" discourse systems like gender and generational discourse systems.

Whether or not the site you are investigating is a workplace or a domain far removed from work, corporate discourse systems exert a profound effect on people's lives. Hopefully the issues raised in this chapter will prompt an examination of these effects on the people you are studying. Questions you might ask are:

Are there explicit or implicit conflicts between the beliefs espoused in private conversations and the ideology of the corporate discourse systems in which they participate?

Are people expected to treat people differently on the job than they do in other situations?

How do people's age and gender affect how they participate in corporate discourse systems?

Are there conflicts between the corporate discourse systems people participate in and the principles or values of the professional groups to which they belong?

It would be useful here, we think, to mention that some of the same difficulties we mentioned above which arise from cross cutting professional and corporate discourse systems also arise for scholars conducting research on corporate discourse systems. Such research usually involves building a relationship and gaining the trust of gatekeepers in these discourse systems who are often highly placed managers or directors, and part of this process of gaining trust involves convincing participants in the discourse system not just that the researcher's goals do not contradict the stated goals of the organization but also that the research might in some way help the organization to further those goals. It is not unusual, however, in such situations for either researchers or members of the organization to come to the conclusion during the course of the research that there is a mismatch in goals or values. The researcher might, for instance, witness practices which he or she might consider in some way unethical, or members of the organization may expect the researcher to provide services to the organization or promote the organization in publications in ways that the researcher is unwilling to do.

Many researchers take the position that the role of scholars is somewhat like that of lawyers, and that they should approach their subjects (or "clients") with an attitude of non-judgmental neutrality. We do not hold this opinion, not only because we doubt that it is possible for research to be truly value-free, but also because we believe that one of the jobs of a researcher, especially a researcher in communication, is to attempt to make people's lives better in any way we can. In his last book Ron Scollon said, "good ethnography is never in my mind a kind of whistle blowing" (Scollon 2008: x). Nevertheless, good ethnography often (if not always) requires one to take a particular stand in relation to a host of ethical issues. How such conflicts should be resolved is a matter best left to the particular researcher in his or her local context. Here it is sufficient simply to point out that such dilemmas are an excellent example of the kinds of conflicts that can arise from cross cutting professional and corporate discourse systems.

Discussion Questions

1   Think back to a job that you have had. Discuss how the organization you worked for socialized new members and the kinds of values expressed in those socialization practices. In particular discuss:
    (a)   What aspects of the socialization were formal and what aspects were informal.
    (b)   Who in the organization took responsibility for different kinds of socialization.
    (c)   What kinds of systems of rewards and punishment existed in the organization.
    (d)   Were members of the organization expected to primarily pursue individual goals or to work as members of teams?

2 Think again about the same job you discussed in the first question. Consider how the beliefs, forms of discourse, and face systems of the organization compare with the beliefs, forms of discourse, and face systems in other groups or organizations you participate in (for example, your family, a religious organization). What are the similarities and differences? Did you encounter any conflicts because of these differences?

3 Go to the recruitment websites of a number of large corporations. (A good example is Apple's recruitment website at http://www.apple.com/jobs/us/.) Discuss how these sites reflect the ideologies, preferred forms of discourse, face systems, and forms of socialization of these corporate discourse systems and how they differ from one another.

References for Further Study

Ron Scollon's study of telephone conversations to which we refer is reported in his 1998 book *Mediated Discourse as Social Interaction: a study of news discourse*. The material on the new work order is taken in part from *The New Work Order: behind the language of the new capitalism* by James Paul Gee, Glynda Hull, and Colin Lankshear (1996). In speaking of the attention economy, we have mentioned the work of Michael H. Goldhaber. Another useful source for information about this concept is Richard A. Lanham's 2006 book *The Economics of Attention: style and substance in the information age*. Much of the material on the role of communication in contemporary workplaces was taken from the work of Deborah Cameron, especially her 2000 book *Good to Talk?: living and working in a communication culture*. Rodney Jones's study on cross-cultural frames for television commercials can be found in his 1996 monograph *Responses to AIDS Awareness Discourse: a cross-cultural frame analysis*. Robert I. Westwood's 1992 *Organisational Behavior: southeast Asian perspectives* provides an excellent study of organizational behavior in Southeast Asia in the late twentieth century. As mentioned before, *Professional Communication in International Settings* by Yuling Pan, Suzanne Wong Scollon, and Ron Scollon (2002) is a very good general introduction to interdiscourse communication in professional and corporate contexts.

10

Generational Discourse

Involuntary Discourse Systems

A person is simultaneously a member of many discourse systems. This is, perhaps, the most important aspect of the concept of discourse systems we have been developing. As we said in the last chapter, a member of a corporate discourse system is normally at the same time a member of a professional or occupational discourse system. The tension between his or her identity as a member of these two discourse systems always presents a potential problem.

In a parallel way, cutting across membership in these voluntary discourse systems are two other involuntary discourse systems in which all of us participate: those of generation and gender. These add two more dimensions of simultaneous participation and therefore of potential conflict among ideologies and identity. These involuntary systems also provide what in the long run are probably even more complex problems of interpretation in communication with members of other discourse systems.

This increased problem of communication arises from the fact that involuntary discourse systems such as those of generation and gender are often invisible to us. After all, we make certain conscious choices in becoming employees of our institutions and in choosing our professions or occupations (though it would be a mistake to exaggerate the extent to which we actually choose our participation in some of these voluntary discourse systems). Furthermore, most voluntary discourse systems are based upon quite conscious and explicit forms of socialization through formal education and credentialization. In contrast, we do not go to school to study how to become a member of our generation or of our gender group; we begin learning the ropes of these identities from our earliest days of life, and, as we will argue below, that early life experience remains the strongest influence toward the maintenance of our sense of membership in these groups.

Since the 1960s it has been part of the common vocabulary, at least in the United States, to speak of a generation gap. This gap is most clearly perceived to have opened up between those in that country born after World War II, the Baby Boom generation, and those born before that time. Today another generation gap is being perceived as those born after 1995,

Intercultural Communication: A Discourse Approach, Third Edition. Ron Scollon, Suzanne Wong Scollon, Rodney H. Jones.

a group we will call the Millennial generation or Generation Y, enters the workforce with very different ideas about work and success than their managers, who are likely to belong either to the Baby Boom generation or to the generation that followed the Baby Boomers, Generation X.

As an example of the relevance of this perception, people writing in management and marketing analysis emphasize the need to recognize these generation gaps both for successful management and for the successful marketing of products. Because generation gaps have been so widely discussed in U.S. society, we will begin our discussion of generational discourse systems with the various U.S. generations that have been described in this research and popular literature. Later, by way of comparison and contrast, we will explore generational discourse systems in the People's Republic of China.

In a discussion between Neil Postman and Camille Paglia on literacy and the electronic media that took place in the early 1990s, the generational difference between these two critics rose to the surface.

> *Postman*:　Now I won't ask you how old you are.
> *Paglia*:　I'm forty-three. I was born in 1947. And you graduated from college in 1953. I checked! I wanted to know, because I think this information is absolutely critical to how one views the mass media. I graduated from college in 1968. There are only fifteen years between us, but it's a critical fifteen years, an unbridgeable chasm in American culture (Postman and Paglia 1991: 47).

This bit of dialogue emphasizes several points. One is that the generation gap is taken as a real and obvious cultural phenomenon in the United States. Another is that this difference in generations is taken to be of considerable explanatory power. The audience to this conversation is expected to accept that one can account for Postman's strong defense of print based literacy not on the internal grounds of his argument but on the grounds of his historical placement among various generations. A third point, which perhaps in the long run is the most significant, is that this view of the generations is advanced by the younger member of the polarity. One might almost say that the belief of the Baby Boom generation in the United States that there was a clear gap between them and their parents became self-fulfilling. At least in this case, Postman, the member of the older generation, chose not to accept this generational explanation as sufficient.

In other words, in contemporary U.S. society, there is a strong belief among many that the experience of having been born at a particular time and in a particular place is taken as giving one "membership" in a particular "cultural group" or, in the terminology we have been using, implicates them as participants in a particular discourse system. It is widely felt that communication between people born after World War II and those born before that time is a form of "intercultural communication," and the same idea is often expressed about communication between today's "wired" young people and their less technology-savvy elders. A Pew Research Center study of generations in the United States released in 2009 found that respondents of different age groups were at such odds over a wide range of political, social, and technological issues as to signal "the largest generation gap since the 1960s" (Taylor and Morin 2009).

At least two theories have been advanced to explain generational differences. The first is known as the generational subculture theory, which posits that the beliefs and social practices of a given generation are shaped by the events that occur during the lives of its members, particularly during their impressionable adolescent years. In other words, generations are "discourse systems" whose participants share a particular worldview, particular forms of discourse, and so forth. The other theory is known as the life-cycle theory, and this suggests that the behavior and beliefs of every generation will evolve through a series of rather predictable stages, with people, for example, universally becoming more conservative and more collectivistic as they grow older. The evidence from research provides some support for both theories. It should not be a surprise to the reader that we will be approaching the issue of intergenerational communication through the framework of the first theory, seeing it primarily as interdiscourse communication. We do not believe, however, that the life cycle theory is without value, and in fact we have already indicated in our discussion on socialization how important the concept of life cycle is to our thinking. We believe it is possible to treat different generations as distinct discourse systems and at the same time to acknowledge that members of these generations typically change their beliefs and behavior as they grow older. In fact, such a position highlights a very important aspect of discourse systems: that they are not static but instead always change and evolve over time.

The Ideologies of Individualism in the United States

Some one hundred and seventy years ago, the French observer Alexis de Tocqueville described people in the United States as highly individualistic. He believed that this individualism was inseparable from the new concept of egalitarian democracy practiced in that country. In the 1830s he wrote: "Not only does democracy make men forget their ancestors, but also clouds their view of their descendants and isolates them from their contemporaries. Each man is forever thrown back on himself alone, and there is danger that he may be shut up in the solitude of his own heart" (Tocqueville 1969: 508). From the point of view of the French Tocqueville, this American democratic individualism was, indeed, extreme. It should be remembered in reading Tocqueville, of course, that the background against which his observations were made, and against which citizens of the United States exercised their individualism, the mid-nineteenth century, was still very traditional in many ways. He was, in fact, observing U.S. individualism just at the point where it was beginning to take on the ideological position of Utilitarianism. "Individualism is a calm and considered feeling which disposes each citizen to isolate himself from the mass of his fellows and withdraw into circle of family and friends; with this little society formed to his taste, he gladly leaves the greater society to look after itself" (Tocqueville 1969: 506). At that time, however, the family was still firmly in place as a grounding social structure. Individuals accepted their places within their families, however democratic and egalitarian they might otherwise have been. The assumption that it was the place of parents or the older generation to lead and of children or the younger generation to follow was unquestioned.

Some one hundred and fifty years after Tocqueville, Robert Bellah and his colleagues (Bellah et al. 1985) found that what was a new term at the time of Tocqueville, "individualism," had become an entire language, which dominated self-analysis in the United States. While they observed a number of forms in which individualism was manifested, the most significant to Bellah and his associates was what they called "ontological individualism," that is, the belief that "the individual has a primary reality whereas society is a second-order, derived or artificial construct" (1985: 334). This form of individualism is very much what

Jeremy Bentham was putting forward when he wrote, "The community is a fictitious *body*" (Bentham 1962: 35).

Ontological individualism is the point of view that all psychological and sociological analysis is based on the primary reality of the individual. Tocqueville argued that historically U.S. individualism developed out of the anti-aristocratic democracy of the United States of America. In other words, in his view U.S. democracy as well as the U.S. individual were defined negatively; they were revolutionary in character. U.S. individualism is based more on what it is not than on any direct expression of what it is. Thus, citizens emphasize that the individual is *not* subject to arbitrary laws without representation, and the individual is *not* subject to domination by historical precedent and preference. The political and social individual is defined negatively by his or her escape from the control of historical and social forces.

This fundamental ideology of individualism in the United States can be summarized in two statements:

1 The individual is the basis of all reality and all society.
2 The individual is defined by what he or she is not.

We ascribe these characteristics to "individualism in the United States" not because we believe that individualism is somehow the unique property of that country: individualism is clearly an important ideology in many societies and social groups, especially those which have been strongly influenced by the Utilitarian discourse system. The point we are trying to make, and which we will elaborate below, is that there are many kinds of individualism, and that it is useful not just to distinguish the individualism that has developed in the United States from that which has developed in other places, but also to distinguish the individualism that dominated the worldview of Americans from one generation from that which dominated the worldview of those belonging to other generations.

In a recent study of discourse on the television show *Donahue*, a popular U.S. talk show that aired between 1967 and 1996, Donal Carbaugh (1989) showed how these two principles combine to form a discourse of negative (or as he calls it "polemical") individualism that has long been embedded in the day-to-day language of people in the United States and has been particularly potent since the 1960s. Carbaugh's analysis of this language is that the person is first symbolized as an individual, that is, ontological individualism lies at the center of the definition of the person. This individual, in turn, has or contains a self. This metaphor of containment is expressed in such phrases as, "I am relatively self-contained," "I have got my self together," "I am trying to put the pieces back together again," "reveal a piece of yourself," "the person inside me," or "There is nothing wrong with getting angry. It's just how you handle it . . . keeping it inside is no good" (Carbaugh 1989: 78–9). Most significantly, and what makes this brand of individualism "polemical," is that this self is understood as being opposed to what are referred to as "traditional social roles." As Carbaugh puts it, "Society and social roles are semantic loci of oppressive historical forces that constrain self" (1989: 92). This polemical code of negative, ontological individualism is expressed in statements such as the quotation below from the *Donahue* show.

> While we're talking about men and women, if people would just concentrate on themselves, and their goals, and being individuals. Society says that you have to earn money [or wash dishes, raise children, be pretty, etc., etc.] to be of any value. I feel that that's very ingrained in men

right now. That is what women are fighting. I feel that I am fighting that right now, myself. (quoted in Carbaugh 1989: 100)

While there is a deeply held belief in the United States that people of different generations in the country are participants in different discourse systems, it is also a widely held belief that what remains constant across generations is the "American ideology of individualism" with the individual assumed to be the central organizing reality for human experience. What has changed across these generations, from the people observed by Tocqueville to those we saw on *Donahue*, and between those who appeared on and watched this program on television back in the 1970s and 1980s and young people today, is the nature of this individualism, the ways the individual is defined and the oppositions against which the individual is observed and expressed.

Six generations of North Americans

Around three decades ago, the behavioral psychologist Layne Longfellow (1978) in his corporate management seminars was using generational differences as a framework in which to analyze productivity in the U.S. workforce. He associated three major lines of psycho-sociological research: studies of changes in child-care practices, studies of developmental stages in the human life cycle, and studies of the modal behavioral syndrome known as Type-A behavior.

The four generations analyzed by Longfellow were as follows:

Authoritarians	1914–28	82–96 years of age in 2010
Depression/War	1929–45	65–81 years of age in 2010
Baby Boom	1946–64	46–64 years of age in 2010
Infochild	1965–80	36–45 years of age in 2010

These divisions were based on practices of enculturation, that is, they were based upon child-rearing and parenting practices in early childhood and upon the impact of significant world and national events at transitional points in the life cycle (secondary socialization). While we will base our analysis on Longfellow's original categories, we will add to his analysis of socialization practices an analysis of ideologies, forms of discourse, and face systems. We will also add to Longfellow's list the more recent generation of the Millennials, those born between 1980 and 1995, sometimes referred to as Generation Y, and those born after 1995, which we call Generation Z.

The Authoritarians, born between 1914 and 1928
Ideology. The Authoritarian generation's view of the world was dominated by war. The first of this generation's members were born during World War I and the bulk of them reached their early adult transition (around eighteen to twenty-one years of age) during World War II.

For the development of U.S. individualism, World War II was significant in several ways. In the first place, as Tocqueville saw so clearly, individualism is greatly strengthened by the breaking of social ties. World War II broke ties for many in the United States simply because, as immigrants and children of immigrants, they found themselves at war with their own countries of origin. The German, Italian, French, and other immigrants who returned to Europe to fight against their own cousins severed forever a tie of loyalty to Europe, which, though it had been weakened by immigration, had never before been so severely tested.

For Japanese-Americans the break was similar, though in most cases they were not put directly into battle with their own cousins but sent to Europe instead (many experiencing confinement in internment camps before being allowed to enlist). Most Japanese-American servicemen along with other Japanese-Americans felt that they were under direct pressure to renounce any suggestion of loyalty to Japan. This cultural separation remains a source of pain to this day.

The separation of the United States from Europe was also completed by World War II in the sense that the United States emerged from that war in a position of economic and political dominance over Europe. By the end of the war there was little sense left of the United States being the poor cousin of the stronger British Empire.

By the time the Authoritarian generation had moved out of World War II into the positions they took in government, business, and education, there was little left to maintain the lingering ties to Europe which had persisted in the country until then. War continued to be the theme for this generation. Just as they came into their mid-life transition period (the early forties or so), the war in Vietnam broke out. As children born into war and as adults who matured as individuals in war, this third war seemed to them to be part of the nature of human society. They did not question it at all. It was their children, the Boom Babies, who questioned it. At this time of life, when it is common to review the course of one's life and to settle into the enjoyment of the benefits of one's work, not only did this generation of Authoritarians find their authority being questioned, but their belief in the past as a major influence on the present was no longer accepted by the younger generation. Although the Authoritarians began the transition from the nineteenth-century individualism described by Tocqueville to the *Donahue*, self-expressive, polemic individualism of the end of the twentieth century, the complete devaluing of trust in authority was more than they were able to accept.

Socialization, enculturation. The psychological anthropologist Martha Wolfenstein studied the sequence of changes in parenting styles as reflected in the extremely popular and widely distributed U.S. government publication *Infant Care* (West 1914; Wolfenstein 1953; Goodrich 1968). In the first period (beginning in 1914) she observed a very strict emphasis on limiting the child's self-exploration. This concern is at direct odds with the sorts of expression found verbalized on *Donahue* in the 1970s and 1980s or in popular culture in present-day America. The very conservative style of parenting of the earlier period is part of a general picture of the nature of infancy which had continued undiminished from the nineteenth century.

In chapter 8 we quoted the New Englander who said that no child has ever been known who did not possess an evil disposition – however sweet it might appear. It is clear enough that the ideological individualism of this oldest generation in the United States was strongly affected by this assumption that human nature was basically evil. The advice given by the U.S. government to new parents is clearly based on this assumption. They were to exercise their parental authority in the strongest way to limit the activities of the child.

Forms of discourse. The world into which the Authoritarians were born had just begun to feel the effects of the first of the electronic media, the telegraph. Radio and movies broke into their consciousness in the 1920s, when they were teenagers. Television did not become the major feature of communication until they were close to mid-life. For the Authoritarians, print literacy and oratory were the principal means of communication in public life. These media carry with them a deeply historical sense of time, the Golden-Age sense we discussed in chapter 6. This historical sense of time ties these Authoritarians both to the past and to the future. They have been avid newspaper readers and have had a high sense of being in the eye of history in their public acts. They have also had a sense of seeing the world degenerate into worse and worse conditions.

Face systems. It is not, perhaps, surprising that the Authoritarian generation developed a very high sense of authority coupled with a very low need for the expression of their own desires. There was a high consciousness of the dangers of both physical and moral dirtiness. The relationship between adults and children was understood as strongly dominated by the adult. From this we can see that, even though there was an emphasis on political egalitarianism, the hierarchical differences between adults and children were to be preserved.

Summary. This generation of U.S. citizens is very much like those observed by Tocqueville. Individualism was best expressed within the narrow confines of family, friends, and business associates. As a polemical form of individualism, they found their identity in being North American, not European or Asian. They further found themselves in opposition to such controlling forces as the government and government regulation. There was, however, as yet no opposition to the control and authority of the ascending generation. The Authoritarians accepted the domination of their parents and assumed that their descendants would accept their authority. While they had become highly individualistic, they had not yet become truly egalitarian.

The Depression/War generation, born between 1929 and 1945

Ideology. The most important life event for the Depression/War generation is, of course, the Great Depression, beginning in 1929 and running through the end of World War II. This is the world into which they were born. As we will see when we look at the primary socialization of this generation, doubt had been expressed by the parents of these children as to whether or not the adult would win out in the battle for dominance. It is significant to see that the parents of these children were actually living under very precarious social and economic conditions. First the Depression had crushed their expectations by eliminating their savings, their jobs, and their faith in the American political process. The great entrepreneurs had lost fortunes; workers were coming close to starvation. Labor unions rose throughout the country to call into question what had seemed obvious – that democratically organized free enterprise was the most productive political and economic system.

At the same time the chaos and terror of World War II, while it did not devastate the continent of North America the way it did that of Europe, left these babies in many cases without fathers. Many of this generation remember the sad, long evenings waiting for news of beloved fathers and older brothers. It was a time in which it was hard to maintain that one's success in life would come as an inheritance from the older generation. It is not surprising, then, to see in this generation the development of the belief that if one was going to succeed, one was going to have to go it alone.

In many ways this Depression/War generation is the transitional one in the United States. The authority of the older generation was no longer simply assumed, and yet there is nothing in this generation of the open self-expression of the Baby Boom generation. Depression/War generation individualism is very much the go-it-alone independence of the "self-made man" who does not identify with either those who went before or those who came after.

Socialization, enculturation. The preceding generation, the Authoritarians, were brought up in a world which assumed that the little infant was basically depraved and needed to be kept from any form of self-pleasure or self-expression at all costs. For babies of the Depression/War generation, the emphasis changed from self-denial to self-regulation and excessive scheduling of behavior. This was most strongly manifested in the emphasis on very early control of the bowels. Infants of this generation were expected, according to government advice, to be bowel trained by six months of age.

Three aspects of this emphasis on bowel training in the edition of *Infant Care* revised for this generation should be noted. First, at least in contemporary pediatric opinion, six to eight months of age is far too early to expect a normal child to complete bowel training. In other words, this is a wholly unreal expectation placed upon the infant. Second, note the battle for dominance between the adult and the child. With the Authoritarians it was taken for granted that the adult was in the position of authority. This was unquestioned. Thirdly, the emphasis on absolute regularity in bowel movements, not varying by more than five minutes from day to day, manifests a society-wide, new emphasis on time-scheduled regularity.

This new emphasis on regularity of timing and control was not by any means limited to childcare. One sees it, for example, in Frederick Taylor's *Scientific Management* (1911), and in the newly popular time and motion studies in American industry. Such studies had led to Henry Ford's production line assembly of cars in Detroit in the 1920s. Cowan (1983) has argued that during the interwar period there was a steady and systematized process which she calls the "industrialization of the home." This widespread mode of thinking penetrated down into such intimate details as the bowel training of infants.

The characteristics of this generation are based on three features of child care of the Depression/War generation: (1) the emphasis on the struggle between the child and the adult, (2) the expectation of absolutely regular behavior (along with the impossibility of achieving it), and (3) the very early time set on this child's achievement of bowel training. These characteristics are strikingly similar to those described by Friedman and his associates for the adult Type-A behavior pattern (Friedman and Rosenman 1974; Friedman and Ulmer 1984).

Major components of the Type-A personality include insecurity of status, the need to control, and a sense of time urgency. Once the connection is made between this behavior pattern and cardiac and other stress-related disorders, it is not difficult to see how the Depression/War baby has been primed from the earliest days for this behavioral syndrome. This person's insecurity of status was first reflected in the doubt shown by the writers of *Infant Care* that the adult could win in the battle for this baby's control. The insecurity was further established in the economic losses and failures of the Depression and the war. To that was added in many cases the absence of many significant men in this child's life. Often those absences were permanent, when fathers and uncles died at war.

The need to control was both modeled by this child's parents in their concern to dominate him or her and emphasized in this child's own need to master bowel control at an age when it was virtually impossible. And, of course, not only was this need to control emphasized, it was timed to within five minutes on a daily basis.

Forms of discourse. This might be called the news generation. Perhaps it was because of the strong influence of World War II, but this generation was the first to grow up with the constant sound of radio news in its ears. One of the manifestations of the Type-A syndrome is an obsession with information and with numbers. This obsession is constantly being fed by both news and sports broadcasts.

At first, of course, these broadcasts were radio broadcasts. This generation was well into its early adult transition period before television became a major factor. What is important, however, is the time sense projected by both news and sports broadcasts. This is a much shorter time sense than that of earlier, literate media. Reality came to be seen as operating in shorter bursts of hours or minutes. As a simultaneous reflection of both the time and motion studies of "scientific management" and of the new electronic media, this generation tended toward a much more compressed sense of time than preceding generations in the United States.

Face systems. The preceding generation, although it expressed an egalitarian ideology, was still basically hierarchical in relationships within the family. This generation, the Depression/War generation, was the one in which the struggle for domination between adults and children in the family is the main theme. As a transitional generation, many of the forms of respectful address of the preceding hierarchical generation remained in place. Nevertheless, underlying these surface forms of respect was an attitude that the younger generation really was more deserving of respect and authority than the older generation. The net result was that for this generation there are frequently mixed signals and less than clear agreement on the appropriate relationships between members of the same or older and younger generations.

Summary. For this generation, the primary opposition by which individualism was maintained was that to the way of life into which they had been born. They were strongly motivated by a vow never to suffer another depression or the poverty of those times. The vow of Scarlett O'Hara never to go hungry again in the movie *Gone With the Wind*, while it was staged as the voice of an earlier period, was certainly calculated to strike a resonant note with the first viewers of this film in 1939, as they themselves were taking the same vow.

Perhaps because of the fear of poverty and struggle, this generation is above all characterized by its insecurity of status. For the Depression/War generation, the breakdown of the authoritarian system made it less clear just what the basis for their individuality was, and at the same time the very clear post-war individualism of the Baby Boom generation had not yet emerged. It might well be said that as a transitional generation, this one has never achieved any clear identity. Being neither Authoritarian nor Baby Boom, they were largely pushed aside by the open conflict between the two generations before and after them.

Cultural observers have noted that in the succession of U.S. presidents, H. Ross Perot was the only candidate from this generation to stage a real presidential campaign. It is characteristic of this generation that Ross Perot's presidential campaign was backed by no established political party or group; he was very much a loner in his quest for the presidency. Significantly, he lost, and the succession skipped from the Authoritarian generation (Presidents Kennedy through George H. W. Bush) to the Baby Boom generation (Presidents Clinton and George W. Bush). Radical ideological individualists, this generation has worked assiduously to spread the Utilitarian discourse system around the world through the medium of international business structures.

The Baby Boom generation, born between 1946 and 1964

Ideology. The post-war boom babies were born into a world of abundance. They were, in fact, part of that abundance. Paradoxically, because of the rapid post-war economic expansion they were born into an increasingly rich country, yet at the same time, because there are so many of them, their share of that richness was never guaranteed. From shortages of diapers in their infancy and a shortage of schools in their childhood they went on to experience shortages in the job market and to fear shortages of social security benefits when they reach old age.

It is probably more significant for the Boom Babies, however, that they were born into a period in which the historical sense of time had been fractured. The understanding of the past was blocked by an older generation who wanted to put the period of the Depression and World War II quickly behind them. At the same time, this generation was born under the shadow of the Cold War and the potential of total world destruction. They are really the first generation in the nation to be born into a world in which humankind had finally reached the possibility of complete technological destruction of the earth.

If asked to name the most important world event in their lives, most members of this generation would name the war in Vietnam. This war came along just as this generation began to reach the early adult transition. This is the period in life, remember, when the individual is expected to firmly begin to establish a life independent of that of his or her parents. This generation, being the first to have been raised in radical, egalitarian, ontological individualism, assumed that it was their right to decide whether or not they would do things, and their decisions were largely based on the extent to which the things they did would bring them enjoyment or at least encourage self-expression.

The war in Vietnam allowed for them neither enjoyment nor self-expression. In their view, that war was the product of a generation with which they had nothing in common, and it quickly became the strongest symbol of the oppression of culture, history, and social institutions. It quickly became the central symbolic threat to their radical individualism, and they quite naturally opposed it fervently.

Here it is useful to remember that ontological individualism, at least in the United States, is negative – the self is defined by what it is not and by what it resists. At this crucial time in the life cycle of the Baby Boom generation, the central definition of the self for this generation was anti-war or anti-establishment. In this resistance to the war of the Authoritarian generation establishment, the Baby Boom generation completed its definition of the individualistic self.

This generation, however, also provides a good illustration of how generational discourse systems develop over time. Radically anti-authoritarian and often anti-capitalist in their youth, members of this generation have now become among the most successful entrepreneurs and strongest proponents of the Utilitarian discourse system in U.S. history. They have gone from being hippies, to being yuppies, to being CEOs. At the same time, behind their entrepreneurialism there often remains a sense of the idealism and the value of creative self-expression that they cultivated in their youth.

Perhaps the quintessential Baby Boomer CEO is Steve Jobs of the Apple Corporation. When Jobs returned to take up the leadership of Apple in 1996 he made a speech which in many ways epitomizes the idealistic entrepreneurialism of his generation. "Marketing is about values," he said. "What we're about isn't making boxes for people to get their job done . . . Apple's core value is that we believe that people with passion can change the world for the better."

In many ways Baby Boomers rival the members of the Depression/War generation in extolling the importance of hard work. The Type A behavior of Depression/War generation, however, has given way to a different kind of workaholism in the Boomer generation, one motivated not by fear of poverty and excessive concern with scheduling so much as by polemical individualism, the constant desire to prove one's worth and to enact one's unique value as an individual. It has become a generation that is in many ways burdened by its own idealism and need for self-expression.

Socialization, enculturation. While the U.S. government's *Infant Care* has continued to be published to this day, the book for the parents of the Boom Babies was *Baby and Child Care* by Benjamin Spock (1976), which turned out to be one of the bestselling books in U.S. history. From its opening words it is clear that a generational, even a historical watershed had been crossed. Indeed, Spock's opening words signal the final, complete victory of negative ontological individualism in the United States. Those words are:

TRUST YOURSELF.
You know more than you think you do (Spock 1976: 1).

This opening paragraph goes on polemically to say that perhaps you have had advice from friends and relatives, from experts in magazines and newspapers, and even from doctors and nurses. His advice is to always trust your own judgment first. This individualism is clearly phrased negatively: "Don't take too seriously all that the neighbors say. Don't be overawed by what the experts say. Don't be afraid to trust your own common sense" (p. 1).

The babies of the baby boom from 1946 to 1964 were brought up in a social environment which was radically different from that of the preceding Depression/War and Authoritarian generations. On the crucial issue of bowel control, Spock says almost nothing. No longer is the parent in control. It is the child who decides, while the parent waits patiently for this decision to be made. The emphasis in Spock's book is on the child's "own free will." The mandate to extend equality to all has now been extended to infancy. From Dr Spock on, no one will be assumed to have the right to make judgments about what is right for another, not even the parents of a child. The right of complete self-determination is asserted by Dr Spock to come into play from birth. The Baby Boom generation is the first completely egalitarian U.S. generation.

The self-exploration which the Authoritarians saw as such a danger for the child is recast by Dr Spock as wholesome curiosity. There is no hint of the "infant depravity" assumed by the Authoritarian generation, though Spock himself was a product of that generation. This Spock Boom Baby was on the path to radical self-discovery and self-expression, so consonant with ontological individualism and so strongly manifested later in such discourses as those seen on *Donahue*.

Finally, it is important to see the relationship of the adult and the child. In a section in which Spock treats the question of security, he suggests the great value in providing "comforters." He writes, "The little girl (or boy) recreates certain comforting aspects of her parents out of the cuddly toy and her thumb for example; *but* it's not a parent who can envelop her or control her; it's a parent *she* can control" (p. 236). What Spock emphasizes here is the great comfort and security the child receives from role-playing her control of the parent. Again, in this detail Spock emphasizes the value of the individual child, which arises directly from that child's control of the world.

Forms of discourse. Could there have been an anti-war movement in the United States without recorded music and without television? Could there have been a civil rights movement without them? Perhaps, but it is very difficult to imagine "the sixties" without either of these media. Much has been written, including the comment quoted above from Camille Paglia, about the nearly complete interpenetration of the idea of a Baby Boom generation and the electronic media, especially recorded music and television. There is little to be added to that discussion here. The one crucial factor from the point of view of the development of U.S. individualism is the flattening of the time perspective that came with these media.

A lead-in to the dialogue between Postman and Paglia describes the latter as follows: "Paglia was born after World War II, an accident to which she ascribes great significance. To hear her talk is to confirm her theory about the influence of the modern media: She speaks in a rush of images, juxtapositions, and verbal jump cuts . . . Television, Paglia says, *is* the culture" (Postman and Paglia 1991: 44). Such beliefs, in fact, are widely held among this generation: that they are the *products* of music and television. They were reflected in the academic work of scholars of the period such as Marshall McLuhan who famously declared "the medium is the message," and are also evident in the opinions of scholars and parents today, most of them members of this generation, when they consider the effect of computers and the internet on their own children. It is a widely promoted view among this generation that electronic media are changing young people's minds in fundamental ways which are impossible for us to control, whether these changes are seen as something to be celebrated or something to be feared.

In any case, the centrality of television for this generation in many ways began a process which has continued with other electronic media of an increasing distrust of traditional forms of argumentation and historical precedent. Ideas for this generation and for those that followed began to have a shorter and shorter shelf-life.

Face systems. One final but important point to be considered about the Baby Boom generation is the rise of the concept of "relationships." One aspect of the Baby Boom lifestyle has been the rise of such loosely knit organizations as relationships, networks, and support groups. These social groups are quite unlike either the traditional relationships of family, community, or business found among the Authoritarian generation or the more limited and highly utilitarian business contacts of the Depression/War generation. The groups and networks of the Baby Boom generation form and disperse along the lines of common interests, needs, and issues, a phenomenon which in some ways paved the way for the rise of computer assisted social networking among young people today. In fact, along with Millennials, it was members of this generation that most enthusiastically joined social networking sites like Facebook when they first became available to the general public.

If we could call the most traditional of relationships, those of the family, hierarchical and vertical (lasting through time across generations), those of the Baby Boom generation might be called egalitarian and horizontal and of insignificant temporal existence. One might almost say that they must of necessity be limited in time so that these network and support group relationships do not come to be perceived as oppressive to the individual. This generation, then, was the one that completed the transition from the hierarchical structures of relationship of traditional European society to the egalitarian and lateral relationships of contemporary U.S. society. As a paradoxical result, one finds simultaneously among this generation a much higher concern for relationships than in any preceding American generation, and a high degree of skepticism about the endurance of any relationship.

Another characteristic of this generation when it comes to relationships is their faith in collective action as a way to solve problems. Partly because of overcrowding in schools, the idea of "getting along with others" was emphasized in their formal education in ways that it had not been for previous generations. They were also encouraged in their adolescence to take part in team sports and join clubs, and the organizational skills they learned in these activities were later further developed as they organized anti-war and civil rights demonstrations. This emphasis on teamwork remains evident in the management styles of Baby Boomer managers and CEOs who prefer to organize their staff into self directed teams rather than exercising authority over them from above.

Summary. The polemic which motivates the Baby Boom generation individual the most is what is usually referred to as "traditional social roles." This is the language of *Donahue*. This opposition began as these Spock babies were brought up in an atmosphere of full and spontaneous self-expression. From the start, anything which might limit or narrow the scope of this self-expression and self-realization was seen as the problem to be challenged and opposed. In the 1960s, the strongest expression of polemical individualism was expressed in opposition to "the establishment." It is significant that often "the establishment" is not more clearly defined, because for this generation, the point is *any* establishment, any *a priori* assumptions about what one ought to do or what one ought to be, are a danger to the full development of the self. As this U.S. generation has reached full maturity, this opposition to tradition has become fully developed in a language where even the choices one makes for oneself are problematic because of the limits they place on one's future. For the fullest self-expression of one's individuality, *all* conceptual limits must be questioned. In a real sense, this Baby Boom generation completed the revolution of American ontological polemical individualism which Tocqueville observed in its first stages.

Generation X, born between 1965 and 1980
Ideology. On February 15, 1961 the Food and Drug Administration approved the drug *Envoid* for contraceptive use, marking the beginning of an era when women in the United States began to assume more control over their reproductive functions and were able to take advantage of a wider range of opportunities to pursue educational and career goals. As a result, many women postponed having children and after 1965 the birthrate in the United States declined precipitously, making the generation that followed the Baby Boomers the smallest living U.S. generation.

In previous editions of this book we referred to this generation as Infochildren, following the original nomenclature of Longfellow. In this edition we will use the more widespread term Generation X, popularized by the Canadian novelist Douglas Coupland in his novel *Generation X: tales for an accelerated culture,* which portrays the apparently shallow lives of a group of under-employed twenty-somethings in the early 1990s. The first members of this generation were born into the time of the Vietnam War, but were much too young to serve or to take much notice. In fact, many observers have noted that this generation seem to see themselves as less affected by world events than any preceding generation in the United States. One author suggested that the most characteristic aspect of this generation in their youth was their apparent lack of interest in entering on the normal path of life's stages (Littwin 1986). She referred to this generation as "the postponed generation," a generation which put off getting out of school, getting into the workforce, and establishing families.

When they did so, however, they distinguished themselves as proponents of self-reliance in the workplace and traditional family values in the home.

Perhaps the most important aspect of growing up for members of this generation is that many of them were alone for much of the time. Nearly half of them lived in households in which either both parents worked or one parent was absent, which meant that they regularly came home after school to an empty house. Their parents were either members of the Depression/War generation who were often at the height of their careers (and the height of their Type A Personality Syndromes) or Baby Boomer parents entering their thirties and becoming more focused on supporting their families and accumulating wealth.

This situation created in many members of this generation a sense of independence and belief that they would have to look after themselves since nobody else seemed available to look after them. At the same time, social and economic conditions also created in many of them a certain skepticism regarding the value of all of this hard work. They grew up in times of economic difficulties, witnessing the stagflation, high unemployment, and long gas lines of the late 1970s, watching many of their parents lose their savings in the October 19 stock market crash of 1987, and entering the job market just as the recession of the early 1990s was at its worst.

This cynicism about economic opportunities was matched by a cynicism about politics. The political consciousness of this generation began with the Watergate scandal and the resignation of President Nixon, and they were teenagers during the malaise of the Carter years and the Iran Hostage Crisis.

Socialization, enculturation. While Dr Spock's *Baby and Child Care* continued to remain very popular, *Infant Care* was revised. By the time these children were born there were two important shifts in such forms of advice to parents. The first shift was in the authorship of *Infant Care*. In the past it had first been written by Mrs Max West (1914 edition), and then later it was revised by individual medical doctors as editors (Wolfenstein 1953). By the time Generation X was born, however, *Infant Care* was written by a committee of over one hundred medical, psychological, and child-care experts (Goodrich 1968). What was once a booklet of housewifely suggestions had become a full-length book of "expert" advice.

This emphasis on expertise was not only seen in the preparation of the book, but was also urged as the path to successful child rearing. The book begins by lamenting that women are not taught child care in public schooling. It goes on to say that one does not need to despair, however, because the ultimate authority, the doctor, is always available.

The theme of professional expertise was reiterated throughout this generation's early life. Their mothers were told that there was nothing much they could do. Not only were most Generation X children expected, like the Baby Boom children, to develop on their own, now the parent was expected to step aside and refer all questions and serious care to hired professional experts. It was emphasized that there is too much information for the ordinary person as a parent to be expected to understand and digest. Generation X was born into a world which was assumed to be complex and quite beyond the scope of any single person's understanding. It is worth remembering that the panel of experts who prepared *Infant Care*, as well as the parents and doctors of Generation X children, were, on the whole, members of the Depression/War generation. This advice to leave the care of these children up to someone else was entirely welcomed by many of them. They were already hurrying themselves into their own world of Type-A-driven success.

Ironically, this resulted in a situation for these children of absent parents that was in some ways similar to what their parents experienced when they were children, albeit usually without the heart wrenching fear that their fathers would never return. And as a result, they developed a belief in self-reliance not unlike that of this previous generation. It is telling that in the 2008 presidential campaign the two generations that supported John McCain most strongly were members of the Depression/War generation and Generation X while Baby Boomers and Millennials were more likely to vote for Barack Obama.

Forms of discourse. In a period in which the highest value was placed on professional expertise, the computer as a medium in many ways came to be the driving metaphor of such objective competence. Members of this generation were the first to grow up with computers. They typically encountered them in the form of rudimentary terminals like the Apple II on which they learned to program with simple computer languages, or in the form of gaming stations like the Atari 2600 which was released in 1976. It was early computer games like Pong, Asteroids, and Pac Man which probably had the greatest impact on the childhoods of members of this generation and contributed to an even further decline in the centrality of print literacy. Significantly, such games lacked the traditional narrative discursivity of either traditional children's books or of the multiplayer online role playing games popular with today's youth; they were, in fact, almost content free, exclusively focused on the logic of speed and movement.

A similar phenomenon could be seen in the television programming of the era. In 1969 *Sesame Street* premiered on PBS, a new kind of children's program that consisted of a series of short sketches, skits, and cartoons each lasting only between ten seconds and a minute presented one after another in rapid-fire fashion. A similar format of rapid-fire montage was later adopted by MTV. Such programming helped to create in this generation well developed visual literacy, and the importance of the image as a communicative mode increased tremendously, affecting nearly every medium, even print media like newspapers and school textbooks.

Face systems. Two factors brought about for this generation an almost complete elimination of any indications of generational hierarchy. For the first time, members of the younger generation had clear cultural and technological dominance in spheres which were widely valued in the society, the uses of computer and electronic technology. As a result of their competence in these areas and of the dependence of modern society on their competence, they felt themselves to be in some ways the equals of members of any other generation in most contexts highly valued by the society.

The second factor was that throughout the period beginning after World War II, there had been a major demographic change in the structure of the family in the United States which resulted in many of the members of this generation growing up in families not of either the traditional extended family type nor the nuclear family type. Their parents were often divorced and sometimes remarried. By the end of the 1970s approximately half of all marriages among Baby Boomers had ended in divorce. As kinship relations between children and their caregivers became more variable and ambiguous, so did the sense of hierarchy between children and adults.

Perhaps in an attempt to create for their children the stable family environments they feel had been denied to them, many members of this generation make it a point to spend time with their children and to reassert more hierarchical (though not authoritarian) relationships with them, evident in the discourse of "setting boundaries" that proliferates in talk about child rearing by members of this generation. Publicly many of them espouse "traditional family values" not unlike those promoted by the Reagan administration that dominated their late adolescence and early adulthood.

Summary. Many have observed among this generation a kind of alienation from political and social life. This should not, however, be seen as an extension of the Baby Boom generation's alienation from traditional social roles. Rather it is something else: a reaction against the idea of society itself. In some ways it is a denial of the faith in teamwork and collective action of the previous generation. In the workplace members of Generation X are known for their resistance to working in teams. Lacking trust in or patience with others, many do not want other people's mistakes to jeopardize their success but prefer to be judged on their own merits. This is not surprising given the fact that many of them spent much of their childhoods alone – watched TV alone, played video games alone, and often went in for more individualistic sports like skateboarding and tennis.

Millennial generation (Generation Y), born between 1981 and 1995
Ideology. In the early 1980s many of the Baby Boomers who had postponed having children decided that it was time to have them before it was too late, resulting in another sharp increase in births. What we are calling the Millennial generation (often referred to as Generation Y) is almost as big as the Baby Boom generation. In 2006 it represented more than a quarter of the U.S. population and more than 35 percent of the workforce (U.S. Census Bureau 2006).

It is safe to say that what characterized the childhoods of members of this generation was an increasing sense among people in the United States that the world is a dangerous place, especially for children. Among the defining events for this generation was the Columbine High School massacre that took place in Littleton, Colorado on April 20, 1999. This event was particularly resonant in that it highlighted the vulnerability of middle class high school students, but it was really just one in a series of acts of seemingly random violence and destruction which included the Rodney King beating in 1991 and the riots that followed the acquittal of the police officers that took part, the FBI killings of members of the Branch Davidian cult in Waco, Texas in 1993, and the 1995 bombing of a federal government building in Oklahoma City. This string of tragedies culminated, of course, in 2001 with the September 11th terrorist attacks on New York City and Washington, DC; but the destruction did not stop there, but continued with Hurricane Katrina in 2005 and the Virginia Tech shootings in 2007. In the midst of these events, however, members of this generation probably experienced the most sheltered childhoods of any generation in U.S. history, often spared from disappointments and challenges by their over-protective Baby Boomer parents. It is not surprising, then, that members of this generation are known for being particularly risk-averse.

Like Generation X before them, this generation also witnessed economic turmoil when they were growing up. Although they were born into the rapidly expanding economy of the late 1990s, many watched their parents lose money when the dotcom bubble burst in 2000. Even more significant was the economic collapse precipitated by the mortgage crisis of 2008, which occurred just as many of them were entering the job market.

Partly as a result of these events, many members of this generation have developed a kind of ideological ambivalence. On the one hand they have an acute awareness of the world's troubles and a keen desire to contribute to fixing them. On the other hand, they expect to have an easy time of it, something that the world is increasingly unable to deliver to them. This paradoxical search for both challenges and security is reflected in a perceived lack of loyalty among members of this generation in the workplace as they move from company to company, career to career in their search of this elusive combination. Of course, the lack of loyalty to employers is in many ways matched by employers' unwillingness to provide the kinds of benefits and job security that many of their parents and grandparents enjoyed (see chapter 9).

Socialization, enculturation. If parents of Generation X children gave much of the authority for parenting over to experts, many parents of Millennials responded to the complexity of child rearing by endeavoring to become experts themselves, reading books, consulting with professionals, and inserting themselves into nearly every aspect of their children's lives. Foster W. Cline and Jim Fay, in their 1990 book *Parenting with Love and Logic: teaching children responsibility*, coined the term "helicopter parents" to describe how many parents of Millennials constantly hovered over their children, waiting to witness their triumphs and to avert any possibility of failure. The absent parents of the 1980s became the "soccer moms" and "stay at home dads" of the 1990s. Much of the leisure time of Millennial children was structured around parent-arranged play dates, music and art lessons, after-school programs, team sports, and other extracurricular activities. The rest of their time was spent on their computers.

As a result one strong characteristic of the socialization of this generation is the blurring of the line between formal and informal socialization. School became more like play, and play was always considered better if it was somehow "educational." The parents of these children adhered to the belief that their role was not to control their children, but to educate them. Thus many endeavored to clearly explain to their children whenever they could the reasons why they should or should not engage in a particular behavior. A resistance to any rules that seem arbitrary and an expectation that the reason for everything will be clearly explained to them has followed many members of this generation into the workplace.

Forms of Discourse. In his original model of generational discourse, Longfellow captured the early exposure to computer technology experienced by members of Generation X by dubbing them "infochildren." While today people are more likely to associate digital technology with the later Millennial generation, we believe the term "infochildren" still fits Generation X in a way that it does not Generation Y. The reason we say this is that while for members of Generation X computers were seen as primarily an *information technology*, a means of processing information, beginning with the Millennial generation computers came to be seen as primarily a *communications technology*, a way of maintaining contact with other people and of creating and maintaining social networks. So, while the earlier generation grew up with relatively linear computer games and programming languages that taught them logic and systematic thinking, members of the newer generation grew up with Web 2.0 and social networking sites which taught them to think of things in terms of complex networks of links and nodes.

Another much commented upon aspect of this generation's preoccupation with digital technology is the increasingly polychronic orientation towards time this has engendered. Millennials multitask more frequently and more successfully than members of any previous generation. Some observers are extremely disturbed by this trend, blaming the increased multitasking made possible by computers and mobile phones for increased behavioral problems and syndromes like attention deficit hyperactivity disorder (ADHD). It is important to note, however, that a chief difference between this behavior among Millennials and the success driven multitasking of Type A members of the Depression/War generation and workaholic Baby Boomers is that for Millennials it seems to be much less related to stress. In fact, members of this generation often engage in multitasking in order to relax and escape from the inevitable stress and frustration brought on by an increasingly unpredictable world.

Face systems. The relationship between members of this generation and their parents continues the flattening of hierarchy that began in the Baby Boom generation. The difference is that whereas in the 1960s the rejection of hierarchy came from children who rebelled against their parents' value system, in the 1990s the rejection of hierarchy came from parents who wanted to be like "best friends" to their sons and daughters (a role their children sometimes resist).

Perhaps the most important change in the way this generation organizes social relationships, however, is the importance many of them give to relationships with their peers rather than their parents and other family members. A recent survey of teenagers reported by McCrindle (n.d.) revealed that the biggest factor determining the choices that members of this U.S. generation make are the opinions of their core group of between three and eight friends rather than the opinions of their parents or their own core values.

Peer groups for members of this generation, of course, typically extend far beyond these core groups to vast networks of hundreds of "friends" managed through websites like Facebook and MySpace. Unlike the loners of Generation X, members of the Millennial generation seem to thrive on constant connectivity. Most of them visit one or more social networking sites at least once a day and many are in constant contact with their network of friends through their mobile telephones.

To a large degree this generation defines themselves in terms of their social networks. It is telling that one of the most conspicuous features of social networking sites like Facebook is that pictures of one's friends and links to their pages are a central aspect of one's online profile. This does not, however, mean that this generation has traded in individualism for a kind of high tech collectivism. Rather they have adopted what we might call "networked individualism," in which one is compelled to enact a unique self online, but a large part of that enactment is displaying how interesting and unique one's social network is.

Another important aspect of this brand of individualism is the ease with which one can alter one's self-presentation using digital technology. The selves of Millennials are by their very nature "works in progress," continually being updated and refashioned as circumstances change and as their social networks grow or evolve. James Gee (2004) refers to members of this generation as "shape shifting portfolio people," and so another way to characterize their brand of individualism might be "portfolio individualism."

Summary. In contrast to the alienation from society exhibited by Generation X, most members of this generation are "hyper-connected" and engaged. Many also share much of the "change the world" idealism of their Baby Boomer parents. At the same time, many are also easily bored and do not react well either to criticism or frustration.

Partly because of values instilled by their parents and partly because of their perception of the real challenges that face them, members of this generation see themselves as socially responsible and prefer to work for companies that exhibit concern for the environment, social justice, and other causes. How much of this social responsibility is deeply felt and how much of it is more a feature of their "profiles" is difficult to tell at this point. Nevertheless, members of this generation have exhibited an unprecedented willingness to volunteer their time and energy to causes they believe in, and this energy and enthusiasm was partly responsible for propelling Barack Obama to the presidency. Corporations have learned that marketing products to and recruiting employees from this generation works best when they speak the language of optimistic social change. One example is Apple Corporation, a company run by Baby Boomers but whose main market and main employee base is the Millennial generation. Working for Apple, their recruitment website (http://www.apple.com/jobs/us/welcome.html) claims, gives young people "license to change the world" and a chance to "forget all the rules." Nowhere can one find a better summary of this generation's blurring of work and play, of social action and having a good time than in the description of working at Apple given here:

> Working at Apple is a whole different thing. Because whatever you do here, you play a part in creating some of the best-loved technology on the planet. And in helping people discover all the amazing things they can do with it. You could call it work, or you could call it a mission. We call it a blast.

Generation Z, born between 1995 and 2010

We will have considerably less to say about this generation, given that at the time of writing most of its members were still children and adolescents. This is a generational discourse system still in the process of imagining itself. Nevertheless, there are still a number of important observations that can be made about it.

Typically children of Generation X parents, this generation was born into a time of growing anxiety about the United States' place in the world, influenced by the specter of terrorism, the rise of other countries like China as major economic competitors, and a sluggish domestic economy. The key events in the lives of members of this generation so far have been the historic election of President Barack Obama and the recession following the stock market crash of 2008. They are the first generation in the United States with no personal memory of the Cold War.

If one can at this point discern an ideology associated with this generation it might be the increased value placed on speed and instant gratification, partly the result of the widespread use of high-speed internet connections. The face systems prevalent among this age group are also to a large degree associated with their media use. They have grown up in online social communities like Facebook, and meeting, befriending, and interacting with people online is second nature to them. They are much more comfortable than their parents in interacting with strangers and with revealing a great deal about themselves to them, a fact that sometimes causes alarm among parents and teachers.

The way the discourse system of this generation is developing, therefore, is inseparable from the development of the high-speed mobile internet and related technology like smart phones and tablet computers. They are the first "digital natives." Unlike members of the Millennial Generation, many of whom remember life before the takeoff of mass technology, most born into this generation were immersed in technology from a very early age. They are also accustomed to using internet technology in a much more active way, regularly posting pictures, comments, and videos using online self-publishing tools.

Because many of the Generation X parents of this generation remember their own "latch-key" childhoods, it is not unusual for them to make the choice to work part time or even become stay-at-home parents so that their children can be raised by them rather than sent to day care facilities or left alone at home. At the same time, however, parenting has become much less focused. The childhoods packed with organized extracurricular activities of the Millennials have been replaced with more time at home with parents and siblings. Much of the socialization of this generation is also taking place online as children are coming of age on social networking sites, constantly being commented upon and commenting upon others.

The shifting ground of U.S. individualism

When we first introduced the notions of individualism and collectivism in chapter 3 we cautioned against overgeneralizations like "Americans are individualistic and Chinese are collectivistic." In this chapter we have so far seen that even when the label of individualism is used to refer to North Americans, the nature of that individualism will be very different depending on when the individuals in question were born and grew up.

The six generations which we have described here are those which have preceded and followed the radical post-war break in U.S. individualism. The Authoritarians were in a sense the last of the "old Americans," the ones described by Tocqueville. There is much in their lives which shows an awareness that change is overtaking them and their world. Their individualism is of the ontological sort that Tocqueville describes, but it is still tempered by the assumption of at least a certain fundamental human grounding in family and tradition. The generation of the Baby Boom, on the other hand, see themselves proudly as being firmly on this side of a radical discontinuity. For this generation there is a clear rejection of tradition and of history in a way that Tocqueville is unlikely to have imagined possible or desirable. Their individualism is the assertive, self-expressive individualism of *Donahue*. The Depression/War generation in this analysis is a transitional generation. They were the generation to suffer the disillusionment of both the Depression and World War II. While they saw little which attracted them in the past and in tradition, they also see little to attract them in the spontaneous, interest-group relationships of the Baby Boom generation. The individualism of this generation is more negative in its strongly go-it-alone nature, in which individual success is upheld as the highest value. Generation X might also be seen as a transitional generation, similarly alienated from the legacy of idealistic individualism of the Baby Boomers and pessimistic about the future. It is the generation that has followed them, the Millennial generation, which has ushered in yet another phase of U.S. individualism, an individualism which combines the need for radical self-expression of the Baby Boom generation with a new sense of the interdependence of people and a reliance on connectivity.

The individualism of the Millennials is in some sense polemical against many of the foundational principles of ontological individualism itself though still embracing the self-expressive aspects of it. Members of this generation blame the selfishness and shortsightedness of previous generations for the state of the environment and the economy. They embrace rather than distrust collective action. At the same time they revel in creative self-expression. The self being expressed, however, is not the "true self" of *Donahue*, but rather a "portfolio self" that changes easily based on changing circumstances. This generation grew up listening to Microsoft's advertising slogan: "Where do you want to go today?" A more apt slogan for them might have been "Who do you want to be today?"

A simpler way to formulate this analysis might be to say that the individualism of the two transitional generations, the Depression/War generation and Generation X, is one that focuses on *self-reliance* and that that of the two largest living generations, the Baby Boomers and the Millennials, is one that focuses on *self-expression*. The danger of such a simplification, however, might be to ignore the interplay of both self-reliance and self-expression in the individualism of all of the generations described.

From this review of generations in the United States, we can draw several conclusions about discourse systems operating within U.S. society. In the first place, it should be clear that it would be impossible to consider the society to be either entirely hierarchical or egalitarian in regard to its assumptions about human relationships. The Authoritarian generation was quite strongly hierarchical in its assumptions, and the Baby Boom generation and the Millennial generation are quite strongly egalitarian. In fact, the stereotypical "American" egalitarian behavior is not at all typical of the oldest generation of North Americans, and the stereotypical "American" attitude of self-reliance and independence is not at all typical of the youngest generation.

If we were to look at another dimension of interdiscourse analysis, the dimension concerning the assumptions made about the functions of language, we would see that the oldest generation, the Authoritarians, would probably take a fairly balanced position and assume that language has both informational and relational functions. The Depression/War generation, however, has a tendency to place a greater emphasis on the informational aspects of language use. The Baby Boom generation, in contrast to these, tends to place a very high emphasis on relationships, as we have said above. For members of Generation X, communication again becomes focused on information with the dawning of the "information age," while for Millennials and for Generation Z, the development of the interactive internet (Web 2.0) has shifted the emphasis strongly back to relationships: the main purpose of communication has become connectivity, the growth, strengthening, and maintenance of social networks.

By developing this generational analysis, we hope to have demonstrated clearly why it is impossible to make such a simple categorization as "the American discourse system" or to speak of things like "American individualism." Within the United States as within every country there exist many competing, overlapping, and inter-nested ideologies.

Communication between generations

When we considered the voluntary discourse systems of corporate structures and of professional or occupational specializations, the problem we posed was for individuals who found themselves caught between the goals, ideologies, and identities of these two different systems. We might think of that as an internal problem, in that it is the individual person who needs to resolve how he or she is going to deal with this conflict in identity. Now we have described some of the differences we find between members of different generational discourse systems.

As a problem in interdiscourse professional communication, we would argue that communication between members of different generations is very much the same kind of problem as communication between employees from different educational or professional backgrounds in a multinational corporation – each approaches situations with a different interpretive framework, and that can sometimes lead to false conversational inferences and ultimately to a difficulty in developing the kind of cooperation people on both sides of the problem are seeking.

The differences between generations are a particularly acute problem in organizational communication. Difficulties, for example, may arise when members of the Baby Boom generation, with the belief among many in teamwork and supportive feedback, manage members of Generation X, many of whom might prefer both to work alone and to be left alone until they have gotten the job done. Similar problems may occur when members of Generation X, who might expect people to be self-directed, are confronted with Millennials who might seem to need constant explanations and crave constant praise.

At the root of these problems is a fundamentally different view of work held by members of these three generations. Meagan and Larry Johnson, authors of *Generations Inc.: from boomers to linksters – managing the friction between generations at work*, sum up this difference as follows: "Baby Boomers live to work. Generation Xers work to live. Generation Yers don't see work and life as any different; they blend into one" (2010: 132).

Six Generations of Chinese

Here we would like to strongly caution against attempting to apply the generational categories we have developed above to generations in other national or regional contexts. Such an approach, we believe, is doomed to gross misunderstanding and misrepresentation, because there is very little in common between the significant historical events, the child-rearing practices, and other life experiences of people in places like Hong Kong, Iran, China, and Japan and those of people in North America.

In order to illustrate this point, we would like to turn to a brief examination of generations in a place where there has recently been a strong interest in studying intergenerational communication and where, because of the rapid pace of change in the past fifty years, such study can yield a very strong sense of the different beliefs and values, different face systems, different forms of discourse, and different processes of socialization of different generations. That place is the People's Republic of China.

The changing nature of collectivism

Earlier we indicated that the Confucian discourse system that has been dominant in China for thousands of years promotes a collectivistic orientation towards the self and society. Now we would like to complicate that observation by proposing that, just as the nature of individualism in North America has changed dramatically over the past half century, so has the nature of collectivism in China.

In many ways these changes are evident in the increased consciousness among people of differences in values, attitudes, and behavior among China's generational discourse systems. In fact, generational discourse has become somewhat of an obsession of the Chinese media and among the general public, with people growing more and more preoccupied with labeling generations and more and more likely to explain the behavior of others with reference to the generational discourse system they participate in. In a 2010 radio documentary on the rising divorce rate in China, for example, many of those interviewed attributed the increase in divorces to "generational factors." One respondent, for example, characterized the generation born after 1980 as "too selfish for marriage," and another said, "This generation is very self-centered, very independent, and they have high expectations as to cost and return; they think, I've paid out, so you have to love me."

Similarly, after a rash of suicide attempts at a Taiwan owned electronics factory in southern China that made international headlines, a China Central Television report explained the incidents as follows:

> The new generation is better educated, has higher dreams, more thoughts, and feels more suffering. The previous generation only thought about how to improve the lives of their family; they were willing to "eat bitterness" and restrained themselves. The younger generation thinks about themselves more, so they can't endure as much as the old generation. Under the heavy workload, they become disappointed more easily, even losing all hope. (Newstex 2010)

Whether or not these perceived differences between generations are actually true, such reports, like the interview between Postman and Paglia quoted above, demonstrate a willingness among people to believe that those born during different time periods have very different views of the world and exhibit different character traits.

Different people have divided up generations in the contemporary PRC in different ways. Business consultant, Tammy Erickson, for example, uses labels similar to those used for U.S. generations, calling them Traditionalists (born after 1928), Boomers (born after 1946), Generation X (born after 1961), and Generation Y (born after 1980), though she describes very different significant life events and characteristics for each of these groups than those we have described for North American generations. From our point of view, recycling these U.S. labels is less than ideal.

Others offer more local labels. Information systems researchers Maris Martinsons and David Ma divide contemporary Chinese in the PRC into only three generations, which they call the Republican generation (born before 1950), the Revolutionary generation (born between 1950 and 1970) and the Reform generation (born after 1970), and sociologists Sun Jianming and Wang Xun classify generations in China based on the major social movements in mainland China of the past sixty years: the generation of the Great Leap Forward, the generation of the Cultural Revolution, the generation that witnessed the beginning of the economic reforms, and the current generation of societal transformation.

The generational "folksonomies" that have developed in the Chinese media and on internet discussion forums over the past few years tend to divide up generations based on decades with terms like "Post-70s," "Post-80s," and "Post-90s," and some people make even finer distinctions, talking of, for example, "the Post-85 generation." One reason for this is that economic, social, and political conditions in China have been changing so rapidly in the past fifty years that even very short periods of time can result in children having very different experiences of the world and undergoing very different kinds of socialization. Another reason for the proliferation of "generations," especially recent "generations," is that much of this discourse comes from Chinese born in the 1980s in the first decade of political and economic reform, who are acutely aware of how different they are from those who have come before them, and also from those who are coming after.

We propose a division of living Chinese in the PRC into six generations which we will call: (1) the War generation, (2) the Great Leap Forward generation, (3) the Cultural

Revolution generation, (4) the Reform generation, (5) the "Post-80s" generation, and (6) the "Post-90s" generation. We remind readers that these categories, like any such divisions, are simply heuristics. There is no uniform group of people that can be identified as the "Post-80s" generation, any more than in the United States there are uniform groups called "Baby Boomers" or "Generation X" about which one can make blanket generalizations. Rather, the "Post-80s" generation is a *discourse system*, a system of historical memories, beliefs, forms of discourse, and patterns of communication and relationships that people come to identify with and participate in, some more fully and some more peripherally. We also must caution that these labels were developed based on the history and experiences of Chinese in Mainland China, and generational divisions in Hong Kong, Taiwan, and Singapore would be very different.

The War generation, born between 1926 and 1935

This generation grew up amidst the war and chaos of the late Republican period, including the War of Resistance against the Japanese and the Civil War between the Nationalists and the Communists. This was probably the first generation that grew up in a China keenly aware of its national identity. Before this, most Chinese identified primarily with their families or clans, and the notion of "nation" was associated primarily with the imperial court. Partly because of the patriotic projects of both the Nationalists and the Communists, and partly because of the sense of unity that came from an invasion by a foreign power, more and more Chinese at this time began to think of themselves as "Chinese."

It is among this generation that one is likely to find the most loyal and sincere "Communists." Despite having witnessed and in many cases been victims of the numerous failed campaigns of the Party, they tend to have remained devoted to it and especially to the memory of Chairman Mao and the principles of self-sacrifice that animated the Long March and the early Revolutionary period.

This is partly a result of their more traditional orientation towards hierarchy and respect for authority, and partly a result of many of them having witnessed even greater suffering and chaos during the immediately preceding periods of the Japanese occupation and the Civil War. In this respect there is a sizable ideological gulf between them and the younger generation of "Post-90s" children who grew up in a time of economic prosperity and cynicism regarding ideological Communism. This gulf is even more evident as these grandparents are often the ones who have become responsible for the day-to-day care of the younger generation.

To say that members of this generation tend to be loyal to the Communist Party, however, is not to say that they are ideologically Marxist. In fact, most of their loyalty to the Party is motivated not by ideology but by the belief that the Party saved them from poverty and rescued the nation from the brink of chaos. Ideologically, they are much more likely to identify with family centered Confucian notions of duty, obedience to authority, and moral rectitude. Extended family connections and traditional Confucian hierarchies remained a central part of life while members of this generation were growing up.

The forms of discourse most members of this generation grew up with were oral. During the early 1940s an estimated 80 percent of the population was illiterate, and over 80 percent was rural. News and information traveled primarily through networks of village and family connections. There was little formal education available for most people, and so the bulk of socialization took place within the family. Child rearing practices remained traditional, with children expected to be totally obedient to their elders. The central value assigned to children was to be *gui*, or "well-behaved," which meant displaying deference, obedience, and behavioral restraint.

The Great Leap Forward generation, born between 1936 and 1950

The People's Republic of China was established when most of the people in this generation were children or young adults, and the childhoods of these individuals were marked by myriad enthusiastic projects by the government to promote the new Communist ideology. As they were growing up they witnessed the nationalization of private enterprise and the first major campaigns to expose and suppress former landlords and capitalists. The most important of these social movements, and the one that had the most profound effect on this generation, was the Great Leap Forward (1957–61). In a quixotic attempt to move China from an agrarian nation to an industrialized nation overnight, the government directed farmers to abandon their fields and turn their attention to setting up small-scale industries like backyard steel furnaces, which, Chairman Mao Zedong proclaimed, would allow China to overtake Britain in production of steel and other products within fifteen years. As a result of this policy, agricultural output declined dramatically leading to widespread malnutrition and famine in which scholars have estimated that somewhere between 16.5 million and 40 million people died.

The defining features of this time in China for those who lived through it were hard work and hunger, though it was also marked by a spirit of idealism and enthusiasm for the "New China" that had finally, as Chairman Mao had announced in Tiananmen Square at its founding, "stood up" and kicked out foreign colonialists and aggressors.

Despite the fact that most members of this generation did not have any formal education, many of them benefited from the mass literacy campaigns begun under the Nationalists in the 1920s and 1930s and continued under the Communists. Such mass education efforts were particularly strong in the early 1950s with peasant reading groups, half-day schools, and "donkey cart libraries" towed from village to village. By distributing simple reading material with strong political contents in the form of "Peasant Literacy Textbooks," the Party was able to both raise the literacy of the masses and indoctrinate them into the new ideology. Around this time Mandarin, declared the official spoken language of the nation, was made more accessible to non-Mandarin speakers through the development of a standard Romanization (*pinyin*) in 1958 and simplified Chinese characters made easier to learn in 1964.

Cultural Revolution generation, born between 1951 and 1965

This is the largest of contemporary Chinese generations, the result of the Party encouraging people to have more children in order to strengthen the country's national defenses. The Great Proletarian Cultural Revolution, which lasted from May 1966 to October 1976, was not just the defining historical event for this generation, but the event that utterly consumed their childhoods and in many ways continues to haunt their adulthoods. Sparked by intra-party conflicts and power struggles among top leaders, Chairman Mao began the movement by mobilizing the masses, particularly teenagers, to take his side in destroying practically all of the existing institutions. What followed was a decade of civil disorder, radical social experiments, political witch-hunts, economic disarray, and extreme poverty for many. Members of this generation started out believing that their loyalty to the state and to the Party would be rewarded only to suffer massive disillusionment.

Socialization for this generation was carried out almost completely through government propaganda and political study meetings. Schools were closed and the authority of the family in providing socialization was seriously undermined. Many of this generation received most of their socialization though membership in the Red Guards and being sent out to the countryside to "learn from the peasants." There were also mass propaganda campaigns like the "Learn from Comrade Lei Feng" campaign initiated by Mao in 1963 to encourage young people to imitate the selfless patriotic attitude of a soldier of the People's Liberation Army who had supposedly died serving the people. Through such exercises young people were schooled in a spirit of self-sacrifice and radical egalitarianism.

The main forms of discourse at this time were what were known as the "four greats" or what Chinese sociolinguist Gu Yueguo refers to as the "four great forms of discursive behavior": (1) *da ming*, meaning to air one's views openly; (2) *da fang*, meaning to speak out freely; (3) *da zi bao*, meaning to write "big character posters"; and (4) *da bianlun*, meaning to engage in great debates. These forms of discourse more often than not manifested as tedious political study meetings, massive public demonstrations, and "struggle sessions" in which those not toeing the Party line were publicly denounced and humiliated. Big character posters were pasted everywhere, even on the bodies of those who were publicly being humiliated and criticized. In theory anyone could engage in these forms of discourse, but in reality only so-called revolutionaries, i.e., Mao's followers, had true access to them.

Perhaps the most radical change in society at this time was a complete overturning of traditional hierarchal face systems as children were instructed to inform on their parents and students paraded their teachers through the streets in dunce caps.

Members of this generation are sometimes referred to as the "Lost generation" because their revolutionary childhoods, usually bereft of formal education, left them largely un-equipped to compete in the society created by the economic reforms instituted after Mao's death. At the same time, the ideology they had so reverently upheld in their youths had failed to deliver the promised rewards. Many members of this generation were victims of the massive layoffs that accompanied the restructuring and privatization of state run indus-tries in the 1980s, and while some were able to make the transition and become successful entrepreneurs, many did not. Members of this generation tend to exhibit survivalist values, moral ambivalence, and an extreme cynicism towards the government. While they may support the government, they are more likely to do so out of pragmatism than idealism. At the same time, there is also evident in this generation a thirst for "something to believe in." They were, in fact, the ones that populated the ranks of the Fa Lun Gong and other new spiritual movements that caused the government so much concern in the late 1990s.

The Reform generation, born between 1966 and 1979

Shortly after Mao died in 1976, Deng Xiaoping emerged as the leader of China and intro-duced a series of economic and political reforms including the Open Door Policy imple-mented in 1979, which after three decades of isolation afforded regular Chinese exposure to the outside world. As we mentioned in chapter 7, the ideology promoted by Deng was marked by a kind of Utilitarianism, which emphasized economic and technological advance-ment. Intellectuals, a group vilified under Mao, were elevated to the status of "mental workers" and portrayed in government propaganda as responsible and productive members of society.

As part of its economic reforms, the government set up special economic zones and encouraged limited private enterprise. By the mid-1980s living standards had risen dramatically and the nation was witnessing the beginnings of a consumer society. Along with this, however, came rampant corruption with friends and relatives of officials being afforded greater access to the fruits of economic reforms than the less well connected masses. It was largely these perceived abuses that motivated the large-scale student demonstrations in Tiananmen Square in 1989, which became for many of this generation the defining event of their youth.

Just as the nation itself was questioning its recent past and searching for the best way to move into the future, for young people this period was also one of intense questioning and, in the words of Chinese sociologist Luo Xu, "searching for life's meaning" in the midst of a flood of new information and opportunities. Advancing their formal education became a priority for most young people, and many even succeeded in going abroad to study, returning with overseas degrees and "western ideas."

Although most households did not have access to television at this time, music became an important form of discourse for young people, particularly previously banned western rock and roll and disco music and Chinese pop songs from Hong Kong and Taiwan. Rudimentary "discos" began to spring up in large and medium sized cities, and young people enthusiastically traded cassette tapes. In the mid-1980s an indigenous youth music scene began to develop led by rock star Cui Jian, whose hit "Nothing to My Name" became the unofficial anthem of the 1989 student protests.

The severe disruption of traditional hierarchical relationships between young people and their parents that occurred during the Cultural Revolution continued to reverberate in relationships between generations during this period. Perhaps the most conspicuous evidence of this came in the famous public confrontation between student leader Wu'er Kaixi and Premier Li Peng in which the younger man refused to accord the expected degree of respect to the Chinese leader, an incident which some believe helped to precipitate the subsequent crackdown.

Despite the student protests, which caught the sympathetic attention of many people throughout the world, it would be a mistake to assume members of this generation were motivated particularly by idealism or commitment to abstract principles like freedom and democracy. Their concerns were for the most part much more practical. What angered them most was the apparent lack of fairness in access to economic and educational opportunities. These values are reflected in a more recent survey of this generation by Martinsons and Ma (2009), who found that they are likely to consider self-interest and majority rights more important than moral principles or the rule of law in resolving ethical dilemmas. Another study conducted in the southern city of Guangzhou found that members of this generation, now most often referred to as the "Post-70s" generation, tend to exhibit more traditional economic values such as saving and valuing hard work compared to the generations that followed.

"Post-80s" generation, born between 1980 and 1989

The most important event for members of this generation occurred before they were born: the 1979 introduction of the One-Child Policy, which meant that the vast majority of members of this generation and the "Post-90s" generation after it would grow up without siblings, often doted upon by their parents and grandparents. They have been characterized as self-centered and pampered "little emperors" (see for example Zhang 2009). At the same time, they tend to be considerably more well-educated, ambitious, and cosmopolitan than their elders.

Among the chief values of many in this generation in China is wealth. Their idols are more likely to be successful business people than scholars or political leaders, and a large number increasingly seek after status symbols like name brand fashions. A survey conducted by the Chinese Communist Youth League and the National Student Federation in Shenzhen and Zhuhai in 2000 reported that the top three ambitions reported by students at the time were (1) to be a millionaire, (2) to be the boss of a multinational corporation, and (3) to be a provincial or municipal leader (Rosen 2004).

As they enter young adulthood, they are exhibiting patterns of consumption that are radically different from those of their parents (many of whom grew up either during the famine of the Great Leap Forward or the ideological severity of the Cultural Revolution), and even of the "Post-70s" generation. They are more willing to buy things on credit and to spend money on luxury or lifestyle goods. In fact, a 2005 survey found that young adults in China were more willing to spend a greater proportion of their incomes on luxury goods than those in the United States and Europe.

Along with this materialistic ideology, members of this generation also tend to exhibit strong nationalism. Although there is little adherence to "Marxism, Leninism and Mao Zedong Thought," members of the "Post-80s" generation, and to some degree the "Post-90s" generation after them, have in some instances proven to be the Party's strongest supporters. During 2008, for example, after unrest in Tibet, young Chinese waged a massive internet campaign against Western media coverage of the protests, and when western leaders make speeches in China about human rights, like British Prime Minister David Cameron did in 2010, it is not just government officials but young middle class adults and university students who criticize them for interfering in China's internal affairs. There is also, however, a large degree of skepticism about the Party and concern, in particular, about corruption. Support for the government and the Party comes from pragmatism – the belief that a strong government is necessary to support the growing economy and promote China's interests abroad – rather than ideology or loyalty.

Formal education, particularly at prestigious schools, has been a major priority for many in this generation. In 2001, among the most popular books in China was a volume entitled *Harvard Girl Liu Yiting*, in which proud parents tell how they systematically prepared their daughter from birth to gain admission to Harvard. The success of this book prompted a rash of similar titles including *Harvard Boy*, *Cambridge Girl*, and *Tokyo University Boy*.

The major forms of discourse for this generation include television, films, and magazines produced by media companies often preoccupied with covering the exploits of the rich and famous. Among the most popular programs are talent shows and variety shows. This is also the first Chinese generation for whom computers and the internet became a major form of discourse, especially the internet "bulletin boards" (BBS) that sprang up on campuses during their university years. These forums played a major role in an opening up of public discourse in China as participants used them to test the limits on more open discussions about things like government policy and sex. Many of the prominent figures of this generation are "bloggers" who made a name for themselves online and then went on to become novelists or journalists. The internet has also been an important tool for educational and career advancement for this generation. Among the most popular forums and discussion boards in their youth were those focusing on how to gain admission to prestigious universities or graduate schools or to get jobs with prestigious companies.

On the whole, members of this generation are seen to be extremely competitive and individualistic. A study by sociologists Sun Jianming and Wang Xun in Shanghai in the early 1990s found respondents who were at that time between the ages of 14 and 18 to be much more likely to regard self-development as more important than making a contribution to the nation or to society, and a study of Chinese managers a decade later found those under 40 to be more likely to orient towards values associated with individualism than more traditional Confucian values. But there is also among members of this generation a sense of searching and an idealism born from the realization that they will be the ones responsible for shaping a nation that will be very different from the China of the past. Many of this age group see themselves as belonging to a transitional generation charged with ushering China into a new era.

At the time this edition of this book was published, members of this generation were just entering their thirties and taking up positions in the government, educational institutions, and private enterprises, and so were also beginning to take control of the public discourse in the media. What has emerged from this discourse is a strong sense of generational identity. In fact, it is members of this generation that are primarily responsible for the proliferation of discourse about generations in the media and for coining the labels "Post-70s," "Post-80s," and "Post-90s" generations. In this discourse they seem very concerned to distinguish themselves not just from their parents, but also from the "Post-90s" generation that followed them.

One major theme emerging from this discourse is a sense of pressure brought on by high expectations and economic competitiveness. While members of this generation have been characterized by their parents as "soft" and "selfish," discourse from members of this generation sometimes emphasizes the unique struggles they must engage in, including the pressures of career achievement and conspicuous consumption. This emphasis can be seen, for example, in the song "Post-80s Wake Up" by the Shanghai rap singer Shou Junchao released in 2011, the lyrics of which include the following lines:

> In the elders' eyes, we are a lucky generation and masters of our fate who live a happy life. But what exactly can take control of our time? Is it power and money or a code of brotherhood? We are the happy generation who can't see where this happiness lies, but have to fight our way, looking for our future. Post-80s, wake up!

"Post-90s" generation, born between 1990 and 1999

Perhaps the most talked about generation today is the "Post-90s" generation, those who have grown up in a strong and economically vibrant China, which, while still ruled by an authoritarian government, has left behind many of the ideological struggles of the past half-century. During their lives, members of this generation have witnessed the return of two former colonies to China, Hong Kong, and Macau, in 1997 and 1999 respectively, China's admission into the World Trade Organization in 2001, and perhaps most importantly, China's successful hosting of the Summer Olympic Games in 2008.

In many ways the ideology associated with this generation is a reflection of the relatively more open, entrepreneurial, and optimistic China in which they are growing up. A 2008 Wuhan University survey, for example, found respondents from this generation to be more "open minded" and "independent in thinking and choosing" than those born in the 1970s and 1980s. They were also, however, found to be less able to cope with frustration (Xinhua 2008).

This is the first truly globalized generation in China, with access to more information and exposure to more cultural products from abroad than any previous one. Many children of the rapidly expanding middle class have actually traveled to other countries, and they are often more likely to seek out foreign entertainment sources than domestic ones. The discourse system that has grown up in the media and in the popular imagination around this generation centers around urban affluence. As a result, many people, although they were born in the 1990s, are marginalized by this discourse system: especially children of the rural poor and migrant workers, who have constructed their own discourse systems around things like narratives of migration to the city to seek their fortunes.

This last point is extremely important not just in discussing this discourse system, but in considering all of the generational discourse systems described in this chapter. In a sense, all of the descriptions of "members" of various generations we have given are essentially caricatures. They are stereotypical representations of certain beliefs, experiences, and forms of social organization that dominated particular periods of history. While all of these discourse systems grew out of some sense of shared experience and worldview among people born at a particular time, they often also expose the fault lines separating other discourse systems, those based on things like region, gender, and class. China and the United States are big countries, and any generation born into these countries is likely to exhibit considerable variety.

If the "Post-80s" generation was often the target of skepticism and doubts from their parents concerning their abilities and values, the "Post-90s" generation has become even more a target of criticism and anxiety. In fact, even a cursory reading of online discussions and media reports might lead one to believe that there is somewhat of a "moral panic" taking place in China over the perceived lack of morals and responsibility of members of this generation. The internet is full of photographs and stories of the "shocking" behavior of members of this generation including cruelty and public displays of sex. In 2009 the national news service *Xinhua* reported widespread cheating on college entrance examinations and other high stakes tests among "Post-90s" students, and a report from the Chinese Academy of Social Sciences released in the same year predicted a serious increase in crime among "the Post-90s generation." Members of this generation are often depicted in the media as difficult to comprehend, strange, degenerate, and sometimes violent. There is a strong sense in China today perhaps more than at any other time since the Cultural Revolution, of a "generation gap." A poll carried out by the Shanghai Teenage Research Center in 2011, for example, found among many young people a difficulty in communicating with their parents and a belief that they are misunderstood by society.

Part of this comes from the embrace by many affluent urban teenagers of unconventional forms of language, music, and fashion, which are characterized by the label *fei zhu liu* (non-mainstream). The individualism of this generation is, in this sense, very different than that of the "Post-80s" generation, for whom the focus of individualism is economic and social competition. The "Post-90s" generation is preoccupied with "self-expression." It is not, however, the kind of self-expression we saw in the Baby Boomer generation in the United States, which was predicated on the idea of a "true self," but rather a kind of self-expression predicated on the idea of the self as a kind of postmodern commodity, a mutable, contingent pastiche of identities.

While many in the "Post-80s" generation have enthusiastically embraced online communication, especially instant messaging, discussion forums, and online "bulletin boards," the "Post-90s" generation is China's first generation of digital natives. Rather than older style discussion forums, they were brought up on social networking sites, online shopping sites, and massively multi-player online games. While there is little evidence that either the socialist ideology or the ideals of self-sacrifice espoused by their grandparents have much relevance to this generation, the Party is nevertheless attempting to respond to the perceived lack of "morals" of young people through propaganda campaigns waged with cultural products. In March 2006, for example, an online game entitled "Learn from Lei Feng Online" was released in China in which players collect points by fighting spies and doing "good deeds" in the form of an avatar representing the revolutionary hero Lei Feng. It is doubtful, however, that this game and cultural products like it will gain much of a following among China's youth.

The shifting ground of Chinese collectivism

What this analysis illustrates is that, just as it is an oversimplification to label Americans individualistic, it is also an oversimplification to call Chinese collectivistic. Over the years the ground of "Chinese collectivism" has shifted considerably. The collectivism of the War generation was more the traditional collectivism of Confucianism, oriented much less towards society as a whole and more towards one's family or clan and founded on strict notions of hierarchy. It was this kind of collectivism that the Party was attempting to transform through mass education campaigns into something more resembling the modern Communist ideology. The collectivism of the generations that grew up during the Great Leap Forward and the Cultural Revolution, on the other hand, though focused on sacrificing individual desires and goals to the good of the collective, bore little resemblance to traditional Confucian collectivism. Rather than hierarchal face relationships, it was predicated on radical egalitarianism that temporarily overturned kinship practices upheld in China for centuries. The collectivism of the Reform generation manifested more as a collective search for national identity and a preoccupation, if not with egalitarianism, at least with fairness.

The collectivism of the "Post-80s" generation actually looks more like individualism than collectivism, though members of this generation do often exhibit a strong sense of loyalty to their families, to their nation. Finally, members of the "Post-90s" generation, at least at this point, seem primarily focused on "self-expression" and perceive themselves as to some degree alienated from their parents.

Largely because of digital technology, members of both the Millennial generation and Generation Z in the United States, and the "Post-80s" and "Post-90s" generations in China share similar experiences, similar forms of discourse and patterns of communication, and similar allegiance to international icons of popular culture like Lady Gaga. Because of this, some have predicted that the continued spread of digital technology will result in a kind of globalized "youth culture." In fact, what now separates the younger generations in nearly every society from their parents is their participation in globalization.

We believe, however, that there is as yet little reason to think that globalization and the internet will result in a homogenized youth culture. Young people in China and the United States still have very different experiences and are faced with very different kinds of challenges. These differences are likely to become important in international relations as these two groups take leadership roles in business and government in their respective nations in the years to come. But, the differences are in many ways very far from what people might expect from their reading of most of the available material on intercultural communication, which continues to perpetuate the individualism/collectivism dichotomy. In contrast to such materials are more recent studies by scholars like Chung and Mallery (1999/2000) who found that in a comparison on seven individualism-collectivism subscales, respondents from the United States were rated as being more collectivist than Chinese respondents on six of the seven scales, and Parker and his colleagues (2009), who found in a survey of U.S. and Chinese University students that the U.S. sample showed higher agreement to statements that seem to reflect principles of collectivism such as, "One of the pleasures in life is to be related interdependently with others," and that the Chinese sample agreed more strongly with statements related to individualism such as, "One should live life independently of others as much as possible."

Such studies and our own analysis outlined in this chapter might lead readers to jump to the conclusion that Chinese are becoming more like North Americans and North Americans are becoming more like Chinese, but this is also, we believe, an unsatisfactory conclusion, for the collectivistic orientation of U.S. Millennials is nothing at all like traditional Confucian collectivism, and the individualism of Chinese "Post-80s" and "Post-90s" generations is still very far from the individualism described by Tocqueville or displayed on *Donahue*. Although very different from their elders, young people in North America still participate in a long tradition of polemical individualism, and young people in China still participate in a strong tradition of collectivism, which is one reason why the "disrespectful" attitude of members of the "Post-90s" generation towards their elders has generated so much discussion in the Chinese media. Having said this, we hope the main effect of this analysis will be to disrupt the notion that individualism and collectivism are mutually exclusive binary opposites and open up space for seeing how both an orientation towards individual goals and towards group harmony co-exist and interact in nearly all discourse systems.

Researching Interdiscourse Communication

Whether or not intergenerational communication is an issue in your site of investigation, attention to generational discourse systems can help you to understand the historical context in which the communication patterns you observe have developed. Elsewhere we have called this process "opening up the circumference" of our investigation.

All communication takes place on multiple timescales. A conversation might be seen as occurring in the scope of the few minutes it takes for the people involved to exchange words, or it might be seen in the wider context of a meeting, or in the even wider contexts of a workday, a workweek, or a particular project. We might open the circumference of our investigation even further to see it as part of the relationship between the people who are speaking which may have been developing over months or years. We might see it as part of the history of the company or the work team. Or we might see it in terms of the life cycles and generations of the people involved.

The idea of "circumferencing" the instances of communication that we are studying is that we try to set the circumference wide enough so that we can include any elements that may help us to understand why people behave the way they do and where potential conflicts might occur. At the same time we must set it narrowly enough so that we can keep our investigation manageable: we cannot refer to the whole history of the world in order to try to understand a single conversation.

In this respect, the notion of generational discourse systems it particularly useful, giving us a reasonable circumference through which to consider the longer timescale of historical events and circumstances that might be influencing the ways people are communicating and the reasons why they might have difficulty communicating.

Discussion Questions

1   Using the outline guide to discourse systems, analyze the ideology, socialization, forms of discourse, and face systems of your own generational discourse system. How do they differ from those of the generational discourse systems we have described in this chapter?

2   Talk to your parents or other people in your immediate environment of your parents' age about formative events in their lives and their values. Would you be able to describe a generation gap? Talk to someone of your own age who grew up in a different social or geographical context and compare their analysis of their generational discourse system with your analysis of your own. Is it more similar to or more different than that of your parents' system?

3   Look at the slogans below:
    • "Challenge the rules"
    • "Follow the rules"
    • "Bend the rules"
    • "Create new rules"
    Which generations in your own social environment would you attribute these slogans to and why? How might the different ideologies and face systems, reflected in these slogans be a source of intergenerational miscommunication?

4   Read the "Top ten reasons you would want to work at Google" below and discuss how they reflect the ideology, socialization, face systems, and forms of discourse of the U.S. Millennial generation. Do you think these reasons would be attractive to participants in your own generational discourse system?
    (a)   **Lend a helping hand.** With millions of visitors every month, Google has become an essential part of everyday life – like a good friend – connecting people with the information they need to live great lives.
    (b)   **Life is beautiful.** Being a part of something that matters and working on products in which you can believe is remarkably fulfilling.
    (c)   **Appreciation is the best motivation,** so we've created a fun and inspiring workspace you'll be glad to be a part of, including on-site doctor; massage and yoga; professional development opportunities; shoreline running trails; and plenty of snacks to get you through the day.
    (d)   **Work and play are not mutually exclusive.** It is possible to code and pass the puck at the same time.
    (e)   **We love our employees, and we want them to know it.** Google offers a variety of benefits, including a choice of medical programs, company-matched 401(k), stock options, maternity and paternity leave, and much more.
    (f)   **Innovation is our bloodline.** Even the best technology can be improved. We see endless opportunity to create even more relevant, more useful, and faster

products for our users. Google is the technology leader in organizing the world's information.

(g)   **Good company everywhere you look.** Googlers range from former neurosurgeons, CEOs, and U.S. puzzle champions to alligator wrestlers and Marines. No matter what their backgrounds, Googlers make for interesting cube mates.

(h)   **Uniting the world, one user at a time.** People in every country and every language use our products. As such we think, act, and work globally – just our little contribution to making the world a better place.

(i)   **Boldly go where no one has gone before.** There are hundreds of challenges yet to solve. Your creative ideas matter here and are worth exploring. You'll have the opportunity to develop innovative new products that millions of people will find useful.

(j)   **There is such a thing as a free lunch after all.** In fact we have them every day: healthy, yummy, and made with love.

(http://www.google.com/intl/en/jobs/lifeatgoogle/toptenreasons/)

References for Further Study

Among the first academic studies of generations was David I. Kertzer's 1983 article in the *Annual Review of Sociology* entitled "Generation as a Sociological Problem." Much of the information on earlier U.S. generations was inspired by the lectures of Layne Longfellow (1978, n.d. 1, n.d. 2, n.d. 3, n.d. 4). Meagan and Larry Johnson's 2010 book *Generations Inc.: from boomers to linksters – managing the friction between generations at work* is an excellent popular treatment of intergenerational communication in the workplace. Donal Carbaugh (1984, 1989, 1990) elaborates in considerable detail the nature of the contemporary U.S. concepts of the self and individualism. *Habits of the Heart* by Robert N. Bellah and his colleagues (1985) followed up the observations of Tocqueville (1969) bearing upon North American individualism. Useful descriptions of the attitudes and behavior of young people in contemporary China can be found in H. Zhang's 2009 article "Problems and solutions of young adults in China" and Stanley Rosen's 2004 article "The state of youth/youth and the state in early 21st-century China." An interesting study of information ethics among three generations of Chinese is presented in Maris G. Martinsons and David Ma's 2009 article "Sub-cultural differences in information ethics across China."

11

Gender and Sexuality Discourse

Gender and Sexuality

The issue of separate systems of discourse associated with particular genders or particular sexualities is complex and contentious, especially since notions of sex and gender are already strongly embedded into the ideologies and social practices of many other discourse systems, including the Utilitarian discourse system and the Confucian discourse system. It is for this very reason, however, that it is so important to explore the place of gender and sexuality in interdiscourse communication; such an exploration will help us to highlight some key aspects of the theoretical framework of discourse systems we have been developing so far and, to some degree, allow us to problematize this framework.

Part of the difficulty of speaking of gender and sexuality discourse systems is coming to terms with what is meant by gender and sexuality in the first place. Don Kulick captures this difficulty well in his ethnography of *travesti* in Brazil. *Travesti* are males who, often from an early age, begin dressing in women's clothing and wearing makeup. They normally engage in sexual relations with heterosexually identifying males in which they take on the role of the one who is penetrated in anal intercourse. They typically congregate in cities as opposed to rural areas. They often work as prostitutes. Although they normally take hormones and other drugs to obtain the secondary sexual characteristics of females and refer to themselves and each other using female pronouns and names, they identify themselves as men and do not endeavor to surgically alter their genitals, as do many who identify as "transsexuals" or "transgendered" people in North America or Europe.

The first question we might ask is whether or not *travesti* participate in a particular discourse system with its own unique ideology, forms of discourse, face systems, and approach to socialization, or is it a group which exists at the *nexus* of multiple, cross-cutting discourse systems including discourse systems associated with a particular region (urban) and profession (sex work). And, if we are ready to posit a *travesti* discourse system, would

Intercultural Communication: A Discourse Approach, Third Edition. Ron Scollon, Suzanne Wong Scollon, Rodney H. Jones.
© 2012 John Wiley & Sons, Inc. Published 2012 by John Wiley & Sons, Inc.

this be a gender discourse system or a sexuality discourse system, or, even more contentious, would we consider it a voluntary discourse system or an involuntary discourse system?

The fact is, convincing arguments could be made for any of these positions. One could very productively analyze the communication and social practices of these men as a discourse system in its own right, showing how the beliefs, ways of communicating, and forms of social organization of groups of *travesti* work together systematically. One could focus on this system from the point of view of gender ideology and gendered behavior, or from the point of view of sexual desire and practices, though neither of these perspectives would make much sense without the other. Or one could approach this community as one existing at the intersection of other cross-cutting discourse systems.

This ambiguity does not undermine the utility of the concept of discourse systems as an analytical tool, but rather demonstrates its flexibility. We said in the very first chapter of this book that when we speak of discourse systems, we are not referring to essential, externally existing entities, but rather to a set of *heuristics* for understanding human behavior and communication. Both treating *travesti* as a discourse system in its own right and treating their social practices as operating within or drawing upon other discourse systems might serve to illuminate different aspects of the behavior and communicative practices of these men and yield valuable information on how they might interact with people who are not part of this group.

The problem is that, when it comes to gender and sexuality, questions of separation and integration, the degree to which a group should be treated as unique, as well as questions of volition, the degree to which one chooses to "be" a certain kind of person, "feel" certain kinds of desires, and engage in certain kinds of practices, are not just academic questions. They are also political questions. The definition of homosexuality, for example, first as a clearly defined discourse system and second, as an *involuntary* discourse system, has, for example, been a central strategy for combating discrimination and establishing rights for people who engage in sexual behavior with members of the same sex in places like North America and Europe.

This, however, is not just true of these discourse systems. In a sense, all discourse systems to some degree define themselves and are defined by others based on their affiliation with or opposition to other discourse systems. That is to say, all discourse systems are to some extent expressions of politics and power relations within a society.

Gender Discourse Systems

The most common argument for considering men and women to be members of different discourse systems is the identification, in a range of studies conducted in North America and other countries in the last four decades, of the unique ways in which men and women talk. In her 1975 book *Language and Woman's Place*, the linguist Robin Lakoff argued that women have a different way of speaking than men, characterized by such features as wider intonation contours and more rising intonation at the ends of utterances, more hedging and imprecise language, more use of expressive forms like adjectives, a more collaborative communicative style, and more attention to linguistic correctness. Since then, similar differences have been noted in many subsequent studies. In 2008, for example, Matthew Newman and his colleagues analyzed a database of over 14,000 text files from 70 separate studies and found that women used more words related to psychological and social processes whereas men referred more to object properties and impersonal topics.

Lakoff's argument at the time she wrote her groundbreaking book in the mid-1970s was *not* that women formed a unique discourse system, but that this way of speaking reflected unequal power relations in the society (and also helped to perpetuate this inequality). It wasn't until later that scholars began to attribute these different ways of using language to "cultural" differences between men and women.

The notion that men and women belong to different "cultures" is usually associated most strongly with the work of Deborah Tannen, whose bestselling book *You Just Don't Understand: men and women in conversation* helped to popularize this theory. Tannen's early work drew heavily on the research of Daniel Malz and Ruth Borker (1982), who adapted to the study of intergender communication a framework developed by the linguist John Gumperz to study interethnic communication. This framework asserted that most cases of interethnic miscommunication are not the result of bad faith, but the result of participants falsely interpreting conversational cues of people from other ethnic groups using the interpretative frameworks of their own groups.

Maltz and Borker extended this notion to communication between men and women, who, they argued, like people from different ethnic groups, grow up with different experiences and operate in different social contexts, and so develop their own norms of communication and frameworks through which to interpret the communication of others. One example they give is the tendency of women to use more minimal responses (like "mm hmm" and "yes") to show listenership, which, they say, results in women believing that men are not listening to them when they fail to use minimal responses with the same frequency, and in men mistakenly believing that women are agreeing with them when they actually are not.

In contrast to this approach is the "dominance" approach, which in many ways continues the line of thinking developed by Lakoff that the main source of the differences in the way men and women talk is the asymmetrical face relationships that exist in most intergender interactions. Advocates of this approach include such scholars as Pamela Fishman, Dale Spender, Candace West, and Don Zimmerman. While proponents of the "difference" approach look for explanations in larger cultural formations, advocates of the "dominance" approach focus on how local instances of verbal interaction between men and women work to construct and maintain hierarchal relations between genders.

It is not our intention to come out on the side of either of these approaches, but rather to consider both perspectives as they relate to the framework of discourse systems we have been developing in this book. Later, we will consider another model for analyzing intergender discourse which attempts to transcend the "difference" and "dominance" dichotomy by focusing on the specific "communities of practice" in which difference and dominance can be observed and on the concrete social practices with which they are associated.

Directness or indirectness?

We will start with an example of a conversation between a man and a woman in order to illustrate these two approaches to gender discourse:

He: What would you like for your birthday?
She: I don't care, anything's OK.

He: No, really, what do you want? I'd like to get you something nice.
She: You don't have to get me anything, besides we can't afford much right now.
He: Well, how about if we just go out for dinner together then?
She: Sure, that's fine. I don't really want anything. You always give me whatever I want anyway.

Both the man and the woman in this conversation feel frustrated by the situation. He really wants to give her something nice, unusual, something she would not otherwise buy for herself because they do not usually spend much money on special things for each other or for themselves. But from this conversation he is not able to figure out what she would like, and he gives up and settles for just going out for dinner – something they have always done and which carries no special meaning for either of them. What has frustrated him is that while he has asked quite clearly and specifically what she wants, she has told him nothing. He is confirmed in his belief that this woman and perhaps all women are "wishy-washy, indefinite, unable to say clearly what they want, or just passive."

The woman in this conversation is also frustrated. She would very much appreciate a special and unusual gift as a symbol of the strength of their relationship. What the gift would be is not the consideration for her at all; what is important to her is that he should know her well enough to be able to tell what would be just the right gift to symbolize this. The fact that he has asked outright indicates to her that he, "like most men," is unobservant, is unable to interpret her feelings, or in the worst case does not really care for her as much as he says. She feels what he has said is just an exercise in pretending to care and that he is really quite satisfied to get out of the situation with nothing but having to go for dinner. The result is that even though he has had the best of intentions in his mind and has sincerely wanted to express his feelings for her, what the man has communicated to this woman is quite the opposite. She feels he does not care for her very much at all.

For her part, the woman has wanted to give him a chance to demonstrate his feelings for her, and so she has been careful not to spoil this by being explicit. For her it is important not to be explicit, and so she carefully disguises any clues that she is really hoping for the nice gift he has suggested. She hopes that in spite of this conversation he will go out and buy something for her, and so is disappointed to find that he has taken her quite literally and they have only had a dinner together.

The likely way proponents of the "difference approach" would interpret this problem is to say that the man and the woman in this example have approached the same situation with very different interpretive frames, with one expecting direct and explicit discourse and the other expecting indirect expression. It is important to say that this interpretation does not mean that men are direct and women are indirect. What is meant is that when one expects directness and the other uses indirectness, wrong interpretations and miscommunication might result. The point is the difference in expectations, not absolute differences in style or behavior.

What can be seen as a contrasting example comes from Donal Carbaugh (1989), whose work we discussed in the last chapter. He has described how on the U.S. television talk show *Donahue*, a woman complained that in some decades or more of marriage her husband had never told her that he loved her. The response many men might make to this complaint is that they have worked hard at their jobs, they have been faithful husbands, they have not wasted money on themselves for years – what clearer expression of their love could they make than years of demonstrating it through their day-to-day behavior? In other words, in this case it seems that what the woman is asking for is an explicit statement, whereas what the man is doing is making an indirect statement through his actions.

In some cases, then, women might use indirect approaches to communication while men are expecting more direct approaches; in other cases, it is women who are expecting a direct statement and the men who are expressing themselves indirectly. The issue is not directness and indirectness; the issue, according to the "difference" approach, is the different interpretive frameworks men and women have which lead them to draw the wrong inferences from language which in another situation would be quite clear and unambiguous.

Those taking the "dominance approach" would look at the conversation above about the birthday gift rather differently, likely focusing more on the face systems that are activated in this exchange. According to the "dominance" perspective, the different ways men and women have of speaking is not so much a matter of different interpretative frames as it is a matter of different positions of power. Here, the man has begun the conversation using an involvement strategy, asking the woman a direct question and showing his interest in what she desires, reproducing for her the traditional subordinate position of being the beneficiary of his generosity. In doing this, he has put the woman in a double bind. Either she can accept this subordinate position by expressing her true desires, or she can resist this positioning by declining to say what she wants or by saying she does not want anything. In doing this, however, she ends up committing herself to using an independence strategy – not imposing on the man – which discursively constructs the very subordinate position within a hierarchal face system that she was attempting to avoid.

In this reading, what makes the man feel dissatisfied is that the woman has not acknowledged his generosity and validated his superior position, and what frustrates the woman is being forced into a subordinate position no matter how she responds.

Similarly, in the case of the woman who complained that her husband never told her he loved her, scholars from the "dominance" perspective might point to the fact that people with power are often less required to engage in interactional work to maintain relationships – they take their relationships and the security of their position in them for granted – whereas people with less power need to constantly work to maintain a feeling of security in their relationships by both expressing affection and soliciting expressions of affection from the other party.

Who talks more?

In organizational communication, from businesses to university and public school classrooms, another difference between the behavior of men and women that has been observed in research in North America has to do with the amount men and women speak. In business meetings consisting of both men and women, it has been observed that most of the talk is dominated by the men in the group. They take the most turns at talk, and when they talk they take longer turns. From this situation one might mistakenly draw the conclusion that men talk more than women, or that women are basically taciturn. On the other hand, a similar business meeting in which the participants are all women finds them highly voluble with rapid exchanges of turns. In university classrooms in which a discussion is being led by a teacher, Tannen (1991) has observed that, again, men dominate the flow of the discussion, with women taking fewer and shorter turns. On the other hand, when the discussion takes the form of separate small groups, women who are silent in the larger setting emerge as having a good deal to say.

Both of these situations are in contrast to the common complaint of women that men at home are sullen, silent, and withdrawn. This once again points up the fact that one cannot make a binary contrast between men and women, saying that women are taciturn and men are voluble. That might be said in the context of a mixed gender business meeting or a large university class discussion. On the other hand, if the context is a same-gender business meeting or a small group discussion, one would have to say that women are if anything more voluble than men. And if the context is the home, one might then want to consider men to be the taciturn ones.

Here a reading that attempts to account for these differences in volubility strictly on the grounds of different communicative habits of men and women would be more difficult to make convincingly. The power difference between men and women which gives men social license to dominate conversations and interrupt women in public situations seems a much more salient factor.

It is important to remember that these two approaches – the "difference" approach and the "dominance" approach – are not necessarily mutually exclusive. In fact, conflicting interpretative frameworks are themselves often a consequence of power differences. The boss who tells a joke forgets that people are laughing because he is the boss, not because he is very funny. Within that framework, his position of power makes his employees more responsive than they might be if he was the mailroom clerk. In order to understand inter-gender discourse, we will have to look at the standing interpretive frameworks within which the discourses between men and women take place. But we will also have to consider how historical conditions of inequality act to support these interpretive frameworks as well as create local conditions that force men and women into certain conversational positions. All of us are the products of our histories and our socialization, and for men and women the most significant aspect of these histories is the asymmetrical differentiation of the roles and status of men and women.

Forms of discourse; functions of language

One of the chief areas on which research from the "difference" perspective has focused is the different functions language supposedly has for men and women. We have discussed differences in this dimension in several places in regard to other social groups. In chapter 5 we said that the use of deductive and inductive strategies for the introduction of topics was related to the question of whether relational or informational functions of language predominated. In that case we were focusing largely on either situational or interdiscourse differences in expectations. In the case of intergender discourse, what some researchers have observed is that in many cases women tend to focus more on relationships than men, who tend to direct their attention to information. Tannen (1990a) has referred to this as the distinction between "rapport" and "report."

One apparent result of this supposed difference is that it leads to intergender miscommunication around the issue of problems and solutions. Everyone, of course, has problems. The difference is in how we respond when others tell us their problems. It has been observed that many women tend to respond to hearing someone else's problems by telling their own problems. This indicates that they understand the situation the other person is in and that they feel sympathetic. Many men, in contrast, are more likely to take it as a request for help and to offer a solution, however pointless the solution might be.

If a woman describes a problem she is having with a client, for example, to another woman, what might happen is that her colleague will say, "Yes. I had one just like that last week. I felt awful, but there was nothing I could do." If she describes this same problem to a male colleague, she might hear, "Well, of course, what you should have done is XYZ." If he is like the "men" described by Tannen and others, he is likely either to offer a reprimand and explanation of what she did wrong, or, in a slightly more helpful case, offer some constructive suggestions about how she might deal with the problem. What he is quite unlikely to do is sympathize with her and share a similar problem.

When a woman uses what Tannen (1990a) calls "troubles talk," that is, the discussion of problems, to emphasize connections, community, and sympathy for others, a man may take this as a request for help and as a display of weakness or ignorance. Consequently, when a man hears problems aired, he is likely to take it as a challenge to his ability, his competence, or his expertise. He is ready to rush in and show how easily he can solve the problem.

What sometimes happens when men and women talk is not a simple problem–solution sequence. If a woman puts forward a problem, she might be looking for a symmetrical exchange of problems and sympathy. This is not what she gets; what she gets is a solution. This suggests to her either that the man has not heard her call for sympathy or that he is attempting to put her down for ignorance as a novice. Because she has not received the sympathy she is looking for, she might increase the emphasis on the problem, and the man might hear this as a failure to accept his solution, which directly challenges his sense of expertise. As each attempts within his or her own framework to continue the discussion, the misinterpretation gets worse until one or the other simply gives up or gets angry.

The reason men and women may take these different positions, of course, is also easily explained as a matter of power and status. By approaching such situations as an opportunity to step into the role of expert, men not only reinforce their position of dominance but also once again position women as being in need of help and advice.

One outcome of this polarity between novice and expert is the polarity between listening and lecture. Women are sometimes accustomed to getting extended lectures from men on a diverse range of subjects. What might trigger these lectures is a woman's attempt to start a round of "troubles talk." As she brings up a problem for sympathy, she is taken as having presented a problem needing a solution. The more she elaborates on the problem, the bigger the problem needing a solution seems to be to the man. The result is that he launches into a full-blown solution when all the woman was looking for was a sympathetic ear. She lapses into silence once she realizes that the more she says about her problem in an attempt to be heard, the longer the lecture is likely to last.

Another aspect of discourse discussed by those who posit that men and women participate in different discourse systems centers on the attention given to messages and to metamessages. This parallels, of course, the difference in attention given to relationship and to information. There is a tendency, it is said, for men to focus on the information given, that is, the message, and for women to pay closer attention to the metamessage, that is, to how the information is to be interpreted.

Attention to messages as opposed to metamessages, as well as to information rather than relationship, of course, is an expression of the Utilitarian ideological position of empiricism and positivism. As a result, the discourse of women who display orientations towards metamessages and relationship is sometimes taken as not just emotional or illogical but also as opposing the ideological basis of this system. Women come to be thought of as willful outsiders. What for a woman is a concern for inequality, very much an expression of one aspect of the Utilitarian ideology, is taken as undermining that ideology. The result is that it is women who are taken to be contradictory, not the ideology of the discourse system which is producing this contradiction.

Face systems

In considering face systems, we can return to one of the problems we mentioned above, the fact that in some contexts men are said to be excessively taciturn and in other contexts it is women who are said to be the silent partners. Women complain that in their intimate relationships, men fail to talk to them. Men sometimes see women in business meetings as quiet and uninfluential. As we have said in chapter 3, taciturnity and volubility are not so much attributes of a person's character, though certainly individuals vary enormously in their personal style on this dimension; they are face strategies of independence and involvement, which to some extent everyone has the ability to use when they are appropriate. That is to say, whatever personal style someone might have, that same person will be more or less voluble, or more or less taciturn, depending on the face relationships he or she is trying to express to others and which the society and social situation makes available to him or her to express.

We believe that the observation by researchers that women tend to be voluble in small and more intimate groups and taciturn in large and more formal or public situations, and that men tend to be more voluble in those more public contexts and fall into taciturnity or monologues in situations of intimacy, is to some degree a direct result of the broader framework of expectations provided by contemporary society and its background of Utilitarian discourse. As this framework grants to men the right (and, of course, obligation) to dominate in public contexts, and since public contexts are ones in which the Utilitarian discourse system expects a face system of symmetrical solidarity, men in these contexts are found to be highly voluble. That is, in these contexts men adopt the face strategies of involvement.

The question then is this: why do men become taciturn in intimate relationships? On the surface of it, it would seem that a man should assume a face system of symmetrical solidarity and feel quite comfortable expressing involvement with his wife or girlfriend. Of course, that would imply equality of status, and that is where the problem lies. In public contexts, at least until recently, the dominating face systems of Utilitarian discourse were taken as the appropriate frameworks. In intimate relationships between men and women, however, there has been an ongoing struggle over the appropriate face system. Although this is changing, men have traditionally assumed asymmetrical status between themselves and women in all contexts. This assumption has been buttressed by claiming the status as wage earner, protector, most informed, expert, and all the other values asserted by the Utilitarian discourse system. Women, on the other hand, have increasingly taken the Utilitarian ideology at its word and claimed equal status as human beings.

In chapter 3 we stated the problem as follows: "When two participants *differ* in their assessment of face strategies, it will tend to be perceived as difference in *power*." Men and women often differ in their assessment of the face systems in which they are currently operating in many societies. When men use face strategies of involvement in speaking to women, they often do so within a face system of hierarchical asymmetry. Women often hear these strategies of involvement as the attempt to assert dominance. To be certain that this dominance is not legitimated, women may avoid using strategies of independence in responding, unless, as in the conversation we analyzed above, such strategies are seen to serve the purpose of resisting being put into a subordinate position. In such a system, men might expect women to respond to them with strategies of independence. When women speak to them with strategies of involvement, men may feel they are being challenged. Such men then have only one of two options. If they continue to respond with involvement strategies, they may feel they will be heard as asserting their unequal status. On the other hand, if they use strategies of independence – taciturnity is primary among them – they may hope to achieve a system of neither symmetrical solidarity nor asymmetry, but a stand-off compromise of symmetrical deference. Unfortunately, this compromise solution men sometimes adopt of avoiding the asymmetry that comes with the use of involvement strategies is not the best way to foster intimacy.

In other words, it is possible to interpret this perennial dilemma for men and women in many societies as arising out of the contradictions of the Utilitarian discourse system, which advocates egalitarian relationships for members only and requires its members to display their membership through its preferred forms of discourse. To the extent one adopts the "male"/Utilitarian values of self-sufficiency, status, exclusion, information, contest, and problem-solving expertise, one can be perceived as a member in good standing. On the other hand, to the extent one expresses the opposite pole of these values: intimacy, connection, inclusion, relationship, rapport, community, problem-sharing, and willingness to learn and to admit one's mistakes, one is more likely to be taken to be a marginal member of the system.

The origin of difference: ideology and paradox

Misinterpretation in communication between men and women is tied up in the historical development of Utilitarian ideology. To put it in a few words, the Utilitarian ideology is based upon the concept that humans are free, equal, rational, economic entities and that all society is based upon free interactions among such individuals. Unfortunately, in practice these rights have been rather selectively distributed.

To be fair, at least one of the founding Utilitarians, J. S. Mill, was among the leaders in the suffrage movement – the social and political movement to grant the right to vote to women. Nevertheless, in practice the conceptual individual at the foundation of Utilitarian thinking was a man.

While Utilitarian ideology is strongly anti-traditional, it has done little to alter the traditional polarization between inside and outside work. In pre-industrial European society, according to the sociologist Ruth Cowan (1983), most economic activity was centered upon the household, particularly the households of large landowners. In fact, the word "economy" was first used in discussions of the management of the resources of such large households. The relatively clear demarcation between the work of men and the work of women was based upon this distinction between outside work, which was the domain of men, and inside work, which was the domain of women. Even though women in many places engage in great numbers in such outside work, and men increasingly engage in inside work, this distinction between inside and outside remains the economic foundation for many of the power differences between men and women.

In this, European society may not have been particularly different from many other traditional agrarian societies. With industrialization and with the rise of Utilitarian ideology, however, two major shifts produced a major asymmetry in the statuses of men and women, which sometimes plays out today in the discourse between them. The first shift came about in the redefinition of economic activity. It came to be defined as just those activities of invention and technologization so idealized by Utilitarian ideology. The second shift was in placing exclusive value on those newly defined economic entities, "productive" individuals.

As creativity and invention came to be valued over tradition in Utilitarian ideology, men came to be associated with the progressive aspects of society and women with the traditional aspects. Early in the period of industrialization, public schools were established as part of the Utilitarian agenda. By the beginning of the twentieth century, however, schools had shifted from being predominantly staffed with male teachers to having mostly women in teaching positions. Men remained in positions of authority as headmasters and principals. At the same time, the moral instruction of children had shifted away from being the father's responsibility to become an integral aspect of the mother's child-rearing practices. Even in families which earlier had given over child rearing largely to servants, the mother was encouraged to take over these tasks.

Ruth Cowan writes,

Experts repeatedly suggested that a mother was the single most important person in a child's life, and that the child raised by nursemaids was a child to be pitied. The young boy raised by servants would never learn the upright, go-getting resourcefulness of the truly American child, would never become a useful member of the egalitarian republic, and would probably fail in the business world. (Cowan 1983: 179)

There are probably many reasons for this reduction in the moral authority of the father in child rearing and education. The story given at that time was that father's time was too valuable. He needed to be at work in business and industry during the days, and after work he needed to stop in the bars to make business contacts. Then, of course, in the wars so many men were lost that this shift in education and child rearing was stabilized as the normal pattern.

Even though women had come to play the major role in socialization, they were denied a role in the structures of authority and decision-making. Despite dramatic advances of women in politics and industry today, there are sill strong remnants of this situation. This attitude toward women was even more severe in government and business, where until recently women had virtually no direct voice in the corridors of power. The net result of these sociological changes, coupled with the growth of the Utilitarian discourse system, was that there came to be a strong identification of the Utilitarian ideology with the discourse of men as it is described by those adhering to the "difference" approach we have described above.

Within the framework of this approach, it would be difficult to establish whether the discourse of men is what it is because of the Utilitarian ideology, or conversely the Utilitarian ideology is what it is because it was developed by men. For our purposes it is sufficient to point out that the similarity the reader will have observed between the characteristics of men's discourse we have given above and the ideology of Utilitarian discourse is not an accidental one; the two discourse systems have evolved together over the past two hundred years or so to the point that in many ways they are indistinguishable from each other.

This, then, is the background against which the misinterpretations between men and women within Utilitarian discourse take place. Men, within this discourse system, often assume that the highest values will be placed upon independence, status, individuality, egalitarianism, the communication of information, competition, problem solving, and displaying technological and other forms of expertise. Furthermore, in many cases quite innocently, they will have come to believe in the ideological egalitarianism of Utilitarian discourse and fail to recognize the clear asymmetries of power which, in fact, still exist between men and women.

On the other hand, women will be much more conscious of the actual asymmetries of power and status, and while they will hold out for the values of intimacy, connection, inclusion, relationship and rapport, problem sharing, and recognition of one's limitations, they will also know that these characteristics are not highly valued within the Utilitarian discourse system. They are likely to be acutely conscious of the contradictions between the equality which is expressed and the asymmetry which is practiced, especially in their discourse with men.

The maintenance of difference: socialization

A question which is often asked in discussions of miscommunications between members of different groups is this: why do people not just modify their behavior once they have realized that some aspect of it is producing difficulties or confusion? The answer we have put forward above is that, to a considerable extent, our sense of who we are as people and of our place in human society is tied up in the patterns of discourse we use in communicating with others. To change our behavior is to change who we are.

But again, the question is asked, "If who we are is producing difficulties, why do we resist undertaking these changes?" The answer to that is that, on the whole, we have been who we are from very early in life and in most cases simply cannot imagine being any different. In other words, our primary socialization is a very powerful framework around what we do for the rest of our lives. We tend to form our concept of the world as well as our own place in it very early in life, and to change that concept of the world is a threatening prospect that few of us are willing to face up to.

There have been an increasing number of studies of how boys and girls learn to become boys and girls, and this research seems to indicate that in many cultural contexts from very early in life we begin to rehearse the roles which we will enact throughout our lives. In studies of the play of boys and girls cited by Maltz and Borker (1982), major differences were observed in their activities which clearly parallel the differences for men and women we have described above. In a major study, Janet Lever (1976), for example, found that the play of girls tended (at that time in North America) to be organized around intimate and small groups of "best friends," who played inside with dolls and other household items. These small groups were hard to join and required constant talk to maintain the strong bonds of intimacy. Boys, on the other hand, tended to play in much larger and much more loosely organized groups which included a wider age range of participants. They played outside in large "packs" in competitive games, chases, and mock fights. These boys' groups were relatively easy to join, but the new members were taken in at the bottom of a rigidly hierarchical structure.

For girls in this study, the main activity was intimate talk about problems. They used their verbal skill to produce intimacy and cooperation and generally avoided fighting and conflict. Through their "troubles talk" they produced tight bonding and felt that they had been successful when a sense of agreement and commonality was achieved. Boys, on the other hand, organized their play around doing things rather than talking. Verbal activities were directed at producing and maintaining a hierarchical structure. They took the form of insults, challenges, and arguments which produced hierarchical bonds. In contrast to girls, boys seemed least satisfied when everyone was in agreement, most satisfied when a struggle for position was in progress.

Another study reported by Tannen (1990b) examined both verbal and non-verbal communication in conversations between females on the one hand and males on the other. In groups from quite young children to young adults, females oriented their bodies and gaze toward each other in what is called direct alignment. The males, on the other hand, sat so that they did not directly face each other, but looked obliquely at some third point. The posture of the females was generally still and collected together into a small space, whereas the males spread themselves out, legs and arms wide, and were very active with much movement of their bodies as they talked.

The talk of these girls and boys paralleled this non-verbal alignment. The girls were highly voluble, but introduced relatively few topics, all of which were quite personal. They tended to focus on one person at a time and thoroughly talk out her problem before going on to the problem of the other person. The boys, on the other hand, talked relatively little and their topics were much more abstracted and diverse. They tended to talk in parallel, largely ignoring the other.

While research on socialization to the roles of men and women is relatively new, it may be that the differences scholars have observed in the language of men and women have some of their foundations in these early behaviors of boys and girls. While the studies we have mentioned say relatively little about what might cause these differences in behaviors, other studies have shown that in primary socialization, quite subtle cues are used by children to determine the wishes of caregivers. It would be quite wrong to think that boys always fight and girls always cry, but it is likely that differential treatment of these two behaviors tells boys and girls what is expected of them. A girl who has just fought with her brother and is crying may be told, "Don't fight. That's not nice." Her brother, on the other hand, may be told, "Don't cry. Boys don't cry about things like that."

Problems with the "difference" approach

There are a number of potential problems with an approach which sees men and women as belonging to different discourse systems, not least of which is the difficulty of generalizing the findings described above, derived mainly from work done with white, middle class participants in North America and Europe, to men and women who have grown up in other contexts. At the very least, one must posit the existence of "women's languages" and "men's languages" as opposed to "women's language" and "men's language" – in other words, despite possible similarities, the gender discourse systems of, for example, Japanese men and women cannot be seen as the same as the gender discourse systems of North American men and women.

Even within North America, there may be important differences based on things like region, religious beliefs, and generation. And so gender discourse systems are defined to a large extent in relation to beliefs, values, forms of discourse, face systems, and patterns of socialization of these other systems. What remains to be proven is the extent to which the women and men of one group might share a discourse system with the women and men of another group. In other words, the question is whether or not women's discourse or men's discourse forms systems which cut across the lines of other discourse systems based on things like class, corporate or professional affiliation, and generational lines.

Another important thing to remember is that the patterns of behavior that have been described above are by no means stable. Like all discourse systems, gender discourse systems are always subject to change. Most of the studies of male/female socialization cited here were conducted several decades ago. Today in North America children grow up in rather different conditions. Two differences are that they are more likely to witness their fathers taking on caretaking roles in the family, and girls are more likely to be given the opportunity to participate in officially sanctioned team sports.

Some scholars have pointed out that research studies which are set up to study the "differences" between men and women tend to find differences as a kind of "self-fulfilling prophecy." In other words, one problem with research from the "difference" approach is that it is based on the assumption that differences must exist and that those differences must be somehow related to gender rather than other things.

Perhaps the biggest complaint advocates of a more critical approach to gender discourse have with the work of scholars like those described above is the "no fault" stance they sometimes take. Differences between the talk of men and women, and even the patterns of socialization that apparently lead to it, are treated as neutral, value-free "cultural differences," and the sources of these differences in deeper structural patterns of inequality are not addressed. In conflicts between men and women, both parties are consistently treated as "innocent," even in cases in which males are clearly asserting dominance.

Compromise: "communities of practice"

The difference between the "difference" and the "dominance" approaches is not really a disagreement about whether or not men and women talk differently but rather about the focus of the analysis. Proponents of the "dominance" approach take it as a given that women will be the less powerful participants in conversations and search for ways in which male dominance or "masculinity" is reflected and reproduced locally. Proponents of the "difference" approach take it as a given that men and women have learned different ways to communicate and search for the source of conflicts in the different interpretative frameworks they bring to interaction. Clearly the assumptions of both these perspectives can be seen as problematic if applied universally and uncritically. A compromise is to focus less on these general assumptions about men and women and more on the particular kinds of interactions that men and women find themselves in and what they are actually trying to accomplish in these interactions. In some situations, dominance might arise as a more salient issue, while in other situations differences might be more prominent.

This is the solution suggested by Penelope Eckert and Sally McConnell-Ginet (1992). They take from Lave and Wenger (1991), whom we briefly discussed in chapter 8, the concept of "communities of practice," which are defined as groups of people who "do things together." What distinguishes "communities of practice" from discourse systems is that "communities of practice" are concrete groups of people involved in concrete social actions whereas discourse systems are more abstract systems of discursive resources that people draw on when they take these actions.

We have said that all individuals participate in multiple discourse systems and when they interact with others they always do so from complex positions of multiple participation. Similarly, groups of people also operate at the intersection of multiple discourse systems when they engage in specific social practices. Elsewhere we have referred to what Eckert and McConnell-Ginet call a "community of practice" as a *nexus of practice*, a site where multiple systems of discourse interact in such a way as to make possible particular social actions and particular social identities.

Such an approach reveals how gender and the systems of discourse and power that are associated with it actually operate differently depending on the other systems of discourse and power that are operating along with it and depending on what the people involved are actually attempting to accomplish.

In their book *Language and Gender* (2003), Eckert and McConnell-Ginet give the example of the confirmation hearings of African American Supreme Court Justice Clarence Thomas in 1991 in which he was accused by former employee Anita Hill of sexual harassment. During the hearings, the ways women and men positioned themselves in relation to these allegations and communicated their positions depended upon a complex set of overlapping and competing alliances. Many middle-class white women at the time wore buttons which said: "We believe her" as a way not only to show solidarity with Hill but to express a united response of "women" against "male" domination and abuse in the workplace. African American women, however, tended to side with Thomas, seeing the accusations as an example of "white racism," thus forming an unlikely alliance with white men and conservative white women who favored the nominee because of his conservative political views. At the same time, liberal white men were also likely to support Hill, not necessarily because they believed her but because they opposed Thomas's politics. Thus, the definition of "we" in the expression "we believe her" became subject to all sorts of cross-cutting and contradictory discourses.

What this example illustrates is that the claims we make to participation in various discourse systems are not just a matter of our socialization, but also a matter of what we are trying to do and the kinds of alliances we are trying to create or avoid in the context of particular situations.

Sexuality

If gender discourse systems are difficult to define and analyze, discourse systems associated with sexuality present even more complications. By sexuality discourse systems we mean systems of communication, social organization, and ideology which arise in relation to different sexual practices. Sexual practices in themselves, however, such as engaging in sexual contact with a person of the same sex, are not usually sufficient to claim participation in such discourse systems. Thus, it is possible to hear people say things like: "He may be a homosexual, but he's not gay." In this case, "homosexual" indexes a particular kind of sexual practice, whereas "gay" signals a discourse system.

This example highlights the fact that in considering sexuality discourse systems we must be careful not to impute participation in particular discourse systems purely on the basis of people's preferred sexual practices or sexual partners. Participation in such discourse systems is less about what people do and more about the meanings that they assign to it.

Although we have referred to sexuality discourse systems, along with gender and generational discourse systems, as involuntary discourse systems, what we mean by this is not that they are biologically determined, but that people are often socialized into them more informally and earlier in their lives, and that these systems are usually seen by participants as somehow "natural" rather than instrumental or goal directed. It is also usually more difficult to cease participation in such discourse systems without suffering some kind of social sanctions or psychosocial pressure. At the same time, we must reiterate that the distinction between voluntary and involuntary discourse systems is extremely contingent. In a sense, all discourse systems can be said to have both voluntary and involuntary dimensions. That is, our participation in all discourse systems is never totally determined or totally free since discourse systems themselves are inevitably shaped by social relations of power.

Whether or not participants in sexuality discourse systems consider their participation to be voluntary or involuntary, in fact, often constitutes an important component of the ideology of such discourse systems. For example, the notion that one is "born that way," a notion celebrated by U.S. pop star Lady Gaga in a recent hit single, is a major ideological pillar of the "western gay discourse system" upon which claims of minority status and civil rights depend. On the opposite side of the spectrum are "political lesbians" who construct participation in a lesbian discourse system as a conscious, goal directed choice. It is not our purpose in this book to consider the degree to which sexual desires are socially conditioned or genetically determined. We are less interested in the source of people's desires as we are in how people communicate about them and manage their social relationships around them. Arguments about nature and nurture are only important insofar as they become tools in this communication and social management.

It is easy to conflate the study of sexuality discourse systems with the study of gay, lesbian, bisexual, and transgender communities. Distinct forms of discourse and social organization have, however, developed around a wide range of sexual practices including things like sadomasochism, exhibitionism, costume play, pedophilia, eating and feeding practices, and even sexual abstinence. Although in what follows we will be focusing mostly on discourse systems that have developed around the practices of gays and lesbians, it would also be a mistake to associate sexuality discourse systems only with what Foucault called "peripheral sexualities." Heterosexuality has also been an important site for the formation of discourse systems.

Many people do not explicitly identify with their sexuality, but that does not mean they are not participating in a sexuality discourse system. Most heterosexuals, for example, do not consciously identify themselves as heterosexuals (in the same way members of the Utilitarian discourse system do not identify themselves as members of that discourse system); instead they simply consider themselves "normal." It is this very assumption of normality, however, that belies the existence of a discourse system whose ideology is very effective in naturalizing certain kinds of social practices and marginalizing others.

"Sexuality" itself is a rather recent invention. Although there are many examples in the pre-modern world of systems of communication and behavior growing up around sexual practices, it was not until the nineteenth century in Europe that the idea that a person's identity could be described by reference to their sexual behavior became popular. In many ways, this idea was a logical outgrowth of the Utilitarian discourse system with its focus on the individual and on classifying and calculating. With the spread of Utilitarianism there came a shift from seeing sex as a moral affair to be policed by religious authorities to seeing it as a medical matter to be policed by doctors and scientists. Perhaps the best expression of this ideological position towards sex can be seen in the work of nineteenth-century psychiatrists and sexologists like Richard von Krafft-Ebing who, in his famous *Psychopathia Sexualis* (1886), presented a systematic classification of a whole host of "normal" and "abnormal" sexual proclivities, coining for the first time terms like sadism, masochism, homosexuality, and heterosexuality.

The most important aspect of this new consciousness about sex was that it shifted attention from sexuality as a set of social actions to sexuality as a quality of particular social actors. As Foucault famously put it in his *History of Sexuality* (1981: 43), "the sodomite had been a temporary aberration; the homosexual was now a species."

Other conditions as well contributed to the growth of discourse systems around this new conception of sexuality, the most important being a general weakening of extended kinship ties in many places due to rapid industrialization and urbanization. The growth of cities where young men and women migrated to seek their fortunes far from the constraints of traditional family ties gave rise to many new forms of non-traditional relationships, many involving sex. Cities also made possible the critical mass and commercial support for groups of people interested in the same sorts of sexual practices to form communities.

This is not to say that non-traditional relationships and practices and communities associated with them did not exist before this time. The point we are trying to make is that many contemporary sexuality discourse systems were made possible by the conditions of modernity – urbanization, industrialization, individualism, and a weakening of traditional kinship ties – conditions which went hand in hand with the spread of the Utilitarian ideology. Today many of the same conditions are helping to bring about the formation of "gay and lesbian communities" in Asia, Africa, and South America, and for many who participate in these new discourse systems, sexuality has become an important aspect in the production of modernity, a marker of sophistication, education, and "westernization."

Sexuality and gender

It is important to state quite clearly that although we are dealing with gender and sexuality discourse systems in separate sections, they are in many ways difficult to separate. As Deborah Cameron and Don Kulick argue in their book *Language and Sexuality* (2003: 5), "Having a certain kind of body (sex), living a certain kind of social being (gender), and having certain kinds of erotic desires (sexuality) – are not understood or experienced by most people in present day social reality as distinct and separate. Rather they are *interconnected.*"

And so, to return briefly to the issue of "women's talk" and "men's talk" which we discussed above, we might consider such features as asking questions, hedging, and focusing more on relationships on the part of women and of interrupting, lecturing, and focusing more on information on the part of men not as a matter of men and women participating in separate gender discourse systems but as a matter of them both participating in the same sexuality discourse system: the heterosexual discourse system, which positions men and women in asymmetrical face relationships in which women, as Fishman (1983) points out, are forced to do more of the interactional "shit work."

In this discourse system, men and women are not only required to be different, but are also required to complement each other in specific ways. Some have pointed out that one of the main weaknesses of the "difference" approach to gender discourse is that it does not take into account the centrality of the institution of heterosexuality through which, for the most part, the very differences this approach points out are produced and enforced.

Sexuality in many societies is an important marker of masculinity and femininity. Both Cameron (1997) in her study of the talk of fraternity brothers and Philipsen (1975) in his ethnography of men in a small industrial town in America have pointed out that the talk of men is often very much preoccupied with showing that one is heterosexual. In fact, in most traditional cultures same sex eroticism is very strongly associated with non-normative gender identities, and many early sexologists of the nineteenth century saw homosexuality as primarily a gender disorder.

Performativity

Here it would be useful to mention an approach to social identity which has not only been extremely influential in the contemporary study of both gender and sexuality, but which also informs our notion of discourse systems in important ways. In the first chapter of this book we suggested that it might be more useful to consider "culture" not as something we *have* but as something we *do*, and throughout the subsequent chapters we have talked of how people use forms of discourse and face strategies to claim participation in various discourse systems in particular social situations. The notion of *performativity*, developed by the cultural critic Judith Butler (1990), highlights this strategic nature of social identities within discourse systems.

The idea of performativity comes from the *speech act theory* of John Austin (1962), who noted that certain speech acts, which he called *performatives*, bring about the state of affairs they describe simply by being uttered. It is by uttering the words "I now pronounce you husband and wife" that a priest or justice of the peace causes two people to be married, and just by saying "you're under arrest," a police officer brings about the state of being arrested. In its application to discourse systems and social identities, the notion of performativity points to the fact that we are not first members of particular discourse systems and then express that membership through discourse, but rather, it is through our use of discourse that we become members of particular discourse systems.

What is so important about this notion is that it reminds us that social identities and the discourse systems which support them are not necessarily unproblematic reflections of who people are and what they believe, but rather performances which people use in all kinds of strategic ways to get things done in the world. Discourse systems themselves, then, can be seen as the result of the strategic positioning of particular groups in society in relation to other groups.

Discourse systems and imagined communities

Another useful concept for understanding discourse systems that develop around sexual practices, and indeed all sorts of other kinds of discourse systems, is that of the "imagined community" as articulated by Benedict Anderson (1991). Anderson was concerned with the formation of the nation-state. How is it possible, he wondered, for the nation-state to come to be a unified and coherent entity when most of the people inhabiting it have never met one another? The answer he came up with is that in order for communities to gain this kind of cohesion, there must be some mechanism through which members can "imagine" themselves as part of a community. This mechanism for Anderson was the circulation of discourse. What made the nation-state possible, he argued, was the invention of the printing press, which enabled people to create discursive representations of the nation and circulate them among disparate individuals.

Above we talked about "communities of practice" as sites where multiple discourse systems intersect around the social practices that people perform together. "Imagined communities" are communities of practice for whom these practices come to take on certain symbolic meanings to the point that members begin to see themselves not just as a group of people acting together, but as a coherent community. They publish newsletters and websites, appropriate various symbols of identity, congregate in various commercial and non-commercial venues, and sometimes mobilize their group identity in the service of various political causes. Through these actions they advance certain kinds of social relationships, legitimate certain preferred forms of discourse, and promote a certain ideology. In other words, they go from being a group of people that exists at the nexus of various other discourse systems to forming a discourse system of their own.

The most important thing about the process through which these new discourse systems come into being is that it does not occur in a vacuum. Imagined communities are formed through various affiliations and oppositions to other discourse systems, by the strategic appropriation of aspects of some already existing discourse systems and strategic rejection of aspects of others. This process takes place both within and outside of these communities, both through members *imagining* identities for themselves, and through others coming to see them as a distinct community and *inventing* identities for them. Imagining myself requires both that I invent a "serviceable other" (Sampson 1993) against which to define myself, and that I to some degree "buy into" the inventions that the other has made of me.

In the analysis that follows we would like to consider this dialectic of imagination and invention in the formation of what appear to be two distinct discourses of gay sexuality, what we will be calling the "western gay discourse system" and the "*tongzhi* discourse system." Both of these discourse systems are historically rather young, one developing in the United States and Europe in the 1960s and 1970s, and the other developing in China, Hong Kong, and Taiwan in the 1990s. Both are undergoing rapid changes as they interact with each other and other discourse systems. How stable or long lasting these two systems of discourse will be is uncertain. And that is not our main concern. Instead what we are concerned with is exploring how these discourse systems, and by extension other discourse systems, come into being as the strategic responses of communities of practice to the material and social conditions they are confronted with.

"Gay Culture" and the Utilitarian Discourse System

One of the authors was once privy to a conversation between a gay man from California and a gay man from Hong Kong which went like this:

U.S. man:	Have you told your parents?
Hong Kong man:	No.
U.S. man:	Why not? Don't you want to be free?
Hong Kong man:	What's that got to do with being free?

We discussed above how the modern notion of sexuality as an aspect of an individual's identity grew out of the ideology of the Utilitarian discourse system and the material conditions of industrial capitalism. What we would like to argue now is that modern gay and lesbian identities as they are practiced and promoted in places like the United States, Australia, and Western Europe (and increasingly other places around the world) are in many ways associated with the most extreme expression of the Utilitarian ideology, the polemical individualism that developed in U.S. society around the 1960s.

Although there have been numerous political movements over the years for the civil rights of men who have sex with men and women who have sex with women, including the formation of various homophile rights groups in Europe in the late nineteenth century, contemporary gay and lesbian identities as most readers will understand them developed in the 1960s and 1970s, primarily in the United States but also in Europe, as part of a broader civil rights movement (which also focused on the rights of racial minorities and women), as an aspect of a broader sexual revolution, and as a direct consequence of the more general definition of U.S. individualism as a matter of self-discovery and self-affirmation which, as we noted in the last chapter, characterized the generation of North Americans born after World War II.

While on the one hand, this period in the United States was associated with a form of individualism which constructed the self in opposition to social roles and identity labels, it was also a period which saw the rise of coalition politics, or what has come to be known as "identity politics," as African Americans, women, gays and lesbians, and other groups began using their membership and shared experience in communities of practice to claim political rights. In other words, members of various groups began to imagine identities for themselves around shared symbols, shared practices, and shared experiences of injustice. For gays and lesbians, for example, the riots at the Stonewall Inn, a gay bar in New York City on June 28, 1969 became a potent symbol around which this new identity could begin to be imagined.

Since the late 1960s, of course, what is known as "gay and lesbian culture" (or the more inclusive "gay, lesbian, bisexual, and transgendered" culture) has developed considerably through specialist media, the rise of various commercial venues, and, in some cities, particular neighborhoods or districts in which a large number of members reside. While it is difficult to posit a stable discourse system in which all of the different sexualities ("LGBT") participate equally, it is possible to speak of discourse systems of gay men, or of lesbians, or of transgendered people which overlap with one another in key ways.

With the spread of the Utilitarian discourse system and the rise of global capitalism, the identities produced by these discourse systems have also spread to other countries. Scholars like Dennis Altman (1996, 2002), in fact, point to the development of a "global gay culture" that has formed as the music, fashions, attitudes, ideologies, and social practices of western gay men and lesbians have circulated throughout the world via electronic media and cultural products. Altman, in fact, points to this global gay culture as "a key example of emerging global 'subcultures,' where members of particular groups have more in common across national and continental boundaries than they do with others in their own geographically defined societies" (2002: 87).

To posit a "western gay discourse system" is in no way meant to deny the considerable variety within gay communities in the west and in "non-western" contexts in which notions of gay and lesbian identity have been appropriated, any more than speaking of the Utilitarian discourse system denies the great variety among the companies and professional groups that participate in and promote this discourse system. At the same time, we can identify particular face systems, forms of discourse, and ideologies that are associated with this sort of "gay culture" to the extent that displaying mastery of these forms of discourse and face systems has come to be seen as a marker of participation both by gays and by straights. What we are really interested in here is not essentializing particular practices and identities, but in understanding how discourse systems themselves are used strategically by people to position themselves in their social worlds.

Ideology

As we said above, the chief ideology of the "western gay discourse system" is polemical individualism in which identities are defined *in opposition* to existing social roles and societal values. From the point of view of gays and lesbians, this primarily means traditional moral values regarding sexual behavior centered around conventional structures of kinship and marriage and often supported by both religious organizations and conservative politicians. In this respect, selfhood is claimed on the basis of being "different." In the 1970s in the United States, gay male "culture" defined itself not just through same-sex sexual practices but through an explicit rejection of the sexual mores of monogamy and sexual restraint associated with mainstream heterosexual society.

At the same time, gay and lesbian identities are also formed in opposition to more recent medical models of sexuality, with their roots in nineteenth-century sexology, which pathologize same-sex eroticism. Indeed among the most important victories of gay rights movements all over the world has been the removal of homosexuality from manuals of pathology and mental disorders. In this respect, selfhood is claimed on the basis of being "normal" or "just like everyone else." It might be argued, in fact, that gay identity, or at least gay politics, has developed in the west at the site of tension between these two constructions of the self – the self as "unique" and the self as "normal" – a fact that is particularly evident in the current debates in the United States and other places around same-sex marriage.

This apparent paradox, however, begins to make sense in the context of American polemical individualism in which the self is defined in opposition to "being defined," whether that definition imputes conformity or uniqueness. That is to say, the value assigned to the self is a function of how successful it is at resisting being fixed or positioned by social institutions like the family, the government, and the church, and even the gay discourse system itself. The proliferation of "subcultures" and identity labels within the gay community and the more recent "queer" movement, which promotes more fluid, postmodern notions of sexuality beyond the "binaries" of gay and straight and male and female, does not represent a break from the ideology of the western gay discourse system but rather a logical extension of the polemical individualism that is at its core. In a sense, "queer politics" might be said to represent the ultimate expression of the American tradition of individualism.

It is important to note, however, that one thing that makes the rejection of these identities possible is the partial appropriation of them. What made possible the gay identities of the late twentieth century, for example, was the very pathologization of homosexuality in the nineteenth century (around what Foucault refers to as the invention of the homosexual person).

Similarly, "queer" identities are predicated on appropriating negative inventions of non-normative sexualities from the mainstream and turning them on their heads.

Face systems

Just as the ideology of the western gay discourse system reflects the polemical individualism of the postwar Baby Boom generation in the United States, its preferred face relationships reflect the radical egalitarianism of this generation. Social roles and relationships of power, rather than being seen as "given," are constantly open to negotiation. Face relationships of symmetrical solidarity between parents and children are promoted and traditional kinship roles are seen as obstacles to self-expression. Despite a rhetoric of solidarity with other gays and lesbians as well as other marginalized groups, individual expression and self-fulfillment are held up as the highest goals.

Forms of discourse

The preferred forms of discourse in the western gay discourse system revolve around self-expression. In fact, as with the guests on the *Donahue* show described in the last chapter, the whole point of discourse is to enact a unique and authentic self, a large part of which involves revealing one's sexual practices and sexual desires to others. As can be seen in the quote from the U.S. gay man above, the public expression of one's sexuality is seen as nothing less than a prerequisite to realizing personal freedom.

The quintessential form of discourse in this discourse system is "coming out," the action of revealing one's gay identity to friends, family members, co-workers, and even strangers through confessions, personal narratives, expressions of "pride," and even public parades. At the core of this form of discourse is a construction of the self built upon the notion of "authenticity."

The key metaphor for the "inauthentic" self is the "closet." To be "closeted" is to be in many ways an imperfect member of this discourse system, and gay men and lesbians who fail to successfully navigate the "coming out" process with their families or who regularly conceal their sexuality from friends and co-workers are often regarded with disapproval or pity.

Of course, what Eve Sedgwick referred to as "the epistemology of the closet" has changed considerably over the years with a greater acceptance of sexual diversity, especially among members of the Millennial generation. Seidman and his colleagues (1999), in fact, argue that the closet is no longer the potent metaphor in the western gay discourse system that it used to be.

At the same time, along with this focus on authenticity, this discourse system is also characterized by a discursive style which in some ways undermines authenticity: "camp," a style which Sontag describes as celebrating artifice and excess. "Camp" discourse, both in the form of explicit performances like drag shows and in the form of more everyday patterns of speech, dress, and behavior, highlights within this discourse system the *performative* nature of sexual (and gender) identities, creating alongside the "authentic" identities of "coming out" an ironic detachment from these identities.

Socialization

When we speak of socialization into the western gay discourse system we are not considering the hackneyed question of how one comes to be attracted to members of the same sex. Such attraction and the sexual practices that ensue from it, as we said above, might be considered conditions for participation, but do not in themselves constitute membership. What we are more interested in is how those who identify themselves as gays and lesbians come to master forms of discourse, face strategies, and ideological positions which they can later hold up as emblems of membership in this discourse system.

For many members, socialization is constructed as a personal journey of self-discovery in which one comes to realize one's "true self." Outwardly it involves mastering the forms of discourse through which this journey can be articulated and this "true self" can be expressed. As gay men and lesbians reach their teens and are more and more exposed to representations of "gay culture" in the media and among circles of like minded friends, they gradually learn to reproduce certain ways of speaking, ways of acting, ways of dressing, and ways of managing social relationships with members of this discourse system and with non-members. It is important to say that there is no one way of "acting gay" within this discourse system. Instead members are presented with a wide array of possible identities associated with different styles and different sexual practices. What unifies all of these various identities and the ways of speaking and acting associated with them is that all of them are constructed as ways of "being yourself."

While to a large extent the western gay discourse system has developed as a response to the marginalization of homosexuals by the wider society, this discourse system, as all discourse systems, also engages in marginalizing those who are unable, for one reason or another, to master its forms of discourse and claim for themselves one of the various identities the discourse system makes available. Despite a rhetoric of inclusivity, a number of observers have pointed to the marginal positions this discourse system sometimes creates for older men and women, men and women of color, men and women from lower socioeconomic strata, and men and women who fail to conform to various ideals of attractiveness or desirability.

We would like to reiterate that by describing this discourse system we are in no way endeavoring to describe the actual condition of gay men and lesbians. Rather, what we are describing is a set of related discursive resources (forms of discourse, face systems, and ideological positions) that has developed over the years around gay and lesbian communities in some societies and which individual gay men and lesbians draw upon in various ways in different kinds of circumstances.

The "*Tongzhi* Discourse System"

In the Hong Kong film *A Queer Story* (dir. Shu Kei, 1997) the main character, played by the popular actor George Lam (Lam Chi Cheung), confesses his homosexuality to his elderly father. "I don't like women, Dad," he says. "I like men." In response his father says nothing and then abruptly tells his son he needs to go home. When the son attempts to give his father money for taxi fare, the father refuses, leaving the son standing on the street bereft as the taxi containing his father pulls away. A few moments later, however, the taxi reappears and the father sticks his head out of the window, says he has forgotten his wallet, and asks his son to give him money for the fare, which the son does happily. The film ends with a shot of the father in the back seat of the taxi smiling down at the money his son has just given him, and then a shot of the son standing on the street, also smiling.

When we have shown this film to our students in Hong Kong, nearly all of our Chinese students express the opinion that this scene has a happy ending. Some of them, in fact, are moved to tears. The students in the class who have come from the United States or Europe, however, tend to be mystified by this reaction. How could this possibly be a satisfactory outcome? Not only has the son failed to gain "acceptance" from his father, but he has ended up having to shell out the taxi fare.

Part of the reason for these divergent reactions is a different conception of communication within the family. In families influenced by the individualism of the Utilitarian discourse system, the best way for children to express their love to their parents is through honesty, revealing to them their "true selves," and the best way for parents to show their love for their children is to "accept them for who they are." In families influenced by the Confucian discourse system, harmony is valued over honesty. Love is shown through the ratification of established roles, with children fulfilling their duty towards their parents and parents nurturing and supporting their children. Expressions of identity outside of these prescribed roles are at best irrelevant and at worst threatening. Expressions of non-normative sexuality are especially threatening if they are seen to preclude marriage and procreation, which are considered among the chief duties of a son or daughter.

The biggest blow to the son in this film is not that his father fails to explicitly "accept" his sexuality, but that the father fails to accept his offer of taxi fare, denying him the opportunity to fulfill his duty as a son. When the father returns and asks the son for money, this communicates a ratification of the son's role in the family and, if not an acceptance of the son's sexuality, an acceptance of the son as a member of the family regardless of anything else. Because of this, our Chinese students judged this outcome to be not only positive but also poignant.

In the last several decades there has been an increasing visibility of gay and lesbian identities in East Asia, particularly in countries and regions like Japan, Hong Kong, Singapore, Thailand, and the Philippines, but also, more recently, in Mainland China. The formation of these communities and identities is driven by many of the same factors that helped create the conditions for the development of the western gay discourse system: industrialization, urbanization, and political and economic liberalization.

Mainstream representations of gays and lesbians have also followed a line of evolution similar to that earlier experienced in the west. In China, for example, images of homosexuality have evolved from the Republican period, when it was portrayed as a foreign perversion that endangered social and familial order, to its portrayal as a symptom of bourgeois decadence in the Revolutionary period, when men who had sex with men were prosecuted under laws prohibiting "hooliganism," to a medicalization of homosexuality in the early Reform period, and finally to more social scientific models of sexuality dominant today.

Along with these changing local conditions, however, another important factor in the rise of East Asian gay and lesbian identities has been economic globalization and the circulation of images of North American and European gay lifestyles through the media and tourism. These images, in fact, have acted as models for many middle class gay men in Asia who regard "western gay identity" as a marker of modernity, education, individuality, and freedom. A gay bar in Hong Kong or Manila, in fact, may be nearly indistinguishable from one in London or San Francisco in terms of the music, the décor, the fashions, and even the dominance of the English language on signs and in the conversation among patrons.

At the same time, this imported model of gay identity – and the ideology of individualism and face relationships of symmetrical solidarity it promotes – is sometimes at odds with traditional kinship roles and hierarchical relationships that are still pervasive in much of

East Asia. This creates for many gays and lesbians a dilemma in which the kind of self made available by one discourse system in which they participate creates a conflict with the kind of self made available by another discourse system in which they participate.

One solution for many gays and lesbians in East Asia has been to orient towards more indigenous forms of gay identity and attempt to formulate new systems of discourse around them, systems which create space for non-traditional sexual practices within the traditional values and kinship roles of their societies.

One example of this kind of "strategic" discourse system is the *tongzhi* movement which has developed in China, Taiwan, and Hong Kong since the mid-1990s. *Tongzhi* is the Chinese word for "comrade," and its appropriation as an identity label for gays and lesbians (an appropriation which has become part of mainstream parlance) emphasizes cultural citizenship rather than individualism. There is, of course, an element of irony as well in the use of a term of address that was earlier associated with the Republican and Communist Revolutions whose governments sought to demonize and criminalize homosexuality.

The imagination of *tongzhi* identities, as opposed to gay and lesbian identities, involves two primary discursive moves. The first is identification with the local culture through the appropriation and re-articulation of traditional Chinese values and Chinese history. Pre-Republican China in this discourse system is romanticized through the selective citation of literary works and historical records that document same-sex relationships among some emperors and members of the nobility in dynastic China as a society tolerant of homosexuality. The Manifesto of the 1996 Tongzhi Conference, held in Hong Kong, for example, declares,

> *Tradition* [sic] *Chinese Society was Tolerant Towards Same Sex Love* Many people mistakenly criticise Chinese culture as sexually repressive and conservative . . . In fact, traditional Chinese culture was tolerant towards same-sex love. Mencius says, "The joy of eating and sex are natural human desires," both of which have no association with sin or guilt . . . Hostility and violence, such as harsh legal punishment, bashing and lynching against same-sex love in pre-modern China cannot be found in historical records. For instance, the introduction of sodomy law in Hong Kong in 1865, which could sentence two consenting male adults to life imprisonment, was the result of British colonial rule. What was brought from the West to China was not same-sex love, but the sin associated with it in the Judaeo-Christian tradition, which significantly contributed to the homophobia found in modern Chinese societies.

Although there is evidence that homosexual practices enjoyed some acceptance and even institutional status in some periods of Chinese history, as documented by Hinsch (1992), it is an exaggeration to portray all of dynastic China as broadly tolerant of homosexuality, and any behavior or identity which interfered with one's duties to the family (including marriage and procreation) would have certainly been severely proscribed. The historical accuracy of these claims aside, this move demonstrates an attempt to construct a gay identity consistent with local Confucian values, and one of the main ways this is done is to adopt the Golden Age orientation towards time characteristic of the Confucian discourse system as opposed to the Utopian orientation of the Utilitarian discourse system (including the "Somewhere Over the Rainbow" utopianism of the western gay discourse system). In this formulation, it is homophobia rather than homosexuality that is constructed as a modern foreign import.

The second discursive move in the imagination of *tongzhi* identity is to define it not in opposition to local moral values, but in opposition to the foreign values of individualism and identity politics promoted by the western gay discourse system. The same Manifesto quoted above continues as follows:

The les-bi-gay movement in many Western societies is largely built upon the notion of individualism, confrontational politics, and the discourse of individual rights. Certain characteristics of confrontational politics, such as through coming out and mass protests and parades may not be the best way of achieving *tongzhi* liberation in the family-centred, community oriented Chinese societies which stresses the importance of social harmony. In formulating the tongzhi movement strategy, we should take the specific socio-economic and cultural environment of each society into consideration.

Again, to portray "confrontational politics" as somehow foreign to a society which brought us the May 4th Movement, the Cultural Revolution, and the Tiananmen Square demonstrations is a bit of an exaggeration. As a strategic move, however, this rejection of Utilitarian forms of discourse and face relationships opens up space within which Chinese gays and lesbians can assume the identities of filial children and legitimate cultural citizens while at the same time inviting tolerance of their sexual practices. This move is of particular strategic value in Mainland China where a confrontational approach to gay liberation would doubtless meet with disapproval from authorities. As it is, this gentler brand of gay politics has enabled gay communities in Mainland China over the last decade to exist openly with a minimum of state persecution and even some state sponsored support around things like HIV/AIDS prevention.

The degree to which gays and lesbians in Chinese societies will "buy into" this new discourse system, and the degree to which they will gravitate towards more "western" expressions of sexuality is unclear. For many men and women these models co-exist as they assume the roles of good sons and daughters at home (often taking an even more central role in the care of elderly parents than their married siblings), and then taking on more individualistic, flamboyant styles in gatherings with their peers. What it means to be "gay" in China, or in any society, is a complex issue which often involves the appropriation and mixing of a wide variety of symbols, histories, and social practices. It sometimes involves taking up the language of the western gay discourse system and sometimes involves borrowing from more local models of sexuality. All of these different ways of "being gay" carry different meanings, signal affiliation to different communities (local, national, and transnational), and create for people different positions within a matrix of overlapping and intersecting discourse systems of age, gender, class, nationality, and ethnicity.

The point of this discussion has been to highlight the strategic, dialogic, and performative nature of sexuality discourse systems. In a sense, however, all discourse systems exhibit these features to some degree. Our participation in discourse systems is not just a matter of our upbringing or "cultural" backgrounds. It is also a matter of positioning ourselves within the multiple communities through which we travel during the course of our lives. The feminist critic Katie King (1992: 82), in discussing the interaction between local and global gay identities, captures this sense of overlapping and intersecting discourse systems well when she speaks of identity formation taking place within "layerings of maps and territories that . . . interact, correct, and deconstruct each other."

Researching Interdiscourse Communication

Throughout this book we have been developing the framework of discourse systems as a way to analyze "intercultural communication" without falling into the trap of naturalizing discursive practices and essentializing social groups, which too often accompanies the use of the word "culture." At the same time we are aware that our concept of discourse systems is also in many ways susceptible to essentialization and reification. In this chapter we have sought to highlight the strategic and performative nature of discourse systems. It is not accidental that we have chosen to thus problematize the notion of stable discourse systems in the context of discussing the two kinds of discourse systems that are most often reified and essentialized: gender and sexuality discourse systems.

We have tried to show in this chapter not only how individuals and communities exist at the nexus of multiple overlapping and intersecting discourse systems within which they seek to strategically position themselves based on specific goals and the contingencies of specific situations, but also how discourse systems themselves develop as strategic responses to social conditions. Here it is useful to remember that we as analysts are not immune to the dialectic of imagination and invention that drives the formation, development, and dissolution of discourse systems. All of the discourse systems we have described in this book, the Utilitarian and Confucian discourse systems, the western gay discourse system, the discourse systems of men and women, and of various professions and various generational groups in certain places are all, in fact, strategic *inventions* which we make use of to imagine our own scholarly discourse system and to position ourselves in relation to various intellectual traditions in the fields of anthropology and linguistics.

At this point, then, in your study of interdiscourse communication in the particular site of investigation you have chosen, it is useful to step back and to destabilize any notions of solid, "natural" discourse systems with clear boundaries that you may have built up during your research. One way of doing this is to consider the performative nature of people's participation in discourse systems, to note how they speak of themselves and others as either affiliated with or excluded from different groups, to observe the ways they imagine identities for themselves and invent identities for other people, and to try to understand the strategic nature of claims and imputations of participation in discourse systems. You might also notice how these claims and imputations are always situated within specific historical moments and material circumstances, and how they are always to some degree responses to specific relationships of power.

Discussion Questions

1   Think of the ways men and women are socialized within the discourse systems in which you participate. Do they grow up having similar or distinct experiences? How does this affect how they communicate? What sorts of ideologies and power relationships underpin these patterns of socialization?

2   Look at the personal ads below and discuss how the writers strategically position themselves within various discourse systems.
   (a)   Sincere Chinese professional, 29, slim, boyish-looking, gentle, dedicated, romantic, naughty, non-scene; Interested in reading, classical music, movie going, travelling, developing genuine friendship; seeks a sincere Western soulmate, 30–42, caring, non-scene, hopefully leading to 121. Photo appreciated, Confidence guaranteed. ALA

(b)　28 SWM, 6'1", 160 lbs. Handsome, artistic, ambitious, seeks attractive WF, 24–29, for friendship, romance, and permanent partnership.

(c)　"I'm gonna rock your world!" If you're big-framed with a big heart, this chubby chaser is ready for you. And if loving you is wrong, I don't wanna be right. Write now, don't just think about it. (No serial killers or sick insects) please.

(d)　Independent SWF, 29, 5'6" 110 lbs., love fine dining, the theater, gardening and quiet evenings at home. In search of handsome SWM 28–34 with similar interests.

(e)　BRITISH ACADEMIC: 30, seeks Western-educated Asian man to explore the theory and practice of sexual dissidence over a bottle of red wine.

(f)　Gujarati Vaishnav parents invite correspondence from never married Gujarati well settled, preferably green card holder from respectable family for green card holder daughter 29 years, 5'4", good looking, doing CPA.

(g)　Gujarati Brahmin family invites correspondence from a well-cultured, beautiful Gujarati girl for 29 years, 5"8", 145 lbs. Handsome looking, well settled boy.

(h)　GYM-LOVER looks for dreamlover. GWM, 25, butch, sporty. Seeks similar (below 35) for friendship or more. Let's work (it) out together. Photo/phone appreciated.

References for Further Study

The culture and sexual practices of the Brazilian *travesti* are described by Don Kulick in his 1998 book *Travesti: sex, gender, and culture among Brazilian transgendered prostitutes*. The concept of the "nexus of practice" is elaborated in Ron Scollon's 2001 *Mediated Discourse: the nexus of practice*. Good introductions to the study of language and gender include Penelope Eckert and Sally McConnell-Ginet's *Language and Gender* (2003), Deborah Tannen's *Gender and Discourse* (1994), and Kira Hall and Mary Bucholtz's 1995 edited volume *Gender Articulated: language and the socially constructed self*. Deborah Cameron and Don Kulick's 2003 *Language and Sexuality* is an excellent introduction to the role of discourse in the construction and expression of sexuality and sexual desire, and their edited volume *The Language and Sexuality Reader* (2006) contains a broad range of articles on related topics. For a more general sociological introduction to sexuality see Jeffery Weeks' 2006 classic *Sexuality* (originally published in 1986). A good anthropological survey of homosexual practices and identities across cultures is Stephen O. Murray's *Homosexualities* (2000). Dennis Altman discusses the globalization of sexual identities in his 2002 book *Global Sex*. For a description of the "*tongzhi* discourse system," see Chow Wah Shan's *Tongzhi/Queer: politics of same sex eroticism in Chinese societies* (2001). For further discussion of the strategic aspects of gay identity in contemporary China, see Rodney Jones's 2007 article "Imagined comrades and imaginary protections: identity, community and sexual risk among men who have sex in China."

12

Doing "Intercultural Communication"

Discourse Systems and the Individual

The problem we have been trying to understand in this book is how a person manages to cope with the complexity of the various different discourse systems in which he or she participates. A person is born a male or a female, in a particular region, whether rural or urban, of a particular country, at a particular time in history. He or she becomes educated within a certain professional sphere, cultivates certain tastes and interests, takes certain political positions, and develops a set of adult family and other interpersonal relationships. In the process of these developments a person learns a set of languages and linguistic varieties. The question is this: how does a person reach a sense of a stable identity and still navigate among all of these competing sources of identity and group membership?

There are two aspects of this problem of discourse systems and the individual which we want to consider: identity and membership. Identity is, of course, a very complex concept, and we recognize that. For our purposes, what we want to emphasize is that part of every person's identity is the discourse systems within which he or she participates. From person to person this will vary, of course, with some individuals taking great pride in their membership in a professional association, for example, while others just pay their annual dues without much further thought to the matter. Even in the case of such deeply permanent identities that are associated with one's home country, one's region, or one's family there will be considerable personal variation.

In research the authors have carried out in Alaska (Scollon and Scollon 1981), it was found that Athabaskan Indians sometimes resist education and literacy within the U.S. school system even though they have clearly stated goals of succeeding within the U.S. economic and political system. The possible reasons given for this resistance were that for Athabaskan Indians to engage in the new discourse systems of U.S. schooling and literacy amounted to a change in identity, and it is this change in identity which was being resisted.

Intercultural Communication: A Discourse Approach, Third Edition. Ron Scollon, Suzanne Wong Scollon, Rodney H. Jones.

At the Earth Summit in Brazil in 1992, it was reported that Third World feminists engaged in extended discussions with North American feminists on the question of cultural and gender identity. As it was reported, the problem was that Third World women felt that U.S. feminists were asking the women of the world to take on aspects of identity which were not, in fact, those of the discourse system of women, but rather the discourse system of North Americans. They argued that these women could not set their North American identity aside and claim to be simply world feminists as a means of escaping responsibility for the worldwide ecological problems which they had gone to the Earth Summit to discuss.

The point we want to make here is that one of the major functions of a discourse system is to give a sense of identity to its participants. The positive side of this function is that participants in a discourse system come to feel comfortable in communicating with other participants in the discourse system. It reduces the ambiguity in interpreting discourse and increases feelings of solidarity and security. The negative side of this function is that it forms a boundary between ingroup and outgroup, and people who are not participants in the discourse system are rejected by participants and find it difficult to achieve even peripheral participation. At the same time the boundary between ingroup and outgroup communication makes it less likely that participants of the discourse system will be able to make themselves understood to non-participants. In extreme cases this may come to seem justified: "Who wants to talk to *them* anyway?"

Each discourse system tends to emphasize certain aspects of face relationships. These, in turn, require certain forms of discourse for their expression. To be sure, participants will have competence in those forms. Socialization practices are instituted within the discourse system, and those socialization practices inculcate certain cultural values. Those values give rise to, support, and legitimate the face relationships expected within that discourse system. Each discourse system, then, forms a circle of enclosure which, on the positive side, gives identity and security to its participants, but, on the negative side, tends to enclose them within its boundaries, so that it is easier for them to go on talking to each other than it is for them to establish successful communication with those who are outside the circle of the discourse system. When this happens, participants are likely to see their participation not as peripheral or contingent (as it always, to some degree, actually is), but rather as a matter of more or less permanent *membership*. That is, they begin to see themselves as *members* of discourse systems (or "cultures") in the same way they see themselves as members of concrete groups and communities.

Identity as a matter of membership in different discourse systems is not something that an individual can come to alone. It is rather a matter of people in a group, often rather self-consciously, imagining themselves to be a group and the discourse system (or combination of discourse systems) that they participate in to constitute a "culture." It is the group which ultimately determines who is or is not a member of the group. It is possible, then for an individual to feel identity with the "culture" of the group and yet be rejected by the group as a non-member. Conversely, one might be considered a member of a group by other members, but not yet come to take it as a part of one's identity.

We wrote in chapter 3 of the study in which it was found that Japanese tended to disapprove of Japanese speaking high or complex forms of Japanese to non-Japanese, no matter what the ability of the non-Japanese with the language might be. This is a case in which participants in a discourse system choose to limit participation by others, even where those others demonstrate serious competence with the forms of discourse associated with the discourse system. In this way, participants in discourse systems transform the notion of participation, which is chiefly a matter of competence, into the notion of membership, which is chiefly a matter of belonging to a particular group of people.

Once this transformation is accomplished by participants, discourse systems come to have requirements for membership. These requirements may vary in their stringency depending on how closely guarded group identity comes to be. In North America in the 1970s and 1980s, for example, there was considerable discussion about whether or not men could be feminists. One position asserted that only a woman can be a feminist, because the feminist discourse system has as one of its basic requirements for membership that one can feel identity as a woman. Others took the position that it is not at all necessary to feel identity as a woman to take on and support the social and political goals and aspirations of women as one's own. In such a case, what was being debated is whether or not feminism is a gender discourse system of women or, in fact, a goal-directed discourse community.

We have used "socialization" as a general term to cover both explicit processes of training and education and implicit processes of learning which take place as part of the ongoing activities within a discourse system. A child born in Hong Kong as the child of Cantonese-speaking parents is socialized into the norms for speaking Cantonese. A person who takes a job with an international corporation usually receives specific training which introduces him or her to the expectations of such a company. In both cases, the new member of the discourse system is given both explicit and implicit expectations of how to behave and how to communicate.

A person is born into a country or region, a family, a gender, a generation, and other such seemingly "natural" groupings which are associated with particular discourse systems. At the same time, a person has been educated for the position he or she has taken within a company. One has both corporate discourse identities and the identities that come with one's professional specialization. One also takes up a variety of interests or hobbies in the course of one's lifetime which one may to varying degrees come to identify with.

We might see these different discourse systems as "toolkits" which contain various discursive tools (that is, ideologies and the interpretative frameworks they create, forms of discourse, and face systems and strategies) which people draw on in different situations. When one is on the job, one is more likely to appropriate tools from one's corporate or professional discourse systems. At home with the family, tools from these discourse systems are less likely to be used. The point is that which tools we use from the various toolkits available to us depends upon the circumstances in which we find ourselves and the people with whom we are interacting. It would also be a mistake to consider this a matter of free and conscious choice. We are, in fact, largely unconscious of how or why we adopt different face systems or forms of discourse in different situations beyond the fact that it simply "feels right." We are also under tremendous social pressure when we find ourselves in certain situations (like workplaces) to appropriate tools that are deemed by others as appropriate to these situations.

Often we draw tools from two or more different discourse systems at once and combine them. This is easy when there are a lot of similarities between the discourse systems, and more difficult when the discourse systems are very different. This is because elements of discourse systems are related to one another in *systematic* ways: certain face systems are expressed and supported by certain forms of discourse which also help to promote particular ideologies.

It should be obvious that not all of these systems will be in agreement about what is proper behavior in every situation. A person will often find himself or herself in conflict over what is the right way to speak, what are the right relationships to express or to maintain, and what are the right forms of discourse to use in any particular situation. This is why we made the claim in the first chapter of this book that interdiscourse communication is just as likely to take place *within* people as it is *between* people.

From the point of view of the analysis of discourse across discourse systems, we might see each system as trying to socialize its participants into its own preferred norms and away from the norms of other systems in which he or she may be a participant. To give an example, contemporary international business has adopted a Utilitarian discourse system which, in many ways, has as one of its goals the elimination of such other forms of discourse that might interfere with its goals. This discourse system, like many other discourse systems, tends to say to participants, "Leave your other ways of speaking at the door."

The result of this is that participation in such systems comes more easily to those whose other forms of identity and membership are less in competition with them. It is a greater problem for those whose other forms of identity are distinctive. For these people, it requires a temporary suspension of their other forms of personal identity and group membership to participate in transactions in these discourse systems.

Intersystem Communication

We hope that we have convinced the reader that there are many kinds of discourse systems, some of which exclude others, some of which are included in others, many of which cut across other systems. All of these discourse systems are defined by features which are shared by some, but not by all, other systems. In any particular communicative situation, participants will simultaneously be members of various discourse systems other than the system that may seem most relevant to that particular communicative situation. To summarize this situation we can say that, from the point of view of the individual, almost all forms of discourse take place at the intersections of several discourse systems, what we described in the last chapter as a *nexus of practice*.

Because of the complexity of human social organization, we believe that communication which takes place exclusively within a single discourse system is the rarest form of communication. Some form of "intercultural" or at least intergroup communication is probably the most normal form of communication. Communicators are regularly faced with complex situations of communication. We began this book by saying that language is always ambiguous, whether it is at the level of the interpretation of words and sentences or at the level of making conversational inferences. This ambiguity is not the result of poor learning; it does not matter how long you study Chinese, or Japanese, or English, the things you say and hear said will never be completely and unambiguously interpretable. This is the nature of language.

Nevertheless, we all depend on achieving some degree of confidence in our communication in order to function in the world. One cannot lie back and simply say that language is always ambiguous, and therefore nothing we can do or study will improve the situation. Throughout this book we have suggested a number of reasons why things might go wrong in communication between people who are participating in different discourse systems. Now we must turn our attention to the broader consequences of miscommunication and what can be done to avoid it.

Cultural ideology and stereotyping

One of the main consequences of the notion of membership we have described above is that it sometimes leads people to form rather rigid opinions about the individuals they are communicating with based on the groups of which these individuals are perceived to be members.

We have said above that a balanced description of any discourse system must take into consideration the full complexity of that system as an interplay of beliefs, relationships, forms of discourse, and practices of socialization. We have also noted that any balanced description of an individual must take into account all of the different, sometimes conflicting discourse systems they participate in, and any balanced description of a situation must see it as a moment when multiple discourse systems come into contact with one another. Whenever one aspect of a discourse system or one discourse system associated with a person or situation is singled out for emphasis, given a positive or negative value, or treated as a full description of a "culture" or a person, we would want to call this an ideological stance rather than a description. A much more common term for such ideological statements is "stereotyping."

One situation in which stereotyping often arises is when someone comes to believe that any two "cultures," or social groups, can be treated as if they were polar opposites. For example, in chapter 5 we introduced the concept of two different rhetorical strategies, the inductive and the deductive strategies, for the introduction of main topics in discourse. There is a danger in such a concept when someone comes to consider, as some researchers have in the past, "Asians" to be inductive and "westerners" to be deductive. That would constitute an ideological statement, by trying to make a clear division between "Asians" and "westerners" on the dimension of rhetorical strategies. As we argued in chapter 5, both strategies are used in all "cultures" and are part of the forms of discourse of all discourse systems that we know of. What might be different is the way communicative situations are established in different societies, and especially the relationships among participants.

Similarly, in our discussion of the differences in the ways time is approached by participants in different discourse systems we observed that the Utopian sense of time is often thought of as "western," associated with the Utilitarian discourse system, and the Golden-Age concept of time is associated with the Confucian discourse system. This binary contrast is obviously too simplistic, since we see so many cases of the Utopian sense of time in societies and organizations heavily influenced by the Confucian discourse system as well as cases of the Golden-Age sense of time in societies and organizations heavily influenced by the Utilitarian discourse system. Stereotypes in "intercultural" comparison are often the result of the fallacy of opposing large "cultural" groups upon the basis of some single dimension, such as the introduction of topics in discourse or the sense of time.

Such general ideological statements, then, focus on simplistic contrasts between groups and then impute to people who participate in these groups or the discourse systems associated with them certain characteristics. The difference between stereotyping and simple overgeneralization is that stereotyping carries with it an ideological position. Characteristics of the group are not only overgeneralized to apply to each member of the group, but they are also taken to have some negative or positive value. These values are then taken as arguments to support social or political relationships in regard to members of those groups.

For example, it is clear that the sense of time urgency is characteristic of many of the residents of Asia's urban capitals, such as Tokyo, Taipei, Hong Kong, Seoul, or Singapore.

It would become an overgeneralization to simply assume that, because someone was a resident of one of these cities, he or she would show a constant sense of time urgency. It becomes stereotyping to assume that this is a particularly good or bad quality of that person upon the basis of his or her membership in the group of residents of that city.

Stereotyping is a way of thinking that does not acknowledge internal differences within a group, and does not acknowledge exceptions to its general rules or principles of discourse systems. Ideologies are largely based on stereotypical thinking, or, to put it the other way around, stereotypes are largely ideological. There is usually a good bit of accurate observation which underlies stereotypes; it is not the accuracy of those observations which is the problem. The problem is that stereotypes blind us to other, equally important aspects of a person's character or behavior. Stereotypes limit our understanding of human behavior and interaction because they limit our view of human activity to just one or two salient dimensions and consider those to be the whole picture. Furthermore, they go on ideologically to use that limited view of individuals and of groups to justify preferential or discriminatory treatment by others who hold greater political power.

Stereotyping is often a matter of conceptually separating people or lumping them together based on limited or superficial differences between the discourse systems they participate in. Some years ago one of us was lecturing at a U.S. campus to a group of teachers from Taiwan who were in America on a cultural exchange program. The purpose of the lecture was to discuss some of the aspects of intercultural communication between Chinese and North Americans. When we took a break for lunch, one of the American women present said that she was struck by how much the differences between Chinese and North Americans were "just like the differences between women and men" that Deborah Tannen had outlined in her book *You Just Don't Understand: women and men in conversation* (1990a).

Even though we were carefully trying to avoid the fallacies of ideological and stereotyping statements – in fact, that was the point of the whole lecture – the form of analysis, contrastive analysis, provided the basis for this woman to make such an intuitive leap. She went on further to ask if it was not the case that the "American" in our analysis was not really better described as "an American man," since she felt the characteristics that we had associated with "Americans" really did not seem to apply to American women, while at the same time the characteristics she thought we had associated with Chinese seemed to fit better.

In a sense there is a kind of surface logic to this woman's analysis. At the same time, it is patently absurd to suggest that all Chinese, men and women, are "just like" U.S. women. The problem we had run into was that of ideological oversimplification, or what we might call "binarism." The lecture had presented contrasts as a way of showing areas where miscommunication might arise. In discussing the differences between communication patterns observed among people in China and the United States in that particular situation, there was little direct cause to wander further afield into other interdiscourse and intergroup comparisons. The audience consisted of Chinese English teachers who were in the United States for the purposes of learning more about English and about "U.S. culture." Their primary concern was not with gender as such, nor was it with other such matters as communication between Athabaskans and Anglo-Americans, or Chinese and Japanese. As a result, the framework which had been set around this presentation was that of a binary comparison.

At the same time, the woman in question had just recently read Tannen's book. The framework set on that analysis by the subtitle on the cover is "women and men in conversation." No matter how careful Tannen may have been to include other intercultural comparisons and to present her analysis within the context of broader sociolinguistic issues, such subtleties were swept aside by her reader, whose own interpretive framework had settled into the ideological binarism of a polarized difference between "American men" and "American women."

The solution to the problem of oversimplification or binarism and "lumping" is twofold. First, it must be remembered that no individual member of a group embodies all of his or her group's characteristics, and no participant in any discourse system is really anything but a partial or "peripheral" participant. As we have said, we all are simultaneously participants in multiple discourse systems; none of us is fully defined by our participation in any single one. One is simultaneously a son or a daughter, a father or a mother, a member of a particular company, a member of a particular generation, and so forth in an indefinite number of discourse systems. Second, comparisons between groups should always consider both likenesses and differences, and they should be based upon more than a single dimension of contrast. In her extremely influential book *Feminism and Linguistic Theory*, Deborah Cameron (1992: 37) asks "why researchers (into gender) have chosen to study sex differences so intensively in the first place (why does no-one study 'sex similarity'?)." Her point could just as easily be made of studies in intercultural communication. Approaching the study of people who participate in different discourse systems with the expectation that one will find significant differences often ends up exaggerating what differences do exist and reinforcing stereotypes. Such an approach, as Cameron points out, is inherently ideological. A focus on difference always seems to serve the interests of one of the two groups under comparison at the expense of the other. In other words, "difference" is often a code word for inferiority.

Negative stereotypes

Any form of stereotyping is potentially an obstruction to successful communication, because it will blind us to real differences and similarities that exist between the participants in an interaction. The most obstructive form of stereotyping, however, is sometimes called negative stereotyping. In such a case, the first step is to contrast two "cultures" or two groups on the basis of some single dimension. For example, someone might say that "all Asians" are inductive and "all westerners" are deductive in their introduction of topics. Such a statement may have some basis in observation, but it ignores the fact that members of both imagined communities use both deductive and inductive strategies.

The second step in negative stereotyping is to focus on this artificial and ideological difference as a problem for communication. Unfortunately, focusing on this assumed therefore ideological difference has become common in what usually passes as the analysis of "intercultural communication," and as a result, a great deal of care is necessary in such analysis to forestall stereotyping. An example of such stereotyping would be to say, following on from the observations described above, that "because 'Asians' are inductive and 'westerners' are deductive, it is difficult for them to communicate with each other easily or successfully."

If we have already forgotten that our first premise was somewhat oversimplified, that is, if we have already forgotten that both inductive strategies and deductive strategies are used by all, and if we have forgotten that we can never classify all "Asians" together and all "westerners" together, it becomes natural at this step to jump to the conclusion that "Asians" and "westerners" will have difficulty communicating with each other. This is false, of course, but at this step in the process it can easily be forgotten, and in fact this kind of reasoning is the problem with much of the work in "intercultural" or "cross-cultural" communication studies.

The third step, then, is to assign a positive value to one strategy or one group and a negative value to the other strategy or group. At this step, for example, a self-described "westerner" might say the problem with intercultural communication between "Asians" and "westerners" is that *they* refuse to introduce their topics so that *we* can understand them. The simple descriptive difference leads to the idea that somehow members of the other group are actively trying to make it difficult to understand them.

The fourth and final step is to regeneralize this process to the entire group. One reasserts the original binary contrast as a negative group contrast. One might say, for example, that *all* "Asians" or *all* "westerners" are like this; "they" always try to obstruct communication. Often one final step is taken; characteristics are assumed to be genetic or racial characteristics.

As we have said, stereotyping such as this is a perennial problem in many popular and even some academic approaches to "intercultural communication." This is because these stereotypes are usually (wrongly) based on some actual observable difference. It is accurate to say that in many instances there will be some difference in topic introduction or other rhetorical strategies between someone from China and someone from the United States. As we have argued above, in chapter 5, this difference does not result from one trying to be indirect or the other trying to be direct. Rather it often is based on deeper assumptions being made about the face relationships one can adopt in certain communicative situations. It would be quite correct to say that in communication between strangers, people socialized to expect a hierarchical face system would be likely to use strategies of independence out of deference and respect for the other person. One of those strategies would be the rhetorical strategy of inductively introducing one's own topics. It would also be correct to say that in communication between strangers, many socialized differently might try to bring the situation around to one of symmetrical solidarity. This would be because of the value placed in their societies on egalitarianism and individualism. One strategy which would be used to do this would be to use a deductive rhetorical pattern for the introduction of topics.

If we forget the deeper reasons why these rhetorical strategies are used, we can easily move into negatively stereotyping participants in discourse systems with different basic assumptions about things like the appropriate face systems to use with strangers than those that we bring to the situation. The result is an overall negative impression of particular individuals or particular groups that comes as a result of communication patterns that are neither a matter of individuals nor of groups, but are instead a matter of systems of discourse.

Positive stereotypes, the lumping fallacy, and the solidarity fallacy

We have mentioned above the woman who thought that our description of "Chinese" characteristics was just the same as Deborah Tannen's description of those for women in the United States. Now we can go back and look at just what led this woman to this conclusion. The point we were discussing which led her to it had to do with the function of language. As we have said above, language has both the function of conveying information and the function of maintaining relationships among participants in speech events. We said that generally speaking, people socialized in the Confucian discourse system tend to be concerned that good relationships are maintained, even if this means that less information may be exchanged, while those socialized to the Utilitarian discourse system will tend to emphasize the exchange of information, even if relationships cannot be easily maintained. Of course this would also depend quite a bit on the circumstances of the communication and the people involved. We have also observed that in interactions with outgroup members such as service encounters, these same people socialized in the Confucian discourse system who before were said to emphasize the relational function of language might focus almost exclusively on information.

Tannen has claimed that in communication between men and women in the United States, there is a tendency for men to emphasize information over relationship and for women to emphasize relationship over information. She characterizes this difference as that between "report" and "rapport," with men emphasizing report and women emphasizing rapport. This, of course, also depends a great deal on the situation and the participants.

While both of these characterizations, that of U.S. women in comparison to U.S. men and that of North Americans to Chinese in general have some basis in actual (though limited) observations, the solidarity fallacy comes into play here when this woman tries to group together U.S. women and all Chinese on this single dimension of information and relationship. The mistake – the solidarity fallacy – is to conclude that because there is some similarity on one dimension, there will be commonality across all or most of the characteristics of these two groups.

No two groups are either polar opposites or exactly identical. The problem of negative stereotyping is one of seeing participants in different discourse systems as being polar opposites. The problem of positive stereotyping is one of seeing participants in different discourse systems as being identical. In either case, it is a problem of stereotyping which arises from making a comparison on the basis of a single, binary dimension of analysis.

When the stereotyping is based on falsely combining one's own group and some other group, we would call it the solidarity fallacy. In the case we have just described, the U.S. woman falsely included her group with Chinese based on the belief that they both have the emphasis on relationship in common, while ignoring the major differences between these groups. When the person making the false grouping is doing so in reference to two other groups, we would call that the lumping fallacy. For example, when someone considers all "Asians" to be members of the same group without taking into consideration the major differences among the many groups that exist in Asia and the many discourse systems people in these groups participate in, this would be called the lumping fallacy. In the same way, grouping together all "westerners" would also be the lumping fallacy. In both cases, positive stereotyping occurs when the person making the categorization takes the characteristics he or she used to make the stereotyping as positive, while negative stereotyping results when the basis of comparison was considered to be negative.

Whether the stereotyping is positive or negative, it should be clear that it stands in the way of successful communication because it blinds the communicator to real areas of difference or similarity. As we said at the very beginning of this book, communication is inherently ambiguous. Effective communication depends on finding and clarifying sources of ambiguity as well as learning to deal with places where miscommunication might occur. Such clarification is impossible when the communicator does not recognize areas of difference among participants, because he or she will assume common ground and mutual understanding. But it can also occur when areas of similarity go unrecognized. The perennial paradoxical situation of interdiscourse communication is that we must constantly be aware of areas of difference between people which may potentially lead to miscommunication, but at the same time constantly guard against assuming differences that do not actually exist.

Othering

Whenever we make claims of participation in a particular discourse system, we are also making claims about non-participants as some kind of "other." It has been argued by some that the identification of "self" is only done through the identification of some "other."

While this is often only an implication, in many cases of interdiscourse communication this is, in fact, the primary goal of the social interaction. We say we are "we" for the purpose of saying they are "they." In our experience, these last two principles are the main occasions by which the idea of "culture" arises in ordinary conversation. In a comparative study of business communication in Hong Kong, Beijing, and Finland, one of the participants in a focus group held in Beijing became rather animated in talking about comparative Chinese and European practices for non-verbal communication. He said that "we" Chinese are taught that we should remain quiet in our bodies and not make a lot of gestures, whereas "we" all know that Europeans and Americans use a lot of gestures all the time.

Three things were striking about this example: first, he used the occasion of talking about non-verbal communication to bring up the idea of "culture." It was clear from the transcript that this person was trying to make a clear distinction between "we Chinese" and "they," the Europeans. We felt that it was not just that he was trying to make clear the "cultural" differences between Chinese and Europeans. We had had much discussion of differences in business and business presentation practices up to this point. On the contrary, it seems to us that the main concern was, in fact, to set up one group, a "we," as the internal or ingroup reference, and to set up another group, a "they," as an external or outgroup reference.

This is somewhat supported because, secondly, this was the only time in a large research project on business communication involving several focus groups in three countries and much interviewing that anybody had brought up the word "culture." Prior to this, nobody had mentioned "culture" as an analytical concept but was quite happy to refer to people as "the people in this videotape" or "the person who made this résumé" or "the person giving that presentation." That is, normally they had referred to the people they were considering quite specifically in terms of the actions they were undertaking in specific cases, not in terms of their group or "cultural" membership.

Thirdly, we believe he was primarily concerned with setting up a broad ingroup/out-group distinction because he was completely wrong in fact. The videotape we had been watching was of a group of Finnish people who were very still on the camera. In fact, even when playing the tape fast-forward there was so little body movement that at points it looked as if the camera had lapsed into freeze frame. These were the "Europeans" to which this man was referring when he said that "they" used a lot of gestures all the time. In contrast to this, this man made rather extreme and wide gestures all the time he was making this comment and at other times as well.

Differences Which Make a Difference: Discourse Systems

In this book, we have reviewed several areas in which researchers have demonstrated that what most people refer to as "cultures" may differ significantly from each other. While we have only touched upon each of these areas with a few examples, we hope it is clear that the potential for misunderstanding in all sorts of interactions is great. At the same time, now that we have reviewed these many areas of potential difference, we want to point out that not all differences are equally problematic in communication. In fact, some "cultural differences" do not make any major difference from the point of view of discourse analysis. The reason for this is that "cultures" as most people understand them tend to be very large groupings with many internal sub-groupings. There is hardly any dimension on which you could compare "cultures" and with which one "culture" could be clearly and unambiguously distinguished from another.

One strategy we have used to overcome this analytical obstacle has been to introduce the notion of discourse systems. Such systems are defined in terms of four interrelated components: ideology, face systems, forms of discourse, and socialization. We believe it is almost impossible to talk about "western culture" in any clear and unambiguous way. On the other hand, it is possible to describe quite clearly the Utilitarian discourse system, its practices of socialization, its assumptions about face and politeness, and the forms of discourse that are used as a result of the face system of symmetrical solidarity. This is because, on the whole, the Utilitarian discourse system is an ideological system which quite self-consciously seeks ideological unity.

It is important to remember, however, that when we are describing the Utilitarian discourse system, we are *not* describing a group of people. We are describing a system of discourse in which all sorts of people around the world participate, some more fully and others more peripherally. Even discourse systems which appear to be associated with specific groups of people such as gender or sexuality discourse systems and generational discourse systems are *not* defined by their membership, but rather they are defined in terms of particular ideological discursive positions that have grown up at particular points in history in relation to particular kinds of social relationships.

As we have shown over and over, there are many characteristics of discourse systems which may influence communication when the expectations of participants in a particular interaction are different in terms of one or more dimensions or factors. For example, if two participants in an interaction are different from each other in their choice of deductive or inductive strategies for the introduction of topics, whether or not they are from different "cultures," they may find themselves confused as to how to interpret what is being said by the other person. What is significant is not the difference in "culture"; it is the difference in that particular rhetorical strategy.

The same argument can be made for differences between any two participants in an interaction on the basis of any of the factors we have just discussed. They could find difficulties in communicating based upon their belief about whether humans were essentially good or evil, their ideas about kinship relationships, their sense of ingroup loyalty, their understanding of egalitarianism and hierarchy, their emphasis on individualism or collectivism, whether they conceive of language as being used primarily for information or relationship, whether negotiation or ratification of those relationships is thought to be primary, or the assumptions they make about the most effective ways of socializing either their children or new members to the group. Their emphasis on group harmony or individual welfare could lead to a different interpretation of such non-verbal aspects of communication as smiles or their use of space. Even a difference in such an abstract factor as their concept of Utopian or Golden-Age directions in the "arrow of time" could lead to problems of interpretation in discourse.

We would be very unlikely to find any two groups or members of any groups who would differ completely from each other on all of these dimensions. As a result, we believe that in discussions of "intercultural communication," we will be more effective by narrowing our focus to discourse systems, where contrasts between one system and another are somewhat more strongly made. From this point of view, we have argued, "intercultural communication" might better be analyzed as interdiscourse system communication.

Intercultural Communication as Mediated Action

Over the years of researching interdiscourse communication we have come to the conclusion that the best way to avoid stereotyping and to capture the true complexity of what is going on is to take our focus off of groups of people and their supposed characteristics and to focus instead on the concrete social actions they engage in with other people.

We began the preface of the first edition of this book with the sentence, "This book is about professional communication between people who are members of different groups." In this case we unfortunately implied that it is somehow possible to know in advance of undertaking research *that* people are members of different groups and of *what* different groups they are members. This implies that the first step in analysis is knowing discourse systems and any particular person's participation in those various systems.

Now we would prefer to begin with a different set of questions that would focus on people taking particular actions together and, starting from these actions, go on to tease out the kinds of identities they are claiming at any particular moment. So the basic research question in "intercultural communication," we believe, should be "what are people doing?" From that then follows the question: how and when and to what effect is the concept of "culture" or the concept of "membership" in groups produced and used within this action?

Any theoretical position will have a natural unit of analysis. Much cross-cultural research takes as its unit of analysis the cultural system of meaning, both linguistic and non-verbal. From our perspective, however, a more productive unit of analysis for research in interdiscourse communication is "people-in-action," that is, the unit of analysis is not just the system of discourse by itself and it is not just the individual person by herself or himself. Our unit of analysis is the person in the moment of taking social action with other people by drawing on the various discursive resources available.

These actions always have the effect of making claims of participation, either implicitly or explicitly, in particular discourse systems. Often such claims are made completely unconsciously. But often such claims are made strategically in order for people to position themselves in particular ways in relation to other people and to the situation. Our view presupposes that all situations are multi- or poly-discursive and, therefore, it presupposes that any action in the social world is interdiscursive. Just as any act positions the actor within a particular combination of discourse systems, it also positions other participants and, through positioning them, produces socialization into some discourse systems as well as exclusion from some others.

The gist of intercultural or interdiscourse analysis, then, is not simply to try to describe discourse systems and to theorize about what might happen if participants in two different systems came into contact. The gist is to focus on people taking action in particular and concrete tasks and then to ask, without presupposing, what is the role of "culture" and of discourse systems in their taking these actions? How are these actions productive of participation in particular discourse systems or membership in particular communities of practice? And how are these actions significant in producing "others," that is, outgroup members, through practices of inclusion and exclusion?

Avoiding Miscommunication

We have in this book implicitly adopted two approaches to improving communication between participants in different cross-cutting combinations of discourse systems. The first approach is based on knowing as much as possible about the people with whom one is communicating. This approach might be called the approach of increasing shared knowledge. The second approach is based on making the assumption that misunderstandings are the only thing certain about interdiscourse communication. This approach might be called dealing with miscommunication.

In increasing shared knowledge, we focused in chapter 2 on the scenes and events in which our communicative actions and activities take place. In subsequent chapters we turned to the question of how our identities as participants in speech events are both developed and maintained in interpersonal communication through the use of particular face strategies and forms of discourse, and how these face strategies and forms of discourse both reflect and produce certain ideological positions. The overall goal of these chapters was to outline the major areas in which shared knowledge can work to reduce the ambiguity inherent in communication.

Much of the substance of this book is given over to detailing the many dimensions along which participants in interaction can either come to share their understandings or fail to understand each other. We have discussed the elements of the grammar of context, face relationships, linguistic resources, conversational inferencing processes including schemata, and rhetorical strategies. Finally, in these last chapters we have shown how all of these factors may combine together into multiple and cross-cutting systems of discourse.

Any communicator will be better positioned for effective communication by learning more about other participants in communicative events in any one of these areas. At the same time, there is always the insoluble problem that, at any one time, one is participating in multiple and possibly conflicting discourse systems. In some of these one will be a fuller participant and in others one will be a more peripheral participant, perhaps only a temporary visitor.

The fact that we are always participants in multiple discourse systems, and the related fact that, particularly in professional communication, we are also often novices or fairly peripheral participants in some of the relevant systems, means that we virtually always communicate under the conditions of potential stress which arises from such role pluralism. To put it in a nutshell, it is sometimes difficult to know just who we are and whom we represent when we speak.

The ideal solution is to share knowledge with other participants in discourse. This is why it is easiest to communicate with people who share with us participation in one or more discourse systems. This is why people so often gather together socially with others who are very much like them. It is easier and more comfortable to communicate when you do not have to do so much work to understand what is going on or to make your own communication clear to others.

Unfortunately, as we have said, in most cases of communication such banding together is impossible, given that we are all simultaneous members of multiple discourse systems. Even within families, interdiscourse communication is the rule. The most fundamental assumption is that all communication is to some extent communication with participants in other discourse systems, and therefore, because we have to assume that in many cases we do not share knowledge, assumptions, values, and forms of discourse with them, we must expect that there may be problems of interpretation. We must look for these problems, anticipate where they will arise, and then plan our communication to be effective not just as ingroup communication but also as outgroup communication.

If we accept that much of our communication is to some extent outgroup communication, we also have to guard against the idea that these other discourse systems are completely different from our discourse system. No single dimension will be sufficient to compare and contrast discourse systems. The problems of ideology arise when we accept the difference between our group and some other group and then come to assume there is a single difference between us which accounts for all of our differences. We must always simultaneously look for differences *and* commonalities. It is the difference in pattern, not any absolute difference, which is significant between participants in different discourse systems.

By being careful to look for both differences and commonalities, we will also avoid the fallacy of lumping. We will not fall into the error of assuming two groups are the same as each other simply because they differ from our own group on some dimension of discourse. Such an analysis will also prevent the fallacy of solidarity, in which we assume that because our group is the same as another group on the basis of a single dimension of discourse, we are the same on all dimensions. Again, it is the difference in pattern which is significant. The key is to note both differences and commonalities.

Sharing knowledge of other groups and other discourse systems is not the same as becoming a member or a participant. As we have pointed out above, many discourse systems are quite resistant to taking on new participants. In developing one's ability in "intercultural communication," it is well worth remembering that it is often quite unlikely that one will ever become a "full participant" in the other discourse system, however much one might learn about that discourse system or come to appreciate it. The point is to learn as much as one can about other discourse systems so that the patterns of differences and commonalities can be appreciated.

This book was originally written for students studying professional communication, and so we would like to conclude with what might seem a paradoxical concept, that is, that the best professional communicator is one who has come to realize his or her lack of expertise. One is, of course, often expert in the discourse systems in which one participates. Nevertheless, professional discourse in most cases produces inherent conflicts between the discourse system of one's corporate culture and the discourse community of one's professional specialization. Furthermore, intercultural professional communication requires outgroup communication in which one is never likely to gain expertise. The dangers all lie on the side of assuming that one is or can be an expert in such outgroup discourse systems. The individual who is sure that he knows all there is to know about communication with "Chinese," for example, is doomed to failure. Such outgroup certainty is virtually always a signal of binarism and stereotyping. On the other hand, a person who understands the outlines of the patterns of differences and commonalities, but fully recognizes his or her own lack of full participation and state of non-expertise, is likely to be the most successful and effective communicator.

We believe that the most successful professional communicator is not the one who believes he or she is an expert in crossing the boundaries of discourse systems, but, rather, the person who strives to learn as much as possible about other discourse systems while recognizing that except within his or her own discourse systems he or she is likely to always remain a novice. We believe that effective communication requires study of discourse on the one hand, but also requires a recognition of one's own limitations.

Researching Interdiscourse Communication

Any research project in interdiscourse communication should end with some kind of attempt to help one's participants become better communicators and to avoid the potential problems that arise when multiple discourse systems come into contact with one another. Elsewhere we have called this stage in the research "changing the nexus of practice," and we believe this stage is essential to any respectable research endeavor. It does not do much good to observe the difficulties people are having and to come to an understanding of their causes if you are not going to share that understanding with those whom you have observed and work with them in converting it into some kind of workable plan of action.

In the past we have used several methods in our capacity as consultants to companies who were sending their staff on postings abroad or employing staff from other countries at home. Companies who might benefit from such consultancies however are not limited to these. Today as workplaces all over the world become increasingly diverse and all business becomes increasingly global in scope, training in interdiscourse communication can be valuable for anyone.

Among the methods we have used are *pre-departure* and *in-country briefings and training* which have actually become common practices in both governmental and business organizations. Although *pre-departure briefings* should by all means touch on such simple, but important, matters as what kinds of food to expect, how the relevant staff would be able to get along linguistically, and what kinds of attitudes they might expect from "locals" to their presence, it is important that such exercises not consist of decontextualized catalogs of "cultural differences" or lists of rather superficial habits or "customs" of the local people. Rather, participants must be made to reflect on the kinds of specific situations they might find themselves in and how different discourse systems – not just discourse systems associated with "national cultures" but also other discourse systems like professional and corporate discourse systems and gender discourse systems – might become relevant in these situations and impact communication.

The counterparts of these pre-departure sessions are *in-country briefings*. Here the primary need is to respond to the complexity which participants may be being faced with and to help to forestall the common reactions which take people to one of two extremes. There are those who come to blindly love everything about the new society they are living in and will admit of no difficulties or complexities, and there are those who come to hate everything. For effective functioning in business, governmental, or personal environments, both of these extremes must be mitigated and in-country briefings and training sessions must emphasize general patterns on the one hand so as to reduce the feelings of complexity, and to introduce diversity to forestall stereotyping and over-simplification on the other.

While most people who seek training expect recipes for dealing with essentialized binary groupings, they must be made aware of the complexity of communication no matter where they are. One of the most valuable things we can do in such situations is to help people to direct their focus on concrete actions, their own and those of others, rather than on broad groups or abstract notions of "culture." These might include the social actions that occur in meetings, on the shop floor, in regional service centers, and at the counter in their retailing operations, among other places. They can then be asked to reflect upon these actions with questions like

- What are we trying to do here?
- Why have we come to take this action?
- Are my motivations for taking it the same as those with whom I am acting?
- What history is this action an outcome of?
- What kind of future situation is it projected towards?
- What resources do I and the people I am acting with have available to us to take this action based on the various discourse systems that we participate in? (Such resources may include various forms of discourse such as genres or styles of speaking and writing, various interpretive frameworks that arise out of ideologies, various strategies for managing relationships, and various ideas about how people learn to be and show themselves to be competent members of a particular group.)
- What degree of choice do I and these other people have in choosing and using these resources in this particular situation?
- How does the combination of discourse systems relevant in this situation not just amplify the resources available but also introduce conflicts or constraints as to which resources I might choose and how I can mix them with other resources?
- How does my choice of particular resources commit me to certain claims of identity or membership in certain groups?
- How do I interpret other people's choice of resources as indicative of their membership in particular groups?
- How am I positioning myself in relation to the various discourse systems that are relevant to this situation?
- How does my position either open up or deny various kinds of positions for the other people involved in the situation?

At the same time, one must also remember that successful training programs are not just about helping people to heighten their awareness and analyze the complex situations in which they find themselves. They also often involve more pedestrian pursuits like training in technical or linguistic skills. As we have argued in chapter 7, many of the skills of writing for international business, for example, which are assumed to be universal skills of "educated" people, are really ideological values of a particular discourse system. It is not at all uncommon for an organization to hire training consultants to "teach common writing skills" when, in fact, what they really want, but do not know they want, is to teach interdiscourse communication skills. Thus, much intercultural training is actually carried out in the service of more basic communication skills. We would argue that virtually any training program has an "intercultural" or interdiscursive component and we have found ourselves and our colleagues very often engaged in intercultural work flying under the colors of much more mundane and traditional technical skills training.

Of course these are just examples of the many kinds of projects people working in inter-discourse communication training might engage in. Intercultural communication specialists work in personnel offices, in marketing departments, in management, in product development, in diplomatic protocol offices, in translation and communication departments, in public relations departments, and in many other organizational functions. As we have just said, intercultural communication or interdiscourse communication is normally a part of almost any organizational or interpersonal communication, and so the world in which these ideas might be applied is a very large world indeed.

Discussion Questions

1   Some people justify stereotyping with statements like "All stereotypes have some basis in truth." Is this a good argument? How would you logically counter this argument?

2   A woman orders coffee in a café in the Tenderloin district of San Francisco. It comes with a plastic straw, while the cup of her male companion does not. Surprised, she asks why and is told that women are given straws because they wear lipstick. This woman is not wearing lipstick. She asks whether transvestites are also treated with this distinction but is informed it is restricted to women. What kind of stereotyping is involved here? If you were the manager, how would you handle the distribution of straws?

3   Think of a time when you or someone you know has been a victim of stereotyping, whether of a negative or positive variety. Try to imagine the process of reasoning that might have taken place in the mind of the person or people who were engaged in this stereotyping. What were the consequences of this stereotyping?

References for Further Study

Some of the recommendations we make in this chapter are based on the research project *Professional Communication Across Cultures* (Scollon et al. 1998, 1999; Pan et al. 2002), independent research of Pan (2000), and earlier work on intercultural communication training which can be found in Ron and Suzie Scollon's 1986 *Responsive Communication: patterns for making sense*.

References

The list of references which follows includes all of the bibliographic sources which are found either in the main body of the text or in the References for Further Study at the end of each chapter. In addition to these references, we have included others which we believe the student of discourse in intercultural professional communication will find useful.

Ahonen, Sirkka 1997: A transformation of history: the official representations of history in East Germany and Estonia, 1986–1991. *Culture and Psychology*, 3(1), 41–62.

Alexander, A., V. Cronen, K. W. Kang, B. Tsou, and B. J. Banks 1986: Patterns of topic sequencing and information gain: a comparative study of relationship development in Chinese and American cultures. *Communication Quarterly*, 34, 66–78.

Allinson, Robert E. 1989: *Understanding the Chinese Mind*. Hong Kong: Oxford University Press.

Altman, Dennis 1996: Rupture or continuity? The internationalization of gay identities. *Social Text*, 48(3), 76–94.

Altman, Dennis 2002: *Global Sex*. Chicago: University of Chicago Press.

American School Board Journal, January 1987.

American State Papers [Declaration of Independence, Articles of Confederation, Constitution] 1990: In Mortimer J. Adler (ed.), *Great Books of the Western World*. Chicago: Encyclopaedia Britannica.

Anderson, Benedict 1991: *Imagined Communities: reflections on the origin and spread of nationalism*. London and New York: Verso.

Anderson, Eugene N. 1988: *The Food of China*. New Haven: Yale University Press.

Austin, John 1962: *How to Do Things with Words*. Oxford: Clarendon Press.

Bakhtin, Mikhail 1986/1936: *Speech Genres and Other Late Essays*. Austin: University of Texas Press.

Barton, David 2007: *Literacy: an introduction to the ecology of written language*. Oxford: Blackwell.

Bateson, Gregory 1972: *Steps to an Ecology of Mind*. New York: Ballantine.

Behler, Ernst (ed.) 1986: *Immanuel Kant: philosophical writings*. New York: Continuum.

Bell, Allan 1991: *The Language of the News Media*. Oxford: Oxford University Press.

Bellah, Robert N., Richard Madsen, William M. Sullivan, Ann Swidler, and Steven M. Tipton 1985: *Habits of the Heart*. New York: Harper and Row.

Bentham, Jeremy 1962: *Introduction to the Principles of Morals and Legislation*. (Mary Warnock, ed.) Glasgow: Fontana Press.

Intercultural Communication: A Discourse Approach, Third Edition. Ron Scollon, Suzanne Wong Scollon, Rodney H. Jones.
© 2012 John Wiley & Sons, Inc. Published 2012 by John Wiley & Sons, Inc.

Bentham, Jeremy 1988: *A Fragment on Government*. Cambridge: Cambridge University Press. (Originally published in 1776.)

Bhatia, Vijay, John Flowerdew, and Rodney H. Jones (eds.) 2007: *Advances in Discourse Studies*. London: Routledge.

Birdwhistell, Ray L. 1970: *Kinesics and Context: essays on body motion communication*. Philadelphia: University of Pennsylvania Press.

Blommaert, Jan 2010: *The Sociolinguistics of Globalization*. Cambridge: Cambridge University Press.

Blum-Kulka, Shoshana, Juliane House, and Gabriele Kasper (eds.) 1989: *Cross-cultural Pragmatics: requests and apologies*. Norwood: Ablex.

Bolton, Kingsley and Helen Kwok 1992: *Sociolinguistics Today: eastern and western perspectives*. London: Routledge.

Bond, Michael Harris 1986: *The Psychology of the Chinese People*. New York: Oxford University Press.

Bond, Michael Harris 1988: *The Cross-cultural Challenge to Social Psychology*. Newbury Park: Sage.

Bond, Michael Harris 1993: Between the Yin and the Yang: the identity of the Hong Kong Chinese. Hong Kong: Chinese University of Hong Kong, Professorial Inaugural Lecture Series 19, Chinese University Bulletin, Supplement 31.

Bond, Michael Harris 1996: Chinese values. In M. H. Bond (ed.), *The Handbook of Chinese Psychology*. Hong Kong: Oxford University Press.

Boswood, Tim 1992: *English for Professional Communication: responding to Hong Kong employers' needs for English graduates*. Department of English, City Polytechnic of Hong Kong, Research Report 20, October.

Bourdieu, Pierre 1977: *Outline of a Theory of Practice*. Richard Nice, trans. Cambridge: Cambridge University Press.

Bourdieu, Pierre 1990: *The Logic of Practice*. Stanford: Stanford University Press.

Brosnahan, Irene, Richard Coe, and Ann Johns 1987: Discourse analysis of written texts in an overseas teacher training program. *English Quarterly*, 20, 16–25.

Brown, Brian and Ly Yu Sang 2003: *Story of Confucius: His Life and Sayings*. Whitefish: Kessinger Publishing.

Brown, Gillian and George Yule 1983: *Discourse Analysis*. New York: Cambridge University Press.

Brown, Penelope and Stephen Levinson 1978: Universals in language usage: politeness phenomena. In Ester Goody (ed.), *Questions and Politeness: strategies in social interaction*, New York: Cambridge University Press. Republished as 1987: *Politeness*. Cambridge: Cambridge University Press.

Brown, Penelope and Stephen Levinson 1987: *Politeness: Some Universals in Language Usage*. Cambridge: Cambridge University Press.

Brown, Roger and Albert Gilman 1960: The pronouns of power and solidarity. In Thomas Sebeok (ed.), *Style in Language*. Cambridge, MA: MIT Press.

Butler, Judith 1990: *Gender Trouble: feminism and the subversion of identity*. New York and London: Routledge.

Cameron, Deborah 1992: *Feminism and Linguistic Theory*. London: Palgrave.

Cameron, Deborah 1997: Performing gender identity: young men's talk and the construction of heterosexual masculinity. In Sally Johnson and Ulrike Hanna Meinhof (eds.), *Language and Masculinity*. Oxford: Blackwell.

Cameron, Deborah 2000: *Good to Talk: living and working in a communication culture*. London: Sage.

Cameron, Deborah and Don Kulick 2003: *Language and Sexuality*. Cambridge: Cambridge University Press.

Cameron, Deborah and Don Kulick (eds.) 2006: *Language and Sexuality Reader*. London: Routledge.

Campbell, John Angus 1987: Charles Darwin: rhetorician of science. In John S. Nelson, Allan Megill, and Donald N. McCloskey (eds.), *The Rhetoric of Human Sciences*. Madison: University of Wisconsin Press.

Carbaugh, Donal 1984: "Relationship" as a cultural category in some American speech. Paper presented at the annual meetings of the Speech Communication Association, Chicago.

Carbaugh, Donal 1989: *Talking American: cultural discourses on* Donahue. Norwood: Ablex.

Carbaugh, Donal 1990: *Cultural Communication and Intercultural Contact*. Hillsdale: Lawrence Erlbaum Associates.

Carrell, Patricia L. 1983: Some issues in studying the role of schemata, or background knowledge, in second language comprehension. *Reading in a Foreign Language*, 1(2), 81–92.

Carrell, Patricia L. 1984a: Evidence of a formal schema in second language comprehension. *Language Learning*, 34(2), 87–112.

Carrell, Patricia L. 1984b: The effects of rhetorical organization on ESL readers. *TESOL Quarterly*, 18(3), 441–69.

Carrell, Patricia L. 1989: Metacognitive awareness and second language reading. *Modern Language Journal*, 73, 121–34.

Castells, Manuel 1993: The informational economy and the new international division of labor. In Martin Carnoy, Manuel Castells, Stephen S. Cohen, and Fernando Henrique Cardoso (eds.), *The New Global Economy in the Information Age: reflections on our changing world*. University Park: Pennsylvania State University Press.

Chai, Ch'u and Winberg Chai 1966: *Li Chi: Book of Rites*. Secaucus: University Books.

Chatman, Seymour 1978: *Story and Discourse*. Ithaca: Cornell University Press.

Chen, Guo-Ming and William J. Starosta 1998: *Foundations of Intercultural Communication*. Boston: Allyn and Bacon.

Cheshire, Jenny 1991: *English Around the World*. Cambridge: Cambridge University Press.

Chinese Culture Connection 1987: Chinese values and the search for culture free dimensions of culture. *Journal of Cross-cultural Psychology*, 18, 143–64.

Chinese Tongzhi Conference 1996: Manifesto of the Chinese Tongzhi Conference. Available at: http://sqzm14.ust.hk/hkgay/news/manifesto.html (retrieved December 21, 2010).

Chow, Wah Shan 2001: *Tongzhi/Queer: politics of same sex eroticism in Chinese societies*. New York: Haworth.

Chu, Godwin C. 1979: Communication and cultural change in China: a conceptual framework. In Godwin C. Chu and Francis L. K. Hsu, *Moving a Mountain: cultural change in China*. Honolulu: University Press of Hawaii.

Chu, Godwin C. 1985: The changing concept of self in contemporary China. In Anthony J. Marsella, George DeVos, and Francis L. K. Hsu (eds.), *Culture and Self: Asian and western perspectives*. New York: Tavistock Publications.

Chu, Godwin C. and Francis L. K. Hsu 1979: *Moving a Mountain: cultural change in China*. Honolulu: University Press of Hawaii.

Chung and Mallery 1999/2000: Social comparison, individualism-collectivism, and self-esteem in China and the United States. *Current Psychology*, 18(4), 340–52.

Cline, Foster W. and Jim Fay 1990: *Parenting with Love and Logic: teaching children responsibility*. Colorado Springs: Pinon Press.

Coates, Jennifer and Deborah Cameron 1988: *Women in their Speech Communities: new perspectives on language and sex*. London: Longman.

Confucius 1971: *Confucian Analects, The Great Learning and The Doctrine of the Mean*. James Legge, trans. Mineola: Dover Publications.

Cook, Guy 1989: *Discourse*. Oxford: Oxford University Press.

Cook-Gumperz, Jenny 1986: *The Social Construction of Literacy*. New York: Cambridge University Press.

Connor, Ulla 1996: *Contrastive Rhetoric: cross-cultural aspects of second-language writing*. Cambridge: Cambridge University Press.

Connor, Ulla, Ed Nagelhout, and William Rozycki 2008: *Contrastive Rhetoric: reaching to intercultural rhetoric*. Amsterdam: John Benjamins.

Coupland, Douglas 1991: *Generation X: tales for an accelerated culture*. New York: St. Martin's Griffin.

Cowan, Ruth Schwartz 1983: *More Work for Mother*. New York: Basic Books.

De Bary, William Theodore 1988: *East Asian Civilizations: a dialogue in five stages*. Cambridge, MA: Harvard University Press.

De Bary, William Theodore and John W. Chaffee 1989: *Neo-Confucian Education: the formative stage*. Berkeley: University of California Press.

Deng Xiaoping 1993: *Selected Readings of Deng Xiaoping*, Vol. 3. Beijing: People's Press.

Dredge, C. Paul 1983: What is politeness in Korean speech? *Korean Linguistics*, 3, 21–32.

Ebrey, Patricia Buckley 1984: *Family and Property in Sung China: Yuan Ts'ai's precepts for social living*. Princeton: Princeton University Press.

Ebrey, Patricia Buckley 1985: T'ang guides to verbal etiquette. *Harvard Journal of Asiatic Studies*, 45(2), 581–613.

Eckert, Penelope and Sally McConnell-Ginet 1992: Communities of practice: where language, gender, and power all live. In Kira Hall, Mary Bucholtz, and Birch Moonwomon (eds.), *Locating Power: proceedings of the Second Berkeley Women and Language Conference*. Berkeley: Women and Language Group.

Eckert, Penelope and Sally McConnell-Ginet 2003: *Language and Gender*. Cambridge: Cambridge University Press.

Erikson, Erik 1950: *Childhood and Society*. New York: Norton.

Erickson, Frederick and Jeffrey Shultz 1982: *The Counselor as Gatekeeper: social interaction in interviews*. New York: Academic Press.

Erickson, Tammy 2009: *Generations in China*. Available at: http://blogs.harvardbusiness.org/erickson/2009/03/generations_in_china.html (retrieved March 28).

Fairclough, Norman 1992: *Discourse and Social Change*. Cambridge: Polity Press.

Fasold, Ralph 1990: *The Sociolinguistics of Language*. Oxford: Blackwell.

Feldstein, Stanley and Cynthia L. Crown 1990: Oriental and Canadian conversational interactions: chronographic structure and interpersonal perception. *Journal of Asian Pacific Communication*, 1(1), 247–65.

Field, Yvette and Yip Lee Mee Oi 1992: A comparison of internal conjunctive cohesion in the English essay writing of Cantonese speakers and native speakers of English. *Regional English Language Center Journal*, 23(1), 15–28.

Fishman, Pamela, Barrie Thorne, Cheris Kramarae, and Nancy Henley 1983: Interaction: the work women do. In Barrie Thorne et al. (eds.), *Language, Gender and Society*. Rowley: Newbury House.

Foucault, Michel 1977: *Discipline and Punish*. New York: Pantheon Books.

Foucault, Michel 1969/1972: *The Archaeology of Knowledge*. Alan Sheridan trans. New York: Pantheon.

Foucault, Michel 1981: *The History of Sexuality, Vol. 1: An Introduction*. Robert Hurley trans. Harmondsworth: Penguin.

Frank, Francine Wattman and Paula A. Treichler 1989: *Language, Gender and Professional Writing: theoretical approaches and guidelines for nonsexist usage*. New York: Modern Language Association of America.

Friedman, Meyer and Ray H. Rosenman 1974: *Type A Behavior and Your Heart*. New York: Fawcett Columbine.

Friedman, Meyer and Diane Ulmer 1984: *Treating Type A Behavior and Your Heart*. New York: Alfred A. Knopf.

Fung, Heidi 1999: Becoming a moral child: the socialization of shame among young Chinese children. *Ethos* 27(2).

Gee, James Paul 1986: Orality and literacy: from "The Savage Mind" to "Ways with Words." *TESOL Quarterly*, 20, 719–46.

Gee, James Paul 1989: Literacy, discourse, and linguistics: essays by James Paul Gee. *Journal of Education*, 171(1).

Gee, James Paul 1990: *Social Linguistics and Literacies: ideology in discourses*. Bristol, PA: Falmer Press.

Gee, James Paul 2004: *Situated Language and Learning: a critique of traditional schooling*. London: Routledge.

Gee, James Paul 2010: *An Introduction to Discourse Analysis: theory and method* (3rd edition). London: Routledge.

Gee, James Paul 2011: *Language and Learning in the Digital Age*. London: Routledge.

Gee, James Paul, Glynda Hull, and Colin Lankshear 1996: *The New Work Order: behind the language of the new capitalism*. Boulder: Westview Press.

Giles, H. and A. Franklyn-Stokes 1989: Communicator characteristics. In M. K. Asante and W. B. Gudykunst (eds.), *The Handbook of Intercultural Communication*. Newbury Park: Sage.

Giles, Howard, Nikolas Coupland, and John M. Wiemann 1992: "Talk is cheap . . . but my word is my bond": beliefs about talk. In Kingsley Bolton and Helen Kwok (eds.), *Sociolinguistics Today: eastern and western perspectives*. London: Routledge.

Goffman, Erving 1955: On Face-Work: an analysis of ritual elements in social interaction. *Psychiatry: Journal of Interpersonal Relations*, 18(3), 213–31.

Goffman, Erving 1959: *The Presentation of Self in Everyday Life*. Garden City: Doubleday Anchor.

Goffman, Erving 1967: *Interaction Ritual*. Garden City: Anchor Books.

Goffman, Erving 1974: *Frame Analysis*. New York: Harper and Row.

Goffman, Erving 1981: *Forms of Talk*. Philadelphia: University of Pennsylvania Press.

Goldhaber, Michael H. 1997: The attention economy and the net. A paper presented at the conference on Economies of Digital Information, Jan. 23, Cambridge, MA. Available at: http://www.well.com/user/mgoldh/AtEcandNet.html.

Goodrich, Frederick W. Jr 1968: *Infant Care: the United States government guide*. Englewood Cliffs: Prentice Hall.

Gu, Yueguo 1990: Politeness phenomena in modern Chinese. *Journal of Pragmatics*, 2, 237–57.

Gu, Yueguo 2001: The changing orders of discourse in a changing China. In Pan Haihua (ed.), *Studies in Chinese Linguistics*, Vol. 2. Hong Kong: Linguistics Society of Hong Kong.

Gudykunst, W. B., Y.-C. Yoon, and T. Nishida 1987: The influence of individualism–collectivism on perception of communication in ingroup and outgroup relationships. *Communication Monographs*, 54, 295–306.

Gumperz, John 1977: Sociocultural knowledge in conversational inference. In M. Saville-Troike (ed.), *28th Annual Round Table Monograph Series on Language and Linguistics*, Washington, DC: Georgetown University Press.

Gumperz, John 1982: *Discourse Strategies*. New York: Cambridge University Press.

Gumperz, John 1991: Interviewing in intercultural situations. In P. Drew and J. Heritage (eds.), *Talk at Work*. New York: Cambridge University Press.

Gumperz, John 1992: Contextualization and understanding. In A. Duranti and G. Goodwin (eds.), *Rethinking Context*. Cambridge: Cambridge University Press.

Gumperz, John J. and Dell Hymes 1972: *Directions in Sociolinguistics: the ethnography of communication*. New York: Holt, Rinehart and Winston.

Günthner, Susanne 1991: *Chines/Innen und Deutsche im Gesprach: Aspekta der Interkulturellen Kommunikation*. Universitat Konstanz: Dissertation.

Günthner, Susanne 1992: The construction of gendered discourse in Chinese–German interactions. *Discourse and Society*, 3(2), 167–91.

Hall, David L. and Roger T. Ames 1987: *Thinking through Confucius*. Albany: State University of New York Press.

Hall, Edward T. 1959: *The Silent Language*. Garden City: Doubleday.

Hall, Edward T. 1966: *The Hidden Dimension*. Garden City: Doubleday.

Hall, Edward T. 1976. *Beyond Culture*. New York: Doubleday.

Hall, Edward T. 1992: *An Anthropology of Everyday Life: an autobiography*. New York: Anchor Books.

Hall, Edward T. and Mildred Reed Hall 1987: *Hidden Differences: doing business with the Japanese*. Garden City: Doubleday.

Hall, Kira and Mary Bucholtz (eds.) 1995: *Gender Articulated: language and the socially constructed self*. New York and London: Routledge.

Halliday, M. A. K. 1989: *Spoken and Written Language*. Oxford: Oxford University Press.

Halliday, M. A. K. and Ruqaiya Hasan 1976: *Cohesion in English*. London: Longman.

Hartzell, Richard W. 1988: *Harmony in Conflict: active adaptation to life in present-day Chinese society*. Taipei: Caves Books.

Hayashi, Reiko 1988: Simultaneous talk: from the perspective of floor management of English and Japanese speakers. *World Englishes*, 7(3), 269–88.

Hayashi, Reiko 1990: Rhythmicity sequence and synchrony of English and Japanese face to face conversation. *Language Sciences*, 12(2/3), 155–95.

Heath, Shirley Brice 1983: *Ways with Words: language, life, and work in communities and classrooms*. New York: Cambridge University Press.

Heritage, John 1989: Current developments in conversation analysis. In Derek Roger and Peter Bull (eds.), *Conversation: an interdisciplinary perspective*. Clevedon: Multilingual Matters.

Hinds, John 1983: Contrastive rhetoric: Japanese and English. *Text*, 3(2), 183–95.

Hinds, John 1987: Reader versus Writer Responsibility: a new typology. In Ulla Connor and Robert B. Kaplan (eds.), *Writing Across Languages: analysis of L2 text*. Reading: Addison-Wesley.

Hinsch, Brent 1992: *Passions of the Cut Sleeve: the male homosexual tradition in China*. Berkeley: University of California Press.

Ho, David Yau-Fai 1976: On the concept of face. *American Journal of Sociology*, 81, 867–84.

Ho, David Yau-Fai 1986: Chinese patterns of socialization. In Michael Harris Bond (ed.), *The Psychology of the Chinese People*. New York: Oxford University Press.

Hobson, John M. 2004: *The Eastern Origins of Western Civilisation*. Cambridge: Cambridge University Press.

Hofstede, G. 1983: Dimensions of national cultures in 50 countries and three regions. In J. B. Deregowski, S. Dziurawiec, and R. C. Annis (eds.), *Explications in Cross-cultural Psychology*. Lisse: Swets and Zeitlinger.

Hsu, Francis L. K. 1953: *Americans and Chinese: passage to differences*. Honolulu: University Press of Hawaii.

Hsu, Francis L. K. 1969: *The Study of Literate Civilizations*. New York: Holt, Rinehart and Winston.

Hsu, Francis L. K. 1973: *Religion, Science and Human Crises*. Westport: Greenwood Press.

Hsu, Francis L. K. 1983: *Rugged Individualism Reconsidered: essays in psychological anthropology*. Knoxville: University of Tennessee Press.

Hsu, Francis L. K. 1985: The self in cross-cultural perspective. In Anthony J. Marsella, George DeVos, and Francis L. K. Hsu (eds.), *Culture and Self: Asian and western perspectives*. New York: Tavistock Publications.

Hu, Hsien Chin 1944: The Chinese concept of "face." *American Anthropologist*, 46, 45–64.

Hwang, Kwang-Kuo 1987: Face and favor: the Chinese power game. *American Journal of Sociology*, 92(4), 944–74.

Hymes, Dell 1966: Two types of linguistic relativity. In William Bright (ed.), *Sociolinguistics*. The Hague: Mouton.

Hymes, Dell 1972: Models of the interaction of language and social life. In John J. Gumperz and Dell Hymes (eds.), *Directions in Sociolinguistics: the ethnography of communication*. New York: Holt, Rinehart and Winston.

Illich, Ivan 1981: *Shadow Work*. Boston and London: Marion Boyars.

Innis, Howard 1951: *The Bias of Communication*. Toronto: University of Toronto Press.

Jefferson, Gail 1989: Preliminary notes on a possible metric which provides for a "standard maximum" silence of approximately one second in conversation. In Derek Roger and Peter Bull (eds.), *Conversation: an interdisciplinary perspective*. Clevedon: Multilingual Matters.

Jobs, Steve 1996: Speech. Available at http://www.youtube.com/watch?v=qjxacrSCYRE&feature= player_embedded (retrieved December 21, 2010).

Johnson, Meagan and Larry Johnson 2010: *Generations Inc.: from boomers to linksters – managing the friction between generations at work.* New York: American Management Association.

Johnstone, Barbara 1991: *Repetition in Arabic Discourse: paradigms, syntagms and the ecology of language.* Amsterdam: John Benjamins.

Jones, Rodney 1996: *Responses to AIDS Awareness Discourse: a cross-cultural frame analysis.* City University of Hong Kong Research Monograph 10. Hong Kong: City University of Hong Kong, Department of English.

Jones, Rodney 2004: The problem of context in computer mediated communication. In Philip LeVine and Ron Scollon (eds.), *Discourse and Technology: multimodal discourse analysis.* Washington DC: Georgetown University Press.

Jones, Rodney 2005: Mediated addiction: the drug discourses of Hong Kong youth. *Health, Risk and Society*, 7 (1), 25–45.

Jones, Rodney 2007: Imagined comrades and imaginary protections: identity, community and sexual risk among men who have sex with men in China. *Journal of Homosexuality*, 53(3), 83–115.

Jones, Rodney 2008: Good sex and bad karma: discourse and the historical body. In Vijay K. Bhatia, John Flowerdew, and Rodney Jones (eds.), *Advances in Discourse Studies.* London: Routledge.

Jones, Rodney 2010: Physical spaces and virtual environments. In Adam Jaworski and Crispin Thurlow (eds.), *Semiotic Landscapes: text, space and globalization.* London: Continuum.

Jones, Rodney, Christopher N. Candlin, and K. K. Yu 2000: Culture, communication and the quality of life of people living with HIV/AIDS. A Report to the Council for the AIDS Trust Fund. Hong Kong: Council for the AIDS Trust Fund, Hong Kong Department of Health.

Kant, Immanuel 1990: The Science of Right. In Mortimer J. Adler (ed.), *Great Books of the Western World.* Chicago: Encyclopaedia Britannica.

Kant, Immanuel 1991: An answer to the question: "What is Enlightenment?" In Hans Reiss (ed.), *Kant: Political Writings.* Cambridge: Cambridge University Press. (Originally published in 1784.)

Kaplan, Robert B. 1966: Cultural thought patterns in intercultural education. *Language Learning*, 16(1/2), 1–20.

Kaplan, Robert B. 1987: Cultural thought patterns revisited. In Ulla Conner and Robert B. Kaplan (eds.), *Writing Across Languages: analysis of L2 text.* Reading, MA: Addison-Wesley.

Kenner, Hugh 1987: *The Mechanical Muse.* New York: Oxford University Press.

Kertzer, David I. 1983: Generation as a sociological problem. *Annual Review of Sociology*, 9, 125–49.

Kim, Ki-hong 1975: Cross-cultural differences between Americans and Koreans in nonverbal behavior. In Ho-Min Sohn (ed.), *The Korean Language: its structure and social projection.* Honolulu: Center for Korean Studies, University of Hawaii.

Kincaid, D. Lawrence 1987: *Communication Theory: eastern and western perspectives.* San Diego: Academic Press.

King, Ambrose Y. C. and Michael H. Bond 1985: The Confucian paradigm of man: a sociological view. In Wen-Shing Tseng and David Y. H. Wu (eds.), *Chinese Culture and Mental Health.* Orlando: Academic Press.

King, Katie 1992: Local and global: AIDS activism and feminist theory. *Camera Obscura*, 28, 78–99.

Kintsch, Walter 1977: On comprehending stories. In Marcel Just and Patricia Carpenter (eds.), *Cognitive Processes in Comprehension.* Hillsdale: Lawrence Erlbaum Associates.

Kintsch, Walter and Edith Greene 1978: The role of culture-specific schemata in the comprehension and recall of stories. *Discourse Processes*, 1(1), 1–13.

Korzybski, Alfred 1948: *Science and Sanity: an introduction of non-Aristotelian systems and general semantics.* Lakeville: International Non-Aristotelian Library.

Kress, Gunther and Theo van Leeuwen 1996/2006: *Reading Images: the grammar of visual design.* London: Routledge.

Kulick, Don 1998: *Travesti: sex, gender, and culture among Brazilian transgendered prostitutes*. Chicago: University of Chicago Press.

Lakoff, George and Mark Johnson 1980: *Metaphors We Live By*. Chicago: University of Chicago Press.

Lakoff, Robin 1973: The logic of politeness; or, minding your P's and Q's. *Papers from the Ninth Regional Meeting, Chicago Linguistic Society*, 9, 292–305.

Lakoff, Robin 1975: *Language and Woman's Place*. New York: Harper and Row.

Lanham, Richard A. 1983: *Literacy and the Survival of Humanism*. New Haven: Yale University Press.

Lanham, Richard A. 2006: *The Economics of Attention: style and substance in the information age*. Chicago: University of Chicago Press.

Lau, D. C. 1970: *Mencius*. New York: Penguin.

Lau, D. C. 1979: *Confucius: the Analects*. New York: Penguin.

Lave, Jean and Wenger, Etienne 1991: *Situated Learning: legitimate peripheral participation*. Cambridge: Cambridge University Press.

Lee, Thomas H. C. 1984: The discovery of childhood: children's education in Sung China (960–1279). In Sigrid Paul (ed.), *Kultur: Begriff und Wort in China and Japan*. Berlin: Dietrich Reimer Verlag.

Leech, Geoffrey 1983: *Principles of Pragmatics*. London: Longman.

Legge, James 1967: *Li Chi: Book of Rites*. New York: University Books.

Lever, Janet 1976: Sex differences in the complexity of children's play and games. *American Sociological Review*, 43, 471–83.

Levinson, Stephen C. 1988: Putting linguistics on a proper footing: explorations in Goffman's concepts of participation. In P. Drew and A. Wootton (eds.), *Erving Goffman: exploring the interaction order*. Oxford: Polity Press.

Levinson, Stephen C. 1990: Interactional biases in human thinking. Working Paper No. 3, Project Group Cognitive Anthropology, Max-Planck-Gesellschaft, Berlin.

Levinson, Stephen C. 2000: *Presumptive Meanings: the theory of generalized conversational implicature*. Cambridge, MA: MIT Press.

Li, David C. S., Wanda W. Y. Poon, Pamela Rogerson-Revell, Ron Scollon, Suzanne Wong Scollon, Brian S. K. Yu, and Vicki K. Y. Yung 1993: Contrastive discourse in English and Cantonese news stories: a preliminary analysis of newspaper, radio, and television versions of the Lan Kwai Fong New Year's news story. Department of English, City Polytechnic of Hong Kong. Research Report No. 29.

Littwin, Susan 1986: *The Postponed Generation: why America's grown-up kids are growing up later*. New York: William Morrow.

Locke, John 1990: *An Essay concerning Human Understanding*. In Mortimer J. Adler (ed.), *Great Books of the Western World*. Chicago: Encyclopaedia Britannica.

Longfellow, Layne A. 1978: *Leadership, Power, and Productivity: doing well by doing good*. Prescott: Lecture Theatre.

Longfellow, Layne A. no date 1: Four American generations: doing well by doing good. Prescott, AZ: Lecture Theatre.

Longfellow, Layne A. no date 2: Changing the rules of our lives: from high school to midlife and beyond. Prescott, AZ: Lecture Theatre.

Longfellow, Layne A. no date 3: Stress: the American addiction. Prescott, AZ: Lecture Theatre.

Longfellow, Layne A. no date 4: Positioning for tomorrow: the emergence of women in the workforce. Prescott, AZ: Lecture Theatre.

Lukes, Steven 1973: *Individualism*. Oxford: Blackwell.

Maltz, Daniel N. and Ruth A. Borker 1982: A cultural approach to male-female miscommunication. In John J. Gumperz (ed.), *Language and Social Identity*. Cambridge: Cambridge University Press.

Mao, Luming 1994: Beyond politeness theory: "face" revisited and renewed. *Journal of Pragmatics*, 21(5), 451–86.

Marsella, Anthony J., George DeVos, and Francis L. K. Hsu 1985: *Culture and Self: Asian and western perspectives*. New York: Tavistock.

Martinsons, Maris G. and David Ma 2009: Sub-cultural differences in information ethics across China: focus on Chinese management generation gaps. *Journal of the Association for Information Systems*, 10, 816–33.

Mauranen, Anna 1993: *Cultural Differences in Academic Rhetoric. a text linguistic study*. Frankfurt am Main: Peter Lang.

McCarthy, Michael 1991: *Discourse Analysis for Language Teachers*. Cambridge: Cambridge University Press.

McCrindle, Mark no date: Understanding generation Y. Available at http://www.learningtolearn.sa.edu.au/colleagues/files/links/understandinggeny.pdf (retrieved December 23, 2010).

McDermott, Ray 1979: Lecture. American Anthropological Association, Cincinnati.

McLuhan, Marshall 1964: *Understanding Media: the extensions of man*. New York: McGraw Hill.

Mehan, Hugh 1983: *Learning Lessons: social organization in the classroom*. Cambridge, MA: Harvard University Press.

Mehrabian, Albert 1972: *Nonverbal Communication*. Chicago: Aldine-Atherton.

Mill, John Stuart 1990: Utilitarianism. In Mortimer J. Adler (ed.), *Great Books of the Western World*. Chicago: Encyclopedia Britannica. (Originally published in 1690.)

Montesquieu, Baron de Charles de Secondat 1990: The Spirit of Laws. In Mortimer J. Adler (ed.), *Great Books of the Western World*. Chicago: Encyclopaedia Britannica.

Murray, Douglas P. 1983: Face-to-face: American and Chinese interactions. In Robert A. Kapp (ed.), *Communicating with China*. Chicago: Intercultural Press.

Murray, Stephen O. 2000: *Homosexualities*. Chicago: University of Chicago Press.

Nakane, Chie 1972: *Japanese Society*. Berkeley: University of California Press.

National Public Radio 2010: China's "Me Generation" sends divorce rate soaring. Broadcast November 17.

Neuliep, James W. 2000: *Intercultural Communication: a contextual approach*. Boston: Houghton Mifflin Company.

Newman, Matthew, Carla J. Groom, Lori D. Handelman, and James W. Pennebaker 2008: Gender differences in language use: an analysis of 14,000 text samples. *Discourse Processes*, 45, 211–36.

Newstex 2010: China worker suicides: a lost generation. *Global Post*, June 14.

Nietzsche, Friedrich 1990: Beyond good and evil. In Mortimer J. Adler (ed.), *Great Books of the Western World*. Chicago: Encyclopedia Britannica. (Originally published in 1886.)

Norris, Sigrid 2004: *Analyzing Multimodal Interaction: a methodological framework*. London: Routledge.

Obelkevich, James 1987: Proverbs and social history. In Peter Burke and Roy Porter (eds.), *The Social History of Language*. Cambridge: Cambridge University Press.

Ochs, Elinor 1979: Planned and unplanned discourse. In Talmy Givon (ed.), *Discourse and Syntax*. New York: Academic Press.

Oliver, Robert 1971: *Communication and Culture in Ancient India and China*. Syracuse: Syracuse University Press.

Ong, Walter 1982: *Orality and Literacy: the technologizing of the word*. New York: Methuen.

Ouchi, William G. 1981: *Theory Z*. New York: Avon.

Paltridge, Brian 2006: *Discourse Analysis*. London: Continuum.

Pan, Yuling 2000: *Politeness in Chinese Face-to-face Interaction*. Greenwich: Ablex Publishing Corporation.

Pan, Yuling and Daniel Z. Kadar 2011: *Politeness in Historical and Contemporary Chinese*. London and New York: Continuum.

Pan, Yuling, Suzanne Scollon, and Ron Scollon 2002: *Professional Communication in International Settings*. Oxford: Blackwell Publishers.

Parker, R. Stephen, Diana L. Haytko, and Charles M. Hermans 2009: Individualism and collectivism: reconsidering old assumptions. *Journal of International Business Research*, 8 (1), 127–39.

Patterson, Lyman Ray 1968: *Copyright in Historical Perspective*. Nashville: Vanderbilt University Press.

Philipsen, G. 1975: Speaking "like a man" in Teamsterville: culture patterns of role enactment in an urban neighborhood. *Quarterly Journal of Speech*, 61, 13–22.

Poole, Deborah 1992: Language socialization in the second language classroom. *Language Learning*, 42(4), 593–616.

Postman, Neil and Camille Paglia 1991: She wants her TV! He wants his book! Dinner conversation. *Harper's*, March, 44–55.

Ralston, David A., David J. Gustafson, Fanny M. Cheung, and Robert H. Terpstra, 1993: Differences in managerial values: a study of U.S., Hong Kong and PRC managers. *Journal of International Business Studies*, 24, 249–75.

Ralston, David A., Carolyn P. Egri, Sally Stewart, Robert H. Terpstra, and Kaicheng Yu 1999: Doing business in the 21st century with the new generation of Chinese managers: a study of generational shifts in work values in China. *Journal of International Business Studies*, 30(2), 415–28.

Redding, Gordon and Gilbert Y. Y. Wong 1986: The psychology of Chinese organizational behavior. In Michael Harris Bond (ed.), *The Psychology of the Chinese People*. New York: Oxford University Press.

Reddy, Michael J. 1979: The conduit metaphor: a case of frame conflict in our language about language. In Andrew Ortony (ed.), *Metaphor and Thought*. Cambridge: Cambridge University Press.

Reichwein, Adolf 1968: *China and Europe: intellectual and artistic contacts in the eighteenth century*. London: Routledge and Kegan Paul.

Richards, Jack C., John Platt, and Heidi Weber 1985: *Longman Dictionary of Applied Linguistics*. Harlow: Longman.

Riley, Philip 2007: *Language, Culture and Identity*. London: Continuum.

Rogers, Everett M. and Rehka Agarwala-Rogers 1976: *Communication in Organizations*. New York: Free Press.

Rosen, Stanley 2004: The state of youth/youth and the state in early 21st-century China. In Peter Hays Gries and Stanley Rosen (eds.), *State and Society in 21st-century China: crisis, contention and legitimation*. New York: Routledge Curzon.

Ross, Steven and Ian M. Shortreed 1990: Japanese foreigner talk: convergence or divergence? Asian Pacific language and communication: foundations, issues, and directions. *Journal of Asian Pacific Communication*, 1(1), 135–46.

Ruesch, Jurgen and Gregory Bateson 1968 [1951]: *Communication: the social matrix of psychiatry*. New York: W. W. Norton.

Samovar, Larry A. and Richard E. Porter 1988: *Intercultural Communication: a reader*. Belmont: Wadsworth.

Sampson, E. E. 1993: Identity politics. *American Psychologist*, 48(12), 1219–30.

Saville-Troike, Muriel 1989: *The Ethnography of Communication*. Oxford: Blackwell.

Sayeki, Yutaka 1983: Joint solving of physics problems by college students. In Michael Cole, Naomi Miyake, and Denis Newman (eds.), *Proceedings of the Conference on Joint Problem Solving and Microcomputers*. La Jolla: University of California, San Diego, Laboratory of Comparative Human Cognition.

Schegloff, Emanuel 1972: Sequencing in conversational openings. In John Gumperz and Dell Hymes (eds.), *Directions in Sociolinguistics*. New York: Holt, Rinehart and Winston.

Schmidt, Richard, Akihiko Shimura, Zhigang Wang, and Hysook Jeong 1996: Suggestions to buy: television commercials from the US, Japan, China, and Korea. In Susan Gass and Joyce Neu (eds.), *Speech Acts Across Cultures*. The Hague: Mouton de Gruyter.

Scollon, Ron 1981: The rhythmic integration of ordinary talk. In Deborah Tannen (ed.), *Georgetown University Roundtable on Languages and Linguistics 1981*. Washington, DC: Georgetown University Press.

Scollon, Ron 1985: The machine stops. In Deborah Tannen and Muriel Saville-Troike (eds.), *Perspectives on Silence*. Norwood: Ablex.

Scollon, Ron 1987: *Time and the Media: notes on public discourse in the electronic age*. Haines: Black Current Press.

Scollon, Ron 1988: Storytelling, reading, and the micropolitics of literacy. In John E. Readance and R. Scott Baldwin (eds.), *Dialogues in Literacy Research*. Chicago: National Reading Conference.

Scollon, Ron 1993a: Cumulative ambiguity: conjunctions in Chinese–English intercultural communication. *Perspectives: Working Papers of the Department of English*, City Polytechnic of Hong Kong, 5(1), 55–73.

Scollon, Ron 1993b: Maxims of stance: discourse in English for professional communication. Department of English, City Polytechnic of Hong Kong, Research Report 26.

Scollon, Ron 1995: Plagiarism and ideology: identity in intercultural discourse. *Language in Society*, 24, 1–28.

Scollon, Ron 1998: *Mediated Discourse as Social Interaction: a study of news discourse*. New York: Longman.

Scollon, Ron 1999: Official and unofficial discourses of national identity: questions raised by the case of contemporary Hong Kong. In Ruth Wodak and Christoph Ludwig (eds.), *Challenges in a Changing World: issues in critical discourse analysis*. Vienna: Passagen Verlag, 21–35.

Scollon, Ron 2001: *Mediated Discourse: the nexus of practice*. London/New York: Routledge.

Scollon, Ron 2002: Intercultural communication as nexus analysis. *Logos and Language: Journal of General Linguistics and Language Theory*, 3(2), 1–17.

Scollon, Ron 2008: *Analyzing Public Discourse*. London: Routledge.

Scollon, Ron and Suzanne Scollon 1980: Literacy as focused interaction. *Quarterly Newsletter of the Laboratory of Comparative Human Cognition*, 2(2), 26–9.

Scollon, Ron and Suzanne B. K. Scollon 1981: *Narrative, Literacy and Face in Interethnic Communication*. Norwood: Ablex.

Scollon, Ron and Suzanne B. K. Scollon 1983: Face in interethnic communication. In Jack Richards and Richard Schmidt (eds.), *Language and Communication*. London: Longman.

Scollon, Ron and Suzanne B. K. Scollon 1984: Cooking it up and boiling it down: abstracts in Athabaskan children's story retellings. In Deborah Tannen (ed.), *Coherence in Spoken and Written Discourse*. Norwood: Ablex.

Scollon, Ron and Suzie Scollon 1986: *Responsive Communication: patterns for making sense*. Haines: Black Current Press.

Scollon, Ron and Suzanne B. K. Scollon 1990: Epilogue to "Athabaskan–English interethnic communication." In Donal Carbaugh (ed.), *Cultural Communication and Intercultural Contact*. Hillsdale: Lawrence Erlbaum Associates.

Scollon, Ron and Suzanne Wong Scollon 1991: Topic confusion in English–Asian discourse. *World Englishes*, 10(2), 113–25.

Scollon, Ron and Suzie Wong Scollon 1992: Individualism and binarism: a critique of American intercultural communication analysis. Department of English, City Polytechnic of Hong Kong, Research Report 22.

Scollon, Ron and Suzanne Wong Scollon 1994: Face parameters in East–West discourse. In Stella Ting-Toomey (ed.), *The Challenge of Facework*. Albany: State University of New York Press.

Scollon, Ron and Suzanne B. K. Scollon 1997: Political, personal, and commercial discourses of national sovereignty: Hong Kong becomes China. In Marju Lauristin (ed.), *Intercultural Communication and Changing National Identities*. Tartu: Tartu University Press.

Scollon, Ron and Suzie Wong Scollon 2003: *Discourses in Place: language in the material world*. London: Routledge.

Scollon, Ron, Suzanne Wong Scollon, Yuling Pan, and Ming Li 1998: Intercultural differences in professional communication: professional communication between Hong Kong and Beijing. Paper presented at SIETAR Congress 98: Asia/Pacific Basin, Tokyo, November 19–24.

Scollon, Ron, Suzanne Wong Scollon, Wenzhong Hu, Liisa Salo-Lee, Yuling Pan, Li Ming, Cecilia Leung, and Zhenyi Li 1999: Professional communication across cultures: a focus group based, three-way cross-cultural comparison. *SIETAR International Journal*, 1(1), 97–108.

Scollon, Suzanne 1995: Methodological assumptions in intercultural communication. Fifth International Conference on Cross-Cultural Communication: East and West, August 15–19. Heilongjiang University, Harbin, China.

Scollon, Suzanne 1997: Metaphors of self and communication: English and Cantonese. *Multilingua*, 16, 1–38.

Scollon, Suzanne 1999: Not to waste words or students: Confucian and Socratic discourse in the tertiary classroom. In Eli Hinkel (ed.), *Culture in Second Language Teaching and Learning*. Cambridge and New York: Cambridge University Press.

Scollon, Suzanne 2003: Political and somatic alignment: habitus, ideology and social practice. In Gilbert Weiss and Ruth Wodak (eds.), *Critical Discourse Analysis: theory and interdisciplinarity*, New York: Palgrave.

Searle, John R. 1969: *Speech Acts*. New York: Cambridge University Press.

Sedgwick, Eve Kosofsky 1990: *Epistemology of the Closet*. Berkeley: University of California Press.

Seward, Jack 1983: *Japanese in Action: an unorthodox approach to the spoken language and the people who speak it*. New York: Weatherhill.

Shroyer, Guy 2004: The presence of the past: enacting time, the nation, and the social self. *Essays in Arts and Sciences*, 33(2).

Smith, Adam 1990: An Inquiry into the Nature and Causes of the Wealth of Nations. In Mortimer J. Adler (ed.), *Great Books of the Western World*. Chicago: Encyclopaedia Britannica.

Smith, Larry E. 1987: *Discourse Across Cultures: strategies in world Englishes*. New York: Prentice Hall.

Sohn, Ho-Min 1983: Power and solidarity in the Korean language. *Korean Linguistics*, 3, 97–122.

Song, Weizhen 1985: A preliminary study of the character traits of the Chinese. In Wen-Shing Tseng and David Y. H. Wu (eds.), *Chinese Culture and Mental Health*. Orlando: Academic Press.

Sontag, Susan 1964: *Notes on Camp* in *Against Interpretation and Other Essays*. New York: Farrer Straus & Giroux.

Spence, Jonathan 1990: *The Search for Modern China*. New York: W.W. Norton.

Spence, Jonathan 1992: *Chinese Roundabout: essays in history and culture*. New York: Norton.

Spender, Dale 1980: *Man Made Language*. London: Routledge.

Spock, Benjamin 1976: *Baby and Child Care*. New York: Hawthorne Books. (Originally published in 1945.)

Stevenson, Harold W., H. Azuma, and K. Hakuta 1986: *Child Development and Education in Japan*. New York: Freeman.

Stewart, E. and J. Bennett 1992: *American Cultural Patterns: a cross-cultural perspective*. Yarmouth: Intercultural Press.

Stover, Leon E. 1974: *The Cultural Ecology of Chinese Civilization*. New York: Pica Press.

Street, Brian 1993: Culture is a verb: anthropological aspects of language and cultural process. In David Graddol, Linda Thompson and Michael Byram (eds.), *Language and Culture*. Clevedon: Multilingual Matters and BAAL.

Sun, Jiaming and Xun Wang 2010: Value differences between generations in China: a study in Shanghai. *Journal of Youth Studies*, 13 (1), 65–81.

Sunley, Robert 1955: Early American literature on child rearing. In Margaret Mead and Martha Wolfenstein (eds.), *Childhood in Contemporary Cultures*. Chicago: University of Chicago Press.

Suzuki, Takao 1986: Language and behavior in Japan: the conceptualization of personal relations. In Takie S. Lebra and W. P. Lebra (eds.), *Japanese Culture and Behavior*. Honolulu: University of Hawaii Press.

Swales, John M. 1990: *Genre Analysis: English in academic and research settings*. Cambridge: Cambridge University Press.

Swann, Joan 1992: *Girls, Boys and Language*. Oxford: Blackwell.

Tannen, Deborah 1982: Oral and literate strategies in spoken and written narratives. *Language*, 58(1), 1–21.

Tannen, Deborah 1984: *Conversational Style: analyzing talk among friends*. Norwood: Ablex.

Tannen, Deborah 1989: *Talking Voices: repetition, dialogue and imagery in conversational discourse*. Cambridge: Cambridge University Press.

Tannen, Deborah 1990a: *You Just Don't Understand: women and men in conversation*. New York: William Morrow.

Tannen, Deborah 1990b: Gender differences in conversational coherence: physical alignment and topical cohesion. In Bruce Dorval (ed.), *Conversational Organization and its Development*. Norwood: Ablex.

Tannen, Deborah 1991: Teachers' classroom strategies should recognize that men and women use language differently. *The Chronicle of Higher Education*, 37(40), B2–B3.

Tannen, Deborah 1993: *Gender and Conversational Interaction*. Oxford: Oxford University Press.

Tannen, Deborah 1994a: *Gender and Discourse*. Oxford: Oxford University Press.

Tannen, Deborah 1994b: *Talking from 9 to 5: how women's and men's conversational styles affect who gets heard, who gets credit, and what gets done at work*. New York: William Morrow.

Tannen, Deborah and Muriel Saville-Troike 1985: *Perspectives on Silence*. Norwood, NJ: Ablex.

Taylor, Frederick 1911: *Scientific Management*. New York: Harper and Row.

Taylor, Paul and Rich Morin 2009: Forty years after Woodstock: a gentler generation gap. *Pew Research Center, Social and Demographic Trends*. Available at: http://pewsocialtrends.org/2009/08/12/forty-years-after-woodstockbra-gentler-generation-gap/ (retrieved December 21, 2010).

Ting-Toomey, Stella 1988: Intercultural conflict styles: a face-negotiation theory. In Young Kim and William Gudykunst (eds.), *Theories in Intercultural Communication*. Newbury Park: Sage.

Tobin, Joseph J., David Y. H. Wu, and Dana H. Davidson 1989: *Preschool in Three Cultures*. New Haven: Yale University Press.

Tocqueville, Alexis de 1969: *Democracy in America*. George Lawrence, trans. Garden City: Anchor Books.

Tönnies, Ferdinand 1971: *Ferdinand Tönnies on Sociology: pure, applied and empirical: selected writings*. Chicago: University of Chicago Press.

Tracy, Karen 1990: The many faces of facework. In H. Giles and W. P. Robinson (eds.), *Handbook of Language and Social Psychology*. Chichester: John Wiley.

Triandis, H. C., R. Bontempo, M. J. Villarcal, M. Asai, and N. Lucca 1988: Individualism–collectivism: cross-cultural perspectives on self–group relationships. *Journal of Personality and Social Psychology*, 54, 323–38.

Tsuda, Yukio 1986: *Language Inequality and Distortion in Intercultural Communication: a critical theory approach*. Amsterdam: John Benjamins.

Tulviste, Peeter 1994: History taught at school versus history discovered at home: the case of Estonia. *European Journal of Psychology of Education*, 9(1), 121–6.

Tulviste, Peeter and James V. Wertsch 1994: Official and unofficial histories: the case of Estonia. *Journal of Narrative and Life History*, 4(4), 311–29.

Tyler, Andrea E., Ann A. Jefferies, and Catherine E. Davies 1988: The effect of discourse structuring devices on listener perceptions of coherence in non-native university teacher's spoken discourse. *World Englishes*, 7(2), 101–10.

Universal Declaration of Human Rights 1948: In *Encyclopedia Britannica* (15th edition), Vol. 12.

US Census Bureau 2006: *American Community Survey*. Washington, DC: US Government.

van Dijk, Tuen 1998: *Ideology: a multidisciplinary approach*. London: Sage.

von Krafft-Ebing, Richard 1990: *Psychopathia Sexualis*. F. J. Rebman (trans.). New York: Rebman. (Originally published in 1886.)

van Leeuwen, Theo 2008: *Discourse and Practice: new tools for critical discourse analysis*. Oxford: Oxford University Press.

Vygotsky, Lev S. 1981: The instrumental method in psychology. In James V. Wertsch (ed.), *The Concept of Activity in Soviet Psychology*. Armonk: M. E. Sharpe.

Waley, Arthur 1943: *Monkey*. New York: Grove Press.

Weeks, Jeffery 2006: *Sexuality* (2nd edition). London: Routledge.

Wertsch, James V. 1991: *Voices of the Mind*. Cambridge: Harvard University Press.

Wertsch, James V. 1997: Narrative tools of history and identity. *Culture and Psychology*, 3(1), 5–20.

Wertsch, James V. and Elena Ivanova 1999: A new generation of historical consciousness in the former Soviet Union. Paper presented at the meeting "History as Equipment for Living" Tartu, Estonia, June 1999. Unpublished manuscript.

West, Candace and Don Zimmerman 1987: Doing gender. *Gender and Society*, 1, 125–51.

West, Mrs Max 1914: *Infant Care*. Washington, DC: US Government Printing Office.

Westbrook Eakins, Barbara, and R. Gene Eakins 1982: Sex differences in nonverbal communication. In Larry A. Samovar and Richard E. Porter (eds.), *Intercultural Communication: a reader*. Belmont: Wadsworth Publishing Company.

Westwood, Robert I. 1992: *Organisational Behavior: Southeast Asian perspectives*. Hong Kong: Longman Group (Far East).

Wetzel, P. 1988: Are powerless communication strategies the Japanese norm? *Language in Society*, 17, 555–64.

Wheeler, L., H. T. Reis, and Michael H. Bond 1989: Collectivism–individualism in everyday social life: the Middle Kingdom and the melting pot. *Journal of Personality and Social Psychology*, 57, 79–86.

White, S. 1989: Backchannels across cultures: a study of Americans and Japanese. *Language in Society*, 18, 59–76.

Whorf, Benjamin Lee 1956: *Language, Thought, and Reality*. Cambridge, MA: MIT Press.

Wolfenstein, Martha 1953: Trends in infant care. *Journal of Orthopsychiatry*, 23, 120–4.

Xinhua News Agency 2008: China's post-90's generation open minded, frustration prone. Available at http://news.xinhuanet.com/english/2008-11/12/content_10347763.htm (retrieved April 20, 2011).

Xinhua News Agency 2009: More than 2,000 found cheating in China's college entrance exam. Available at http://news.xinhuanet.com/english/2009-07/03/content_11649354.htm (retrieved July 3, 2009).

Xu Chuiyang (ed.) 1990: *Three Character Classic*. Singapore: EPB Publishers.

Xu, Luo 2002: *Searching for Life's Meaning: changes and tensions in the worldviews of Chinese youth in the 1980s*. Ann Arbor: University of Michigan Press.

Young, Linda Wai Ling 1982: Inscrutability revisited. In John Gumperz (ed.), *Language and Social Identity*. New York: Cambridge University Press.

Young, Linda W. 1994: *Crosstalk and Culture in Sino-American Communication*. New York: Cambridge University Press.

Yu, Anthony C. 1977: *The Journey to the West*. Chicago: University of Chicago Press.

Yum, J. O. 1988: The impact of Confucianism on interpersonal relationships and communication patterns in East Asia. *Communication Monographs*, 55, 374–88.

Zhang, H. 2009: Problems and solutions of young adults in China, *International Studies of Education and Society*, 6(2), 77–89.

Zhu Yunxia 2005: *Written Communication across Cultures: a sociocognitive perspective*. Amsterdam: Benjamins.

Index

Intercultural Communication: A Discourse Approach, Third Edition. Ron Scollon, Suzanne Wong Scollon, Rodney H. Jones.
© 2012 John Wiley & Sons, Inc. Published 2012 by John Wiley & Sons, Inc.

CPSIA information can be obtained
at www.ICGtesting.com
Printed in the USA
BVHW080714270619
552068BV00006B/137/P

9 780470 656402